TWO LIVES
Edmund Campion – Ronald Knox

TWO LIVES

Edmund Campion – Ronald Knox

Evelyn Waugh

CONTINUUM
London and New York

Continuum

The Tower Building, 11 York Road, London SE1 7NX

370 Lexington Avenue, New York, NY 10017-6503

www.continuumbooks.com

First published in this edition 2001

Edmund Campion first published Longman 1935
Ronald Knox first published Chapman & Hall 1959

British Library Cataloguing in Publication Data

A catalogue record for this book is available from the British Library.

ISBN 0-8264-5726-6 (hardback)

Designed and typeset by CentraServe Ltd, Saffron Walden, Essex
Printed and bound in Great Britain by Biddles Ltd, Guildford and King's Lynn

CONTENTS

Publisher's Introduction   vii

I   *Edmund Campion*   I

II   *Ronald Knox*   129

PUBLISHER'S INTRODUCTION

Evelyn Waugh is widely recognized as one of the finest English prose stylists of the twentieth century. Each generation of readers since his death in 1966 has been drawn to read widely in his *oeuvre*. However, in recent times two of Waugh's biographies, *Edmund Campion* and *Ronald Knox*, have been difficult to obtain.

Edmund Campion, first published in 1935, tells the dramatic life of the Jesuit priest and scholar who was martyred in 1581. As befits the life of a man whom Waugh admired greatly as a hero and exemplar, *Campion* (in contrast with his earlier novels) is written simply, gracefully – even romantically. Waugh's *Campion* was admired by many, including Graham Greene, and was awarded the prestigious Hawthornden Prize in 1936.

Monsignor Ronald Knox, a close and influential friend of Evelyn Waugh, combined great erudition with a celebrated wit that was both subtle and keen-edged. He was a prolific writer, whose greatest literary labour was a translation of the Bible, and his book *Enthusiasm* was described by Waugh unrestrainedly as 'the greatest work of literary art of the century'. On Knox's death Waugh began to absorb himself completely in the biography that was to take nearly two years to write and was published in 1959 to much critical admiration. With energy and elegance, Waugh skilfully masters his strong sympathy for his subject, maintaining a clear-sighted understanding of Knox's gifts and shortcomings.

The hope of the publishers is that this edition will restore to the general reader two works that are an essential part of the library of any admirer of Evelyn Waugh.

EDMUND CAMPION

by

EVELYN WAUGH

CONTENTS

Preface to Second Edition   5

  I. The Scholar   7

 II. The Priest   33

III. The Hero   60

IV. The Martyr   94

Appendix I
Campion's Brag   123

Appendix II
List of Books Consulted   126

PREFACE TO SECOND EDITION

In 1934, when Campion Hall, Oxford, was being rebuilt on a site and in a manner more worthy of its distinction than its old home in St Giles's, I wished to do something to mark my joy in the occasion and my gratitude to the then Master, to whom, under God, I owe my faith. A life of the Blessed Edmund Campion seemed the most suitable memorial. The alternatives were either a drastic revision of Richard Simpson's excellent work, which had long been out of print and had been corrected in many particulars by subsequent research, or to attempt an entirely new book. I chose the latter, but Simpson's strong foundations support my structure, and it is to him that I owe the greatest debt. I received invaluable help from Father Basset and Father Booth, of Campion Hall, from the late Father Watts of Stonyhurst, Father Hicks of Farm Street, and Mr Douglas Woodruff. I was privileged to use the copious collection of notes and documents collected by one of the Fathers at Farm Street for what would have been, had he lived, the definitive biography.

There is great need for a complete, scholar's work on the subject. This is not it. All I have done is select the incidents which struck a novelist as important, and relate them in a single narrative.

It shall be read as a simple, perfectly true story of heroism and holiness.

We have come much nearer to Campion since Simpson's day. He wrote in the flood-tide of toleration when Elizabeth's persecution seemed as remote as Diocletian's. We know now that his age was a brief truce in an unending war. The martyrdom of Father Pro in Mexico re-enacted Campion's in faithful detail. We are nearer Campion than when I wrote of him. We have seen the Church drawn underground in country after country. In fragments and whispers we get news of other saints in the prison camps of Eastern and Southeastern Europe, of cruelty and degradation more savage than anything in Tudor England, of the same, pure light shining in darkness, uncomprehended. The haunted, trapped, murdered priest is our contemporary and Campion's voice sounds to us across the centuries as though he were walking at our elbow.

EVELYN WAUGH   1946

Chapter One

THE SCHOLAR

In the middle of March 1603 it was clear to everyone that Queen Elizabeth was dying; her doctors were unable to diagnose the illness; she had little fever, but was constantly thirsty, restless, and morose; she refused to take medicine, refused to eat, refused to go to bed. She sat on the floor, propped up with cushions, sleepless and silent, her eyes constantly open, fixed on the ground, oblivious to the coming and going of her councillors and attendants. She had done nothing to recognize her successor; she had made no provision for the disposal of her personal property, of the vast heterogeneous accumulation of a lifetime, in which presents had come to her daily from all parts of the world; closets and cupboards stacked high with jewellery, coin, bric-à-brac; the wardrobe of 2,000 outmoded dresses. There was always company in the little withdrawing room waiting for her to speak, but she sighed and sipped and kept her silence. She had round her neck a piece of gold the size of an angel, engraved with characters; it had been left to her lately by a wise woman who had died in Wales at the age of 120. Sir John Stanhope had assured her that as long as she wore this talisman she could not die. There was no need yet for doctors or lawyers or statesmen or clergy.

Lord Admiral Howard was one of her visitors. He knelt beside her and, with tears, implored her to take a little nourishment. They brought a bowl of broth and the Admiral coaxed her to take a spoonful or two from his own hands. But when he urged her to go to bed she refused angrily, breaking into a confused and violent tale of her nightmares.

'If you were in the habit of seeing such things in your bed, as I do when in mine,' she said, 'you would not persuade me to go there.'

But she had not the strength to sustain her rage, and, when Cecil and the lawyers had left her, she shook her head piteously, saying, 'My lord, I am tied with a chain of iron about my neck.'

The Admiral reminded her of her wonted courage, but she replied, desponding, 'I am tied, I am tied; and the case is altered with me.'

The Council sent the Archbishop of Canterbury to her; he came with several other divines, eloquent, circumspect men who had made a great career in her church, to offer the consolations of religion; but their appearance roused her to fury. She rated them and sent them packing, crying that she was no atheist, but she knew full well they were but hedge priests.

The women about her tried to attribute causes to her melancholy; it was due to the execution of Essex, the execution of Mary of Scotland, the pardon of Tyrone. She herself confided to Lady Scrope that, before the Court moved from Whitehall, she had seen a hideous vision of 'her own body, exceeding lean and fearful in a light of fire'. She had asked, too, for a 'true looking-glass', which she had not seen for twenty years, and when it was brought fell exclaiming at all the flatterers that had so much commended her.

All her life she had been surrounded by plots; plots to implicate her in Wyatt's rebellion, plots against her life, to murder her with fire balls, to poison the pommel of her saddle; many of them real enough, some fomented by *agents provocateurs*, some the inventions of forgers and informers, plots that had no existence except in the brains of Walsingham and the Cecils. Now in her last illness they took shape again, and assassins lurked for her in the darkness and behind the curtains.

So she lay for nearly two weeks, until, lapsing into a stupor, she was carried to bed, where she died without speaking. The Archbishop returned to her at the end, and a movement of the hand was interpreted by her ladies-in-waiting as her consent to his presence.

In these circumstances the Tudor dynasty came to an end, which in three generations had changed the aspect and temper of England. They left a new aristocracy, a new religion, a new system of government; the generation was already in its childhood that was to send King Charles to the scaffold; the new, rich families who were to introduce the House of Hanover were already in the second stage of their metamorphosis from the freebooters of Edward VI's reign to the conspirators of 1688 and the sceptical, cultured oligarchs of the eighteenth century. The vast exuberance of the Renaissance had been canalized. England was secure, independent, insular; the course of her history lay plain ahead; competitive nationalism, competitive industrialism, competitive imperialism, the looms and coal mines and counting houses, the joint-stock companies and the cantonments; the power and the weakness of great possessions.

What was in Elizabeth's mind as she lay there through the silent hours, sane and despairing? The thought of another England that it had been in her hands to make? Or did she contrast her present state, an old perjured woman, dying without comfort, with those early years when the future had been compact of hope and adventure; see the light on the river and hear again the splash of oars as Leicester's barge rode between green banks and pollarded willows, and the flowered damask trailed out in the water behind them; the torchlight at Kenilworth and Rycote, the extravagant, irresponsible dances before the royal suitors, the bonfires kindling from crest to crest as the news travelled across country of the Armada's failure? . . . It had been a life of tumultuous drama, and it was ending, now, in silence; among all its incidents did she recall the afternoon of high summer when she had moved in a great retinue from Woodstock to Oxford, and, for the first time, held her court among the scholars of the university?

The visit had been twice postponed. Two years earlier − in 1564 − she had been to Cambridge, where the whole university had exerted itself in her entertainment, some of the more enthusiastic members even following her on the first stage of the return journey and attempting to make themselves agreeable to her − unsuccessfully, as things turned out − by performing a burlesque of the Mass, in which one of them, dressed as a dog, capered about the stage with a Host in his mouth. She had meant to proceed to Oxford at that time, but the plague, brought over by the defeated garrison from Dieppe, still hung about the city, and it was not until the summer of 1566 that it was thought safe for the eagerly expected visit to take place.

Although it was vacation time, practically the whole university remained in residence for her coming. The Court was at the Palace of Woodstock, a short journey away, and at the end of August, on an afternoon of heavy rain, Leicester, who was now Chancellor of the University, Sir William Cecil, and a few companions rode over to make the final arrangements. Two days later − Saturday 31st − the Queen followed them, attended by most of the Court and the Spanish Ambassador. Leicester came to meet her at Wolvercote, the boundary of the University Liberties; with him were the Vice-Chancellor and the Heads of Houses in their academic robes.

It was a formidable afternoon. From the moment that the gay and chattering procession crossed into university ground, the character of their reception became manifest. That day, at any rate, there was to be no levity; nor was there to be any haste. The cavalcade halted while the Provost of Oriel pronounced in laboriously polished Latin an address of welcome, which can have been intelligible to very few of the attendant ladies and gentlemen – the Earl of Warwick, Leicester's brother, a tough, middle-aged soldier; Edward de Vere, Earl of Oxford, aged 16, Cecil's son-in-law, but a child of the old nobility, soon to get into trouble for murdering a servant; young Edward Manners, Duke of Rutland – all sitting patiently on their horses while the phrases of the oration rose and fell in the best Ciceronian style. At length it came to an end, compliments were exchanged, and the procession moved off. A few miles further on another little cluster of notables was assembled – the Mayor of the City and the civic dignitaries. Here the speeches were in English, but at the North Gate another don was in wait for them, Mr Deal of New College, with an oration in Latin. From the gate to Carfax the way was lined with kneeling and applauding scholars; this was the kind of thing to which the Court was accustomed, but at Carfax came another check, Lawrence the Regius Professor, with a composition in Greek. It was the finest oration, the Queen said, that she had ever heard in Greek; she was prepared for an exchange of pleasantries in the same language, but, in pity for the evident distress of her followers, she consented to postpone it until they reached their lodgings. The company moved on again, litter and hackney, but the speeches were not yet over. At the gates of Christ Church Mr Kingsmill, the University Orator, was ready to welcome them. The Queen heard him to the end, but, grown slightly testy by this time, merely remarked in acknowledgement, 'You would have done well had you had good matter.'

The Court crossed the threshold of the House; they were now among the very buildings where most of them were to be quartered, but their hosts had not yet done with them. Four Doctors in their scarlet robes were observed advancing upon the royal party across the quadrangle, carrying a canopy; under this Elizabeth was led to church where, in sonorous English, prayers were offered in thanksgiving for her safe arrival; an anthem was sung to the music of cornets; after the anthem there were more prayers. At last, late in the evening, the weary courtiers were allowed to disperse, to see to their baggage and their beds, to wash and refresh themselves, while the young Queen stole away to her lodgings through the gathering shadows of Dr Westphaling's garden.

The visit lasted for six days. There were some lighter moments: a Latin play in Christ Church Hall, called *Marcus Geminus*, which the Queen did not attend (the Spanish Ambassador spoke so highly of it that she resolved to lose no more sport thereafter); an English play acted in two parts named *Palemon and Arcyte*, at the first night of which the stage collapsed, killing three people and injuring five more; on the second night a pack of hounds was introduced into the quadrangle, which moved the young scholars, confined to the upper stories, to such excitement that the Queen expressed her fear that they would fall out of the windows; there were several elaborate dinners; but for the most part the entertainment was strictly academic; orations, sermons, debates, the presentation of Latin verses translated from the Hebrew, the conferring of honorary degrees.

It was not until the third day, Tuesday, 3 September, when the senior members had played their parts, that Edmund Campion made his appearance. He was then 26 years old, seven years younger than the Queen, but already a person of outstanding importance in the university. At the age of 17 he had become a Fellow of St John's, and almost immediately attracted round him a group of pupils over whom he exerted an effortless and comprehensive influence; they crowded to his lectures, imitated his habits of speech, his mannerisms, and his clothes, and were proud to style themselves 'Campionists'. There had been a certain difficulty in choosing suitable subjects for debate, for the subject in everyone's mind at Oxford and on everyone's tongue was the Queen's change of religion; Cecil had carefully edited the list of propositions, eliminating Jewel's attempt to bring matters to an issue; it was well known that Oxford, and particularly St John's, was predominantly Catholic in sympathy; the last thing that he wanted was to embarrass the occasion by arousing the theological passions that had flamed into disorder when Peter Martyr had been Professor of Divinity. Discussion was confined to strictly secular subjects, and to Campion fell the task of proposing 'that the tides are caused by the moon's motion', and 'that the lower bodies of the universe are regulated by the higher'.

Throughout his career Campion preserved a naïve interest in natural science, and later, in the dark hours when he was fighting for his reputation in Hopton's Hall, he was willing to prove to his judges that the heavens were as hard as crystal. Now he seems to have treated the question at issue as a subordinate matter; all his eloquence, the delicate accent, the terse, stylish antitheses, the strong and accurate diction, that made him the model of the schools, was devoted to the praise of the Queen and the Vice-Chancellor. Speaking in Latin, he began: 'One thing only reconciles me to the unequal contest, which I must maintain single-handed against four pugnacious youths; that I am speaking in the name of Philosophy, the princess of letters, before Elizabeth, the lettered princess.'

He praised the learning of her ancestors and her condescension in visiting her poor scholars; then he turned to the Earl of Leicester, who sat beside her, and reminded him that it was due to his godly and deathless benefactions that the university had thrown off its lethargy and was once more advancing in hope.

'May God preserve these benefits to us; may He preserve,' bowing left and right, 'your Majesty, your Honour; you our mother, you our protector – *te quae haec facis, te qui haec mones*,' at which the Queen, turning smiling in her seat towards the Earl, said: 'You, my lord, must still be one.'

The balanced compliments succeeded one another, until, remarking that the poor scholars had no fit present to offer their visitors except what was within them, something from 'the veins and bowels of philosophy', Campion proceeded to his subject and briefly expounded the theory that the sea was constantly blown out with vapours, like water boiling in a pot.

The speech was the success of the afternoon. The Queen warmly applauded and commended Campion to Leicester, and later, when the Spanish Ambassador remarked that, though laudable, the speeches were, after all, well prepared beforehand, and the Queen assembled the most notable orators for an extempore debate at Merton, Campion was among them, and spoke on the subject of 'Fire' in a way to confirm her highest opinions of him. Before leaving Oxford, both Cecil and Leicester saw Campion privately, and promised him their patronage.

He could hardly have been offered two more different patrons – the secretary, purposeful, cautious, self-controlled, indefatigable, middle-class, the man of the desk and the Council table; and the flamboyant courtier, swarthy and swaggering, magnificent, impulsive, a spectacular horseman, a soldier; descended on one side from the great families of English history, Talbot and Beauchamp, on the other from the reckless, bloodstained house of Dudley; three generations of Dudleys, his grandfather, his father, and his brother, had died on the scaffold; perhaps no one in Oxford doubted that Amy Robsart, whose obsequies four years before they had piously celebrated, had been murdered at his orders. At any hour he might become the Queen's husband. His was all the glamour of the great world that lay beyond the University Liberties; the pageantry and the high politics of the new reign. It was to him that Campion immediately attached himself.

And Leicester did not neglect his satellite. At Woodstock and Rycote, when the Court felt the need for a serious interlude, it was often Campion who was summoned to minister to them. For, though to the dazzled young scholar their world might seem something intangibly remote, those in power knew very well that they had need of men like Campion. There had been a grave purpose behind the visit to Oxford.

For the past twenty-five years education in England had been in a state of disorder which threatened at any moment to become chaos. At the beginning of the century Erasmus had placed English scholarship above that of France or the Germanies, second only to Italy in its breadth of culture. It was to England that the University of Leipzig had turned for its professor of Greek; Colet, Grocyn, Lynacre, and More were able to converse on terms of equality with the leading men of Padua, and under their temperate and profound influence Oxford was emerging gradually, steadily, by a process of organic growth, from the cloistered formality of the Middle Ages into the spacious, luminous world of Catholic humanism. With the Pope's encouragement Wolsey had taken over monastic revenues for the endowment of Christ Church; Fox, Bishop of Winchester, instituted the first Greek lectureship in the foundation of Corpus; the faction of 'Trojans' who were opposed to the new learning were being gently pressed into acquiescence by the King and the Bishops. Close correspondence was kept with the great teachers of Italy, and the foundations were laid of a Renaissance which, illuminated by the poetic genius native to the country, might, in a generation, have been one of the glories of Europe.

All this ended abruptly and violently at Henry's break with the Pope. When the Church was in undisputed authority she could afford to wink at a little speculative fancy in her philosophers, a pagan exuberance of taste in her artists; now, when she was driven to defend the basis and essential structure of her faith, there was no room for indulgence; controversy took first place among the Arts, and scholars became famous for their views on the Mass rather than their appreciation of classical poetry.

More than this, the confiscators of ecclesiastical property made havoc of university finance. Education all over the country was dependent upon monastic and chantry foundations, and at their suppression grammar-school education in many districts came utterly to an end. Here and there the revenues of the dispossessed religious were kept for public services, and a few reorganized grammar schools survived under charters of Edward VI, but in the great majority of cases the estates went direct to the courtiers. At Oxford the colleges were a comparatively new institution, and a large part of university life still centred in the halls which the various abbeys and priories maintained for their students. These were all emptied; the undergraduates dependent on monastic exhibitions were turned adrift and the colleges themselves entertained well-founded apprehensions of how long they would be allowed to survive. The courtiers both of Henry VIII and Somerset had pressed for their abolition; the demand, in both cases, was resisted and rebuked, but the thirst for plunder was not slaked and it is possible that, if Edward VI had lived some years longer, both universities would have come to grief. As it was, the visitors of Edward VI suppressed many of the exhibitions for poor students which had survived the acts of confiscation, and only the strenuous protests of the citizens saved Magdalen Grammar School from extinction. The college chapels were ransacked of Popish ornaments; the great reredos of All Souls was destroyed, and New College windows only survived on the Fellows' promise to have them out, as soon as they could afford to replace them with plain glass; but it was upon books that the Anglicans particularly turned their disapproval. The whole of Duke Humphrey's library was gutted and the shelves sold in the streets; the illuminated office books in Magdalen choir were hacked up with choppers, and from every college cartloads of books were removed to be burned or sold as waste paper; a coloured initial was enough to convict the contents of Popery; a mathematical diagram of magic. When the visitors left, the collections of centuries had been irretrievably ruined.

Better order was restored under Mary. Two new colleges, St John's and Trinity, were founded, but the past could not be recalled. There was another upheaval at Elizabeth's succession, and numerous Catholics lost their chairs and fellowships; no one felt confidence in the rewards of scholarship. Politics and theology continued to sway university elections. A great tradition had been broken. Not for a hundred years was the university to know security, and it was to emerge from its troubles provincial, phlegmatic, and exclusive; not for 300 years was it to re-emerge as a centre of national life.

Elizabeth and Cecil were well aware of these conditions. They had a genuine and deep respect for learning, and one object of the visit had been to assure the scholars of royal favour. In this they were successful; the numbers taking degrees show a marked increase from this time. But there was another and more delicate mission.

From its earliest days the university had been primarily a place for the training of churchmen. By the statutes, Holy Orders were obligatory on aspirants for almost all the important offices. Sons of the aristocracy might keep term in the interests of culture, but the general assumption for the poor scholars was that they were qualifying as priests. Now Cecil and Elizabeth were finding it very hard to get suitable candidates for ministry in the new church. By the first acts of the reign they had made the Mass illegal and issued a Prayer Book based on the two experimental books of Edward VI. This had been done against the unanimous vote of Convocation, and it was followed by the resignation or deprivation of a considerable number of the clergy. It is impossible, through the absence of many of the records, to estimate at all accurately the number of parish priests who gave up their cures and drifted into penury or other employment – probably about 500 – but the names of most of the higher clergy have been preserved, and these include the entire episcopate, with the exception of Kitchen of Llandaff, 15 heads of colleges, 10 deans, 12 archdeacons, and 47 prebendaries. The new church was thus starting its history with a painful shortage of qualified leaders. Those who preferred to accept the change and make careers for themselves in the establishment against which they had protested were not the most desirable of the old body; reluctant acquiescence was the best for which Cecil and Elizabeth could hope, except from one quarter where support was wholly unwelcome. They had no more taste for the extremists of their own party than they had for the Catholics. Elizabeth's personal inclinations were towards something mildly ceremonious in public worship; she kept a cross and candles in her chapel, she preferred her ministers to be celibate and suitably vested, she liked to think that her church had retained something from the tradition of her ancestors. Had she been born in an age which offered no alternative, she would have conformed complacently enough, for, apart from a pronounced deficiency in faith, hope, and charity, she had in many ways a naturally Catholic temperament; Cecil, though more austere in taste, already divined in the theocratic system of Geneva and the wild oratory of St Andrews the spirit that was later to wreck the monarchy; neither had any use for the fanatical Puritans. They needed, to guide their church through her difficult infancy, a new kind of cleric; sober, decently educated men, with a proper devotion to the Crown and the Council, men of common sense who could see where their advantage lay, men of high repute who could override the suggestion that religion had fallen to the management of knaves and eccentrics. Inevitably, it was to the younger members of the universities that they turned; Campion seemed a man eminently suitable to their purpose. His charm and attainments were easily apparent; he was sprung from just that stock of London tradespeople where the chief strength of Protestantism lay; he was completely without resources, and had his way to make in the world.

There was another young Oxford man who attracted their particular attention, a Fellow of Christ Church named Tobie Matthew. He was younger than Campion, barely 20 years old, and had had no part in the debates in the schools. It was not until Elizabeth's last day in Oxford that he was presented to her, when he made a farewell oration which attracted her so much that she nominated him her scholar. Cecil looked after him well; a splendid career lay before him. He became Canon of Christ Church four years later; in 1572, at the unusually early age of 26, he was made President of St John's, where he set himself to release the college from its obligation to receive poor scholars elected from the Merchant Taylors; four years later he was Dean of Christ Church, later Vice-Chancellor; from there he turned to the greater world, became successively Dean and Bishop of Durham, and, finally, Archbishop of York. He was a talkative little man, always eager to please, always ready with a neat, parsonic witticism; the best of good fellows, everywhere, except in his own family. When, on the Council of the North, he was most busy hunting down recusants, he was full of little jokes to beguile his colleagues. He was a great preacher. At first he kept no count of his sermons, but later, realizing their importance, he scored them punctually in a book; between his elevation to the Deanery of Durham and his death he preached 1,992 times. In James's reign he saw the trend of the times, and, alone among the bishops, voted in favour of conference with the lower House. He married admirably, a widow of stout Protestant principles and unique place in the new clerical caste, which had sprung naturally from the system of married clergy; Frances Barlow, widow of Matthew Parker, Junior; she was notable in her generation as having a bishop for her father, an archbishop for her father-in-law, an archbishop for her husband, and four bishops for her brothers. Tobie Matthew died full of honours in 1628. There, but for the Grace of God, went Edmund Campion.

The visitors departed and the university settled down to its normal routine. At St John's work started early with a lecture in logic at half-past six; at nine there was a Greek lecture; rhetoric at one or two; there were also university lectures once or twice in the week on divinity, grammar, physics, and metaphysics. Mathematics was left to vacations. In hall the college dined at three tables, the Fellows and masters at one, bachelors and third-year undergraduates at another, the choristers and students at a third; recreation was limited to the bow and arrow. At night the scholars slept in a single, large dormitory, two in a bed, until they were over 16 years of age. The Fellows and tutors had their own rooms, which they shared with a scholar deputed to work for them. Every scholar was put under the particular supervision of a tutor, who directed his studies, saw that his hair was trimmed and his manners orderly, and, when necessary, corrected him with the birch. The founder of the college, Sir Thomas White, had lived until 1564, and up to his death he saw to it that the rules he had laid down were properly observed. He was a city magnate of modest education and simple piety; a childless old man who devoted the whole of his great wealth to benefactions. The last years of his life were quite overclouded by the change of religion; he collected the sacred vessels from the college chapel and stored them away in his own house for a happier day, and was obliged to stand by helpless while the authorities perverted the ends of his own foundation; he saw the poor scholars whom he had adopted and designed for the priesthood trained in a new way of thought and ordained with different rites, for a different purpose. He had set down in his statutes that the day was to begin with Mass, said in the Sarum use; at Elizabeth's accession it ceased, never to be restored; he saw three of his Presidents, Belsire, Elye, and Stork, deposed by the authorities for their faith. He died a comparatively poor man, out of favour at Court, out of temper with the times, and was buried according to Protestant rites; Campion speaking the funeral oration in terms which appear rather patronizing.

Perhaps in secret a Mass was said for him; it is impossible to say. There were still many priests in Oxford, and at this time the greater part of St John's was Catholic in sympathy, but no record survives of any such act, and it seems probable that from the early days of Elizabeth until the counter-reformationary period, fifteen or twenty years later, Catholicism at Oxford was largely a matter of sentiment and loyalty to the old ways, rather than of active spiritual life. The best men, like William Allen, had left the university and the country. Those that remained honoured the Church in much the same way as the dons of the eighteenth century were to honour the House of Stuart. At Merton they enjoyed singing Popish hymns round the fire at night, as a later generation were to sing Jacobite songs. But the saying of Mass was a different matter. Whatever the sectional differences between the various Anglican groups, they were united in their resolve to stamp out this vital practice of the old religion.

They struck hard at all the ancient habits of spiritual life – the rosary, devotion to Our Lady and the Saints, pilgrimages, religious art, fasting, confession, penance, and the great succession of traditional holidays – but the Mass was recognized as being both the distinguishing sign and main sustenance of their opponents. The objects specially connected with it, the vestments, plate, and missals, were singled out for destruction; the altar stones were taken for paving and cheese presses; they ridiculed the Host in broadsheets and burlesques, called it by derisive nicknames, 'Round Robin', 'Jack in the Box', and 'Wormes Meat'. 'Massing priests' is the phrase constantly used in Cecil's correspondence to designate the Marian priests; the right to have Mass said in a private chapel was one of the main questions at issue in the negotiations for Elizabeth's marriage with her Catholic suitors; one of the terms suggested for peace with Mary Stuart was that she should 'abandon the Mass in Scotland and receive Common Prayer after the form of England'. It was one of the complaints against de Quadra that he had allowed strangers to hear Mass in the Embassy Chapel. Other instances of the kind can be quoted almost interminably; many will occur in the course of this narrative. On occasions the feeling found extravagant expression. In July 1581 the congregation in St Peter's at Rome was startled by an infuriated Anglican tourist who attempted to snatch the Host from the priest's hand, while in November of the same year another Englishman upset the chalice and attempted to strangle the priest in S. Maria del Popolo.

Opinion differed on the significance of the 'Lord's Supper or Holy Communion' service which had been composed in its place; it was employed as an occasional service for communicants only, not as the central act of worship; the wording was devised so as to embrace, as far as possible, the conflicting theories of Luther, Calvin, Zwingli, and Bucer, but it was explicit in its dissociation from the Catholic Mass. It was on this very point – not of the Papal supremacy – that the condemned heretics of Mary's reign went to the stake; men and women of noble resolution to whom the new church looked back as martyrs, worthy of the same veneration which Catholics paid to Fisher and More, and the record of whose sufferings, in Foxe's highly inaccurate chronicle, was placed beside the Bible in the churches.

The law at this period (1559–70) was mild in comparison with what it subsequently became; the priest, for saying Mass in public or private, was liable at the first conviction to one year's sequestration from his benefice and six months' imprisonment; at the second, to deprivation and a year's imprisonment; at the third, to imprisonment for life. Anyone inducing him to offend in this way was fined 100 marks in the first case, 400 in the second, and in the third forfeited his entire property and was imprisoned for life. But there do not appear to have been any convictions under this Act at Oxford. Later, in 1577, when the penalties were far heavier and more rigorously imposed, a Mr Etheridge was arrested for having Mass said in his house; there seems, too, at that time, to have been a regular chapel frequented by Catholics in the cellars under the Mitre Inn, but during the time that Campion was in residence submission on this point may have been complete; the ambiguous attitude of himself and his contemporaries is easily explicable on the assumption that throughout the whole of this period they were entirely deprived of the sacraments.

He probably had taken the oath of supremacy when he became B.A. in 1560; he must have put in a fairly regular appearance at the Protestant services in the college chapel; in 1568 he committed himself more gravely by accepting ordination as deacon at the hands of his friend Cheney, Bishop of Gloucester. But it seems clear that he took this step to avoid rather than to invite prominence in ecclesiastical affairs. In this confused and ill-documented decade, the Catholics, left without effective leadership, appear to have been dealing with the problem of conformity, each in his own way. It was one which varied greatly in different parts of the country. Some refused the oath and went into exile; some paid the penalties of the law. Some, who were popular or locally powerful, avoided, year after year, taking the oath at all; some took the oath and meant nothing by it. That generation was inured to change; sooner or later the tide would turn in their favour again; a Protestant coup, such as was spoken of, to enthrone the Earl of Huntingdon might inflame a national rising and restore the old religion; the Queen might die and be succeeded by Mary Stuart; she might marry a Catholic; she might declare for Catholicism herself. In any case, things were not likely to last on their present unreasonable basis. It was one thing for a Government to suppress dangerous innovations – that was natural enough; but for the innovators to be in command, for them to try and crush out by force historic Christianity – that was contrary to all good sense; it was like living under the Turks. At the worst there would soon be a truce, and both parties would practise their religions without interference. So they muddled along, waiting for better times to come. In many places the priest would say Mass in his own house for the Catholics before proceeding to read Morning Prayer in the parish church; occasionally, it is said, he would even bring consecrated wafers and communicate his Catholic parishioners at the same time as he distributed to the Protestants the bread blessed according to the new rite.

At Oxford the division was more sharply defined; there was a Catholic party in the majority, and a Protestant party in the ascendant. Campion hesitated between the two, reluctant to decide. What he wished was to be left in peace to pursue his own studies, to discharge the duties which soon fell on him as proctor and public orator, to do his best for his pupils. But he was born into the wrong age for these gentle ambitions; he must be either much more, or much less. By the statutes of the college he was obliged, if he wished to make his career in the university, to proceed to the study of theology and the acceptance of Holy Orders. He put it off as long as he could, concentrating at first upon Aristotle and natural theology, where there was little to entangle him in the controversies of the day, but in 1567 he had, in the normal course, to proceed to the study of the Fathers. Here every sentence seemed to bear a topical allusion, and the deeper he penetrated into the minds of the Doctors, the further he seemed from the Anglican Church which he was designed to enter. He fled and doubled from the conclusions of his reason; nothing but ill was promised for him by the way he was being drawn; he prayed fervently, he consulted those about him. Shrewd little Tobie Matthew was recognized as a specialist on the subject. Earnestly, man to man, Campion asked him how, with his deep knowledge of the Fathers, he could take the side he did.

'If I believed them as well as read them,' Matthew replied, 'you would have good reason to ask.'

It was no longer a question of theology, but of morals. Campion could not, like Cheney of Gloucester, affect to recognize in Cecil's establishment the ancient church of Augustine and Thomas à Becket; nor could he, like Grindal, find it probable that the truth, hidden from the world for fifteen centuries, had suddenly been revealed in the last few years to a group of important Englishmen. Elizabeth and Cecil had refused their co-operation in the Council of Trent. England had been represented there, but by the dispossessed and fugitive Bishop Goldwell of St Asaph. The continuity of English Catholicism survived, but in the secret, illegal congregations of the remote countryside and among the ever-growing colonies of refugees in Rome, the Netherlands, and the Channel ports. The official Anglican Church had cut itself off from the great surge of vitality that flowed from the Council; it was, by its own choice, insular and national. The question before Campion was, not whether the Church of England was heretical, but whether, in point of fact, heresy was a matter of great importance; whether in problems of such infinite magnitude, human minds could ever hope for accuracy, whether all formulations were not, of necessity, so inadequate that their differences were of no significance. Tobie Matthew's way lay smooth before him; it was not on his responsibility that the changes had been made; perhaps they were regrettable, but, since that was the condition of the times, it was the duty of a loyal Englishman to throw in his lot with the Government and make the best of what was left. The new services were written in language which any man of culture might delight to enunciate; the points of variance, compared with the similarities, were not numerous. Campion loved his country and his countrymen; the way was easy for him to live among them in honour and authority; the ancient Cathedrals were still standing, scarred and scoured perhaps, but fine prizes in the Government's gift – massive, visible tokens of unity with the past; titles of honour were still to be won which had been borne by the saints and scholars of antiquity. In a world where every thing was, by its nature, a makeshift and poor reflection of reality, why throw up so much that was excellent, in straining for a remote and perhaps unattainable perfection?

It was an argument which might be – which was – acceptable to countless decent people, then and later, but there was that in Campion that made him more than a decent person; an embryo in the womb of his being, maturing in darkness, invisible, barely stirring; the love of holiness, the need for sacrifice. He could not accept.

Now, when Campion most required tranquillity in which to adjust his vision to the new light that was daily becoming clearer and more dazzling, events outside his control, both at Oxford and in the world at large, became increasingly obtrusive. Throughout the country discontent with Cecil's policy became consolidated. Under the Tudor system of government there was no place for a legitimate opposition; it was forced into conspiracy or rebellion. Leicester was deeply involved in intrigue with the Duke of Norfolk and the Conservative peers; this party, though led in part by Protestants and impelled primarily by feudal distaste for the Queen's low-born advisers, looked to the Catholics as their main source of support. At the same time the Government was drifting towards an antagonism to Spain which could only result in war. In the spring of '68 Mary Stuart took refuge and was imprisoned in England; in the winter the Queen confiscated a fleet of Spanish treasure ships which had put into harbour in Plymouth and Southampton, carrying half a million ducats to the Duke of Alva. England and Spain were confronted with precisely similar problems in Ireland and the Netherlands, and both had reason to fear the damage the other would do to them among their disaffected subjects. In the event of war abroad or rebellion at home, Cecil felt that the Catholics constituted a grave menace. They were proving more stubborn in their faith than had at first seemed likely. Books of controversy, printed by the English exiles abroad, were finding their way into the country in disturbing quantities; up till now the Catholics had spent little time in detailed argument; when in power, they had judged their opponents on the grounds of authority and obedience; now the old faith was being restated in new and persuasive terms, applicable to a generation who had grown up without the heritage of instinctive respect for tradition, terms of reason, and research. It would have been easy to show lenience to a moribund superstition, the sentimental regrets of an old generation that was rapidly dying out; here was something unexpectedly vigorous and up to date, which must either suffer decisive and immediate defeat, or conquer. Accordingly, all over England the commissioners and magistrates were instructed to take a firmer line; at first no new legislation was used, but the law which before had been administered with some tact was everywhere more sternly enforced. More Catholics went into exile, among them Gregory Martin, Campion's closest friend for thirteen years, who had left Oxford to act as tutor in the Duke of Norfolk's family. The repression had begun which was to develop year by year from strictness to savagery, until, at the close of the century, it had become the bloodthirsty persecution in which Margaret Clitheroe was crushed to death between mill stones for the crime of harbouring a priest.

Campion, although a deacon and nominal member of the Church of England, had made no secret of his spiritual wanderings; he had taken his doubts eagerly to anyone who he hoped might resolve them. He was not a reserved man; he loved argument; ideas, for him, demanded communication, and it was his particular genius to give them expression in lucid and memorable phrases. No one in Oxford can have been in any doubt of the way in which his mind was leading him.

But even had this not been his method; had he, instead, gone gravely about the duties of his office, lecturing, preaching, giving his advice at college meetings, and all the time waged a deep, interior argument, hearing anyone's views, never committing himself, until one day, his mind made up, he could startle his associates by a calm renunciation of all he had seemed to represent, he would have come under suspicion, now, when everyone watched his neighbour for signs of heterodoxy, by his familiarity with Richard Cheney of Gloucester.

It was in this Bishop's library and at his table that half Campion's opinions were at this time formed. He was a virtuous, mild, learned, deeply embarrassed old gentleman of utterly different mind from his busy colleagues. He was the first high-churchman. His clergy regarded him as little better than a Papist, for he supported the Lutheran doctrine of consubstantiation, which affirmed the miraculous character of the Mass, and differed from Catholic teaching on points to which only metaphysicians could attend; he believed in the freedom of the will and the efficacy of good works, and was denounced for preaching 'very strange, perilous, and corrupt doctrine, contrary to the Gospel'. He was excommunicated by his fellow-bishops. He employed against his opponents just those arguments from the Fathers and Councils which the Catholics could turn against him. Later from Douai, in 1572, Campion wrote to him one of his most eloquent letters, exposing the ignominy of his position.

. . . You are sixty years old, more or less, of uncertain health, of weakened body, the hatred of heretics, the pity of Catholics, the talk of the people, the sorrow of your friends, the joke of your enemies. Against your conscience you falsely usurp the name of bishop, by your silence you advance a pestilential sect which you love not, stricken with anathema, cut off from the body into which alone the graces of Christ flow, you are deprived of the benefit of all prayers, sacrifices, and sacraments. What do you think yourself to be? What do you expect? What is your life? Wherein lies your hope?

He urges him, with all the strength of his own new-found spiritual confidence, to make his surrender. But it needed more than a gentle heart and pious disposition to make a Catholic in that age; the old man stayed in his palace, increasingly lonely, maligned, distracted; deep in debt, sued by the Crown for 'tenths'; he died, as far as is known, undecided, and was buried without tomb or memorial in his own Cathedral; he was succeeded, first, by a dunce, next, by an absentee; the little work he had accomplished to preserve decency and toleration was quite undone, and thereafter there were few dioceses in England where the persecution was more ruthlessly pursued than in Gloucester.

Early in the gathering storm, pressure was brought upon Campion to declare himself. A part of his income was derived from an exhibition paid by the Grocers Company of the City of London. As rumours of his Popish sympathies began to spread, a demand was made by them that he should come to London and clear himself by preaching at St Paul's Cross before Candlemas. At first Campion asked for a postponement, and the ordeal was put off until Michaelmas, when he would have had leisure to prepare his arguments.

He was proctor at the time, an office which then involved heavy obligations in university and town. He resented this attempt of the city merchants to dictate to his conscience, and protested that declarations of the kind demanded were neither their business nor his; his duty lay at Oxford where he was a 'public person . . . charged with the education of divers worshipful men's children'. They suggested a less conspicuous place for his confession, the pulpit of St Stephen's Church, Walbrook. He still refused and the company accordingly deprived him of his exhibition.

There was no injustice in the sentence, nor did it involve any great hardship, for Campion was now in possession of a benefice given him by Cheney; he was fully alive to the ambiguity of the position into which he had put himself by becoming a deacon. It was daily becoming more difficult for him to remain in England. Gregory Martin was writing to him from Douai, urging him to leave, before he compromised himself further. On 1 August 1569, Campion's term of office as proctor came to an end. He punctually fulfilled his last duties, set things in order for his successor, and delivered the customary account of the year's work in his elegant, Ciceronian Latin. It was his last public act in the university.

A period of uncertain duration followed before he left Oxford, and then he did not go at once to join Gregory Martin at Douai; he does not appear to have contemplated becoming a priest at all; it is improbable, indeed, that he was as yet formally reconciled to the Church; by canon law he had put himself in a state of excommunication, and it is highly unlikely that, placed as he was, he could get into touch with anyone possessed of the necessary faculties to absolve him. He was, however, openly Catholic by conviction, and recognized as one by friends and opponents. It remained to be tried, whether it was possible to readjust his life on this basis; whether there was any honourable life open to a Catholic layman. Only by slow stages was it revealed to Campion how complete was the sacrifice required of him. He had powerful friends and a brilliant reputation. Surely with these it must still be possible to make a career in the world, without doing violence to his religion? Surely it was not expected of him to give up *all*?

The present of a book turned his thoughts towards Ireland; it was from Richard Stanihurst, one of his most devoted pupils; the boy's own first composition, a commentary on Porphyry. Stanihurst's father was Recorder of Dublin and Speaker in the Irish House of Commons, a prominent man in the project, then on foot, to establish an Irish University. Here, it seemed, was an opportunity exactly suited to a man of Campion's attainments and antecedents. He was known to Sir Henry Sidney, the Lord Deputy. According to reports, the Reformation had, so far, made little stir in Dublin; laws of supremacy and uniformity had been enacted, but no great pains were taken to enforce them. Sidney was known to be tolerant, if not sympathetic, and, except for the Anglicized official class, everyone of importance still adhered to the old belief. Accordingly, with Leicester's approval, Campion repaired to Dublin, where he was warmly received by the Stanihursts. Sidney promised him protection from police interference. He was given lodging in the Stanihursts' Dublin house. Besides Richard, there was a daughter who later married Ussher, a clerk of the Court of Chancery, and became mother of a future archbishop; and an elder brother, Walter, already married, but apparently living at home. The company they kept was drawn from the official Government class, partly civil servants sent out from England, partly the sons of Anglo-Irish families, most of whom had been educated across the channel. They were on cordial terms with the neighbouring gentry, such as the Barnewells, and Richard later married one of the Barnewell daughters, thus allying himself to the Dunsanys and other prominent families of the Pale. Campion was accepted on terms of warm familiarity. At an early age his education had separated him from his own family; though he had two brothers of his own and a sister, they seem never to have played any part in his life; apparently he never had the inclination to marry; the school-room, the college dining-hall, the common room, the cloister, were his constant surroundings. He had seen something of the splendid, formidable life of the Court. With the Stanihursts, for the first and last time in his life, he tasted the happiness of a normal, cultured household. Here he shared the daily experiences of a busy and affectionate home circle; he enjoyed intelligent, topical conversation; there was a good library and a study set apart for him to work in, and, ahead, the promise of distinguished employment, when the projected university took form. He settled in happily; he was at peace with his conscience, and, once more, on good terms with his surroundings. The ambition of serene scholarship and gentle, sympathetic society, so rudely disturbed at Oxford, seemed once more attainable; outside, beyond the mountains, among bog and rock, raged the tumultuous, tribal life of the Irish people, Geraldines, Butlers, and McCarthys prosecuting their endemic feuds; here, apart from all that, apart from the rancorous jostling and the dark, high intrigues of the English Renaissance, lay the cosy, colonial world of the Pale; no hate, no bloodshed . . .

He worked daily, coaching his old pupil, for his religion never overclouded his enthusiasm for learning and its rewards. 'Proceed with the same pains and toil,' he had written on receiving Richard Stanihurst's *Porphyry*, 'bury yourself in your books, complete your course . . . keep your mind on the stretch . . . strive for the prizes which you deserve. . . . Only persevere, do not degenerate from what you are, nor suffer the keen eye of your mind to grow dark and rusty.' With the project of the Irish University in his mind, he prepared a discourse *De Homine Academico*, an elaborate portrait of the ideal student. This paper has not survived in its original form, but we have an oration delivered shortly afterwards at Douai on the same subject, which was probably derived from it. Here he insists upon the virtues of piety, modesty, kindness, obedience, upon grace of deportment and civility of manners. The student's pronunciation must be specially cultivated, his mind 'subtle, hot, and clear, his memory happy, his voice flexible, sweet, and sonorous; his walk and all his motions lively, gentlemanly, and subdued'. His recreations are painting, playing the lute, singing at sight, writing music with facility and correctness.

His first years at school are devoted to Latin, the rudiments of Greek, and the control of his own language, in which he must compose verses and epigrams. Later he must become a finished debater in philosophy, modelling himself upon Cicero; by his sixteenth year he must be able to write Greek iambics. He must master all histories, classical and modern, the ethics and politics of Aristotle and Plato, logic and natural science, so as to deserve the title of 'oracle of nature'.

His habits of study must be regular and collected, he must not 'dull himself with unseasonable vigils' but allow seven hours' sleep at night and a proper attention to toilet and appearance. He must neither write licentious and amorous verses, nor fall into the puritanical extreme of eschewing the great literature of the past which occasionally bore this character. He must be a dialectician, an orator, an astronomer, and in his last year of study a master of Hebrew. He must be respectful to his superiors, generous in judgement of his equals, courteous and helpful to the obscure. This catalogue no doubt defines the aim which Campion was setting himself and, to a great extent, realizing at this period.

Soon afterwards he began work on a history of Ireland. Recorder Stanihurst's library contained numerous uncollated scraps, journals, annals, books of correspondence; his conversation, too, was full of information of doubtful historical value. Campion knew no Gaelic; nor, probably, did anyone in his circle. His attitude towards the 'mere Irish' was derived from the people among whom he lived, who were confident of their own superiority and the beneficence of their rule; they spoke of the unadmin-istered, alien territories almost exactly as their countertypes, the colonial officials of the nineteenth century, might speak of the bush lands of Africa; they retailed anecdotes of native savagery and superstition, and saw in English education the only cure for them; in Campion's own words, Ireland was 'much beholden to God for suffering them to be conquered, whereby many of their enormities were cured, and more might be, would themselves be pliable.'

The short history, begun at leisure but hastily scrambled together in the end, under pressing distractions, is remarkable as being Campion's only complete work which has survived in the English language. The rest of his published work was in Latin. The sermons, upon which his contem-porary fame most depended, were never taken down, and we can only guess at their character from rare, fragmentary quotations. *The History of Ireland* is a superb piece of literature, comparable in vigour and rhythm to anything written in his day. With all its imperfections of structure and material, it is enough to show that, had Campion continued in the life he was then planning for himself, he would, almost certainly, have come down in history as one of the great masters of English prose. From the lovely cadence of the opening sentences, describing the physical character of the country which 'lieth aloof in the West Ocean, in proportion like an egg, blunt and plain at the sides, not reaching forth to sea in nooks and elbows of land as Britain doth', to the balanced, Ciceronian speeches at the end it is manifestly the work of a stylist for whom form and matter were never in conflict; there is no shadow of the effort and ostentation which clouds all but the brightest genius of the period.

Three extracts, chosen almost at random, must suffice to suggest the flavour of the work:

> The people are thus inclined: religious, frank, amorous, ireful, sufferable, of pains infinite, very glorious; many sorcerers, excellent horsemen, delighted with wars, great almsgivers, passing in hospitality. The lewder sort, both clerks and laymen, are sensual and loose to lechery above measure. The same, being virtuously bred up and reformed, are such mirrors of holiness and austerity, that other nations retain but a show or shadow of devotion in comparison of them.

> Clear men they are of skin and hue, but of themselves careless and bestial. Their women are well favoured, clear coloured, fair headed, big and large, suffered from their infancy to grow at will, nothing curious of their feature and proportion of body.

> 'Look, sir King; eye us well; it is not light prowess that has caused these valiant bodies to stoop. Scythians were we, and the Picts of Scythia – great substance of glory lodgeth in these two names.'

Campion's superiority to his contemporaries is well illustrated by comparing his work with another, anonymous, history written at about this time and collected later by Holinshed. They are both paraphrasing from the same chapter by Giraldus Cambrensis.

The one writes 'And here you may see the nature and disposition of this wicked, effrenated, barbarous and unfaithful nation who (as Cambrensis writeth of them) they are a wicked and perverse generation, constant always in that they are always inconstant, faithful in that they be unfaithful,' and so on for the length of a column.

Campion renders it in two sentences 'Covenant and indent with them never so warily, yet they have been found faithless and perjured. Where they are joined in colour of surest amity, there they intend to kill.'

So easily, inevitably, through page after page of this little book, barely more than a pamphlet, the melodious phrases fall into place. What a translator for the Vulgate was lost in Campion!

The work was dedicated to Leicester – for Campion still looked to him as his patron – in an inscription of exquisite grace.

> There is none that knoweth me familiarly, but he knoweth withal how many ways I have been beholden to your lordship. . . . How often at Oxford, how often at the Court, how at Rycote, how at Windsor, how by letters, how by reports, you have not ceased to further with advice, and to countenance with authority, the hope and expectation of me, a single student. Let every man esteem in your state and fortune the thing that best contenteth and serveth his imagination; but surely to a judgement settled and rectified, these outward felicities which the world gazeth on, are there and therefore to be deemed praisable when they lodge those inward qualities of the mind, which (saving for suspicion of flattery) I was about to say are planted in your breast. Thirteen years to have lived in the eye and special credit of a prince, yet never during all that space to have abused this ability to any man's harm; to be enriched with no man's overthrow, to be kindled neither with grudge nor emulation, to benefit an infinite resort of daily suitors . . . these are indeed the kernels for which the shell of your nobility seemeth fair and sightly. . . . This is the substance which maketh you worthy of the ornaments wherewith you are attired.

Admirable prose, redolent of the security and good humour in which it was written; tender, and big with promise for the future.

But this happy interlude proved brief and all the warm prospects illusory. A few subscriptions were raised for the new university; a site was suggested for it and a name – Plantolinum, in compliment of the Boleyn family; it was constantly discussed, but during the discussions it became clear that there were two parties in Dublin, on the one side Sidney, Stanihurst, and Campion, on the other the Protestant clergy under the leadership of the Chancellor, Dr Weston. The question was referred back to Cecil and nearly a generation elapsed before the scheme at last took form in the institution of Trinity College.

Anti-Catholic feeling, which at first had been scarcely perceptible in Ireland, was brought into life by the events of the succeeding months.

In the winter of 1569 the rebellion of the Northern Earls had taken place in England; though feudal in essential character, it assumed a religious aspect when, as each place fell to the rebels, the Mass was restored there. Leicester had deserted the conspirators some time before; the Duke of Norfolk surrendered himself, and what had at one time threatened to be a widespread conservative reaction ended in a local adventure which never extended beyond a day's march of the traditional Percy and Neville territories; it was the last, forlorn protest of pre-Tudor chivalry. Mary Stuart was moved to the Midlands; the feudal levies melted away, and the Government forces settled themselves to a leisurely campaign of hanging in the affected areas. It had not caused serious alarm in Whitehall, but it had the effect of planting in the public mind the association of Catholicism with political treason which was to prove ineradicable for generations; the first sparks of that fierce and almost fatal conflagration which, stoked by Ridolfi and Guy Fawkes, was to smoulder on, through the Titus Oates conspiracy and the Gordon riots, almost until modern times.

In the spring of 1570 there occurred another event that completely recast the Catholic cause; Pope Pius V excommunicated the Queen. It is possible that one of his more worldly predecessors might have acted differently, or at another season, but it was the pride and slight embarrassment of the Church that, as has happened from time to time in her history, the See of Peter was at this moment occupied by a Saint. Pius was a Dominican friar of austere observance and profound spiritual life; as the Duke of Alva complained, he seemed always to expect events in the world to take place without human agency. He chose a life of great loneliness; he lived in a little set of rooms removed from the great state apartments of the Vatican; he confided in no one and took counsel from very few; the Turks were threatening Christianity in the rear, her centre was torn by new heresies, his allies were compromising and intriguing, their purpose distracted by ambitions of empire and influence; in long vigils of silent, interior communion, Pius contemplated only the abiding, abstract principles that lay behind the phantasmagoric changes of human affairs. He prayed earnestly about the situation in England, and saw it with complete clarity; it was a question that admitted of no doubt whatever. Elizabeth was illegitimate by birth, she had violated her coronation oath, deposed her bishops, issued a heretical Prayer Book and forbidden her subjects the comfort of the sacraments. No honourable Catholic could be expected to obey her. The Emperor, the Duke of Alva, the King of Spain, were shocked at his decision. He consulted nobody; he acted without any regard to the events of the moment. He had heard of the rising of the Northern Earls and had been delighted with it; he did not know whether it had succeeded. Every government maintained its own secret lines of communication; his were far from efficient; it took three months or more for him to get a letter from England. He knew that there had been a rising, and that by now it was probably decided, one way or the other; rumours had, perhaps, reached Rome of its failure; he did not wait to hear them. The formalities were observed; in the first week of Lent a Court of Enquiry heard the evidence of twelve trustworthy English witnesses; Elizabeth was charged and found guilty on seventeen counts; on 12 February Pius pronounced the sentence which on the 25th was embodied in the Bull *Regnans in Excelsis*. Elizabeth was excommunicated and her subjects released from the moral obligations of obedience to her.

Three months later, on Corpus Christi Day, 25 May, a manuscript copy of the document was nailed to the door of the Bishop of London's palace, in St Paul's Churchyard, by Mr John Felton, a Catholic gentleman of wealth and good reputation. He was tortured and executed. On the scaffold he made a present to the Queen of a great diamond ring which he had been wearing at the time of his arrest, with the assurance that he meant her no personal harm, but believed her deposition to be for her own soul's good and the country's. He was the first of the great company of Englishmen who were to sacrifice their entire worldly prospects and their lives as the result of Pius V's proclamation.

His contemporaries and the vast majority of subsequent historians regarded the Pope's action as ill-judged. It has been represented as a gesture of medievalism, futile in an age of new, vigorous nationalism, and its author as an ineffectual and deluded champion, stumbling through the mists, in the ill-fitting, antiquated armour of Gregory and Innocent; a disastrous figure, provoking instead of a few buffets for Sancho Panza the bloody ruin of English Catholicism. That is the verdict of sober criticism, both Catholic and Protestant, and yet, as one studies that odd and compelling face which peers obliquely from Zucchero's portrait at Stonyhurst, emaciated, with its lofty and narrow forehead, the great, beaked nose, the eyes prominent in their deep sockets, and, above all else, the serene and secret curve of the lips, a doubt rises, and a hope; had he, perhaps, in those withdrawn, exalted hours before his crucifix, learned something that was hidden from the statesmen of his time and the succeeding generations of historians; seen through and beyond the present and the immediate future; understood that there was to be no easy way of reconciliation, but that it was only through blood and hatred and derision that the faith was one day to return to England?

★

That year, at any rate, the Bull came most opportunely to Cecil. There was now the best possible evidence to confirm anti-Catholic feeling. He drew up the list of members for the new House of Commons and secured a body of uncompromising, Calvinistic opinion. Up till then Elizabeth had resisted his imposition of the Thirty-nine Articles; now she was forced to give way, and the Parliament won the first of their long series of Puritan victories over the monarchy. The measures against Catholics were tightened by another twist of the screw. Naturally enough, the importation of copies of the Bull was forbidden, but into the same Act a clause was introduced providing that 'if any person after the same 1 July should take upon him to absolve or reconcile any person . . . or if any shall willingly receive and take any such absolution or reconciliation' he incurred the penalties of high treason – execution and the confiscation of property. Gradually the discharge of the penal laws was put into new hands, and instead of the old-fashioned justices who usually knew and quite liked their Catholic neigh-bours and distrusted the innovations from Westminster, there rose to eminence a set of strict officials, party men put up by the Government with, at their back, a more odious rabble of spies and informers.

All this was reflected in Ireland, and, with Sidney about to retire, Campion's security became increasingly precarious. It was finally upset by the first brief incursion into serious history of the preposterous and richly comic figure of Mr Thomas Stukeley. Even to the generation of Drake, Ridolfi, and Hawkins he seemed a shady and irresponsible person. He was a middle-aged pirate of gentle West Country origin, who, in the spring of 1570, put into harbour at Vivero de Galicia in Spain and, calling himself a son of Henry VIII, offered to conquer Ireland for the Spanish throne. The King was but mildly interested in the suggestion; nevertheless, at request of an Englishwoman, sometime lady-in-waiting to Mary, the Duchess of Feria, with whom Stukeley had ingratiated himself, he consented to pay off the arrears of wages to Stukeley's crew, who had never expected to come to Spain, and were threatening mutiny. Stukeley hung about the Court and the Duchess's drawing-room all that year, but could persuade very few people to take him seriously; the ecclesiastics doubted the sincerity of his religious conversion, and refused to receive him into the Church; eventually Philip knighted him and sent him away, and for the time being he disappeared from diplomacy.

But the reports of his activity served Cecil, in the alarmed state of the country, as material for a scare of invasion in Ireland. The authorities in Dublin were instructed to arrest suspected Catholics, and at the beginning of March 1572 Campion, with his *History* still unfinished, became a fugitive. The Stanihursts took him out of town to the Barnewells at Turvey, a house naturally protected by water from surprise attack. There is no clear record of his movements in the next few months; he appears to have dodged back to Dublin in May, and from there to Drogheda; no doubt he lodged in the houses of various friends he had made, slipping away by night at news of the pursuivants' arrival, avoiding making any record that would be likely to incriminate his hosts. Finally, at the end of May, he embarked for England at the little port of Tredake, twenty miles from Dublin, disguised as a lackey and calling himself Mr Patrick, in the service of Melchior Hussey, steward to Lord Kildare.

Before sailing, the ship was searched by police officers. Campion himself escaped detection, but they rifled his luggage and confiscated the manuscripts. Among them was the hastily completed *History*. There were other manuscript copies in existence, and eight years later, shortly before his removal from Prague, he was in correspondence to recover one of them; probably it arrived too late. He assumed that his own copy had been destroyed, but it lay about in various offices and passed from hand to hand until, some years after its author's death, it appeared, mutilated, in Volume II of Holinshed's *Chronicles*. As the ship gathered way and rolled through the stormy passage of the Irish Channel, Campion may well have seen in the loss of his book, with its elegant dedication to the Earl of Leicester, his final severance with the old life. Whatever achievement lay ahead of him was not to be the achievement at which he had once aimed; the glory, transcendent and undying, not what he had sought.

He spent a few weeks, unobstrusively, in England, and was in the crowd at Westminster Hall to witness the trial of Dr Storey, a refugee whom Cecil had had kidnapped at Antwerp and brought home to suffer in old age under an insupportable charge of treason for the prominent part he had taken against the Protestants in Queen Mary's reign. The condemned man was executed on 1 June with peculiar ferocity; Cecil and the chief ministers stood close by while he was being disembowelled; the cries of agony made an agreeable theme for popular preachers such as Fulke, who quoted them as showing that their victim was 'manifestly void of patience, and no martyr, as the Papists did mightily boast of him'. But on that day Campion was in mid-Channel on his way to Douai. There was a check in his journey; his boat was stopped, and he was taken aboard the *Hare*, an English frigate, and so back to Dover, but the captain was more concerned to keep Campion's purse than get his prisoner to London, so they parted company at the coast. Campion travelled to some friends in Kent, raised some money, and eventually crossed to Calais without further interference.

Chapter Two

THE PRIEST

The English College at Douai, to which Campion now went, had already, in the three years of its existence, become a rallying point for Catholic refugees of the most varying characters and antecedents. When the first emigration took place at Elizabeth's accession, the exiles had dispersed all over Europe, going wherever they saw the best chances of employment or support; but, from the first, the Spanish Netherlands had attracted the greatest number, both by reason of their accessibility from England and the connexions long established between the two countries by the wool trade. Several English scholars had been received at Belgian schools and cathedrals, and when Philip II carried out his father's project of founding a university at Douai, where his Flemish subjects might receive an education in their own tongue independent of French influence, an Englishman, Dr Richard Smith of Merton, was made Chancellor, while later, another, Dr Richard White, was made head of the law school established there by the Abbey of Marchiennes. Early in the history of the new university a house was formed for English students, where, in a very modest fashion, the great seminary had its origin.

The founder and first President was Dr – later Cardinal – William Allen of Oriel, a gentleman of ancient Lancashire family, 36 years old at the date of the foundation, 1568, who had left Oxford at the first religious changes, become a priest in Louvain, and had already attracted notice as a controversialist in defence of the doctrines of purgatory and indulgences. The object of the college was primarily to supply priests for the Catholic population of England, for, since the bishops were all either in prison or under detention, it was impossible for them, except very rarely with the connivance of their gaolers, to ordain priests; the system of education imposed by the Government made it increasingly difficult to train candidates for orders in England; in a few years the Marian priests would begin to die out and, as Cecil foresaw, the old Church would quietly expire with them; that Catholicism did in fact survive – reduced, impoverished, frustrated for nearly three centuries in every attempt at participation in the public services; stultified, even, by its exclusion from the universities, the professions and social life; but still national; so that, at the turn of opinion in the nineteenth century, it could re-emerge, not as an alien fashion brought in from abroad, but as something historically and continuously English, seeking to recover only what had been taken from it by theft – is due, more than to any other one man, to William Allen.

His was a compelling and elaborate character. His prodigious power in human intercourse is clear from the uninterrupted success of the English college. He was dealing with men of every age and position; elderly ex-professors and heads of houses; raw, embarrassingly enthusiastic converts; old-fashioned priests, schooled and ordained under the Marian regime, who came to him when they found their simple, rule-of-thumb dialectics insufficient to cope with their trained opponents; bitter fanatics whose fathers and brothers had died on the scaffold; later, when the seminary was recognized as a menace at Whitehall, spies, sent over by Walsingham to discover the secrets of the organization – all these it was Allen's task to sift out and control; to estimate their capabilities and vocations, to turn some to work writing tracts and translating, to keep some as lecturers and send some across the Channel to martyrdom. Besides them, there were at Douai an increasing number of Englishmen and women who regarded the college as their centre, and its President as their leader; some were passing through, others more or less permanently settled; great ladies like the widowed Countess of Northumberland; humble, homeless artisans, all looked to Allen for encouragement.

Throughout the whole period he was in constant anxiety about money and he was living among a foreign people. At Douai the exiles, at first popular enough, became, after a time, identified by the anti-Spanish faction with the vice-regal Government; at Rheims, where he moved for a time, they were disliked as Englishmen. Only by unremitting caution could the students avoid becoming embroiled in the local disturbances. But never was the regime of the college interrupted; whatever doubts secretly harassed the President, however tumultuous the immediate circumstances, however desperate the future, everything went on as before, English and imperturbable.

Mass for the whole college was at five, all the priests celebrating daily; there was weekly confession and communion; twice a week they fasted, and even on ordinary days the fare was so meagre that two Belgians who had originally joined quickly removed elsewhere. The students were assumed to have some Latin before their arrival; they learned Greek and Hebrew; they took dictation from the scriptures; during the course they went through the New Testament sixteen times. The teaching was counter-reformatory; in theology and exegesis they concentrated almost entirely upon controversial texts; in their spiritual exercises they were prepared for sacrifice; they were being trained not as scholars and gentlemen, but as missionaries and martyrs. Within a few years of its foundation the seminary was sending about twenty priests a year to England, of whom, before the end of Elizabeth's reign, 160 had died on the scaffold. To critics at the time this yearly despatch to almost certain imprisonment or death, of relays of the finest youth of the Church, seemed a gruesome and intolerable waste. In 1584, the Jesuit General Aquaviva was to write that 'to send missionaries in order to give edification by their patience under torture might injure many Catholics and do no good to souls'. But Allen knew that the devotion of his seminarists, so gallantly squandered, sometimes, in a few weeks of ministry, was of more value than a lifetime of discreet industry. His was the humbler task of composing their epitaphs. One aim was paramount to him, whatever its cost; the Church of Augustine, Edward the Confessor, Thomas of Canterbury, and Thomas More must go on.

But there was another side to Allen's activity; besides being a great university administrator, he was a man of affairs, the last of the English cardinal-politicians. There were unexplained absences, when, after a cautionary address, the President would leave his college for three months or so at Rome; there was a voluminous correspondence, written in cypher, with the great men of the age; the Duke of Guise, the Cardinal of Como, Don John of Austria, with Philip himself; there were secret visitors, of whom the students knew nothing except the clatter of hooves and the appearance of strange liveries in the courtyard; there were Mr Egremont Radcliffe and an anonymous poisoner who, at their several times, came to assassinate him; a sure sign, in that century, of political eminence.

From all these high affairs Allen's students were rigidly excluded. Political discussion was forbidden absolutely; Elizabeth's name was never mentioned in school or recreation, and in their lectures the Pope's deposing power might not be explained, even in hypothetical examples. As the door closed behind Sir Francis Englefield or the Papal nuncio, Allen would gather up the notes and cryptograms, the lists of disaffected noblemen, the tables tracing the descent of the Infanta Isabel-Clara from John of Gaunt, lock them away in his despatch box and turn with equal

mind to the kitchen accounts of the college refectory or to some
particularly promising thesis which one of the tutors had left for his notice.

The end was single, but the means devious and distinct. In that regular
and generous mind there was no confusion.

The college was still in its earliest phase at the time of Campion's arrival.
It had not yet been granted the Papal subsidy which made possible the
rapid expansion of the next few years. Seven priests and thirteen candidates
for orders, living sparsely and precariously, constituted the entire permanent community. Some were dependent on remittances sent out from
England, others on grants from Philip and local patrons. There were other
English students reading secular subjects at the university, who lived near
the college and resorted to it for their religious and social needs. Visitors
and refugees came and went. Probably the total number of English in
Douai at this time varied between 100 and 150.

For Campion exile from England meant reunion with many old friends.
There was Gregory Martin, who had twice written him urgent invitations
to accept the duty that was now thrust upon him, and Richard Bristow,
of Exeter, who had appeared before Elizabeth in the same debate, and on
the same side as Campion, during her memorable visit to the university.
These two were to devote the rest of their lives to the college, leaving
behind them the great Douai Bible, the most accurate English translation
of the Scriptures that had then appeared. There were also Risdon, White,
and Darell, all Oxford men, in whose sympathetic and appreciative
company many of the asperities of exile disappeared.

For nearly two years Campion conformed to the congenial routine of
the place. He read for his baccalaureate in Divinity, and at the same time
acted as professor of rhetoric, delivering model orations on most of the
important occasions of the year, and having as one of his pupils Cuthbert
Mayne, who was to be the first martyr of the seminary priests. He received
minor orders, and, in the normal course, would have proceeded direct to
the priesthood. Responsible work lay at hand for him at Douai, pamphlet-
eering, lecturing, translating, the very tasks which he had sought in vain
at Dublin, and from across the Channel the continuous, insistent summons
to the highest destiny of all. The copy of the Summa which Campion was
using at this time survives at Manresa College, Roehampton; it is annotated in his own hand and opposite an argument on baptism by blood
occurs the single *mot prophète et radieux*, 'Martyrium'. The persecution in
England was still comparatively mild; the new Church attracted little
enthusiasm, and the governing party proceeded with caution and reluc-

tance; violent sentences were uncommon and, where they occurred, could more often be attributed to motives of personal greed than of religious intolerance. But none knew better than Dr Allen the fate that lay ahead of his seminarists. So long as the Church seemed to be on her death-bed, Cecil was content to cut off the necessaries of her life and leave her to die in peace. Deprived of the sacraments, England would be lost to the Faith in a generation. But as soon as the young priests, now patiently conning their text books abroad, began to appear in their own country, to appeal to the old loyalties that lay deep in the heart of the people, to infuse their own zeal into the passive conservatism over which the innovators had won a victory too bloodless to be decisive, the character of the Government would change. Martyrdom was in the air of Douai. It was spoken of, and in secret prayed for, as the supreme privilege of which only divine grace could make them worthy.

But it was with just this question, of his own worthiness, that Campion now became preoccupied. There is no record of the date of his formal reconciliation with the Church, but it is reasonable to assume that it occurred immediately on his arrival from England. From then onwards he was admitted to the sacraments without which he had spent the past ten or twelve years of his life. From then onwards, for the first time in adult life, he found himself living in a completely Catholic community, and, perhaps, for the first time, began to have some sense of the size and power of the world he had entered, of the distance and glory of the aim he had set himself. The faith of the people among whom he was now placed was no fad or sentiment to be wistfully disclosed over the wine at high table, no dry, logical necessity to be expounded in the schools; it was what gave them daily life, their entire love and hope, for which they had abandoned all smaller loyalties and affections; all that most men found desirable, home, possessions, good fame, increase, security in the world, children to keep fresh their memory after they were dead. Beside their devotion Campion saw a new significance in the evasions and compromises of his previous years. At Oxford and Dublin he had been, on the whole, very much more scrupulous of his honour than the majority; he had foresworn his convictions rarely and temperately; when most about him were wantonly throwing conscience to the winds and scrambling for the prizes, he had withdrawn decently from competition; but under the fiery wind of Douai these carefully guarded reserves of self-esteem dried up and crumbled away. The numerous small jealousies of university life, his zeal for reputation, his courtship of authority, the oaths he had taken of the Queen's ecclesiastical supremacy, the deference with which he had given assent to Cheney's view of conformity, his melodious eulogies of the Earl of Leicester, above all 'the mark of the beast', the ordination which he had accepted as an Anglican deacon, now appeared to him as a series of gross betrayals crying for expiation, fresh wounds in the hands and feet of Christ.

He had come to Douai as a distinguished immigrant. At the time of his departure Cecil remarked to Richard Stanihurst, 'It is a great pity to see so notable a man leave his country, for indeed he was one of the diamonds of England.' Allen received him as a sensational acquisition. He had left England, it may be supposed, in a mood of some pride and resentment; he was casting off the dust of ingratitude, taking his high talents where they would be better appreciated.

Now in this devout community, at the hushed moment of the Mass, he realized the need for other gifts than civility and scholarship; he saw himself as a new-born, formless soul that could come to maturity only by long and specially sheltered growth. There was now no question in his mind of finding scope for his abilities, but of preparing himself laboriously in self-knowledge and the love of God, to become capable of the lowest service. This could not be done at Douai among his old friends of the senior common-rooms, and, as his course of studies drew to their close, his mind turned more and more towards the selfless discipline and vigilance of the rule of St Ignatius, to the complete surrender sought in the prayer *Suscipe, Domine, universam meam libertatem. Accipe memoriam, intellectum, atque voluntatem omnem* . . . Only thus, if ever at all, could he be worthy of the hangman and the butcher.

Accordingly, soon after he took his degree on 21 January 1573, he left for Rome with the intention, if God willed it, of entering the Society of Jesus. He travelled on foot, alone, as a poor pilgrim.

Allen did nothing to hinder him. A less spacious mind might have resented the decision. In its earliest years, with its prestige still uncertain, his college was losing its most notable convert; the community were bereft of a magnetic and inspiring companion; it was possible that Campion would be permanently lost to the English Mission, for there was no English Province in the Society and, although several English and Irishmen had joined the Society since its foundation, none had as yet been sent to work in their native countries. But to Dr Allen the matter admitted of only one question: where would Campion best satisfy his particular spiritual needs? He knew that Douai had given him much, and that there was between them a bond of love and gratitude which separation could not weaken. His struggling mission was in need of everything, and he knew that Campion's prayers would be for them, whether he was despatched to America or China, or confined for the rest of his days in the philosophy schools of Central Europe. Campion could help the English Mission best by realizing his own sanctity. The ways were involved and manifold, but the goal was one.

It was probably towards the end of February when Campion arrived in Rome. We do not know the exact date, nor have we much information about his life there until his departure at the end of June. We know that he visited Cardinal Gesualdi, was well received and offered preferment in the event of the Society deciding against his vocation. He had some conversation with the Cardinal on the subject of the Bull *Regnans in Excelsis* which will be referred to later. In his letters he mentions Father Ursnar and his old tutor, John Bavand, as his chief benefactors at this time. It is recorded that he performed the customary devotions of the pilgrimage with great zeal. He does not appear to have had an audience at the Vatican.

Pius V had died early in the previous year, his last months illumined by the great victory of Catholic arms at the battle of Lepanto. The danger which darkened the whole of the period, that in its distracted state Europe might fall to Islam, as North Africa and the Eastern Empire had fallen, though still grave, was no longer desperate. Calvinism in France and Lutheranism in Central Europe had reached their widest expansion. The Tridentine reforms were becoming effective in every branch of the Church's life. Pius's reign ended, if not in triumph, in hope more substantial than had been known for a generation. To the end he maintained his energy and austerity. His last public appearance, a few days before his death, was to make the arduous visit of the seven churches; one of his last acts was to check this procession in order to exchange a few words about their country with some English pilgrims.

He was succeeded by Gregory XIII, a lawyer and efficient man of affairs who had taken orders late in life, after the birth of an illegitimate son. He had then come into contact with Borromeo and Philip Neri, and was profoundly influenced by the spiritual life which centred round them. He took up the work of Pius, pursuing it with method and discretion, reinforcing on all fronts the resistance to the Turks and the Reformers. Under him the new Calendar was introduced, which, denounced at first in all Protestant countries as an invention of anti-Christ, was gradually accepted in the subsequent 200 years by each of them in turn. He was a friend of the Jesuits and remitted Pius's decree that they should sing the office in choir, thus preserving for them one of the characters given by their founder, which particularly distinguished modern from medieval piety. In domestic government he encouraged a good standard of private morality by advancing men of orderly lives, but did not continue the more severe, puritanical measures of his predecessor under whom a wealthy layman had been publicly flogged for adultery and a drove of harlots turned loose on the Campagna to be massacred by bandits. His chief minister was Galli, Cardinal of Como, who played a more important role in the foreign politics of the period than Pius allowed to any subordinate.

These two Popes, the saint and the administrator, may be taken to typify the change which had come over the Holy City, and was to determine her character through the succeeding centuries; the luxury and scepticism had gone, but with them something of the former chivalry and culture. The Popes were no longer patrons of art; their revenues were directed into strictly practical channels, to build missions and to subsidize theological colleges; their entourage ceased to be of courtiers and connoisseurs, but was composed, instead, of soft-footed, bureaucratic clergymen; no buffoon was kept in the Vatican after the Council of Trent to remind the Pontiff of his human follies; instead, at his elbow there was always a confessor.

At the time of Campion's visit to Rome the antiquities were already out of favour. Both Paul and Pius had regarded pagan sculpture with detestation, and a large part of the Vatican collection had escaped destruction only by being bundled out of sight. The ruins, lately the resort of the dilettanti, which everywhere challenged the pilgrim's attention, were now valued by the moralist for their edifying witness to the mutability of human achievement. Archaeology found its place in the new order when, five years later, the first of the catacombs was excavated; here was something in the new fashion; all Rome crowded to the sunless galleries, promenading by candlelight between the interminable shelves of skeletons; scrawls were brought to light of first-rate controversial importance, affirming dogmas now in dispute, and were greeted with the enthusiasm which an earlier generation, secure in its orthodoxy, had squandered on the bronzes and marbles of ancient Greece.

A few years before, Campion might have found something to regret in the modern attitude, but now it commanded his whole sympathy.

Make the most of Rome,

he wrote later to Gregory Martin.

> Do you see the dead corpse of that Imperial City? What can be glorious in life, if such wealth and beauty has come to nothing? But who has stood firm in these wretched changes – what survives? The relics of the Saints and the chair of the Fisherman.

We do not know where he lodged; perhaps with Father Ursnar. Writing, some years later, to John Bavand, he recalls the kindness he was offered and the spirit in which he received it.

> When I was in Rome did you not spend your entire self on me? On one from whom, to your knowledge, there could be no repayment; one just embarking from the world; in some sort, a dying man. It is a work of high compassion to bury the dead . . . you were munificent to me as I went to my rest in the sepulchre of religion.

These words, heavy with the imagery of the Ignatian exercises, were written when he was a professed priest, but they may well represent the mood in which he accepted the weeks of delay. In his mind he eagerly anticipated the noviciate; it was no reluctance on his part which held him in Rome, but the circumstance that the third General of the Jesuits, Francis Borgia, had recently died and that the congregation was assembled to elect his successor.

The Society had now been in existence nearly thirty-three years, and in that time had drawn to itself men from every degree of life – Faber the shepherd, Borgia the Duke of Gandia, Polanco the Jew. The first three Generals had been Spanish, but the membership included nearly every nationality; there had been several Englishmen, Br Lambert, a lay brother in the time of Ignatius Loyola, Fr Darbyshire, Fr Good, Fr Heywood, all three Oxford men with whom Campion probably had some acquaintance, Fr Rastall, a great-nephew of Sir Thomas More, and others. The Society knew no bounds to its work but those of the human race; its missionaries penetrated to India, China, Japan, Abyssinia, and the New World; in the lecture halls of the ancient universities, in obscure provincial day schools, guarding the consciences of great ladies at court and of dying seamen on the bullet-swept decks at Lepanto, among galley-slaves and lepers, in council with Cardinals and men of affairs, wherever there were souls to be saved, these men of single purpose were making a way.

In government the Society was, and is, a highly centralized autocracy under a General, elected for life; by the constitutions he is chosen not for any pre-eminent intellectual attainments or influence, but for 'the habit of union with God' and experience in the Society's affairs. An Admonitor is appointed with him to be always at hand supervising and, when necessary, correcting his private conduct. He is resident in Rome, and direct to him come reports of the Society's work from all parts of the world; from him issue appointments and orders. The congregation which elects him consists of the Provincial of every Province accompanied by two priests chosen by their fellows.

As has been stated above, the congregation, thus composed, was assembled in Rome by the beginning of the year 1573, and after it had elected a Fleming, Mercurianus, as General, on 23 April it proceeded among other business to review the candidates for entry and apportion them to their respective Provinces. No difficulty was made about Campion's reception – indeed his biographers claim that there was some competition for him – and it was eventually decided that he should join the Austrian Province under Fr Magius. He was offered the series of questions addressed to every postulant:

> Are you willing to renounce the world, all possessions and all hope of temporal goods? Are you ready if necessary to beg your bread from door to door for the love of Jesus Christ? Are you ready to reside in any country and to embrace any employment where your superior may think you to be most useful to the glory of God and the good of souls? Are you willing to obey in all things in which there is evidently no sin, the superiors who hold towards you the place of God? Do you feel resolved generally to renounce without reserve all those things which men in general love and embrace, and will you attempt and desire with all your strength what our Lord Jesus Christ loved and embraced? Do you consent to put on the livery of humiliation worn by Him, to suffer as He did and for love of Him, contempt, calumnies, and insults?

He assented and was received as a novice.

In the middle of June the congregation dispersed, and Campion, in company with certain Spanish and German Fathers, travelled with his Provincial to Vienna, where they arrived in August. The noviciate was stationed at Prague, where, accordingly, Campion was now sent in company with Father James Avellanedo, the newly chosen confessor to the Empress. After two months there he was moved to Brunn in Moravia with five other novices, where he remained until September 1574, when he was again removed to Prague, which was to be his home for the succeeding six years.

It was no part of the Jesuit system to station its forces in remote or congenial country. Other religious orders, training their members for other ends, have built their houses in the desert, on cliffs and desolate promontories above the sea, or high in secluded valleys where crest upon crest of tranquil upland stretch uninterrupted to the horizon and dispose the mind to peace. The Jesuits' work lay in the crowded cities, wherever the conflict was hottest and the issue least sure, and it was for these very reasons that Prague and Brunn were chosen for the Austrian noviciate.

Until the Hussite disorders at the beginning of the preceding century, Prague had been the centre of Middle-Europe for scholarship and culture. Inspired by Wycliffe, John Huss taught that 'Universities, studies, degrees, colleges, and professorships are pagan vanities, and of no more use to the Church than the devil', and during his brief period of eminence he was able to reduce the ancient university to ruin. Like the culture which it fostered, the university was international. Appealing to the particularist sentiment, in which the reformers of the next century were to find their chief support, Huss succeeded in driving out the foreign students who formed the strength and life of the place. To the number of several thousand they left the country and founded the University of Leipzig, while Huss was left rector over a few hundred Bohemians. This easy success tempted him to greater energy in the denunciations of Catholic teaching and organization, which he had already begun from the pulpit of the Bethlehem Church. His counsels made for disorder rather than revolution, for, unlike Calvin and Luther, he suggested nothing to replace the system which he was attacking, and his conformity with some points of Catholic doctrine was as capricious as his dissent from others. But his supporters, by the prerogatives which he himself affirmed, were at liberty to select and amplify whatever they found personally sympathetic in his teaching. His execution at Constance inflamed the anti-clerical and anti-royal sentiment of the Bohemian nobility who were soon at war with their king and with one another. Hostilities, lasting fifteen years, impoverished the country and resulted in a decisive defeat to the extremists and a treaty generally acceptable to the more moderate reformers. The monarchy, however, was fatally weakened, became elective, and finally, in 1526, passed into the hands of Charles V, who absorbed it into the Empire. Fifty years of comparative peace followed, but the university never recovered its dignity.

Lutheran teaching achieved an immediate popularity, and at the time of the Jesuits' arrival there the country was predominantly, if apathetically, Protestant. They came, at the Emperor's invitation, to take up the Church's battle on a losing front.

From the time of Ignatius until the present day the Jesuit's training has retained its essential structure. The postulant is assumed to have attained a respectable standard of education before admission. For the two years of his noviciate his studies cease, and he devotes himself entirely to a routine designed to develop the character in holiness and obedience, after which he takes his first vows and resumes his studies for the priesthood. Campion, with his ample attainments in philosophy, rhetoric, and divinity, was able to complete the course in five years, and said his first Mass on 8 September 1578.

His exterior life during these five years is easily told. The routine was hard, but without the extreme physical austerities of some other systems. The first month of the noviciate, following the precept from which there has been no deviation, was spent in absolute solitude; here, disturbed by no human intercourse except that of his director, he followed the *Spiritual Exercises*, in meditation and scrupulous examination of conscience, and erased all previous experience in a detailed confession of his whole life. He then resumed the companionship of the other novices and shared with them the manual labour of the household, of which he has left an enthusiastic description in a letter written from Prague after he had become a professed priest.

> How could I help taking fire at the remembrance of that house (Brunn) where there were so many burning souls – fiery of mind, fiery of body, fiery of word with the flame which God came upon earth to send, that it should burn there always? O dear walls, that once enclosed me in your company! Pleasant recreation-room, where we talked so holily! Glorious kitchen, where the best of friends – John and Charles, the two Stephens, Sallitzi Finnit and George, Tobias and Gaspar – fight for the pots in holy humility and charity unfeigned! How often do I picture it; one returning with his load from the farm; another from market; one sweating, sturdy and merry, under a sack of refuse, another toiling along on some other errand! Believe me, my dearest brethren, your dust and brooms, chaff and loads are beheld with joy by the angels. . . . Would that I had never known any father but the fathers of the Society; no brothers but yourselves and my other brothers; no business but that of obedience; no knowledge but Christ crucified.

At Brunn their work brought the novices into frequent contact with the Moravians round them, who, like the Bohemians, were for the most part disaffected in religion. It was hoped that the enthusiasm of the Jesuits in their midst might prove infectious, and the young novices, following the classic 'Experiments', were sent out to converse with them, begging from door to door, labouring in the hospitals and sick rooms, and tramping among the outlying villages to teach the catechism to children. This work, whose importance the Bishop of Olmutz particularly urged, brought back some converts, but not in any remarkable number, and it soon became clear to the Provincial that his end would best be served by opening in that part of the Empire one of the schools which were already becoming famous throughout Europe. He chose Prague for its seat; accordingly, in September 1574, Campion was recalled there, and became Professor of Rhetoric, the first of a series of important posts which he held at the new school.

From now, until his summons to Rome in 1580, Campion's activities were entirely educational. The Jesuits may fairly be said to have created a new system in teaching; their schools were the best equipped and the best staffed; their text books were the most modern and their curriculum the widest, but, more than anything else, it was their classroom method that won them the supremacy which they enjoyed throughout Europe from this period until the eve of the French Revolution, so that even at times of the sharpest religious difference Protestant parents could be found sending their sons to them. Their own acute training gave them particular insight into the habits of the mind, and to them may be credited the discovery and application of the principle, now universally accepted, that a pupil will be able to retain more in his memory when he has acquired it in a mood of curiosity and imagination. However admirable the higher achievements of medieval scholarship, its primary and secondary education had been pedestrian; a matter of teaching by rote an unvaried syllabus of rules and citations, and of enforcing defective attention with the rod; the facts and principles of knowledge were treated as the stones, laboriously laid, of a work whose nature would appear only towards the end of the building. The Jesuits sought to present everything as having an immediate significance and intrinsic interest; they fostered competition and argument with the result that the driest grammatical questions became the subjects of hot debate. Wherever they went they encouraged oratory and acting; they paid particular attention to style of language and dexterity of wit, but chose the material of their exercises so that, in the course of them, knowledge was acquired, almost without effort.

During his six years at Prague, Campion worked tirelessly in the community and in the school. He was Professor of Rhetoric and later Professor of Philosophy, Praefectus Morum, Praefectus Cubiculi, Director of the Sodality of the Immaculate Conception, and Latin preacher; he gave frequent displays of oratory and wrote and produced plays, some of great length, for all important occasions. When he became a priest, he was in great demand in the town as preacher and confessor, and still found time for visiting the prisons and hospitals. It became the fashion to employ him for important funeral orations. In 1577 a tragedy of his, on the subject of Saul, was produced with great splendour at the expense of the municipality before Elizabeth, the widow of Charles IX of France; it played for six hours, and was repeated next day at the request of the Emperor.

During this time he received the news of six of his Oxford friends entering the Society, but the only Englishman with whom he appears to have had any contact (beside Father Ware, who was at the college with him), is Philip Sidney, who arrived in 1576 as English Ambassador to congratulate the Emperor Rudolph on his accession. It was natural that he should call upon Campion, who had been an associate of his father's in Dublin, and as a fellow-Englishman living near the centre of local affairs would be able to supply him with much information of the kind which Walsingham required, but he was embarrassed to do so openly for fear of the spies who had already made mischief for him at the time of his visit to Venice. They did meet, however, more than once, and enjoyed long and serious discussions. Campion was left with the conviction, whether as a result of Sidney's impressionable nature or merely of his engaging manners, that his visitor was at heart a Catholic and solicited John Bavand to pray for 'the poor, wavering soul' of the magnificent young Englishman.

He kept up a correspondence, of which part has survived, with and about his old friends and pupils. The references to English affairs are rare. No doubt his unhappy country was frequently in his prayers, but, as far as his own life lay, the severance seemed complete; the probability was that he would remain at Prague until his death, following the same routine year after year, extending himself to the utmost in the work that lay immediately at hand. During his last months at Prague he was engaged in procuring a copy of his *History of Ireland*, with the intention of revising it and preparing it for publication.

These were the externals of his Jesuit vocation; of the other, interior life, the penances and rapt meditation, the prayer and communion, the inner struggles and victories, we know nothing except as their results appear in his life. To the superficial observer there might seem to be little change. He was leading the old life which he knew and loved, living in a celibate community, maturing and polishing his scholarship, instructing, expounding, disputing as he had done before, more tenderly, perhaps, and more thoroughly, without trace of vanity and emulation, but to all appearances much the same man as he had been at Oxford and Dublin.

The precise discipline of the Ignatian *Exercises* had served only to confirm him in the habit of life he had originally chosen.

Then comes the interruption, for the origin of which it will be necessary to notice some recent events in Rome, and Campion suddenly emerges as a hero.

It was an age replete with examples of astounding physical courage. Judged by the exploits of the great adventurers of his time, the sea-dogs and explorers, Campion's brief achievement may appear modest enough; but these were tough men, ruthlessly hardened by upbringing, gross in their recreations. Campion stands out from even his most gallant and chivalrous contemporaries, from Philip Sidney and Don John of Austria, not as they stand above Hawkins and Stukeley by finer human temper, but by the supernatural grace that was in him. That the gentle scholar, trained all his life for the pulpit and the lecture room, was able at the word of command to step straight into a world of violence, and acquit himself nobly; that the man, capable of the strenuous heroism of that last year and a half, was able, without any complaint, to pursue the sombre routine of the pedagogue and contemplate without impatience a lifetime so employed – there lies the mystery which sets Campion's triumph apart from the ordinary achievements of human strength; a mystery whose solution lies in the busy, uneventful years at Brunn and Prague, in the profound and accurate piety of the Jesuit rule.

The letter which first informed Campion that he was going to England came from Dr Allen, and in order to understand the circumstances of the mission it is necessary to review some of the events which had occurred in the lives of the English immigrants at Douai and Rome since his departure. Cardinal Allen's College had increased greatly in size and importance, and was now in receipt of a large Papal subsidy which enabled it to support an average membership of rather more than 100. Thirty or forty priests were ordained yearly, more than half of whom managed to cross the Channel into England, from where they sent reports of the great enthusiasm with which they were received by people of all classes, the hunger for the sacraments which still survived, and the eagerness with which they were sought by penitents desiring reconciliation. As a result of their labours, more Englishmen every year were coming abroad with the intention of becoming priests. It was to deal with some of this immigration that Pope Gregory decided to found an English seminary in Rome. There already existed a pious foundation of the Middle Ages, the Hospice in the Via di Monserrato, which housed numerous English exiles; it was now proposed to amplify this and create a regular seminary on the lines of Douai. The matter was put in the hands of Dr Owen Lewis, sometime Fellow of New College, later a colleague of Allen's at Douai, Canon of Cambrai, a distinguished jurist, who was in Rome at the time on legal business for his Chapter. Despite his education at Winchester and Oxford and his long sojourn abroad, Dr Lewis still retained a predominant devotion to his native Wales, and a wistful, Celtic strain in his character, which made him uneasy among the rigid Tridentine clergy who surrounded him. At his and Bishop Goldwell's suggestion, a fellow-Welshman, Dr Morys Clynog, was appointed Rector, a kindly, chatty, homesick, old man, whose emotional patriotism was not balanced, as in Dr Lewis, by very weighty scholarship. Up to this time he had been in charge of the old-fashioned English Hospice where neither his discretion nor business ability had been very severely taxed. He had a deep affection and loyalty to men of his own blood, and it was his great joy to welcome them to the college; by 1579 he was able to number seven Welshmen among his students, with most of whom, in his Celtic enthusiasm for genealogy, he was able to claim personal kinship. For the thirty-three Englishmen who composed the remainder of the community he could feel only the most tepid sympathy.

The greater part of these had been sent to him from Douai, for during the years 1576–9 the position of the English students in the Netherlands had become insecure. The Spanish Government was faced with a situation very similar to that which confronted Elizabeth in Ireland, and her advisers, despite her own expressed reluctance, had been quick to provide the Prince of Orange with help of the kind which later Philip was to give to the Earl of Desmond. The Calvinists in Douai were a small minority, but the richly deserved unpopularity of the Spanish garrisons aided their cause. The English students, being under direct Papal and royal patronage, and being moreover physically defenceless, found themselves an easy target for popular insult. The streets of the town became dangerous to them. It soon became clear that they would have to find a temporary home elsewhere. Cardinal Allen, accordingly, took as many of them as was possible into French territory at Rheims and sent the remainder to Rome.

These young martyrs in training were of different mettle from the ordinary, docile seminarists of the Roman colleges, and the unremitting tact by which Dr Allen managed to keep them all harmoniously at work was attested by their behaviour as soon as they were removed from his control.

At the end of October 1578 two Italian Jesuits – Fathers Navarola and

Capecius – were added to the staff of the Roman college; the English students could not fail to contrast their up-to-date efficiency with the slipshod, ramshackle mentality of their Rector, nor could the Fathers fail to prefer their keen-witted, generous English pupils to the moody Celts, but there is no reason to believe that they had any share in encouraging the disorders. The endemic antagonism of Welsh and English which, as the malcontents naïvely remarked in a petition to the Holy Father, dated from the days of King Arthur, was inflamed by the shameless advantage which the Rector gave to his countrymen in anything that lay in his power: better food, better rooms, better clothes. The English were soon in open rebellion; the ringleaders marched to the Pope, and were refused admission; they went to the Cardinal of Como, who referred them to Cardinal Morone; Cardinal Morone told them to go back to their books. Accordingly, after a scene in the dining-hall, which came near to blood-shed, the whole body of them, at the beginning of Lent, 1579, marched out, with the intention of making their way back to Dr Allen at Rheims. The Jesuits openly sympathized with them, and began raising a collection to provide for their journey. At this juncture the Pope intervened and promised a change of management. They asked first for Dr Morton or Dr Bavand as Rector, but were refused; they then suggested the Jesuits, and this was allowed them; for nearly 200 years the college remained under the control of the Society; an italian, Father Agazzari, was the first Rector.

Allen was invited to Rome to help in the settlement. The disturbance had caused great anxiety to him and to Dr Lewis, though it is typical of this godly man that he had made no reproach to the students for their ingratitude to himself, who had been the chief benefactor of the college, but was distressed only at the scandal that might be caused and the danger to the students if they undertook the journey to Rheims without proper precautions. Dr Allen was on the whole in favour of entrusting the college to the Jesuits, but in the three months of his journey south, the temper of the students was again excited against their authorities.

This time the complaint was more sober: that the Fathers, by their superiority to their predecessors, were gaining too great an influence over the more zealous students and would end by turning them into Jesuits instead of into English priests. Allen had already seen several of his most promising students, Campion among them, drawn into the Society away from direct participation in the English mission. In each case he had submitted, thinking it was for the individual's highest good, but it was another matter to expose an entire seminary college to this influence. If there was to be extensive recruiting for the Society among his students, it was fair that they should take their part in the work in England. In a series of long discussions with the General and the superiors of the Society, Allen pleaded his case and secured their agreement. In future English Jesuits should co-operate with Allen's priests, and arrangements were made for the immediate disposal of two fathers for the next mission. On 5 December he wrote with great joy to inform Campion that he was one of those who had been chosen to go.

> Our harvest is already great in England: ordinary labourers are not enough; more practised men are wanted, but chiefly you and others of your order. The General has yielded to all our prayers; the Pope, the true father of our country, has consented; and God, in whose hands are the issues, has at last granted that our own Campion, with his extraordinary gifts of wisdom and grace, should be restored to us.

It was not until March that the Austrian Provincial would allow his departure. In the time of waiting Campion continued without interruption in the normal order of the school, but there was the aura about him of one devoted to another destiny. A Silesian Father, James Gall, an ecstatic, came to the door of Campion's cell, on the eve of his departure, and inscribed above it *P. Edmundus Campianus Martyr*. Some days before another Father had painted the emblem of martyrdom, a garland of roses and lilies, on the wall at the head of Campion's bed.

Campion left Prague on 25 March, and travelling sometimes on foot, sometimes on horse, sometimes by coach, as the chances of the journey allowed, arrived in Rome on Easter Saturday, 9 April 1580. He remained there until 18 April. During this time he made or renewed the acquaintance of his companions on the mission. Of these by far the most important both in Campion's life and the future history of his generation was the fellow-Jesuit, Robert Persons. They had met before at Oxford, and had lately exchanged letters. At their first encounter Campion had been proctor and Persons, as an undergraduate, six years his junior, had been required by the university rules to take the Oath of Allegiance and Supremacy before him. He was known to have Catholic sympathies, and Campion had been ready to excuse him, but other authorities intervened and Persons took the oath, which he was to repeat later on becoming Fellow of Balliol. He was now, at Campion's earnest request, appointed his superior during their mission.

The materials for writing a life of Persons are not yet accessible, and until that day is thought to have arrived he must remain a shadowy and enigmatic figure. The little that is known of him is mostly derived from the utterances of his enemies. He was of humble, and, it was generally believed, illegitimate birth at Nether Stowey, in Somerset. He was educated by the help of the parish priest, who was reputed to be his father, first at Taunton and later at St Mary's Hall, Oxford, where he showed acute intelligence, if not scholarship, and inspired very strong feelings in all he met, either of affection or dislike. In 1574 he was obliged to resign his Fellowship in circumstances in which religion had no share. He had apparently succeeded in antagonizing the other dons by his popularity as a tutor and the licence he allowed himself in ridiculing them, but there is no reason to suppose that the charges which brought about his dismissal, of misappropriating college funds, were ever proved. He went to Padua to study medicine, but on the way stopped at Louvain, where he encountered Father William Good, under whose direction he seems to have experienced a profound and permanent conversion. He left Padua for Rome, entered the Jesuit noviciate on 24 July 1575, and was ordained priest there three years later. He became Penitentiary at the Vatican, where he rapidly attracted the notice of his superiors, and was employed for a short time at the English college in the transition period between Clynog's administration and the assumption of management by the Society. After Campion's death he never returned to England, but busied himself in ecclesiastical and secular politics, in which his projects were seldom wholly successful. Legends inevitably accumulated about him, magnified by the extreme expressions of his friends and enemies, and in the vague and slightly sinister form in which he has descended to posterity he forms the prototype, rarely repeated, of the 'subtle Jesuit' of popular superstition.

It seems certain that in later life he interpreted very loosely the strict Jesuit rule against interference in politics; he seems, too, to have worked under the conviction that all affairs, civil and ecclesiastical, could be more efficiently and conveniently managed by the Fathers of the Society. As a politician he proved wrong, but often, apparently, through ill-luck rather than bad judgement, as when the Raid of Ruthven upset his plans in Scotland; as an ecclesiastic he ended by antagonizing a great body of the more responsible clergy. But in all these matters the details, and perhaps the true facts, are hidden from us. We do know, however, that he completely captivated a man as astute in his human judgements as Dr Allen; that he founded the school for English boys at St Omer, which preserved Catholic education for three centuries of Englishmen and is the direct ancestor of Stonyhurst College, and that he composed the *Spiritual Directory*, which has proved a text book of sturdy piety to thousands of Catholics up to the present day.

In the few days of preparation and leave-taking which succeeded Campion's arrival in Rome, the purpose on which they were being sent was fully and precisely explained to the two missionaries. A large part of their instruction was concerned solely with their vocation as members of the Society, for it had been the chief anxiety of the General, which had for so long made him hesitate in his decision to send men to England, how it would be possible to lead the life of a Jesuit in the peculiar conditions that prevailed there. They would be obliged to abandon their habits and travel in disguise, living among laymen under assumed names and false professions of their business; they would be alone for long periods of time, entirely deprived of the corporate strength which was the chief advantage of membership of an organized Society; they would be without supervision and direction in a country where the ecclesiastical government had fallen into chaos and the only surviving bishop lived in imprisonment; they would be hindered, if not absolutely prevented, from making the periodic retreats in which they recuperated their spiritual powers. But the General had decided to commit them to these dangers, and accordingly he drew up a special code of rules for their work.

The objects of the mission were clearly defined and limited. It was for 'the preservation and augmentation of the faith of the Catholics in England'. So far from active proselytizing among heretics, the missionaries were charged not only to avoid disputes with them, but to shun their company. They might treat with Catholics who had lapsed through compulsion or ignorance, but this work was subordinate to their primary duty of ministering to those who remained constant. They were forbidden, absolutely, to involve themselves in questions of state or to send back political reports. They must permit no conversation against the Queen in their presence, except perhaps in the company of those whom they held to be exceptionally faithful, and who had been tried a long time; and even then not without serious cause. At this point a definition was required by the Fathers of the precise position of Catholics towards Queen Elizabeth. As early as 1573, during his first visit to Rome, Campion had had some conversation with Cardinal Gesualdi and had represented to him the difficulty in which loyal Englishmen had been placed by the Bull of Deposition. After Pius's death an inquiry had been sent to Rome to discover whether the Bull was still in force, and had elicited the following replies: that it had been issued in the hope of the kingdom being immediately restored to Catholicism, and in view of that occasion, and that as long as the Queen remained *de facto* ruler, it was lawful for Catholics to obey her in civil matters and co-operate in all just things; that she might honourably be addressed with her titles as Queen; that it was unlawful for any private person, not wearing uniform and authorized to do so as an act of war, to slay any tyrant whomsoever, unless the tyrant, for example, had invaded his country in arms; that in the event of anyone being authorized to put the Bull into execution, it would not be lawful to Catholics to oppose him. These judgements were now confirmed and epitomized in the statement 'that the Bull should always bind the Queen and the heretics; on the other hand that it should in no way bind the Catholics, as things then stood, but only in the future when the public execution of the Bull could be made'.

It was possible to deduce from this decision that the Catholics were a body of potential rebels, who only waited for foreign invasion to declare themselves. This was the sense in which Cecil read it, for he was reluctant to admit the possibility of anyone being both a patriotic Englishman and an opponent of his regime. The Catholics, however, concerned very little with matters of high politics and very much with their ordinary day-to-day relations with their neighbours, accepted it eagerly, as permission to deny the royal authority only in so far as it forbade them the practice of their religion, and in all other matters to arrange their lives in harmony with their fellow-countrymen. It was in this sense only that the question interested Persons and Campion. It was the very antithesis of their mission to instruct Catholics in their duty in the hypothetical event of King Philip suddenly appearing among them at the head of a victorious army; they came to treat with distressed consciences, and Gregory's pronouncement enabled them to reassure scrupulous penitents who feared that by performing the normal duties of citizenship they had incurred the penalties of excommunication.

A lay brother of the Society, Ralph Emerson, was appointed to accompany the two Fathers. With him, the party leaving for England now numbered fourteen, and represented all ranks of the Church; there was the aged Bishop Goldwell of St Asaph, who with Dr Morton, the Penitentiary of St Peter's, travelled ahead by horseback; there were two laymen, one of them, John Pascal, a young gallant who had lately been hanging about the Vatican and making himself noticeable by his debonair manner; four elderly Marian priests from the English Hospice, one of them the old Prior of Manchester; and three young priests from the college; so that the expedition began to assume the air of a crusade. Before leaving they were received in audience by the Pope, and given special faculties for their work; they also visited Philip Neri and received his blessing. When the actual day for their departure came, they were attended by Sir Richard Shelley, the Prior of Malta, and almost the whole of the English colony of Rome, as well as a large number of Italian sympathizers, as far as the Ponte Molle, where solemn and affectionate leave was taken. These circumstances, far from unobtrusive, were duly notified to Walsingham by his agents, and the English Government was well aware what was on hand before the missionaries had reached the Channel ports.

The first ten days of the journey were accomplished in heavy rain and over roads which were barely passable. The way led through Viterbo, Siena, Florence, Bologna, Modena, Parma, Piacenza, and Milan. At Siena and Florence they were able to obtain lodging at Jesuit colleges; at Bologna, where they were delayed some days by an accident to Persons, they were entertained by Cardinal Paleotto, the Archbishop; after dinner Campion was called upon to preach, which he did in his old academic manner, beginning with a quotation from Pythagoras, and comparing the ardours and consolations of the Christian life with those of the pagan.

At Milan they spent eight days in the palace of Cardinal Borromeo, where a daily discourse was required of Campion. That huge and princely establishment was well accustomed to visitors of every degree; it numbered over 100 members of the regular household; there were Chamberlains, Almoners, Stewards, Monitors, Oblates, Discreets of the Confraternity, Prefects of the Guest Chambers, all maintained and graded in hierarchic order under the Praepositus, the Vicar, and the Auditor-General. Three hundred guests a month, on an average, passed through these hospitable courts; there all the ways and passages of the vast, ecclesiastical labyrinth seemed to intersect, and in the centre of it all, living in ascetic simplicity among the lavish retinue, eating his thin soup, sleeping on his folding bedstead, wearing his patched hair shirt, moving with halting gait, chilly even in the height of summer, speaking in a voice so subdued that it was barely audible, grave and recollected as a nun, was the dominating figure of the great Cardinal. The pilgrims were received, entertained, blessed and sent on their way, and the immense household went about its duties; in its splendour and order and sanctity, a microcosm of the Eternal Church.

From Milan the party passed through Turin, crossed the Alps by the Mont Cenis hospice, and descended into Savoy, where they met the vanguard of a great rabble of Spanish troops, returning from Flanders. They pressed on as far as Aiguebelle, where it became clear that they would have to change their course, for not only was there a continuous stream of soldiers blocking the roads and commandeering provisions, but, they learned, the country round Lyons was in a state of anarchy as a result of the Huguenot rebellion. Accordingly they struck east of their original route, along the road through Geneva. As they approached the home of Calvinism, they put out of sight all evidence of their profession and disguised themselves, Campion with characteristic humility taking the role of Pascal's lackey. When, however, they were examined by the magistrates they admitted that they were Catholic. 'Of that we marvel,' was the reply, 'for your Queen and all her realm are of our religion.' But no difficulty was made of their admission, and they were led to an inn where, with the genius of the race, they were made exceptionally comfortable.

So far from being subdued by the kindness of their reception or the delicacy of their position in a hostile town, six of the younger members, Campion and Persons among them, set out after dinner in a mood of exuberant high spirits to interview Theodore Beza, the prominent Calvinist, who at the moment enjoyed an international reputation as a theologian, greater, perhaps, in England than anywhere else. He was then an old man; in early life his ambitions had been purely literary, and he had earned considerable popularity in the composition of lubricious verse; later, falling in with Calvin and being disposed to settle down, he had married one of his mistresses, the wife of a Parisian tailor, and was now one of the nine elders of the Church of Geneva. His lady, Candida by name, opened the door and admitted them to the courtyard, where the old scholar came to see them, a venerable figure with long beard, dressed in black gown and skull cap, with a starched white ruff at the neck. The magistrates had told him of their arrival, and after an exchange of compliments he expressed his regret that they were not of the religion of their country.

Persons, who presumably understood the injunction they had received 'to avoid all sarcasm and prefer solid to sharp answers', as applying only to their behaviour in England, proceeded by a series of questions to show that, since the Calvinists admitted no inequality in ministry and governed their Church theocratically, while Elizabeth had appointed bishops and usurped for herself the entire jurisdiction of the Pope, the English Protestants were heretical even by his own standards.

The ground of the discussion then shifted, and Beza recounted a number of stories, which subsequently proved to be false, about the iniquities of the Duke of Guise; but Campion, standing impatiently by in his servant's livery, could retain himself no longer and insisted on bringing the subject back to essentials, offering to demonstrate numerous features of the Elizabethan church that were out of accordance with Beza's views. But Beza was not in the mood to waste an afternoon in his courtyard being catechized by a servant on questions of which there was little hope of agreemeet, so he called his wife to bring him another packet of letters, and took leave of the Fathers with remarkable courtesy of manner, promising to send them an English pupil of his, the son of Sir George Hastings, next-of-kin to the Earl of Huntingdon, who had greater leisure than himself for such discussions.

Hastings never arrived, but in his place there came to visit them at their inn a Mr Brown and a Mr Powell, two keen Anglicans, with whom the priests struck up a relationship of some cordiality, arguing well into the night, promenading the streets, breakfasting together, and eventually enjoying their company for the first mile or two of the journey north.

It was by Mr Powell's advice that Persons was dissuaded from challenging Beza to a public disputation, the loser of which should be publicly burned alive in the market place. Thanks to him they left Geneva without embroiling themselves with the authorities, but could not be restrained from baiting an unfortunate clergyman whom they encountered, placidly conning a sermon, a mile out of the town. Campion and Fr Bruscoe were ahead, and without introduction accosted the man and tackled him on the subject of Church government; at first he took them for sympathetic enquirers, but was speedily tied up on the question they had put to Beza of Elizabeth's ecclesiastical supremacy; he turned for support in his confusion to the rest of the party, who fell upon him with relish, contradicted him, tripped him up in his arguments, and left him breathless with indignation, his fingers vainly fluttering the pages of his sermon, while Mr Powell attempted to excuse the eccentricities of the strange company in which he had been found.

At the summit of a hill overlooking the city, the pilgrims paused and sang a *Te Deum* in acknowledgement of the enjoyable time they had spent there; and then, perhaps slightly in doubt of whether they had behaved with complete politeness, went out of their way over rough ground to do penance at the shrine of St Claude, a place which, until its destruction during the French Revolution, was a great centre of devotion in that part of the country. From there they continued the journey in buoyant spirits and, until near the end, excellent health, to Rheims, where they arrived on the last day of May, having spent about six weeks on the way from Rome.

While they were on the road it was Campion's practice to say his Mass very early, and then, after reciting the *Itinerarum* with the others, to push on ahead for a few hours' solitary devotion, reading his breviary, reciting the Litanies of the Saints and telling his beads. When this was over he would allow the rest to overtake him, and would spend the day laughing and talking until evening, when he would again slip away from them for his meditation and prayers. One of his particular jokes, in which they all shared, was the terror with which they looked towards England and the probability of a painful death.

When they reached Rheims and caught up with Bishop Goldwell and Dr Morton, they found that what had been fun to them had become a very grave matter to the Prelate. He was in his eightieth year and far from hardy; all his life he had been accustomed to soft living and deferential treatment. It had seemed easy enough during the wave of enthusiasm at Rome to volunteer for the expedition; he had left in an atmosphere of personal popularity which was novel and entirely agreeable to him; but the weeks of jogging along through waterlogged high roads, of putting up at inns where the accommodation seemed totally inadequate for a person of his dignity, of not being recognized, of getting wet and having nothing dry to change into, above all of reflecting as he lay sleepless on the wholly unsuitable beds which he was obliged to occupy, that each day's painful journey was taking him further from the life which he understood and nearer to those sufferings which had sounded so edifying when read aloud in the refectory, had effected a serious derangement of the bishop's system. At Rheims they received him with the utmost kindness; they were continually kissing his ring; but when they sought to be most complimentary they would applaud his courage by recounting with something very like relish the appalling severity of the new penal laws on the other side of the Channel. After a few days of it he took to his bed and began writing to the Pope to express his doubts, whether he were precisely the best person for the work in hand. He had already written from Bologna, saying it had come to his ears that the Bishop of Lincoln was now out of prison; was there any object in his going on? The answer conveyed to him by the nuncio in Paris was sharp; that even if the rumour were true, there was room in England for two bishops. Now he wrote twice, mentioning his willingness to go anywhere and endure anything at His Holiness's command, but suggesting an alternative plan; why should not one or two of these courageous young priests be made bishops? It was not a question of money; they would be content to live in the poverty of the primitive Church.

To make matters worse, before there was time for a reply, plague broke out in Rheims, and the Bishop's agitation became frantic. Accordingly he settled matters for himself and returned to Rome without permission, where he was greeted by a somewhat cold reception from the Cardinal of Como. Dr Allen allowed himself no recriminations, merely remarking that 'it was better the old man should yield to fear now than later on, on the other side'.

The other, more disturbing, piece of information which greeted the pilgrims at Rheims was that, at about the same time as their departure from Rome, Dr Nicholas Sander had been despatched as Papal nuncio, with five ships of men and arms, to assist the Geraldine rising in Ireland. The prudence of this step was more in doubt than the strict legality, for Ireland stood in a very different relation to the Holy See from that of England and Wales. Although it had once, in extremity, been admitted by King John, the Pope's feudal jurisdiction over England had been constantly and resolutely denied. Ireland, however, was, in feudal law, unquestionably a Papal fief, and had always been recognized as such by the English monarchy; moreover, it had never been effectively conquered or administered; outside the Pale English control had been negligible. The Pope had a legal right of interference, such as Elizabeth never enjoyed in the Netherlands, but to Campion, whose acquaintance with the country derived entirely from official circles in Dublin, the expedition seemed a shocking alliance with anarchy against the decent order of English jurisdiction, while to all the priests it was clear that Cecil's policy of identifying their cause with political treason would be greatly facilitated.

They learned moreover that Walsingham's agents had provided him with very complete descriptions of all the party, and that the Channel ports were being closely watched for their arrival.

How little this intelligence depressed the optimism of the party may be judged by the fact that before they had been more than a few days at Rheims the defection of Bishop Goldwell and Dr Morton had been made up by two volunteers from the college, Dr Ely and Father John Hart, and by Father Thomas Cottam, an invalid, who had been obliged by ill health to leave the Jesuit noviciate.

Campion as usual was called upon to preach; he did so, and the sermon is notable as being the first time for many years that he had spoken in public in his native language. Dr Allen awaited the issue with some anxiety, but any difficulties he may have expected were completely overcome, and Campion spoke as fluently and correctly as though he had never left England. The text which he chose was *Ignem veni mittere in terram*; once more employing the fire motive which appears frequently in his utterances, from his second debate before Elizabeth, through his letters to the novices at Brunn, to this memorable occasion when he cried the word so loudly that, Bombinus records, passers-by in the street took alarm and hastened to the water buckets.

He had long conversations with Dr Allen in which it was clear that neither of them expected to meet again. 'As for me,' said Campion, 'all is over . . . I have made a free oblation of myself to His Divine Majesty, both for life and death, and I hope He will give me grace and force to perform; and this is all I desire.'

In this mood the missionaries separated to make their way, as best they could, in pairs and small companies, across the Channel. Dr Brombury and Father Bruscoe went to Dieppe, Sherwin and Pascal to Rouen, Gilbert, Crane, and Kemp to Boulogne, Ely, Rishton, Kirby, Hart, and Cottam to Dunkirk. Persons, Campion, and the lay brother Emerson went to the Jesuit house at St Omer. There were several English fugitives there; they and the Flemish Fathers attempted to discourage the crossing, saying that the vigilance at Dover was now so great that their immediate arrest was inevitable, but Mr George Chamberlain, a man of some consequence, was more hopeful and, since it was clear that whatever dangers awaited them would tend to become more, rather than less, grave with delay, Persons decided on immediate action. Disguised as a soldier with buff and gold braid and a soldierly, swaggering manner, Persons set out from Calais commanding Campion and Emerson to wait, get what information they could at the quayside of their superior's fortune, and, if all had turned out well, follow without delay.

For nine days they waited at St Omer without news. Then a letter arrived, addressed by Persons to Campion in the capacity of jeweller, which he had decided to assume, urging him to come at once to London and market his wares. Accordingly Campion and Emerson set out, found a ship, and after four days in harbour waiting for a favourable wind, crossed on the evening of 24 June and landed at Dover before it was daylight.

Chapter Three

THE HERO

In the nine years of Campion's absence from England William Cecil's position had become steadily stronger. He had been created Lord Burghley in 1571, and in the summer of the following year took the office of Lord Treasurer. He still kept control of the Star Chamber and of foreign affairs, while in 1574 he secured the appointment to his old position as Secretary of Sir Francis Walsingham, a man in absolute sympathy with himself in the aims and methods of Government. In 1572 Norfolk had gone to the scaffold; with him had died the hopes of the Conservative Party. Mary Stuart's cause had come to final ruin in Scotland with the surrender and death of Kirkcaldy and Maitland; she was a prisoner on English soil, and Cecil knew that with tact and patience he would, one day, persuade his mistress to order her execution. The Queen increased daily in popularity, particularly in London, the home counties, and the ports, where she was accorded something nearly approaching divine honours. Cecil had her complete confidence. The Dudley circle, where it was now fashionable to be anti-French and Calvinist, might regard him with distrust, but the Queen drew a fairly clear distinction between the company with whom she amused herself and those whom she allowed to manage the affairs of State.

On the other hand, in foreign politics Cecil had not been so successful. He had not foreseen the massacre of St Bartholomew's Day, 1572, which had broken the supremacy of the Huguenots; deprived of French help, the insurgents in the Spanish Netherlands were being reconquered, and he had counted upon them to distract Spanish attention from the unremitting provocation offered by the English buccaneers. A Spanish war was to the interest of neither country. So far from being, as he appeared to many of Campion's contemporaries, the Catholic Genghis Khan, sweeping irresistibly over Europe, Philip, we now know, was an intensely conscientious and far from competent bureaucrat, whom vast inherited dominions kept constantly embarrassed. No one knew better than himself the weakness that lay behind the elaborate façade of the Spanish monarchy; how vital despatches got delayed and lost in the huge secretarial system of the Escurial; how revenues melted away as they passed from hand to hand between their source and the Treasury; how officials in his remote territories wilfully misconstrued their orders; how posts requiring the highest abilities were distributed by titles of birth; how priests were continually interfering and admonishing about his responsibilities and destinies, how his own stiff conscience was always prompting him into courses radically opposed to common sense, how the salaries and pensions were in arrears, troops mutinying for lack of pay, and pious foundations petitioning for subsidies which he could not find heart to refuse. The last thing he wanted was to go to war, particularly with the English, whose formidable spirit he knew from the days when he had been their king.

But the provocation had been continuous, from the earliest days when Cecil had sent Dr Man as ambassador, a person of atrocious manners who had referred to the Pope in front of half the court as 'a canting little monk'. Then there had been the treasure which he had unloaded at Plymouth and Southampton, to convey under Elizabeth's safe conduct for re-embarkation at Dover. She had rescinded the safe conduct and commandeered the entire booty. Then there were the slave traders. In accordance with his stern moral code Philip forbade his American colonists from enslaving the native Indians and from importing Negroes. They resented this, and readily bought from Hawkins, although trade of any kind was forbidden them except with their Mother Country. Not only was Elizabeth cognizant of this contraband business, she was a partner in it. She had lent a ship of her own, unsuitably called the *Jesus*, for this very purpose. Bristol grew rich once more with the trade that St Wulstan had suppressed there in the eleventh century. English galleys, laden with human cargo, plied regularly between America and West Africa, and on their return journeys, as often as not, stopped to sack a Spanish outpost or board a treasure ship.

At this very time, the summer of the Jesuits' arrival, Drake was coming into home waters after three years of sensational good fortune in the Indies; Cecil had done all in his power to discourage the expedition, even to insinuating an agent of his own into the crew with instructions to raise a mutiny and conjure unfavourable winds, but the man had been detected and hanged from the yard-arm, and Drake's arrival with a hold full of plunder was acclaimed as a national triumph by the Queen herself. At present Philip was occupied in Portugal, where the English as usual had been intriguing with the pretender; when that was settled he would have to turn his mind to a punitive expedition.

There were numerous disturbing portents recorded on the eve of the Jesuits' arrival. In April the great bell of Westminster tolled of itself without human agency. In June there were thunderstorms of exceptional violence. A woman named Alice Perin, at the age of 80 years, gave birth to a prodigy with a head like a helmet, a face like a man, a mouth like a mouse, a human body, eight legs, all different, and a tail half a yard long, while in the same year another monster was reported from Stowe that was both male and female, with mouth and eyes like a lion. In May a pack of hounds was clearly visible hunting in the clouds over Wiltshire, while over the border in Somerset three several companies of sixty men each, dressed in black, marched in procession through the sky. Cecil, Elizabeth, and most of the Court took serious notice of auguries and the events caused great anxiety for the Government's security.

There was also the question of the Queen's projected marriage with the Duke of Anjou. In a general way, so long as Mary Stuart remained alive, everyone wished to see the Queen married, but the objections to every suitor, royal or common, seemed insuperable. For some years now, Castelnau, the French Ambassador, had been pressing forward the claims of the French prince. A personable agent, Simier, had been wooing her assiduously, and with some response. Elizabeth had already been warned that the Duke was not physically prepossessing, but his appearance, when finally he arrived, in the summer of 1578, startled the court. He was dwarfish in stature, with bandy legs, an enormous cleft nose and a profusion of pock marks. He was sexually perverted, and twenty years the Queen's junior. Contrary to all expectation she was enchanted with him, played with him by the hour, fondled him, and called him 'her little frog'. They formed a macabre pair, for Elizabeth was now in middle age, her face was shrunken, revealing the large, masculine bones beneath it, she was extravagantly painted and dressed, while over all towered a crimson wig, stuck with jewellery, which, it was reputed, covered a head that was totally bald. The flirtation, however, was carried to extremes of demonstration, and the general opinion held that at last the Queen's capricious heart was finally won. But the difficulty, as with so many of her suitors, lay in the question of their faith. The Duke's mother, Catherine of Medici, was impatient of religious scruples, but the little fellow held out for his Mass, and negotiations were protracted until, four years later, the project was at last abandoned. Meanwhile, however, in the year with which we are dealing, the Catholics watched the affair with tragic eagerness, for it was in that grotesque alliance that they saw the single, frail hope of their own survival.

It is still generally believed in England that Elizabeth's anti-Catholic legislation was remarkable for its leniency, and that in an age of savage intolerance she and Cecil stood out as unique examples of enlightenment and moderation. It may, therefore, be convenient to approach the English Catholics by means of a summary of their legal position.

Some of these measures have been mentioned above. By the two Acts of Supremacy and Uniformity which established the Church of England, there was imposed a fine of one shilling for non-attendance at the parish church, the proceeds of which were to go to the poor of the parish. It was also made illegal to hold any service, except those contained in the Prayer Book. An oath of submission to the Queen's spiritual supremacy was formulated, which might be tendered to all officials and to anyone found attending an illegal service. The penalty for a second refusal of this oath was death.

A later ordinance provided that anyone engaged in education, either as a schoolmaster or as a private tutor, must receive licence from the Bishop of the Diocese. A passport system at first hindered, and later prohibited, parents from sending their children to school abroad.

This was the situation up till 1570, the date of the Bull of Excommunication. It was then made high treason (punishable, of course, with death) to bring into the country 'any bull, writing, or instrument obtained from the Bishop of Rome', 'to absolve or reconcile' any of the Queen's subjects, or to be absolved or reconciled. To bring into the country or receive any object of devotion, 'tokens, crosses, pictures, beads or such like vain things from the Bishop of Rome', was punishable by the confiscation of property.

In 1581, to meet the emergency of Campion's mission, a further act was passed 'To retain the Queen Majesty's subjects in due obedience'. It reaffirmed the principle that it was high treason to reconcile anyone or to be reconciled to the Church and imposed a new scale of fines. For hearing Mass the penalty was 100 marks (£66 13s. 4d.) and a year's imprisonment.

This clause is notable because it is the first time that the Mass is specifically proscribed. Hitherto the offence had been 'to sing or say any common or open prayer or to minister any sacrament otherwise than is mentioned in the said book' (the Elizabethan Prayer Book). The same Act provides that the penalty for not attending church shall be £20 per month, per head, for those over 16 years of age.

The object of this legislation was to outlaw and ruin the Catholic community. It will be seen that under the new code a family of four adults who elected to lead a regular Catholic life, attending Mass on days of obligation and eschewing the Protestant services, were liable, if they were fortunate enough to keep out of prison, to a total yearly payment of over £15,500 (or in modern currency about £93,000). This sum was to be divided into three parts, one of which went to the Treasury, one to the informer, and one to the poor of the parish, but there is no single instance on record of this last humane provision having been put into effect. There was scarcely an estate in the country capable of sustaining an imposition of this size, nor, in fact, was any obliged to do so, for the Masses were said in secret, the vessel kept behind sliding panels, and the priests smuggled in and out of doors through concealed passages, but one infraction of the code could not in its nature be kept hidden – the refusal to attend Protestant services – and from 1580 onwards the enormous tax of £240 (about £1,440 modern value) yearly for each adult member of a Catholic household was pretty regularly exacted; none but the wealthiest had any choice between submission and destitution.

The other penalties could not be enforced consistently. Some recusants were continually in and out of prison, some were left undisturbed for years together. The system was full of incongruities, such as Mass being regularly said in Marshalsea prison. Some provisions, such as that any man might be convicted of high treason who twice refused the oath of supremacy, seem never to have been put into force. Raids for proscribed objects – rosaries, religious pictures, crucifixes, etc. – took place capriciously. First one district would be combed out and then another. Everything depended on local goodwill and the activity of the professional informers.

Of these the best known and most successful was Richard Topcliffe, who first appears in history in 1578. From then onwards he was in regular employment under the Government hunting out Catholics. To him was accorded the privilege unique in the law of England, or, perhaps, of any country, of maintaining a private rack in his own house for the more convenient examination of prisoners. Only once did he fall into discredit, towards the end of his public life, in 1594 when he was brought to court by a colleague, Thomas Fitzherbert. 'For whereas Fitzherbert entered into bonds to give £5,000 unto Topcliffe, if he would persecute his father and his uncle unto death together with Mr Bassett, from whom he expected legacies, Fitzherbert pleaded that the conditions were not fulfilled because they died naturally and Bassett was in full prosperity.' Evidence was given by Mr Bassett himself that Topcliffe had done everything in human power to entrap him, and Coke, the Queen's attorney, confirmed him, testifying that Topcliffe had assiduously accused all three of Popery, but the court held that Topcliffe, for once, had been remiss in his duty and sentenced him to a short term in prison, of the injustice of which he complained bitterly, saying that it was enough to make the bones of Father Southwell dance for joy.

He and others like him now proceeded about the country levying blackmail where they could, spying, bribing servants, corrupting children, compassing the death of many innocent priests and the ruin of countless gentle families.

The Catholics were defenceless at law, for their whole inherited scheme of life had been dubbed criminal; they lived in day-to-day uncertainty whether they might not suddenly be singled out for persecution, their estates confiscated, their families dispersed and themselves taken to prison or the scaffold. Three examples of the manner in which the law was enforced even in the milder days before the coming of the Jesuits may be taken from the accounts of Elizabeth's progress through Norfolk in 1578.

The county was particularly strong in Catholics and they welcomed the opportunity to show their loyalty to the Queen. At Euston Hall, near Thetford, lived Edward Rookwood, a Catholic squire in the early twenties, newly married. Although there were many more magnificent houses in the neighbourhood, the Queen chose to come out of her way to stay at Euston. The house was ill-equipped for the accommodation of her large retinue, but the young couple exerted themselves to the utmost and, until the last morning, were hopeful that the visit had proved a success. When, however, Rookwood presented himself to kiss his guest's hand, he was roughly told to stand aside, was rated for being a Catholic, put under arrest, and marched away to Norwich gaol.

At first his Norfolk neighbours were inclined to attribute Rookwood's disgrace to the simplicity of his entertainment, but four days later the Queen crossed into their county to visit the former Lady Elizabeth Style, now married to Thomas Townshend of Braconash. Townshend had taken the oath of spiritual supremacy, but was related to several recusants and was on friendly terms with others. He lived in baronial splendour and the Court were here treated with the extravagance they expected, but the Queen took the opportunity of a party to have nine of her fellow-guests arrested under her host's roof and sent, like Rookwood, to Norwich, where the Court followed shortly.

About a mile from the city a gentleman named Downes rode out to meet them. He was a Catholic of ancient family, lord of the manor of

Erlham, which he held from the Crown by Petit Serjeantry or service of a pair of spurs. Mr Downes presented the Queen with the spurs, fashioned in gold, and began to recite some complimentary verses of his own invention. He was curtly ordered to stand aside and follow the party into Norwich, where he was clapped into prison.

These were the conditions of life, always vexatious, often utterly disastrous, of the people to whom the Jesuits were being sent, people drawn from the most responsible and honourable class, guilty of no crime except adherence to the traditional faith of their country. They were conditions which, in the natural course, could only produce despair, and it depended upon their individual temperaments whether, in desperation, they had recourse to apostasy or conspiracy. It was the work of the missionaries, and most particularly of Campion, to present by their own example a third, supernatural solution. They came with gaiety among a people where hope was dead. The past held only regret, and the future apprehension; they brought with them, besides their priestly dignity and the ancient and indestructible creed, an entirely new spirit of which Campion is the type; the chivalry of Lepanto and the poetry of La Mancha, light, tender, generous, and ardent. After him there still were apostates and there were conspirators; there were still bitter old reaction-aries, brooding alone in their impoverished manors over the injustice they had suffered, grumbling at the Queen's plebeian advisers, observing the forms of the old Church in protest against the crazy, fashionable Calvinism; these survived, sterile and lonely, for theirs was not the temper of Campion's generation who – not the fine flower only, but the root and stem of English Catholicism – surrendered themselves to their destiny without calculation or reserve; for whom the honourable pleasures and occupations of an earlier age were forbidden; whose choice lay between the ordered, respectable life of their ancestors and the faith which had sanctified it; who followed holiness, though it led them through bitter ways to poverty, disgrace, exile, imprisonment, and death, who followed it gaily.

Campion's first action on landing on English soil was to retire out of sight of the men, fall on his knees and commend his cause to God; then as dawn was breaking he and Brother Ralph went to interview the 'searcher', whose business it was to inspect all immigrants. Persons, as they learned later, had got through with his usual adroitness, not only unsuspected by the officials, but on terms of easy cordiality with them. Campion was less successful; there had been a warning to watch the ports for the arrival of

Gabriel Allen, Dr Allen's brother, who was reported to be on his way to visit his family at Rossall. Campion and Ralph were therefore brought before the Mayor of Dover and interrogated; at first he seemed disposed to send them under guard to London, but unexpectedly changed his opinion and allowed them to go in freedom. They travelled by boat up the river to Hythe, in some doubt as to what their procedure should be on arrival in London; but Persons had arranged everything, and, as soon as they were moored to the quay, a man stepped on board, greeted Campion as 'Mr Edmunds' and led them immediately to a house in Chancery Lane where Mr George Gilbert had lodgings.

This was probably Campion's first meeting with Gilbert, but he was well known to him by repute. He was a wealthy layman, aged at this time 28, whose large properties in different parts of the country had been preserved and augmented during his long minority. He had been educated at London and Cambridge in strict Calvinist principles, being at one time particularly under the influence of Dr Edward Dering, a prominent Anglican divine. At his coming of age he was handed over the unrestricted use of his fortune and sent abroad for the completion of his education. He was a good athlete, horseman, and fencer, and his interests seem to have been mainly sporting until, at Paris, he came into contact with Father Thomas Darbishire, who converted him to Catholicism. He went to Rome, where he put himself under the direction of Persons, and rapidly became absorbed in his new religion. He wished to make a pilgrimage to the Holy Land, but Persons deflected his enthusiasm to England, where he now returned and made himself the centre of a group of Catholic laymen of his own kind. They took into their pay the London pursuivants and were able to meet and hear Mass freely; the house in Chancery Lane where he was now living belonged to Adam Squire, the chief pursuivant and son-in-law of the Bishop of London. He was on the point of marrying an heiress at the time of the Fathers' arrival, but now took a vow of chastity until England should publicly return to the Faith. One of the blessings with which Pope Gregory had charged the Fathers was to this association of laymen, who were bound together by a vow to devote themselves to furthering the Church's progress, but do not appear to have constituted a sodality of the kind which was becoming common under Jesuit missions.

Persons was away in the country at the time of Campion's arrival and had left word for him to await his return. During these eight or ten days Campion made the acquaintance of most of the chief Catholics and Catholic sympathizers in London. On the Feast of St Peter and St Paul,

29 June, he preached on the historic text *Tu es Petrus* before a large audience in the hall of Lord Norreys' house, hired for the occasion by Lord Paget, and daily interviewed a great number who came to him for advice. There seems to have been a friend or agent in Court, for he was successfully protected from the informers who attempted to get access to him in the guise of penitents, among the most dangerous of whom was one Sledd, who had been a servant in Rome and knew by sight many of the missionaries. Persons and Campion had two narrow escapes from this man, in one of which Father Robert Johnson, a Marian priest, was taken and later executed. It had become clear that the Fathers could not remain hidden for long in London, and on Persons's return he set about preparations for their work in the country.

But first it was necessary to define the aims of the mission to the existing clergy and to discuss various topics of importance with the leading Catholics. Accordingly a conference, which has later been dignified with the name of the Synod of Southwark, was called in the second week of July at a small house on the south side of the river near St Mary Overies. There were three or four Marian priests still at large in London, ministering in secret to the Catholic community; these — the names and exact number are not known — assembled under Father George Blackwell, the future Archpriest, with several of the seminary priests who had arrived in safety, and some of the laity — a combination which old-fashioned professional churchmen, such as Bishop Goldwell, might have regarded askance.

The questions debated were typical of the situation which confronted the missionaries. Persons was in charge of the proceedings. He first read to the meeting the instructions under which the missionaries were working, emphasizing the prohibition of political action and declaring on oath his ignorance, until his arrival at Rheims, of Dr Sanders's expedition in Ireland.

The next question was one of vital importance to the laymen: the rule governing their attendance at Protestant services. A committee of the Council of Trent had already given a decision, but there had been no official promulgation of it (except to individuals here and there by Dr Sanders) and many had found it convenient to profess ignorance. They could plead, with some reason, that there was nothing specifically anti-Catholic in the Morning Prayer, which would secure them immunity from persecution; it consisted of the recital of a creed identical with their own, readings from the scriptures, psalms and prayers mostly translated from Catholic sources. In a great number of places the newly

appointed clergy had no authority to preach, but had to content themselves with homilies, exhorting their flocks to virtue in unexceptional
terms. But no compromise was allowed. By the very importance which
the Government attached to it, attendance at the new service constituted
an act of adherence to the Elizabethan settlement; it was not merely
participatio in sacris, but a formal admission of the spiritual supremacy
of the State. Accordingly Persons pronounced an absolute prohibition
which placed anyone observing the law outside the Catholic body, in
the words, 'So public an act as is going to the church, where profession
is made to impugn the truth and to deface, alienate, and bring into
hatred Christ's Catholic Church, is the highest iniquity that can be
committed.'

If anyone had remained in doubt of the missionaries' innocence of
political motive, this verdict should have reassured them. If the object in
their secret coming and going from house to house had been conspiracy;
if, as was said by their enemies, they were using the confessional to
prepare a concerted insurrection in support of Spain, they would have
instructed their followers to equivocate with 'mental reservations', to lie
low, to attend the services, take the oaths, and then at the appointed signal
fall upon their unsuspecting neighbours; nothing would have been more
recklessly imprudent, or fatal to their purpose, than to make their
adherents advertise themselves publicly to the authorities.

The next question was ecclesiastical. Up to the Reformation there were
various slight differences of rite in different parts of the country, the Sarum
use being the predominant one. There were now no more Sarum books
printed and the priests arriving from abroad were all trained in the Roman
rite. The old English one, moreover, was considerably stricter in matters
of fasting than that generally followed on the Continent. The missionaries
were asked whether any rule was to be observed universally throughout
the country. The decision was that nothing should be altered from the old
customs, but that each district should retain its traditional observance.

There were various particular cases cited for discussion. Father Cottam
had been arrested at Dover and sent to London in charge of a fellow-
traveller. The fellow-traveller was his colleague, Dr Humphrey Ely, who
under the name of Haward had crossed the Channel several times before,
was well known at the port, and had a friend in the town who entertained
him in ignorance of his identity. Dr Ely allowed Cottam to escape, but as
a result had been arrested himself, and, with him, his host at Dover, who
had gone surety for him. Father Cottam asked whether it was his duty to
give himself up and release his sureties; after some uncertainty the Synod

decided he might; he did so with great cheerfulness, was imprisoned, and later died on the scaffold.

There was also the case of Father Bosgrave, another Jesuit, who had joined the Society sixteen years before and had since been working in Poland, far out of touch with the course of events in England. Now, at his superiors' bidding, he returned to England, sent, by a singular irony, for the good of his health. He was arrested immediately he landed, and taken for examination to the Bishop of London, who asked him whether he would go to church. 'I know no cause to the contrary,' he replied, and did so, to the great pleasure of the Protestant clergy, who widely published the news of his recantation. The Synod had only time to express their shame at his action before it broke up. The Catholics all shunned him, and Father Bosgrave, who retained only an imperfect knowledge of English, wandered about lonely and bewildered. Eventually he met a Catholic relative who explained to him roundly the scandal which he was causing. Father Bosgrave was amazed, saying that on the Continent scruples of this kind were not understood, but that a Catholic might, from reasonable curiosity, frequent a Jewish synagogue or an Anabaptist meeting-house if he felt so disposed. As soon as it was made clear to him that the Protestants had been claiming him as an apostate, he was roused to action, and, saying that he would speedily clear up that misunderstanding, wrote a letter to the Bishop of London which had the effect of procuring his instant imprisonment. He was confined first in the Marshalsea and later in the Tower, from which he was moved only to his trial and condemnation for high treason, a sentence that was later commuted to banishment. He then returned to Poland and resumed his duties there, having benefited less by his prolonged stay in England than his superiors had hoped.

As the little Council was coming to an end of its work a proclamation was issued by the Government which gave promise of further severe steps against the Catholics. This was dated 15 July; it announced, without giving confirmation of them, that there were rumours abroad of a Catholic League organized by the Pope and the King of Spain against the realm, and warned all loyal subjects to be 'in good readiness, with their bodies and arms' while those 'who have any unnatural affections are charged not to irritate Her Majesty to use the rod or sword of justice against them, from which, of her own natural goodness, she has a long time abstained. It was in fact, the preface to the Act already quoted 'for retaining the Queen Majesty's subjects in their due obedience', which was passed early in the following spring. The existing law was everywhere more rigorously enforced. Recusants who had been let out of prison on surety were now re-arrested. Watson, the aged Bishop of Lincoln, and Feckenham, the Abbot of Westminster, together with several other deposed dignitaries of the old Church, who had been allowed from time to time a measure of uneasy liberty, were now taken to Wisbech Castle and entrusted to men very different from the easy-going and corruptible gaolers of the Marshalsea; no visitors were allowed them; no books except the Bible; they were kept apart from each other except at mealtimes, when their conversation was limited to bare civilities; they were obliged to find the expenses not only of themselves but of an Anglican chaplain who harangued them regularly in their cells and whose visits were as unacceptable as that of the harlot who was, on one occasion, locked up among them, not with the kindly, if misguided, notion of relieving their depression, but in order to damage the reputations of these aged men with the charge of incontinence.

The common gaols were soon full, and in all parts of the country castles were appointed for the reception of recusants – Banbury, Tremingham, Kimbolton, Portchester, Devizes, Melbourne, Halton, and Wigmore – and in their catalogues may be found many famous names which survive among the Catholic community today – Tichborne, Stonor, Arundel, Throckmorton, and countless others.

In these circumstances the Fathers left London for the provinces. Gilbert equipped them magnificently, giving each a pair of horses, a servant, the clothes suitable to a travelling gentleman, and the substantial sum of £60 in ready money. He himself accompanied Persons for the first stage of his journey, while Campion went with another of the association, Mr Gervase Pierrepoint. All travelled together for the first day and spent the night at Hoxton, at that time a village outside the city, at the house of a Protestant, perhaps Sir William Catesby, whose wife was Catholic. They arrived at nightfall and were about to start out again next morning when they were met by Mr Thomas Pounde, who had slipped prison and ridden after them. Pounde was a devout and intelligent man, of pronounced eccentricity. The circumstances of his religious conversion were remarkable. He had been born with wealth and powerful family connexions, and for the earlier part of his life lived modishly and extravagantly at Court; his particular delight was in amateur theatricals, for which the fashion of the reign gave him ample scope. On one occasion he performed an unusually intricate *pas seul* before the Queen; it made a success with her and she called for a repetition. He complied, but, this time, missed his footing and fell full length on the ballroom floor. The Queen was more than delighted, gave out one of her uproarious bursts of laughter, kicked him, and cried 'Arise, Sir Ox.' Pounde picked himself up, bowed, backed out among the laughing courtiers with the words 'Sic transit gloria mundi,' and from that evening devoted himself entirely to a life of austere religious observance. Various attempts, friendly and penal, failed to draw him back to his former habits, and in 1574 he was put into prison, after which date he was seldom at liberty, except on rare occasions like the present one; his cell at the Marshalsea became a resort of Catholic society, and it was there, in fact, that Persons had, on his arrival in London, first got into touch with Gilbert and the other members of the association.

It is not clear how Pounde was able to get away from prison, perhaps by a trick or by bribery, but it is most probable that he was let out on parole, for the regime at the Marshalsea was notoriously lax, and cases are even recorded of priests being allowed to spend the entire day at liberty, returning in the evening to sleep.

He came with a very wise suggestion. The prisoners had been discussing the Jesuits' mission and the probability sooner or later of their capture; they feared that they might be taken and summarily executed without having the chance to plead their true intentions; the Government would be able to give their own account, forge confessions of treason, and no one would be in a position to contradict them. Accordingly Pounde asked the Fathers to draw up a written statement of their aims, which he would keep by him and publish in case of emergency. Persons and Campion agreed, and, sitting down there and then, each composed his own apologia, which Pounde carried back with him to the Marshalsea.

Even now, after the passage of more than three centuries, when the battle is on another ground and against other enemies, it is impossible to read *Campion's Brag* without emotion. At that day, to the ruined men at the Marshalsea, who for years had heard no news except of failure and betrayal, no arguments except those of the Puritan chaplains, whose triumphant, derisive, substantially documented sermons they were often obliged to hear; men cut off from the vivid Catholic life of Douai and Rome, who followed a loyalty which they themselves could not explain, against not only the fashion and authority, but what seemed to be the massed scholarship and reason of their age – the letter was intoxicating. As has been said above, it was composed in great haste, when the saddle bags were already packed and the horses waiting to take Campion on his journey; he needed no time for reflexion, for the matter had been ceaselessly in his thoughts since he left Prague; it is the work of half an hour.

To the Right Honourable Lords of Her Majestie's Privy Council, it begins:

> Right Honourable,
>
> Whereas I have come out of Germanie and Boëmeland, being sent by my Superiours, and adventured myself into this noble Realm, my dear Countrie, for the glorie of God and benefit of souls, I thought it like enough that, in this busie, watchful and suspicious worlde, I should either sooner or later be intercepted and stopped of my course. Wherefore, providing for all events, and uncertaine what may become of me, when God shall haply deliver my body into durance, I supposed it needful to put this writing in a readiness, desiring your good Lordships to give it yr reading, for to know my cause. This doing, I trust I shall ease you of some labour. For that which otherwise you must have sought for by practice of wit, I do now lay into your hands by plaine confession.

He proclaims that he is a priest and a Jesuit, sent under obedience to England, to preach the gospel, minister the Sacraments, and instruct the simple,

> in brief, to crie alarme spiritual against foul vice and proud ignorance, wherewith many my dear Countrymen are abused.
>
> I never had mind, and am strictly forbidden by our Father that sent me, to deal in any respect with matter of State or Policy of this realm, as things which appertain not to my vocation, and from which I do gladly restrain and sequester my thoughts.

He then states with extreme simplicity that the Catholic case is unanswerable. Up till then the issue had chiefly depended upon sentiment, anti-Spanish feeling on the one hand, loyalty to tradition on the other. He now makes the claim, which lies at the root of all Catholic apologetics, that the Faith is absolutely satisfactory to the mind, enlisting all knowledge and all reason in its cause; that it is completely compelling to any who give it an 'indifferent and quiet audience'. This was something which had been consistently denied to it by the Elizabethan Government; accordingly he now appeals for a hearing before the Privy Council, with regard to its effect on 'the common weal', before the Doctors and Masters of the universities for its theology, and before the judicature for its legality. He concludes with a peroration, every sentence of which is aflame with his own fiery spirit:

> Many innocent hands are lifted up to heaven for you daily by those English students, whose posteritie shall never die, which beyond seas, gathering virtue and sufficient knowledge for the purpose, are determined never to give you over, but either to win you heaven, or to die upon your

pikes. And touching our Societie, be it known to you that we have made a league – all the Jesuits in the world, whose succession and multitude must overreach all the practices of England – cheerfully to carry the cross you shall lay upon us, and never to despair your recovery, while we have a man left to enjoy your Tyburn, or to be racked with your torments, or consumed with your prisons. The expense is reckoned, the enterprise is begun; it is of God, it cannot be withstood. So the faith was planted: so it must be restored.

If these my offers be refused, and my endeavours can take no place, and I, having run thousands of miles to do you good, shall be rewarded with rigour, I have no more to say but to recommend your case and mine to Almightie God, the Searcher of Hearts, who send us His grace, and set us at accord before the day of payment, to the end we may at last be friends in heaven, when all injuries shall be forgotten.

It was characteristic of the two priests that Persons sealed his paper, while Campion left his open. Pounde read it that evening at the Marshalsea. Perhaps he showed it to some of the other prisoners. The effect, at any rate, upon his own somewhat volatile nature was instantaneous. There and then he set about the composition of a challenge on his own account, modelled upon Campion's; in the first instance, a brief thesis giving three reasons why Scripture should not be taken as the sole grounds of faith, which he followed, shortly afterwards, with an appeal for a formal dispute before the Bishops and Council.

Throughout the summer the prisoners at the Marshalsea had been obliged to listen to occasional exhortations from visiting Anglican divines. Now, on 16 August, the Bishop of London detailed two clergymen, Mr Tripp and Mr Robert Crowley, to act as regular chaplains. Little is known of Mr Tripp; Mr Crowley was rapidly rising to prominence as a leading low-churchman; he was above the average of his fellows as a scholar and had attracted favourable notice by his detestation of his surplice, which he described as his 'conjuring garment'. Former missionaries had found their audience at the Marshalsea torpid and indisposed to argument. Mr Tripp and Mr Crowley met with lively opposition and, unwilling to miss any opportunity for pushing himself forward, Mr Crowley set about a pamphlet in reply to Pounde's *Three Reasons*. But the Bishop of London had no desire to see the Marshalsea prison turned into a school of theological debate, and he quickly silenced Pounde by removing him to chains and solitary confinement in a cell in the half-ruined palace at Bishop's Stortford. In these circumstances, if not before, Pounde passed on the text of *Campion's Brag* to his fellow-prisoners. Copies were made and circulated rapidly from hand to hand; visitors to the Marshalsea carried them into the city and the countryside. They came to the notice of the Bishop of Winchester, the Sheriff of Wiltshire, and other Government men; whenever found they were destroyed and their possessors arrested, but the paper spread rapidly among friend and enemy. The document originally intended as a final vindication in case of Campion's arrest or summary execution thus became, as by its spirit and form was eminently suitable, the manifesto of his mission.

The result, both for good and ill, was a vast augmentation of Campion's fame. This, obscured now by his long absence abroad, had, even in the old days before his exile, been local and limited; he was known at the universities and at Court, among scholars, men of affairs, and men of fashion, but it is improbable that his name had ever reached the market towns and remote manors, where now it became fabulous.

Both sides now looked upon him as the leader and spokesman of the new mission; his membership of the Society of Jesus cast over him a peculiar glamour, for, it must be remembered, the Society had, so far, no place in the English tradition. Many Englishmen could remember the day when the great estates were religious property; when friars tramped the roads from village to village, and monks, tonsured and habited, drove their animals to market and dispensed alms and hospitality to the destitute; many had had their earliest lessons from Dominican or Benedictine in the drowsy village schools; the desolate monuments of the old orders stood in every county; their names were familiar and their memory still sweet with the gentleness and dignity of a lost age. But 'Jesuit' was a new word, alien and modern.

To the Protestants it meant conspiracy. The countryman knew for himself the virtues and defects of the old monks; he had seen the methods by which the Royal Commissioners obtained their evidence, and he understood their motives perfectly; but of the Jesuits he knew nothing, except distorted and monstrous reports; that their founder was a Spaniard and that they were sworn to another allegiance than the Queen's. Stories of Spanish atrocities were eagerly devoured; the Jesuits were the vanguard of Spanish invasion; their business was to murder the Queen and the Council, and set the country in anarchy so that Philip could march in with the tortures of the Inquisition. Preposterous tales obtained credence of the Jesuits' rule and training and the enormous crimes daily committed behind their walls. The news that disguised Jesuits were now at large in the English countryside caused indignation and alarm, and those who had been apathetic in helping the authorities when the quarry was a Marian priest, now joined fiercely in the hunt.

To the Catholics, too, it meant something new, the restless, uncompromising zeal of the counter-Reformation. The Queen's Government had taken away from them the priest that their fathers had known; the simple, unambitious figure who had pottered about the parish, lived among his flock, christened them and married them and buried them; prayed for their souls and blessed their crops; whose attainments were to sacrifice and absolve and apply a few rule-of-thumb precepts of canon law; whose occasional lapses from virtue were expected and condoned; with whom they squabbled over their tithes, about whom they grumbled and gossiped; whom they consulted on every occasion; who had seemed, a generation back, something inalienable from the soil of England, as much a part of their lives as the succession of the seasons – he had been stolen from them, and in his place the Holy Father was sending them, in their dark hour, men of new light, equipped in every Continental art, armed against every frailty, bringing a new kind of intellect, new knowledge, new holiness. Campion and Persons found themselves travelling in a world that was already tremulous with expectation.

We have few details of this expedition. The two priests separated at Hoxton and met again three months later at Uxbridge; in the intervening time Persons had passed through Gloucester, Hereford, Worcester, and up into Derbyshire; Campion had been in Berkshire, Oxfordshire, and Northamptonshire. Both they and their hosts were careful to leave no record of their visits, and the letters in which the Jesuits reported progress to their superiors maintain strict anonymity for their converts; edifying anecdotes are related of 'a certain noble lady' who was offered her liberty on the condition of once walking through a Protestant church, but indignantly refused; of 'a young lady of 16' who was flung into the public prison for prostitutes on account of her courageous answers to the 'sham Bishop of London'; of a 'boy of, I believe, 12 years' who was inveigled into acting as page at a Protestant wedding, was inconsolable with shame until he was able to make his confession to a priest – but nothing is said to identify the protagonists. The only names that can be given with any certainty as Campion's hosts during this journey are Sir William Catesby of Ashby St Leger, Lord Vaux of Harrowden, and Sir Thomas Tresham, a man of exceptional character, eventually brought to ruin for his faith, whose singular and brilliant taste in architecture may still be seen in the exquisite, unfinished mansion at Lyveden and the unique, triangular pavilion, planned and intricately decorated in honour of the Trinity, which stands, concealed and forlorn, among the trees that border the park at Rushton. It is possible, however, to form a tolerably clear, general impression of the journey from the letters already mentioned and the numerous sources of information about Elizabethan conditions.

He travelled in fair comfort, mounted and equipped as befitted a gentleman of moderate means. He was attended by his servant, and more often than not by one or more of the younger members of the household where he had last stayed, but it was his habit for most of the way to ride in silence at some little distance from his companions, praying and meditating as he had done on the road to Rheims. Changes of horse and clothing were provided for him at different stages; he was constantly on the move, rarely, for fear of the pursuivants, stopping anywhere for more than one night. He must in this way have visited fifty or more houses during the three months.

Along his road the scenes were familiar enough, but he was seeing them with new eyes; the scars of the Tudor revolution were still fresh and livid; the great houses of the new ruling class were building, and in sharp contrast to their magnificence stood the empty homesteads of the yeomen, evicted to make way for the 'grey-faced sheep' or degraded to day-labour on what had once been their common land; the village churches were empty shells, their altars torn out and their ornaments defaced; while here and there throughout his journey he passed, as, with a different heart, he had often passed before, the buildings of the old monasteries, their roofs stripped of lead and their walls a quarry for the new contractors. The ruins were not yet picturesque; moss and ivy had barely begun their work, and age had not softened the stark lines of change. Many generations of orderly living, much gentle association, were needed before, under another Queen, the State Church should assume the venerable style of *Barchester Towers*. But if the emotions of the journey were shame and regret, hope and pride waited for him at the end of the day. Wherever they went the priests found an eager reception. Sometimes they stayed in houses where only a few were Catholic. There was constant coming and going in the vast, ramshackle households of the day, and an elaborate hierarchy in the great retinues; there were galleries where the master never penetrated. It was natural enough that any respectable wayfarer should put up there for the night, whether or no he had any acquaintance with his host.

> We passed through the most part of the shires of England,

wrote Persons,

> preaching and administering the sacraments in almost every gentleman's and nobleman's house that we passed by, whether he was Catholic or not,

provided he had any Catholics in his house to hear us. We entered for the most part, as acquaintance or kinsfolk of some person that lived within the house, and when that failed us, as passengers or friends of some gentleman that accompanied us; and after ordinary salutations we had our lodgings, by procurement of the Catholics, within the house, in some part retired from the rest, where putting ourselves in priests' apparel and furniture,

they heard confessions, perhaps preached, and very early next morning said Mass, gave communion and started on their way again, leaving the rest of the household in ignorance of their identity.

At Catholic houses they found themselves guests of the highest honour, and there they sometimes prolonged their stay for a few days, until the inevitable warning of the pursuivants' approach drove them once more on to the road. In recent years most of the houses had been furnished with secret cupboards where were stored the Mass vestments, altar stones, sacred vessels, and books; these 'priest-holes' were usually large enough to provide a hiding-place for the missionaries in case of a sudden raid; in some cases there were complete chapels with confessionals and priest's room. Many houses sheltered one of the old Marian priests who had left his cure at Elizabeth's succession, and now lived in nominal employment as secretary and butler. At this early date these seculars had no quarrel with the Fathers of the Society. The Jesuits, fresh from Rome and the Continental schools, were as welcome to them as to their flocks; cut off, as they were, from episcopal control, from their reading and from intercourse with other clerics, they constantly found themselves confronted with problems to which their simple training afforded no solution; all these were brought to Campion and Persons. Their prayers were always for more Jesuits.

The priests of our country,

wrote Campion,

being themselves most excellent for virtue and learning, yet have raised so great an opinion of the Society, that I dare scarcely touch the exceeding reverence all Catholics do unto us. How much more is it requisite that such as hereafter are to be sent to supply, whereof we have great need, be such as may answer all men's expectation of them.

And Persons:

It is absolutely necessary that more of our Society should be sent . . . who must be very learned men, on account of the many entangled cases of conscience, which arise from no one here having ample faculties, and from the difficulty of consulting the Holy See.

Campion found his Catholic hosts impoverished to the verge of ruin by the recusancy fines; often the household were in mourning for one or more of their number who had been removed to prison. 'No other talk but of death, flight, prison, or spoil of friends,' yet everywhere he was amazed at the constancy and devotion which he found. The listless, yawning days were over, the half-hour's duty perfunctorily accorded on days of obligation. Catholics no longer chose their chaplain for his speed in saying Mass, or kept Boccaccio bound in the covers of their missals. Driven back to the life of the catacombs, the Church was recovering their temper. No one now complained of the length of the services, a priest reported to Father Agazzari; if a Mass did not last nearly an hour they were discontented, and if, as occasionally happened, several priests were together, the congregation would assist at five or six Masses in one morning.

Word would go round the countryside that Campion had arrived, and throughout the evening Catholics of every degree, squire and labourer and deposed cleric, would stealthily assemble. He would sit up half the night receiving each in turn, hearing their confessions and resolving their difficulties. Then before dawn a room would be prepared for Mass. Watches were set in case of alarm. The congregation knelt on the rush-strewn floor. Mass was said, communion was given. Then Campion would preach.

It needs little fancy to reconstruct the scene; the audience hushed and intent, every member of whom was risking liberty and fortune, perhaps his life, by attendance. The dusk lightened and the candles paled on the improvised altar, the tree tops outside the window took fire, as Campion spoke. The thrilling tones, the profusion of imagery, the polish and precision, the balanced, pointed argument, the whole structure and rich ornament of rhetoric which had stirred the lecture halls and collegiate chapels of Oxford and Douai, Rome, Prague, and Rheims, inspired now with more than human artistry, rang through the summer dawn. And when the discourse had mounted to its peroration and the fiery voice had dropped to the quiet, traditional words of the blessing, a long silence while the priest disrobed and assumed once more his secular disguise; a hurried packing away of the altar furniture, a few words of leave taking, and then the horses' hooves clattered once more in the cobbled yard; Campion was on his way, and the Catholics dispersed to their homes.

The danger was increasingly great.

I cannot long escape the hands of the heretics,

said Campion, in the letter quoted above,

> the enemy have so many eyes, so many tongues, so many scouts and crafts.
> I am in apparel to myself very ridiculous; I often change my name also. I
> read letters sometimes myself that in the first front tell news that Campion
> is taken. . . . Threatening edicts come forth against us daily. . . . I find many
> neglecting their own security to have only care of my safety.

More than once while Campion was sitting at dinner strangers would
be heard at the outer doors. 'Like deer when they hear the huntsmen' the
company would leap to their feet and Campion would be rushed into
hiding. Sometimes it proved to be a false alarm; sometimes the pursuivants
would enter, question the inmates, and depart satisfied. The party would
resume their meal and the interrupted conversation. Events of this kind
were now a part of his life, but by the loyalty and discretion of his friends,
and by his own resources, he escaped unmolested through the three-
month journey, and his report ends in a triumphant mood.

> There will never want in England men that will have care of their own
> salvation, nor such as shall advance other men's; neither shall this Church
> here ever fail so long as priests and pastors shall be found for their sheep,
> rage man or devil never so much.

London was the centre of danger for the priests; the meeting of Campion
and Persons was therefore brief. They reported progress, discussed plans,
redistributed their resources, and parted again after the mutual confession
and renewal of vows which was customary in the Society. There were
other priests, seminarist and Marian, and probably several of their lay
supporters at the Uxbridge meeting. The names have not been recorded.
Father Hartley and Father Arthur Pitts were sent to the universities. (Both
were caught later by the authorities. Father Hartley was hanged.) There
was some discussion of a project towards Scotland, later put into effect by
Father Holt, which has no part in Campion's story. His instructions were
to proceed north to Lancashire, where many Catholic families were
petitioning for his services, and if circumstances permitted, to produce a
literary work, a Latin tract addressed primarily to the universities, which
should follow up with solid argument the sensation made by the *Brag*.
Persons remained in and about London. The search for him was incessant.
A few weeks brought the news that Ralph Sherwin, most charming and
devoted of the seminarists, had been taken, preaching in the house of a Mr
Roscarock. Bosgrave, Hart, and Cottam were already in prison; Bruscoe

was arrested on Christmas Eve. By constant changes of disguise and name and daring effrontery in his choice of residence, Persons succeeded in remaining at liberty; sometimes he attached himself to the Spanish Ambassador, sometimes he bribed the pursuivants and lodged with them, on one occasion at least he seems to have stayed in one of the royal palaces. All the time he pushed on the work with unremitting zeal. A great need of the Catholic party in the controversy which their activity had aroused was a printing press. The difficulties were formidable; every transaction, even the purchase of paper, was fraught with danger, and we shall see, when we come to examine Campion's *Ten Reasons*, how meagre the apparatus was, but a press of a kind he was able to procure, which he set up first at East Ham and later at Stonor Park, near Henley. The first production was an English composition of his own, the *Reasons Why Catholiques Refuse* to attend the Protestant services. There is no evidence that this work attracted much attention, but its successor was more sensational.

On 30 December and 3 January, respectively, there appeared pamphlets by two Anglican clergymen, Mr Charke and Mr Hanmer. Hanmer was a Welshman, who in 1567 had been chaplain of Christ Church at Oxford, and later became vicar of St Leonard's Church in London, where he tore up and sold the memorial brasses. He seems to have been a cheerful, bombastic person, free from malice, with small sympathy for his Puritan colleagues. 'A poor, dear soul,' Father Fitsimon later described him, 'much given to banqueting and drinking and jesting and scoffing.'

Charke was a protégé of Burghley's, and a man of far stricter disposition. He had got into trouble at Cambridge for declaring the episcopal system to be the invention of Satan. In the disputations at the Tower he was later to prove one of Campion's most ill-mannered antagonists.

As might be expected, Charke's pamphlet was the more likely to prove damaging. It is entitled *An Answer to a Seditious Pamphlet lately cast about by a Jesuit*, and affords an instructive comparison both in style and matter with Campion's *Brag*. Briefly summarized, Charke's points are:

(1) The Church of Rome is the Church of Anti-Christ and her priests the priests of Anti-Christ, who take upon them 'against the manifest word of God to offer a sacrifice for the quick and the dead'. Campion had described himself as an 'unworthy' priest; 'to judge an evil servant by his own mouth, he, that is unworthy of so foul a priesthood, what shall he be worthy of?'

(2) In old time the friars and monks used to name themselves Franciscans, Dominicans, etc., after 'base and beggarly friars'. Campion has the blasphemous presumption to take the name of Jesuit.

(3) 'They preach not the Gospel but against the Gospel ... their ministry of the Sacraments is the saying or singing of mass and corrupt baptism.

(4) 'Religion and politics in England are, through God's singular blessings, preserved together in life, as with one spirit; he that doth take away the life of the one, doth procure the death of the other. . . . Because he carrieth no sword he would be thought to carry no weapon. But is not the trumpet worse than many swords?'

(5) Natural and moral reason, to which Campion appealed, are 'the two great enemies of true religion and the great nurseries of Atheism and Heresy'. Canon Law is 'ludicrous'.

(6) Campion speaks of 'innocent hands'. How can they be innocent when 'they crucify the Son of God again every day in their most blasphemous sacrifice of the Mass'?

This was the Anglican case which the Jesuits were called to meet. Except in its fourth section, it was not formidable, but the author must have felt confident that in the state of the censorship and the fugitive condition of his opponents, they would find it impossible to publish a reply. Within a week Persons had his answer written and printed. His *Censure* of Hanmer and Charke was adequate to the occasion, though it affords little interest to a modern reader. Even in its own day its chief importance was the fact of its appearance. It was suddenly brought home to the Government that there was in their midst an effective machinery working against their interests, that their pamphleteers could no longer pour out whatever abuse and misrepresentation they pleased without fear of correction. The speed of Persons's reply made it clear that he was on the spot; this was not one of the tracts emanating from the seminaries abroad. Their alarm found expression in the proclamation dated 10 January 1581, for 'recalling her Majesty's subjects which under pretence of studies do live beyond the seas both contrary to the laws of God and of the realm, and against such as do receive or retain Jesuits and massing priests, sowers of sedition and of other treasonable attempts'.

By this proclamation the relatives of seminarists had to recall them, or lose all civil rights. It was illegal to send them any supplies. Jesuits and priests must be surrendered; anyone knowingly harbouring them was guilty of sedition and treason.

The Jesuits were already outlaws, and as regards the legal position of them and their hosts the proclamation made little change, but its significance was that by forcibly reaffirming the existing law, the Council was giving warning of a further increase of severity in its application. Already,

on 10 December, the Council had started in the case of Kirby and Cottam
what was henceforth to be its consistent policy, of putting their religious
prisoners to the torture. In the next four weeks, Sherwin, Johnson, Hart,
Orton, Thomson, and Roscarock were racked, Sherwin on two succeeding days. On 25 January Sir Walter Mildmay, in the House of Commons,
rose to move the Bill for 'the retaining of Her Majesty's subjects in due
obedience' quoted at the beginning of this chapter.

News of these events reached Campion in Lancashire and Yorkshire.
About six months passed between the Conference at Uxbridge and
Campion's return to London. They were spent, as before, in visiting
Catholic houses of whose names we have some fragmentary information.
He spent Christmas with the Pierrepoints of Holme Pierrepoint; on the
Tuesday after Twelfth-night he was in Derbyshire at Henry Sacheverell's,
from whom he went to Mr Langford, to Lady Folambe of Walton, and to
Mr Powdrell, where he met George Gilbert, and perhaps received copies
of Hanmer's and Charke's pamphlets. From there he visited Mr Ayers of
the Stipte. All this time he was under the conduct of Gervase Pierrepoint;
in the third week of January Mr Tempest took him in charge and led him
into Yorkshire. On 28 January he was at Yeafford as the guest of Mr John
Rookby. In the succeeding weeks he visited Dr Vavasour, Mrs Bulmer,
Sir William Bapthorpe of Osgodby, Mr Grimston (probably Mr Ralph
Grimston of Nidd, who was hanged seventeen years later for harbouring
Father Snow), Mr Hawkeworth, and Mr Askulph Cleesby. Tempest was
then succeeded by a Mr Smyth, who took him to his brother-in-law's,
Mr William Harrington of Mount St John, where Campion made a stay
of twelve days, and so impressed William, one of his host's six sons, that
he became a priest, and was later hanged. From Mount St John he
travelled with a Mr More and his wife into Lancashire, where almost the
whole county was Catholic in sympathy. Here he stayed with the
Worthingtons, Talbots, Heskeths, Mrs Allen, widowed sister-in-law of the
Cardinal, Houghtons, Westbys, and Rigmaidens. In the middle of May he
was summoned to return to London.

These names are taken from Burghley's list, drawn up after Campion's
arrest. It is far from complete, as will appear later from his letter to Lord
Huntingdon. Probably twice its number remained undetected, if, as it is
reasonable to suppose, Campion maintained the practice of constant
change of residence. It is significant that much of Burghley's information
seems to be of places where Campion remained some days and thus risked
attracting the attention of Protestant informers; other names, such as Sir
William Bapthorpe's and Dr Vavasour's, were already well known to the

authorities; Vavasour had been in prison at Hull in the preceding August, and Bapthorpe had given a bond of £200 to the Archbishop for his good behaviour.

His work in the north was apostolic, as it had been in the Midlands. Nearly a century later Father Henry More found that the tradition of Campion's passage was still fresh in Lancashire, and that Catholics still spoke of his sermons on the Hail Mary, the Ten Lepers, the King who went on a journey, and the Last Judgement. Perhaps he was more free in his movements, as danger lost its novelty; he seems to have preached more openly and to larger audiences than he had dared do during his first journey.

Besides this he was employed in writing the *Ten Reasons*. As we have noticed, the project was discussed at Uxbridge. Various suggestions had been made for its title, until Campion had proposed *De Haeresi Desperata* – 'Heresy in Despair'; it was a suggestion typical of the spirit of the missionaries; on every side heresy seemed to be triumphant; the Queen's Government was securely in power; the old Church was scattered and broken; they themselves were being hunted from house to house in daily expectation of death; their very existence was a challenge to the power of the State to destroy a living Faith. Leading Catholics, such as Francis Throckmorton, were discussing a treaty with the Government in which they proposed to compound their fines for a regular subsidy on condition of being allowed the quiet practice of their religion. All despaired of the restoration of the Church and only begged sufferance to die with the aid of her sacraments. It was at this juncture that Campion gently proposed to examine the despair of heresy and show that all its violence sprang from its consciousness of failure.

It is not certain why he changed his mind. Perhaps he felt that the issues were too grave for a display of high spirits; Charke, Hanmer, and other Anglican critics had made great play with his 'insolence' in taking upon himself, in the *Brag*, to challenge the combined scholarship of his country; it was necessary to show that his confidence was founded on the strength of his case, not of his own skill. Whatever the reason, the book, when it appeared, bore the title *Decem Rationes*, 'Ten Reasons, for the confidence with which Edmund Campion offered his adversaries to dispute on behalf of the Faith, set before the famous men of our Universities.' It was composed, for the most part, at Mount St John, and the manuscript was sent to Persons soon after Easter. It was primarily for the purpose of seeing it through the press that Campion was called back to London at Whitsun.

The difficulties of production were very great. The margins were copiously annotated with textual references, all of which would be scrutinized by his opponents; accuracy was of vital importance, for any slip would be eagerly advertised as evidence of dishonesty. A young convert, Mr Fitz-Herbert, who was so far unsuspected by the Government and was therefore able to work without embarrassment, undertook to verify the references, but both Campion and Persons were anxious that the author should have the final reading. Before the date of Campion's arrival in London, it had been found necessary to move the press from East Ham, for the search was closing in. In March, the servant of Roland Jenks, a stationer who helped supply Persons with materials, turned informer; Persons's lodgings were raided and most of his personal possessions seized; more serious still, Father Briant was arrested in a neighbouring house and taken to the Tower, where, after more than usually savage torture, he emerged only for his execution. Shortly afterwards, one of Persons's workmen was arrested while on an errand in London, and racked, without success, to make him reveal the hiding-place of the press. In these circumstances Persons removed to Henley, where Dame Cecilia Stonor, mother of the Sir Francis of the day, put her house at his disposal. It was well suited for the purpose, being hidden in woods and easily accessible by river from London and Oxford. Here the *Decem Rationes* was printed, under the supervision of Stephen Brinkley, who, with the four workmen, was subsequently arrested.

Only four copies of the first edition are known to exist; one is in the possession of the Marquess of Bute, another is exhibited in the library at Stonyhurst; a third was in the possession of a Canon of Windsor in 1914; a fourth was discovered in 1936 in the sixpenny-box of a second-hand book shop and is now in Campion Hall library. At first sight the little volume – it is barely 20,000 words in length – shows little evidence of the difficulties under which it was produced. It has an elegantly spaced title page, decorated with a sacred emblem; the press-work is regular and the composition free from misprints. An expert examination has revealed certain peculiarities. Since the work is in Latin, Roman type had been used (Persons's English tracts were in black letter), but the printers were working at the disadvantage of great poverty of materials; after the first pages the diphthong 'Æ', which occurs frequently, runs out, and is replaced by the italic '*Æ*', by 'E', and even by '*E*'. These substitutions become more frequent as we approach the end of signatures C, H, and I, while at the beginning of the next signature the fount Æ reappears, suggesting that the sheets were printed off and the type distributed and reset three times during the printing. There is no Roman query sign; black letter is used in its place. There is no Greek fount; Campion's Greek quotations have to be given in Roman italics.

It is not surprising that, in these circumstances, the book took several weeks to print off, but it was ready in time for Commencement at Oxford, Tuesday, 27 June. The distribution was made by Father Hartley, the priest mentioned above, who was in close association with Persons at this period. Copies were introduced into St Mary's Church and placed on the benches. Campion's name was still well remembered in Oxford. The polished Livian style of the essay and the romantic manner of its appearance made an appeal to the University, where repeated repressive measures had failed to destroy traces of the old Faith, and, from the first, it became the centre of controversy.

In the present century it is difficult to understand the sensation which was aroused. The Church has vast boundaries to defend, and each generation finds itself called to service upon a different front. The apologetics of another century seem to be concerned with truisms and trivialities, and modern Catholics are unlikely to find much that is useful in the *Ten Reasons*. The thesis may be analysed as follows:

(1) All heretics have been obliged to mutilate Holy Scripture in their own interest. The Lutherans and Calvinists have done this in several instances. (2) In other cases they retain the text, but pervert the clear meaning of the passage. (3) The Protestants by denying the existence of a visible Church, deny, for all practical purpose, the existence of any Church. (4) The Protestants pretend to revere the first four General Councils, but deny many of their doctrines. (5) and (6) The Protestants are obliged to disregard the Fathers. (7) The History of the Church is continuous. The Protestants are without living tradition. (8) The works of Zwingli, Luther, and Calvin contain many grossly offensive statements. (9) The Protestants are obliged to employ many empty tricks of argument. (10) The variety and extent of Catholic witness are impressive. This section contains the eloquent passage: 'Listen, Elizabeth, most powerful Queen . . . I tell thee; one and the same heaven cannot hold Calvin and the Princes whom I have named' (Elizabeth's ancestors, and the great heroes of Christendom). 'With these Princes then associate thyself, and so make thee worthy of thy ancestors, worthy of thy genius, worthy of thy excellence in letters, worthy of thy praises, worthy of thy fortune. To this effect only do I labour about thy person, and will labour, whatever shall become of me, for whom these adversaries so often augur the gallows, as though I were an enemy of thy life. Hail, good Cross. There will come,

Elizabeth, the day that will show thee clearly which have loved thee, the Society of Jesus or the offspring of Luther.'

It was a work of its own day, and the measure of its quality was the effect which it had on Campion's contemporaries. Burghley took up the matter as one of gravity and instructed the Bishop of London to produce an answer; the Regius Professors of Divinity at both Oxford and Cambridge were enlisted, and before 1585 no less than twenty works had appeared, dealing either with the *Brag*, the *Ten Reasons*, or the Disputes in the Tower, which were their direct consequence. Catholic theologians, who are notoriously critical of each other's work, combined to praise it. It was commended by the Cardinal Secretary of State, and Marc Antoine Muret, who, after a dangerous youth, was now established in honour at Rome, and enjoyed international pre-eminence as a Catholic humanist, described it as *Libellum aureum, vere digito Dei scriptum* – 'a golden little book, truly written by the finger of God'. Since his day it has been reprinted nearly fifty times.

We have no exact information of Campion's movements in the two months which he spent in and about London. He was certainly at Stonor for part of this time, revising the proofs of the *Ten Reasons*. He appears to have frequented three lodgings in London, Mrs Brideman's in Westminster, Mr Barnes' in Tothill Street, and Lady Babington's in the White Friars. He also visited the Bellamys at Uxendon Hall, Harrow-on-the-Hill, and made a few expeditions into the Midlands, to the Prices at Huntingdon, Mr William Griffith at Uxbridge, Mr Edwin East of Bledlow, Bucks, Lady Babington at Twyford, Bucks, Mr Dormer at Wynge, and a Mrs Pollard. The hunt was working nearer to him. The raid on Persons's headquarters in Bridewell had seriously embarrassed the two fathers. Since the new year there had been, as was mentioned above, a series of arrests in their immediate circle, and it was in a mood of resignation that Campion awaited the doom which, with the pitiless step of ancient tragedy, came daily closer to him. Persons records how, at this time, he and Campion sat up most of one night, reviewing their situation and speculating how they would acquit themselves when the ordeal came.

Persons was to live on; his destiny was to lead him through many byways; his work was to be multifarious, obscure, inconclusive, there were to be days of tumult and of impenetrable silence, ceaseless effort, partial victory, fame that was spread in doubtful accents. For Campion there was only glory; a name of triumph and pure light. But as the figure of Persons recedes from view down the gloomy corridor of the Escurial, it is Campion's rope that he wears, knotted about his waist.

With the publication of the *Ten Reasons* the first part of Campion's task was accomplished. He had been in England, now, for over a year; that was his achievement, that in all her centuries the English Church was to count one year of her life by his devotion; others were now ready to take over the guard; since Easter thirty of Allen's priests had crossed the Channel and landed successfully; the work would go on; Mass would still be offered in England, the growing generation would still learn the truths of the Faith; the Church of Augustine and Edward and Thomas would still live; for Campion there remained only the final sacrifice. His road to Harrow took him past Tyburn gibbet, and here, Persons records, he would often pause, hat in hand, 'both because of the sign of the Cross and in honour of some martyrs who had suffered there, and also because he used to say that he would have his combat there'.

On Tuesday, 11 July, Campion took his leave of Persons, intending to collect some papers which he had left at Mr Houghton's house in Lancashire, and then proceed into Norfolk upon another round of visits. They made their mutual confessions and renewal of vows, and on parting exchanged hats – as, on leaving Prague, Campion had exchanged his gown with the rector, Campanus – a gesture, perhaps, signifying a particular solemnity and finality in the occasion. But in a short time Campion was back, to ask his superior's permission to break his journey at a house which lay almost directly on his route, Lyford Grange, near Faringdon in Berkshire. The proprietor, Mr Yate, was then in London, a prisoner for his religion, and his mother lived at Lyford in the company of two priests named Ford and Collington, and some Brigittine nuns to whom he was giving protection. Yate had more than once begged Campion to visit them, but the household was notorious, and, since it was already liberally supplied with priests, Campion had hitherto declined. Now, however, that he was to pass so near them, Campion asked permission to stop there the night. Persons distrusted the plan. He knew Campion's gentle courtesy and the tenacity of pious women. They would never let him leave. Campion's heart was set upon the visit; he promised to stay exactly as long as Persons ordered; he offered to put himself under obedience to the lay brother Ralph Emerson, who was to be his companion to Norfolk. On these terms Persons gave his permission, and the two parted, this time for life.

All went well at Lyford. Campion behaved with complete discretion; he refused to preach or to be displayed in any way to the neighbours; he conferred with the good women, quietly, one by one, said Mass for them early next day, and departed unobtrusively towards Oxford in the company of Father Collington, before anyone outside the house got wind of his arrival.

Lyford, with its nuns and its two chaplains, was the religious centre of the district. That afternoon there were callers. Catholic gossip began, and the women could not contain their news; the famous Father Campion had been there; he had said this and that; he had dressed in such a way; this was how he had heard confessions; it was thus he had said Mass; they might have passed him on the road; he was barely thirty miles away at the moment.

The neighbours were chagrined at what they had missed; how could the women have been so churlish as to keep their guest to themselves? And he had not preached? Everyone said it was the experience of a lifetime to hear him. Father Campion must be brought back.

Ford was mounted and sent after him. They met that evening at an inn near Oxford, where he was already in discussion with a group of undergraduates and masters of the university. He was weary of danger, and took risks in these last days that he would not have allowed himself a year before. The company had already tried to get a sermon out of him. Now Ford arrived with his entreaty to return to Lyford. Campion referred them to 'the little man', his superior. They all turned upon Brother Ralph, arguing and coaxing. Obedience must be tempered with good sense; the object of Persons's order was the good of souls. Here was an unrivalled opportunity. He had allowed Campion to waste a day among a handful of pious women; now he was offered a large and eager audience. Brother Ralph pleaded the necessity of the road. Here he was undone. Persons had expressly forbidden Campion to preach or visit in Lancashire; for him the journey was an unnecessary risk and waste of energy. Let him stay at Lyford over the week-end, while Brother Ralph fetched the papers from Mr Houghton. Campion could leave on Sunday and meet him at a Catholic gentleman's house on the borders of Norfolk. Brother Ralph yielded and rode on alone into Lancashire. Campion returned, joyfully attended, to the house at Lyford.

The Grange still stands, reduced in size and importance, but still a house of poignant association to the Catholic visitor. At this date it occupied four sides of a courtyard with a gate-tower, long since demolished, facing a drawbridge. Mrs Yate's room and the priest's cell have disappeared, and there is no good reason for identifying the long room as the chapel. The moat and drawbridge posts can still be seen and a line of trees marks the avenue which once constituted the main approach. Originally the moat enclosed a large area which included a dove-cot, probably other outbuildings, and a dense orchard and fruit garden. The fact, which will be seen later, that it employed sixty men seven or eight hours to search it, attests the size of the place.

Friday and Saturday passed without alarm. Campion was lionized and cosseted by the good ladies; scholars came out from Oxford, and the Catholic neighbours flocked to see him. On Sunday, in obedience to Brother Ralph, he was to start for Norfolk. That morning Mr George Eliot arrived. He was a typical member of the class of professional priest-hunter whom Cecil and Walsingham now employed. Originally a man-servant of low character, he had worked in the households of Mr Roper of Orpington, in Kent, and the Dowager Lady Petre, mother of Sir John Petre of Ingatestone, Essex, both of whom were Catholic. While in their service he had professed himself of their Faith. He got into trouble for rape and homicide and left Lady Petre's employment for gaol. From there, he wrote several letters to Leicester, offering information against his former employers, giving a list of prominent Catholics, and in particular accusing Father Payne, who lived in Roper's house under the title of steward, of a 'horrible treason' by which the priest proposed to levy a certain company of armed men, fall upon and despatch Leicester, Walsingham, and Burgh-ley, use Her Majesty in such sort as neither modesty nor duty would suffer him to rehearse and raise a general cry everywhere of 'Queen Mary! Queen Mary!' No anti-Catholic tale was too extravagant or insubstantial to interest the Council; Eliot was summoned to Leicester House, given his freedom and a general commission to seek out and arrest any Jesuits or massing priests whom he could discover. A man named David Jenkins was appointed to assist him. Profiting by his former Catholic connexion, he was able to attend and report a Mass said at Haddon, in Oxfordshire, on 2 July, and, still on the same errand, returned to the neighbourhood at the time of Campion's visit. Lyford was well known as a Catholic centre, and in the hope of finding a Mass there on the Sunday morning he and Jenkins arrived, quite unaware of the sensational coup they were about to make.

On their approach at about eight in the morning, they found the gates barred and a watchman on guard. Thomas Cooper, the cook, had been a fellow-servant with Eliot at Mr Roper's. Eliot asked for him by name, and the watchman, who at first had received them with suspicion, went in to fetch him. Eliot and Jenkins waited in their saddles outside the gates. Presently the cook came out. They greeted each other as old friends. Eliot explained that he was on his way to Derbyshire, and must now be off.

'No,' said the cook, 'that you shall not do before dinner.'

Eliot and Jenkins made a show of reluctance, but at length allowed themselves to be persuaded; dismounted, and accompanied the cook to the buttery, where he drew them a jug of ale.

Presently after,

Eliot records,

> the said Cook came and whispered with me, and asked, Whether my friend (meaning the said Jenkins) were within the Church or not?
>
> To which I answered, 'He was not; but yes,' said I, 'he is a very honest man, and one that wishes well that way.'
>
> Then said the Cook to me, 'Will you go up?' By which speech I knew he would bring me to a Mass.
>
> And I assured him and said, 'Yea, for God's sake, that let me do; for seeing I must needs tarry, let me take something with me that is good.'

Accordingly they left Jenkins in the buttery with his beer mug, and passing through the hall, the dining parlour and two or three other rooms, came to a 'fair, large chamber' where Mass was in progress. Father Ford – who was known to Eliot by the name of Satwell – was at the altar; the congregation consisted of three nuns, in their habits, thirty-seven lay people, Collington and Campion. Eliot slipped into a place and followed the service with a suitable display of familiarity and devotion. When Ford's Mass was finished, the people remained on their knees while Campion vested, said his Mass,

> and at the end thereof, made holy bread and delivered it to the people there, to everyone some, together with holy water; whereof he gave Eliot part also.
>
> And then was there a chair set in the chamber something beneath the Altar, wherein the said Campion did sit down; and there made a Sermon very nigh an hour long; the effect of the text being, as I remember, 'That Christ wept over Jerusalem, etc.' And so applied the same to this our country of England for that the Pope his authority and doctrine did not so flourish here as the same Campion desired.

The text was from the gospel of the day; from that morning every phrase of the reproach was indelibly written in the hearts of Campion's audience, 'Jerusalem, Jerusalem, thou that killest the prophets.' It was the Tenebrae of his Passion. Never, it was remembered, had his eloquence been more compelling than in this last sermon.

While he listened Eliot's hand strayed, he tells us, to the pocket where he kept the Queen's commission; it was half in his mind to produce it there and then; but he prudently sat the sermon out, and as soon as he decently could, hurried back to Jenkins in the buttery. There was no time now to stay for dinner, and making what excuses they could to the hospitable cook, the two galloped off with their news to the nearest Justice.

Seven or eight of the visiting Catholics remained for dinner, and they were still at the table, at about one o'clock, when the alarm was given, that the house was completely surrounded. Mr Fettiplace, a neighbouring magistrate, Eliot, Jenkins, and a squadron of soldiers sat their horses outside the main gate demanding admission, while the watchmen reported armed men posted in a circle round the moat. Campion wished to surrender himself, in the hope that, content with his easy capture, the magistrate might leave the others unmolested. Mrs Yate insisted that the house was well provided with hiding-places, and that there was a fair prospect of escape; in any case his presence there would ruin them all, whether he surrendered or was discovered. The three priests were led to a secret room, where there was just space for them to lie side by side on a couch; some provisions were put in with them and the panelling slid into place; meanwhile the nuns hastily put themselves into ordinary costume; books, beads, pictures were hidden away; Edward Yate, brother of the master of the house, and two yokels, locked themselves in the pigeon house; it was half an hour before Fettiplace was admitted. He was then greeted by Mrs Yate and her guests – five gentlemen, one gentlewoman, and the three nuns in lay attire – who demanded indignantly to know the reason for the disturbance. Eliot accused the entire party of having been present at a Mass that morning. They flatly denied it, and Fettiplace found himself in the difficult position of having to choose between the word of a professional informer and of a number of local gentry. Perhaps he knew that Eliot was telling the truth, but he had no particular zeal to prove it. Eliot insisted on a search, and the men marched through the house, glancing under beds and behind curtains. Nothing was found; the magistrate had done his duty and was ready to apologize and withdraw. But, says Eliot, 'I eftsoone put Master Fettiplace in remembrance of our Commission.' The magistrate protested that he had no warrant to do any damage in the house. Eliot produced his commission and began to read an authorization for this very purpose. One of the men, looking over his shoulder, discovered that he was inventing. Eliot challenged the magistrate to arrest him as a comforter of Jesuits. They were now outside the gates, arguing the matter on the drawbridge; within, the household was jubilant at their escape. Suddenly the party were observed to waver and to turn back; they were demanding readmission. Eliot had won. Fettiplace recognized that he was a dangerous man; a malicious report to Leicester might bring about his own ruin.

Eliot and Jenkins took charge of the raid. Edward Yate and the two countrymen were discovered in the dove-cot. It was now useless to pretend that nothing unusual had been on foot. Methodically, room by room, they went through the house, sounding the panelling and splintering it where it seemed hollow; they found several secret places, but no trace of the priests. The afternoon drew in, and Fettiplace's men became sulky. Eliot sent to the High Sheriff, Mr Foster, and to another Justice, Mr Wiseman, for further help. Foster, who had no liking for this sort of procedure, sent back word that he could not be found; Wiseman arrived before dark with a posse of a dozen of his own servants 'very able men', according to Eliot, 'and well appointed'. That night a guard of sixty was set about the house, while others slept on the premises; Mrs Yate gave them supper.

The cell where the priests lay opened out of 'a chamber near the top of the house; which was but very simple; having in it a large shelf with divers tools and instruments both upon it and hanging by it; which they judged to belong to some cross bow maker'. Shelves hung across the door. Mrs Yate had her bed made up in a room close to this workshop, and during the night Campion came out and addressed a few words of encouragement there to the household. As they were leaving her room one of them stumbled; the guard was alarmed, but the priests got back to their hiding-place without detection.

At daybreak the search began again, but by now even Eliot was losing heart. He knew that Campion had been there, and had meant to remain to dinner, but it seemed probable that he had changed his plan – perhaps alarmed by Eliot's precipitate departure – and had escaped while his pursuers were summoning Fettiplace. When they were 'in effect clear void of any hope', Jenkins noticed a chink of light in the well over the stairs, and seizing a crowbar, revealed the back of the cell,

> the priests lying all close together upon a bed of purpose laid for them; where they had bread, meat, and drink sufficient to have relieved them three or four days together.
>
> The said Jenkins then called very loudly, and said 'I have found the traitors!' and presently company enough was with them; who there saw the said Priests, when there was no remedy for them but *nolens volens* courteously yielded themselves.

Chapter Four

THE MARTYR

As soon as the news of the discovery reached him, the High Sheriff, Humphrey Foster, rode over from Aldermaston to take charge of the house. He saw to it that Campion and the other prisoners were decently used, and despatched a messenger to the Court for further instructions. Eliot, however, had anticipated him, arrived first with the news and was given, as was very clearly his right, full credit for the capture. Before Thursday he was back at Lyford with authority to bring Campion and the men taken with him to London as his own prisoners. The Sheriff was instructed to provide a guard. In Eliot's absence there had been another arrest, of a fourth priest named William Filby, who, unwittingly, came to call at Lyford and found the magistrates in possession.

The party set out on the 20th, passed through Abingdon, and rested the first night at Henley. At every stage of the journey large numbers turned out to see them, some with open sympathy. Persons was still in hiding at Stonor; he sent his servant to see how Campion was looking, and the man brought back word that his gentleness and charm had already put him on easy terms with his captors. The party dined together at the same table. Campion chatted easily with them and with several members of the university who were allowed to approach him.

Eliot was ignored; neither magistrates nor soldiers troubled to hide their dislike of the man; once or twice on the road there had been hostile movements in the crowd as the informer passed, and cries of 'Judas'; his first elation was exhausted; the praise which he had received at Court sounded faint and distorted; it was almost as though this were Campion's triumph, and he the malefactor. At last he could bear Campion's neglect no longer, and so broke out: 'Mr Campion, you look cheerfully upon everyone but me. I know you are angry with me for this work.'

Then, perhaps for the first time since Sunday morning, when Eliot had knelt before Mass to receive the holy bread from his hands, Campion turned his eyes on him. 'God forgive thee, Eliot,' he said, 'for so judging of me; I forgive thee and in token thereof, I drink to thee.' He raised his cup, and then added more gravely, 'Yea, and if thou repent and come to confession, I will absolve thee; but large penance must thou have.'

According to Eliot, Campion warned him that no good would result from the service he had done; which prediction Eliot, as was his nature, took as a threat of Catholic vengeance; from that day he imagined he was being followed and bewitched, and, though no attempt was ever made at reprisal, went in fear of his life, so that the report gained credence that he had lost his wits.

At Henley, that night, after they had all retired to bed, there was a sudden wild shouting; the guards took alarm that an attempt was being made to rescue the prisoners; torches were brought and it was found that Father Filby was suffering from nightmare; he had dreamed that someone was ripping down his body and taking out his bowels.

They spent the succeeding night at Colnbrook and there, on special instructions from the Council, the character of the procession was altered. The prisoners were pinioned on their horses; their elbows being tied behind them and their wrists in front; their ankles were strapped together under the horses' bellies. Campion was driven on in front with a paper stuck in his hat reading CAMPION THE SEDITIOUS JESUIT. In this way they were paraded through the London streets, crowded for the Saturday market. At Cheapside, the statues at the foot of the old cross were all defaced by the Protestants, but the cross itself still stood beyond their reach. As he passed it, Campion made a low reverence. Finally they reached the Tower, where the Governor, Sir Owen Hopton, took them into his custody. Before he parted with the Berkshire guard, who had had no responsibility for his humiliation, Campion thanked them and blessed them. Then the gates of the Tower shut behind him.

The conditions of imprisonment in the Tower were very different from the sociable, haphazard life at the Marshalsea. The regulations for solitary confinement are on record; the windows were blocked up; light and ventilation came through a 'slope tunnel', barred at top and bottom, so that nothing could be conveyed to the prisoner from outside. The lieutenant had to be present whenever a keeper entered the cell, and it was rarely possible, and then only under the strictest supervision, for prisoners to receive a visitor. In some cases, no doubt, severity was tempered by venality, but Campion was a prisoner of the highest import-ance, suspect of having wide, subterranean connexions, and Hopton treated him with more than customary harshness. He was placed in the Little Ease, the cell, still an object of interest in the Tower dungeons, in which it was impossible for a full-grown man to stand erect or lie at full length. Here, crouching in the half-dark, he remained for four days. Then the cage was opened and he was summoned to emerge; under a strong guard he was led up to the level of the ground, out into the air and sunshine, across the yard to the water gate, where a boat awaited them; they rowed up-stream among the ferrymen and barges and busy river traffic. Presently they reached Leicester House.

We cannot know what hopes may have stirred in Campion's heart as he recognized the home of his old friend and patron; as the guard led him through the familiar, frequented anterooms to the Earl's apartment. The doors were thrown open; the soldiers at his side stiffened; they were in the presence of the Queen. Beside her chair stood Leicester, Bedford, and two Secretaries of State. The guards stood back and Campion advanced to make his salutations.

It was a singular meeting.

The grime of the dungeon was still on Campion; his limbs as he knelt were stiff from his imprisonment.

The vast red wig nodded acknowledgement; the jewels and braid and gold lace glittered and the sunken, painted face smiled in recognition. They received him courteously, almost affectionately. 'There is none that knoweth me familiarly,' Campion had written to Leicester ten years earlier, 'but he knoweth withal how many ways I have been beholden to your lordship. How often at Oxford, how often at the Court, how at Rycote, how at Windsor, how by letters, how by reports, you have not ceased to further with advice and to countenance with authority, the hope and expectation of me, a single student.' Campion had followed other advice, recognized another authority, in those ten years; he had lived in a different hope and expectation; he stood before them now as an outcast, momentarily interrupted in his passage from the dungeon to the scaffold. But, for the occasion, politeness was maintained.

They questioned him about his purpose in coming to England, about Persons, about his instructions from Rome. He answered easily and quietly; he had come for the salvation of souls. The harsh, peremptory tones of Elizabeth broke in; did he acknowledge her as his Queen or no? Campion replied that he did indeed recognize her as his lawful Queen and governess, and was bound to her in obedience in all temporal matters. She pressed him with the question of her deposition. He answered, with perfect candour, that it was a subject upon which theologians were still divided, and began to explain the distinction between the *potestas ordinata* and *potestas inordinata* of the Papacy, and quoted the text, 'Render unto Caesar the things that are Caesar's.'

But the politicians were not in the mood for a debate upon Canon Law. They were satisfied that he had no treasonable designs, and told him that they had no fault to find with him except that he was a Papist.

'Which is my greatest glory,' Campion replied.

They then made the proposal for which he had been summoned. The past ten years should be forgotten; the road of preferment was still open; if he would publicly adjure his Faith and enter the Protestant ministry there was still no limit to the heights he might reach. The offer was kind in its intention. They had no desire to kill the virtuous and gifted man who had once been their friend, a man, moreover, who could still be of good service to them. From earliest youth, among those nearest them, they had been used to the spectacle of men who would risk their lives for power, but to die deliberately, without hope of release, for an idea, was something beyond their comprehension. They knew that it happened; they had seen it in the preceding reign, but not among people of their own acquaintance; humble, eccentric men had gone to the stake; argumentative men had gone into exile in Germany and Geneva, but Elizabeth and Cecil and Dudley had quietly conformed to the prevailing fashion; they had told their beads and eaten fish on Fridays, confessed and taken communion. Faith – as something concrete and indestructible, of such transcendent value that, once it was held, all other possessions became a mere encumbrance – was unknown to them; in rare, pensive moments shadows loomed and flickered across their minds, sentiment, conscience, fear of the unknown; some years Leicester patronized the Catholics, at others 'the Family of Love'; Elizabeth looked now on the crucifix, now on a talisman; Bible and Demonology lay together beside her bed. What correspondence, even in their charity, could they have with Campion?

He returned to the Tower, and, five days later, Leicester and Burghley signed the warrant to put him to the torture.

From now until 1 December, when he was dragged out to Tyburn, Campion disappeared from the world. He was seen again at the Conference in September with the Anglican clergy, and at his trial in November, but of the agony and endurance of those four months we have only hints and fragments of information. The little that we know was hidden from his contemporaries, and rumour was busy with his name.

First it was said that he had turned Protestant, had accepted a bishopric, and was about to make a public avowal of his apostasy and burn the *Ten Reasons* at St Paul's Cross. Hopton himself seems to have been responsible for this report, and so authoritatively that it was made an official announcement at many of the pulpits of London. Then it was said that he had taken his own life; then that he had purchased his safety by accusing his former friends of treason. No one was allowed to see him. All over the country gentlemen were being arrested and charged with Catholicism on Campion's authority. His friends were thrown into despair and shame. The Protestants taunted them with their champion's treachery. Then he reappeared, at the Conferences, at his trial, at Tyburn. In those brief glimpses they recognized the man whom they had known and trusted, the old gentleness, the old inflexible constancy. Opinion veered again; the confessions were challenged and could not be produced. They were denounced as forgeries. Only in recent years, when the archives are open and the bitter passions still, can we begin to pierce the subterranean gloom and guess at the atrocious secrets of the torture chamber.

Two things seem certain, that Campion told something and that he told very little. The purpose of his captors was to make him convict himself and his friends of treason, and in this they failed absolutely. Hardened criminals, at the mere sight of the rack, would break down and testify to whatever their gaolers demanded. Campion, the gentle scholar, was tortured on three occasions and said nothing that was untrue; nothing to which he was bound in secrecy by the seal of confession; nothing which, in the actual event, brought disaster to anyone. He seems, however, to have made certain admissions with which his scrupulous conscience, always more ready with accusation than with excuse, troubled him on the scaffold.

These all dealt with the hospitality he had received during his mission. His first examination took place on 30 or 31 July, and immediately afterwards Burghley wrote to Lord Shrewsbury that 'he would confess nothing of moment'. The subject upon which the Council particularly desired a 'confession' was the sum of £30,000 which he was reputed to have conveyed to the rebels in Ireland, how the money had been collected, how transferred. On this topic they could obtain no information. Immediately afterwards, however, they had knowledge of names of several people associated with Campion. On 2 August Burghley drew up a list of his hosts in Lancashire, on the 4th in Yorkshire, the 6th in Northamptonshire, and the 7th and 14th in Derbyshire. He attributed these to Campion's confessions. Thirty-two persons in all were questioned as a result of the lists, but in no case was the evidence considered strong enough for a conviction.

What importance Campion's admissions had in the compilation, and how those admissions were extorted, cannot be certainly known, but it is possible to make a conjecture.

The examiners were men proficient in every trick of their profession, and they were already well informed from other sources. For months the pursuit had been closing in; there had been other arrests; the two servants, taken at Lyford, had turned Queen's evidence. For over a year spies had been at work all over the country bribing and threatening; indiscreet conversations at the Marshalsea had been overheard; scraps of information from countless sources had been collected and arranged. Before the examination began the Crown lawyers had a fair idea of Campion's movements.

All the devices of cross-examination were then employed. They would pretend to certain knowledge, where they had only a suspicion. – 'When you were at such-and-such a house you spoke about Mary Queen of Scots'; 'No, we spoke only of religion'; 'Then you *were* at that house.' – They would quote to him spurious confessions of others; they would tell him of arrests that had not been made, of false betrayals. All the bluffs and traps which, in a court of law, will confuse a witness, cool headed and protected by counsel were now, used upon a man stretched in the last extremity of physical agony.

It is certain that neither then, nor in his subsequent examinations, did Campion ever break down. He never blurted out all that he knew, anything his tormentors required of him, only so that he might be released from the unendurable pain. There are no signed depositions. It was the custom of the time for the clerk, seated beside the rack, to record all that the witness said; then, when he was released, as soon as his fingers could hold a pen, he was required to put his name at the foot of each sheet. The pitiful, straggling, barely recognizable signatures were then admissible as evidence. In Campion's case they could produce no such testimony; if in the last minutes before the senses failed, in the delirium of pain before unconsciousness gratefully intervened and he was taken inert from the rack; as the pitiless questioning went on and on and the body lost its dependence upon the will – if then he spoke of things that should have been kept secret, his first conscious act was to repudiate them; the confessions were useful as a bluff to use against other prisoners, but they were valueless in a court of law.

And, even so, it was very little that was wrung from him. A page survives in Burghley's handwriting summarizing the investigation.

Henry Perpoynt esquire.

Jervis Perpoint his brother.

Campyon. That he was there all the last Christmas and tarried there until the tewsday after twelfth day, brought thither by Jervis Pierpoynt.

Confessed by bothe the Pierpoynts he said masses and confessed Jervis every week once.

Henry Sacheverell esquire.

Campyon. That he was there aboute the wednesday after twelfth day last, tarried there one night.

Confessed by Mr Sacheverell and that he said one masse.

The Lady ffuljames.

Campyon. That he was there one night about Saturdaie after twelfth day last.

Jervis Perpoynt that they stayed there two nights and said two masses.

And so on. These are not the confessions of a man whose courage has failed; it was not the kind of information that the rack-master was trying to wring from him; the Council wanted tales of Spanish gold and poisoned bodkins if the execution were to be popular.

It was recognized that the itinerary was incomplete and the details inadequate. On 7 August the Council despatched to the Earl of Huntingdon a list of some of Campion's Yorkshire hosts with instructions to examine

> bothe of them and others of their familyes and neighbourhood . . . how long he continued in their said houses or anie others, from where he came, whither he went and with whom; how often he or anie other jesuite or priest said anie masse in their houses . . . whether they themselves or anie other have heard masse or been reconciled or confessed.

On the back of the letter was a list similar to the one quoted:

> Campion confesseth he was in the City of York at the house of D. Vavasour. Thither resorted soche of the neighbours as Mrs Vavasour called her husband being then in prison. He was also at the house of one Mrs Boulmer. He hath forgotten who brought him thither neither did he know the company, etc.

The Vavasours were notorious recusants; their house would be under surveillance; Dr Vavasour was in prison for his religion; it was a common practice to shut up a spy with the prisoners to gain their confidence; a secret note from his wife may have fallen into the gaoler's hands. There are many ways in which the Council might have information about Campion's visit. But of the details which only Campion could tell, the waverers who conformed in public to the State Church but came to him secretly for advice, there is not a word. 'He hath forgotten who brought him thither.' One can guess what efforts were made to stimulate his memory; what endurance and triumph is recorded in that phrase.

It will be seen from the above quotations that Campion very rarely admitted to having performed any priestly office, and without that admission the case against his hosts was extremely slender. The recent proclamation had made it treasonable to harbour a priest, but Campion had travelled in disguise and under an assumed name. In the open hospitality of the age, the mere fact of Campion having slept under a certain roof was not enough to convict the master of complicity. Persons's letter, quoted in the preceding chapter, shows that he frequently stayed, unsuspected, in the houses of irreproachable Protestants.

But the men who were now arrested and questioned on the authority of Campion's 'confessions' had no means of judging the weakness of the case against them. They were told that Campion had betrayed them. The news reached Pounde in prison, and, impetuous as ever, he wrote a letter to Campion, which his gaoler accepted a bribe to deliver. The whole incident is obscure. He may have written in reproach or in enquiry about the authenticity of the 'confessions'. In any case, the message was shown to Hopton who, having read it, told the man to deliver it to Campion and bring him back the answer. This note has not been preserved, nor have we any exact transcript of its terms; it was quoted at the trial of Lord Vaux, Tresham, Catesby, and others before the Star Chamber as follows: 'A letter produced, said to be intercepted, which Mr Campion should seem to write to a fellow prisoner of his, namely, Mr Pound; wherein he did take notice that by frailty he had confessed of some houses where he had been, which now he repented him, and desired Mr Pound to beg pardon of the Catholics therein, saying that in this he rejoiced, that he had discovered no things of secret, nor would he, come rack, come rope.' Without Pounde's letter, to which it was a reply, this message is capable of more than one interpretation. Its value to the Council was as evidence of conspiracy, 'the things of secret' being taken as a political plot. The plainest and most probable meaning would seem to be that by 'frailty', either of endurance or astuteness, Campion had been forced into admissions which he now repented, but that he had merely confirmed what they already knew and had given no new information to the inquisitors – nothing that had hitherto been secret to them. His anxiety was not to defend his own reputation, but to warn his friends against an attempt to bluff them, as he had himself been bluffed.

One other point must be noticed with regard to the 'confessions'. At the beginning of his Conferences with the Anglican clergy there was some discussion of Campion's treatment on the rack. Beale, the Clerk of the Council, asked if he had been examined on any point of religion. Campion answered, 'that he was not indeed directly examined of religion, but moved to confess in what places he had been conversant since his repair into the realm.' Beale replied, 'that this was required of him because many of his fellows and by likelihood himself also, had reconciled divers of her Highnesses subjects to the Romish Church.' To which Campion replied, 'that forasmuch as the Christians of old time being commanded to deliver up the books of their religion to such as persecuted them, refused so to do, and misliked with them that did so, calling them *traditores*, he might not betray his Catholic brethren which were, as he said, the temples of the Holy Ghost.'

Now Beale himself had been present at the racking; Hopton, Hammond, and Norton, the other examiners, were present in the Conference room. The chief purpose of the meeting was to discredit Campion publicly in every way they could. And yet when he made this provocative comparison of himself with the Christian martyrs in ancient Rome, no one retorted that he *had* betrayed his brethren, the temples of the Holy Ghost, and out of his own mouth was condemned as *traditor*. Instead the question was immediately dropped. The examiners did not wish to give Campion the opportunity of challenging the 'confessions' that were being circulated under his name.

The Conferences referred to above were four in number. They were held at the express orders of the Council, who were anxious that Campion's challenge, contained in the *Brag* and the *Ten Reasons*, should not seem to go unanswered. Aylmer, Bishop of London, chose the disputants.

The first took place in the Tower of London on 1 September. No opportunity was given to Campion to prepare himself; he was aroused without warning, unfettered, and led from his cell. Sherwin, Bosgrave, Pounde, and some other Catholic prisoners were waiting under escort. They may well have supposed that their hour had come, and that they were being taken to summary execution. Instead they were marched to the chapel, where they found a formidable array drawn up to meet them. On one side a state box had been erected in which lounged members of the Court and Council; opposite stood a table littered with books and papers, behind which were enthroned two clergymen, in starched linen and voluminous, academic robes. They were Nowell, the Dean of St

Paul's, and Day, the Dean of Windsor; round them sat a number of chaplains and clerks, helping to arrange the notes and mark the passages to be quoted. Another table, and other high chairs, accommodated Charke and Dr Whitaker, the Regius Professor of Divinity at Cambridge, who were to act as notaries. The Governor of the Tower sat with the rack-master and other officials; a large and varied audience filled every available space, for theological dispute was a popular recreation of the day. Some Catholics were in the crowd, one of whom took notes which furnished Bombinus with the material for his description. The official reports, both of this and the subsequent Conferences, were not published until two years after Campion's death. The Anglicans had then the opportunity to revise them, and one editor, Field, admitted in his preface, 'If Campion's answers be thought shorter than they were, you must know that he had much waste speech, which, being impertinent, is now omitted.' Through-out all the Conferences Campion shows constant anxiety that he is not being reported justly.

A little stool was set for him among the soldiers in the body of the court. He had now been in solitary confinement for five weeks; his second examination under torture had taken place ten days before and, though he was gradually recovering the use of his limbs, his health was broken. The Catholic witness reports that his face was colourless, 'his memory destroyed and his force of mind almost extinguished'. With unconscious irony the Dean of St Paul's opened the discussion by blandly rebuking Campion for having, in his *Ten Reasons*, dared to accuse the Queen's most merciful Government of *inusitata supplicia* 'uncommon cruelty' – and the Anglican bishops of offering *tormenta non scholas* – 'tortures instead of conference'.

Campion replied by protesting against the manifest inequality of the contest, his own lack of preparation, his deprivation of texts and notes. It was here that the subject of his 'confessions' was raised, and hastily shelved, as described above.

The Deans then proceeded to the debate, the scheme of which was that they should propose the subjects, taken from the *Ten Reasons*, should state their argument in the form of a syllogism, and Campion should answer them. In this way, with a recess for dinner, they continued until nightfall. The chief topic was the Anglican defence of Luther's doctrine of Justification by Faith alone. The report makes tedious and shameful reading, and the results were inconclusive. Campion was freely insulted, described as *os impudens* and *miles gloriosus*, and any demonstration in his favour was instantly checked by the soldiers. Only twice did he seem clearly to be in the wrong. He was unable to verify his quotation from Luther, describing the Epistle of St James as 'a thing of straw'. It occurred in the Jena edition, from which he had taken it, but not in the expurgated Wittenberg edition, with which he was now provided. The second occasion was when he became confused in a passage from the Greek Testament, and refused to continue the argument. His opponents eagerly seized upon this, and both now and later asserted that his much-advertised scholarship was spurious. Apologists have suggested that the type was too small for him to read, but the simplest explanation is that his Greek was, in fact, rather rusty. He was pre-eminently a Latinist. He had read Greek at Oxford and Douai, could quote it familiarly and write it in a clear and scholarly hand – of this there is abundant proof – but he had used it little at Prague, and, when he did so, spoke it with the Bohemian accent which was confusing in England. He regarded the Conference as a test of the truth of his creed, not of his own accomplishments, and he was unwilling to compromise his case by straying on uncertain grounds. At the end of the day, when the Catholics returned to the cells and the Deans to their comfortable lodgings, both sides were satisfied that they had had the best of it.

Eighteen days passed, but Campion, in his sunless dungeon, had lost count of time, and, lying in constant prayer, thought that it had been only a week, when he was again led out to debate. This time his opponents were Dr Goode, the Provost of King's College, Cambridge, and William Fulke, the popular preacher whose delight at the execution of Dr Storey has been reported earlier in this narrative. Fulke was a contemporary of Campion's, and had been his unsuccessful rival for the silver pen offered to the prize boy at the City schools. He was an enthusiastic opponent of the surplice, and had inflamed a riot at the university on that subject which led to his being sent down; he was triumphantly reinstated in 1567, but was again expelled for conniving at an incestuous marriage; Court favour did not fail him, and in 1569 he was restored to his fellowship, became Leicester's chaplain, a Doctor of Divinity by Royal Mandate, and Master of Pembroke Hall, where he augmented the Master's stipend by cutting down the number of fellowships. From 1580 he was in regular employment as an official Anglican controversialist, both against Catholics and the more extreme Protestants of the 'Family of Love'.

On this occasion the Conference took place in greater privacy, in Hopton's Hall, but the method was the same as before, the Anglicans stating their arguments and Campion objecting. In the morning the Anglicans set themselves to deny the existence of a visible Church; in the afternoon to prove that the Church was capable of error. As before, Campion was forbidden to take any lead, and when he attempted to press an argument was sharply reprimanded. 'It is your part to answer, not to oppose,' and Campion replied wearily, 'I have answered, but I wish to God I had a notary. Well, I commit it all to God.'

In the afternoon the dispute veered again to Justification by Works. Campion asserted that children who died without sin were saved. The Anglicans maintained the contrary doctrine that they were damned unless specially 'elected'; that baptism had no power to save.

Only at rare moments did the dialogue become animated:

Goode: 'Can you love God above all things and your neighbour as yourself? Can you love him with all your heart, with all your soul and with all your strength?'

Campion: 'I can. For when I prefer God before all things and love him chiefly, I love him above all.'

Fulke: 'Note that blasphemous absurdity.'

Goode: 'If a man may fulfil the law to justification, then Christ died in vain . . .'

Campion: 'Why think you the law was given to no purpose? I am sure it was given to be fulfilled, and we are not bidden to keep it, if it were impossible.'

Fulke: 'The law was given for another case . . . namely to show us our infirmity, that we may be convicted of sin.'

Campion: 'You will give me leave to declare my meaning.'

Fulke: 'Belike you have an ill opinion of the audience that they can understand nothing except you tell them twenty times over. If you will not suffer me to proceed, I must desire Master Lieutenant to command you.'

Campion was never allowed to forget the difference of position between himself and his opponents.

Later in the afternoon the Anglicans were denying the Real Presence in the Mass, saying that the doctrine denied the bodily resurrection of Christ. Campion broke out impatiently, 'What? Will you make him a prisoner now in Heaven? Must he be bound to those properties of a natural body? Heaven is his palace and you will make it his prison.'

Goode: 'They are the words of the Holy Ghost. It becometh not you to jest at them and specially considering your state being a prisoner.'

It is clear, however, even in the official report that Campion acquitted himself the better. Once he was tripped up in his Greek, giving the wrong name to the tense of κεκλειομένον, but the general debate had been of the broad and humane truths of the ancient faith, rather than of small details of text and verse, and the disadvantage of his circumstances oppressed him less.

The debate was continued five days later. Both sides were now out of patience with one another. 'You are very imperious,' Campion complained. 'You come, I bow, to prove me as a grammar scholar and to take me up with check at your pleasure. I know no cause why I should take it at your hands. I am the Queen's prisoner, not yours.'

As before, the form of the syllogism was used:

Fulke: 'Whatever is in the sacrament is void of sense or insensible: But Christ is not insensible: Ergo Christ is not in the sacrament' – but there was now little pretence of serious academic dispute. The farce had to be played out; that was the Council's order; but neither side hoped for any profit at the outcome.

Campion was consistently refused the courtesies of debate. 'If you dare, let me show you Augustine and Chrysostom,' he cried at one moment, 'if you dare.'

Fulke: 'Whatever you can bring, I have answered already in writing against others of your side. And yet if you think you can add anything, put it in writing and I will answer it.'

Campion: 'Provide me with ink and paper and I will write.'

Fulke: 'I am not to provide you ink and paper.'

Campion: 'I mean, procure me that I may have liberty to write.'

Fulke: 'I know not for what cause you are restrained of that liberty, and therefore I will not take upon me to procure it.'

Campion: 'Sue to the Queen that I may have liberty to oppose. I have been now thrice opposed. It is reason that I should oppose once.'

Fulke: 'I will not become a suitor for you.'

So the futile debate continued until dusk; Campion was led back to his cell; the divines collected their notes and sauntered home to supper, to boast to their womenfolk how they had rattled the Jesuit; but under their windows the chapmen and ballad-mongers were already hawking a different version:

> A Jesuit, a Jebusite? Wherefore I you pray?
> Because he doth teach you the only right way?
> He professeth the same by learning to prove
> And shall we from learning to rack him remove.
>
> His reasons were ready, his grounds were most sure,
> The enemy cannot his force long endure,

Campion, in camping on spiritual field,
In God's cause his life is ready to yield.

Our preachers have preached in pastime and pleasure,
And now they be hated far passing all measure;
Their wives and their wealth have made them so mute,
They cannot nor dare not with Campion dispute.

Still the Council was not satisfied, and a fourth Conference was arranged. Two new Anglican champions, Dr John Walker and Mr Charke, were put forward. Walker began the day with a denunciation of Campion as 'an unnatural man to his country, degenerate from an Englishman, an apostate in religion, a fugitive from this realm, unloyal to his Prince', who had returned 'to plant secretly the blasphemous Mass'. The old questions of Justification by Faith and Sufficiency of Scripture were proposed. There was little public interest now in the controversy, and when the meagre audience, shamed and bored, attempted to leave, Charke had the doors shut on them so that they should hear him out. He proved Campion wrong in a reference to Tertullian; that was the full extent of his triumph. It was the most ignominious display yet made by the Government party, and after that evening Burghley gave instructions that the Conferences should be discontinued. Campion was left in peace, to prepare himself for death.

A majority in the Council had decided in favour of Campion's execution; under the recent laws his office as priest made him guilty of high treason, but respect for public opinion, both in the country and abroad, made them hesitate to bring him to the scaffold upon this charge alone. Walsingham was in Paris that summer, on an embassy connected with the Queen's marriage; he employed his leisure in interviewing various inform-ers and renegade émigrés, and on 20 August he was able to report to Cecil a Popish plot for the conquest of Scotland which was being offered for sale at twenty crowns, but the Council do not seem to have found it suitable. Campion's fate was now curiously linked with that of Anjou, the Queen's 'little frog'. During that summer and autumn the exigencies of foreign policy brought the French marriage into increasing prominence. It was a matter of the greatest delicacy. Catherine of Medici, the Queen Mother, was pressing her son to give up all idea of Elizabeth and to marry a Spanish princess; there was a danger that Elizabeth, who throughout the reign had made it her policy to keep the precarious balance between Spain and France, might find herself isolated against an alliance of the two traditional enemies. Her throne was threatened from both sides, for, at home, it rested upon her personal popularity with her people, and it was doubtful how long her glamour could survive so grotesque a romance. Resentment at the proposal had become vocal, two years earlier, among subjects as different in character as Sir Philip Sidney and Stubbs, the printer. Stubb's mutilation was remembered by the low-church party. It was rumoured that the Queen was again falling into the hands of the Papists. An emphatic assertion of her Protestant principles was demanded; the death of her Catholic prisoners would conciliate just those elements of the population whom Stubbs's punishment had antagonized. But this would embarrass her negotiations with Anjou; somewhere in his twisted mind the little monster concealed, like the jewel in a toad's head, a genuine loyalty to his Faith. It would be ungracious to greet him on his arrival in England – he was coming on 1 November – with the execution, on purely religious grounds, of a fellow-Catholic of international repute. It was essential to convict Campion of some specific treasonable intent. Accordingly, on 31 October, while Anjou was in the Channel, Campion was again put to the rack in the hope that, at the last moment, he might extricate the Council from their difficulty by confessing to one or other of the plots they had devised for him. So savage were the torturers on this occasion, Campion informed a friend with whom later he had a few words of conversation, that he thought they intended to kill him. He never recovered from this racking; when his keeper asked him next day how he felt, he answered 'Not ill, because not at all,' and three weeks later he was unable to lift his hand high enough to take an oath. But Lord Hunsdon reported that one might sooner pluck his heart out of his bosom, than rack a word out of his mouth that he made conscience of uttering. The Council therefore decided to proceed with the trial without further scruple.

The first indictment proposed was that Campion 'did traitorously pretend to have power to absolve the subjects of the said Queen from their natural obedience to her majesty, with the intention to withdraw the said subjects of the said Queen from the religion now by her supreme authority established within this realm of England to the Roman religion, and to move the same subjects of the said Queen to promise obedience to the pretensed authority of the Roman See to be used within the dominions of the said Queen,' and proceeded to particularize an individual so absolved. The space for this man's name was left blank until a suitable informer could be found to give evidence.

But the considerations suggested above moved the Council to change their ground, and a fresh indictment was drawn up, upon which Campion was finally brought to trial. In this it was asserted that William Allen, Nicholas Morton, Persons, and Campion had, at Rome on 31 March of the preceding year, at Rheims on 30 April, and on other unspecified days before and after, both at Rome and Rheims, formed a conspiracy to murder Queen Elizabeth; that at Rome, on 20 May and on other dates, they had exhorted foreigners to invade the country; that they had decided to send Persons and Campion into England to stir up a rebellion in support of the invading force.

A further emendation was made, by whose hand it is impossible to tell, and in the margin were inserted the names of Bosgrave, Filby, Ford, (Cottam, Lawrence, Richardson, Collington, Sherwin, Kirby, Johnson, Rishton, Briant, Short – the entire bag of priests then in custody – and Orton, a layman, to be tried on the same charge. This addition removes any possibility of believing in the sincerity of the prosecution. It is conceivable that some of the Council believed in the guilt of Allen, Morton, Persons, and Campion. That Ford and Collington, who had been in England for the last four or five years, whose only connexion with Campion was that they had been serving a handful of nuns at the house where he was arrested, and Filby, who had dropped in to call, had been dodging about Europe in his company at Rome on 31 March, at Rheims on 30 April, back at Rome again on 20 May – was a charge which the most cursory investigation must instantly disprove. It was on this indict-ment, however, that the trial took place.

On Tuesday, 14 November, Campion, Sherwin, Kirby, Bosgrave, Cottam, Johnson, Orton, and Rishton were arraigned at the bar of Westminster Hall, and the preposterous charge was first read to them.

'I protest before God and his holy angels,' Campion replied, 'before heaven and earth, before the world and this bar whereat I stand, which is but a small resemblance of the terrible judgement of the next life, that I am not guilty of any part of the treason contained in the indictment, or of any other treason whatever.'

The jury was empanelled for the following Monday. 'Is it possible,' Campion said, 'to find twelve men so wicked and void of all conscience in this city or land that will find us guilty together of this one crime, divers of us never meeting or knowing one the other before our bringing to this bar?'

'The plain reason of our standing here is religion and not treason,' said Sherwin.

Sir Christopher Wray, Chief Justice of the Queen's Bench: 'The time is not yet come wherein you shall be tried, and therefore you must now spare speech . . . wherefore now plead to the indictment whether you be guilty or not.'

When they were called to take the oath, Campion, as was mentioned above, could not lift his arm; his crippled hands were tucked into the cuffs of his gown, whereupon one of his companions drew up the sleeve, kissed his hand and raised it for him.

Next day Collington, Richardson, Hart, Ford, Filby, Briant, and Short were arraigned in the same manner on the same charge.

The trial took place on 20 November. Three gentlemen, originally empanelled as jurymen, refused their attendance, because they doubted that justice would have a free course that day; their places were filled with less scrupulous substitutes. Only one of the twelve dishonoured names has come down to us, one William Lee, the foreman, who was himself an informer and a fanatical Calvinist. Chief Justice Wray presided with gravity and temperance; William Ayloff and, probably, Thomas Gawdy sat with him. Prisoners at this time were never defended by counsel. The prosecution was in the hands of Mr Anderson, Queen's Counsel, John Popham, the Attorney-General, cadet of a family already rich in monastic lands, who was later rewarded for his services to the Government by his elevation to the post of Chief Justice of the Queen's Bench, and Thomas Egerton, Solicitor-General, founder of the Ellesmere fortunes.

When the indictment was read, Campion, who acted as spokesman for the prisoners, requested that they might each be given a separate trial. The plea was disallowed.

'I could have wished,' Wray admitted, 'that everyone should have had his special day assigned him, had the time so permitted; but since it cannot be otherwise, we must take it as it is.'

The trial then proceeded in accordance with the Council's instructions.

Anderson opened the case with a general denunciation of the Pope as the Queen's chief enemy, and 'professed scourge of the Gospel'; the prisoners, he said, had lived on the Pope's bounty abroad and were now sent to England as his agents.

Campion indignantly asked whether Mr Anderson was there as an orator, or as a counsel submitting evidence to a court of law.

The Lord Chief Justice: 'You must have patience with him . . . for they, being of the Queen's Council, speak of no other intent than of duty to Her Majesty.'

Campion again protested that evidence should be brought. 'The wisdom and providence of the laws of England, as I take it, is such as proceedeth not to the trial of any man for life and death by shifts of probabilities and conjectural surmises, without proof of the crime by sufficient evidence and substantial witness. I see not to what end Mr Serjeant's oration tended or if I see an end I see it but frustrate; for be the crime but in trifles, the law hath his passage; be the theft but a halfpenny, witnesses are produced. He barely affirmeth; we flatly deny. . . . Who seeth not but these be odious circumstances to bring a man in hatred with the jury and no necessary matter to conclude him guilty? . . . This word soundeth not a lawyer's usage. . . . These matters ought to be proved and not urged, declared by evidence and not surmised by fancy. Wherefore, in God's behalf, we pray that better proof may be used, and that our lives be not brought in prejudice by conjectures.'

Anderson next asserted two oaths taken at the seminaries, one to the Pope, the other to the propositions in a book called Bristow's *Motives*. The confusion resulting from the joint trial was then apparent; it had not yet been proved that any of the prisoners had been to a seminary; in point of fact some had been and some had not; Campion pointed out that in any case the oath was not administered to any except striplings; Bristow's pamphlet was used as a text book only in the elementary course for those who came to the seminary without previous academic training, so that it was entirely beyond the point to argue whether or no it could be held to contain treasonable matter. Kirby protested that of his conscience there were not four copies of Bristow's *Motives* in all the seminaries. There was a general murmur among the prisoners that it was for their religion that they were being tried, not for treason, which Campion voiced, saying that, since they had been offered their liberty on condition of their attending the Anglican services, their Faith was the sole cause of their being there.

The question of Bristow's book and the seminary oath was not pressed. Anderson proceeded: 'All of you jointly and severally have received money from the Pope to spend in your journeys. Was such liberality of the Pope's without cause? No, it had an end; and what end should that be but your privy inveighings and persuasions to set on foot his devices and treacheries?'

Campion replied that the end was solely to preach the Gospel.

The first Crown witness was then produced, a man named H. Caddy, of whom little can be traced. He asserted that when he was abroad he was told of a holy vow made between the Pope and 200 English priests for the restoration of Catholicism. Also that Sir Ralph Shelley, Knight of Malta, had been approached by the Vatican to lead an invading fleet against England and had refused, saying he would sooner drink poison.

Campion easily disposed of this point. 'Two hundred priests made an holy vow to labour for the restoring of religion. It seemeth, by all likelihood, that we made up the number, and therefore privy and parties to the treason; here is a conclusion without a jot of affinity to the premises; first an holy vow, then an establishing of religion. What colour is there left here for treason? All the treason rehearsed was reputed to Sir Ralph Shelley; not one syllable thereof was rehearsed to the priests. But granting, and which the witness has not deposed, and namely, that we are some of the 200 priests; you see Sir Ralph Shelley, a Catholic, the Pope's captain, a layman, would rather drink poison than agree to such treason; is it like that priests . . . would in any wise consent to it. This deposition is more for us than against us.'

It was by now abundantly clear that there was to be no fair trial; that the Lords of the Council were demanding a death sentence and that the conviction had to be for treason. But Campion kept up the defence; the trial was being watched all over England. If the Government could announce that the priests had been proved guilty of conspiracy, the Catholic cause would be prejudiced; worse still, the elements among the Catholic laity whose loyalty was already strained by the persecution, would be encouraged in the extreme measures which eventually in the next generation brought about their ruin. The Gunpowder Plot was still at a distance.

Doubtless the priests had heavy secrets to guard; what the rack-master could not discover, we shall never learn. The priests knew far better than their accusers, the conflict that was rending every Catholic heart in the country. They knew what had been said at those night-long sessions before the morning Mass; what plots they had forbidden in Christ's name; what reasons they had urged to men rendered reckless by injustice; how in private converse and in the inviolable secrecy of the confessional, they had wrestled with desperate consciences, holding up the cross, cease-lessly commanding patience, trust, submission, the way of truth that could never be the way of blood. It was these with whom Campion was pleading in the tedious, futile, assertion and denial, perjury and disproof, of the mock-trial. He and his fellows were to die, but the world must know the cause.

They accused him of having made himself privy to the Bull of Excommunication, by discussing it with the Cardinal of St Cecilia; they accused him of association with the Bishop of Ross, whom he had never met; they accused him of private conversation with Dr Allen, who had been in communication with Dr Sanders, who was with the Irish rebels.

Campion replied: 'I cannot deny but that I dined with Dr Allen at Rheims, with whom also after dinner I walked in his garden, spending a time in speeches referred to our old familiarity and acquaintance; during the whole course thereof (I take God to witness) not one jot of our talk glanced to the Crown or State of England; neither had I the least notice of any letters sent to Dr Sanders.'

He was accused of having dissembled his identity, of calling himself 'Hastings', of wearing a velvet hat and a feather, a buff leather jerkin and velvet venetians; of having 'wrought a hugger-mugger'. They read Campion's note to Pounde, quoted above, in which he denied having revealed any 'secrets'. They produced papers found in some of the houses where he had visited, containing a form of oath against Her Majesty. Campion replied: 'Neither is there, neither can there be anything imagined more directly contrary or repugnant to my calling than upon any occasion to administer an oath. But, admit I am authorized, what necessity imported that reason, that neither being set down in my handwriting nor otherwise derived by any proof from myself, but only found in places where I resorted, therefore I should be he by whom they were ministered? This is but a naked presumption (who seeth it not?) and nothing vehement nor of force against me.'

The two rack-masters, Norton and Hamond, gave evidence that, under torture, Campion could not be brought to a clear answer on the Bull for the Queen's excommunication. Eliot was called; he described his visit to Lyford, and reported that in Campion's sermon he had spoken of 'a great day' that was shortly to come.

Queen's Counsel: 'So, what would you wish more manifest? The great day is threatened, comfortable to them and terrible to us; and what day should that be but that wherein the Pope, the King of Spain, and the Duke of Florence have appointed to invade this realm?'

Campion: 'O Judas! Judas! No other day was in my mind, I protest, than that wherein it should please God to make a restitution of faith and religion. Whereupon, as in every pulpit every Protestant doth, I pronounced a great day, not wherein any temporal potentate should minister, but wherein the terrible Judge should reveal all men's consciences and try every man of each kind of religion. This is the day of change, this is the great day which I threatened.'

A witness named Anthony Munday was called. He was a professional informer who had recently hung about Dr Allen's seminary, practising as a Catholic, and seeking to gain the confidence of the *émigrés*. He published reports of Campion's capture, of the trial and of the execution; some years later he wrote a play rehabilitating Sir John Oldcastle's reputation, which, until the imposture was detected, he ascribed to Shakespeare; he attached himself to Topcliffe's staff, but got into trouble for robbing a widow of £40 under colour of searching her house for *Agnus Dei*s. Munday testified that the English at Rheims spoke treason and that Campion had at a later time had conference with Allen; the charge to which he had already replied.

This concluded the case against Campion, for which he was to go to the gallows. Of the detailed plot to murder the Queen of which he was indicted, no evidence had been offered. Treasonable papers (whether genuine or not it is impossible to say with any certainty) had been found in some houses where he had stayed; he had dined with Allen and walked about the garden with him after dinner; he had received financial assistance for his mission from the Pope; he was a priest who had travelled about the country in lay attire. This was the case on which the Crown lawyers were demanding the death penalty.

A letter was then read – the author is not named in the report – saying that Sherwin at the fireside of the seminary had been heard to remark that one Arundel, in Cornwall, could levy a great army, and that St Michael's Mount would be the best landing place for an invasion. Sherwin took an oath that he had never said any such thing.

It was alleged of Bosgrave that he had heard some rumours abroad of a projected invasion and, by not disclosing them, had made himself privy to treason. Campion interposed in his favour '. . . Who findeth it not by daily experience, how that in every city, every village, and in most barber's shops, in all England, many speeches, both of estates and commonwealths, be tossed, which were never meant nor determined of in the court? If it be so in England shall we not look for the like in Italy, Flanders, France and Spain? . . . Were it not then a great point of credulity for a man divided from England with a many seas and lands, upon a matter only blazed among the vulgar people, either by journey or letter to certify the Queen's Council or commonalty of things never purposed, much less put into practice? . . . Supposing he had done as you would have had him, what had come of it? Marry, then, greater danger for slandering the realm, and how little thanks for his false information.'

Cottam was accused of possessing a book named *Tractatus Conscientiæ*, containing advice for making equivocal answers. Eliot gave evidence against Johnson that he had adjured him, at Lady Petre's house, to keep secret any plots which Payne had disclosed to him. Johnson denied any such conversation.

Munday gave evidence against Rishton that he had great cunning in the manufacture of fireworks, and that he was about to burn the Queen in her barge with 'a confection of wild fire'; an enterprise which was to be followed by the general massacre of all who were ignorant of the password 'Jesus Maria'. Rishton denied all pyrotechnic knowledge.

Sledd, the informer mentioned in the preceding chapter, who had at one time been a daily communicant at Rome and Rheims, testified against Kirby, that he had come to his, Sledd's, bedside when he was ill and told him of the projected invasion, had attended a sermon of Allen's in which the priests were advised to prepare the English for the invaders, had spoken of Elizabeth as the Whore of Babylon, and expressed his intention of murdering her. Kirby denied the entire allegation.

Munday deposed against Orton that he had told him at Lyons that Elizabeth was not lawfully Queen. Orton denied ever having met Munday at Lyons or anywhere else. This concluded the evidence.

Throughout the day the Chief Justice had conducted the trial with an appearance of impartiality. The gang – Sledd, Eliot, Munday, and Caddy – had sworn to the evidence for which they had been paid; the prisoners had been given the opportunity of denying it; everything had been done in order. Only once had the semblance of legality broken down, when Sherwin was comparing his work under a hostile Government to that of the Fathers of the primitive Church under the pagan Emperors. Then one of the justices – Ayloff? – had forgotten his part, and, assuming the role of prosecutor, interposed: 'But your case differeth from theirs in the primitive Church, for those Apostles and preachers never conspired the death of these Emperors.'

No one protested. No one hoped for anything in that shabby pantomime. The verdict had been decided many days before; the real judges and the real jury were in the Council room occupied with other business.

Campion was now allowed to speak to the jury; he did so courteously, reasonably, hopelessly.

'What charge this day you sustain, and what accompt you are to render at the dreadful Day of Judgement, whereof I could wish this also were a mirror, I trust there is no one of you but knoweth. I doubt not but in like manner you forecast how dear the innocent is to God, and at what price He holdeth man's blood. Here we are accused and impleaded to the death. We have no whither to appeal but to your consciences.' He showed how the most part of the evidence was general and vague, a matter of conjecture and capricious association. Only a few particulars had been precise and damning, and those had emanated from the gang. 'What truth may you expect from their mouths? One hath confessed himself a murderer' – Eliot – 'the other' – Munday – 'a detestable atheist, a profane heathen, a destroyer of two men already. On your consciences, would you believe them – they that have betrayed both God and man, nay, that have left nothing to swear by, neither religion nor honesty? Though you would believe them, can you? . . . I commit the rest to God, and our convictions to your good discretions.'

The jury retired. Ayloff was left alone on the bench, and, pulling off his glove, found all his hand and signet ring bloody, 'without any wrong, pricking or hurt'. The jury returned with the inevitable verdict. The Lord Chief Justice demanded whether there was any cause why he should not pass sentence of death upon the prisoners.

It was then that Campion's voice rose in triumph. He was no longer haggling with perjurers; he spoke now, not merely for the handful of doomed men behind him, nor to that sordid court, but for the whole gallant company of the English counter-Reformation; to all his contemporaries and all the posterity of his race:

'It was not our death that ever we feared. But we knew that we were not lords of our own lives, and therefore for want of answer would not be guilty of our deaths. The only thing that we have now to say is, that if our religion do make us traitors, we are worthy to be condemned; but otherwise are, and have been, as good subjects as ever the Queen had.

'In condemning us you condemn all your own ancestors – all the ancient priests, bishops and kings – all that was once the glory of England, the island of saints, and the most devoted child of the See of Peter.

'For what have we taught, however you may qualify it with the odious name of treason, that they did not uniformly teach? To be condemned with these lights – not of England only, but of the world – by their degenerate descendants, is both gladness and glory to us.

'God lives; posterity will live; their judgement is not so liable to corruption as that of those who are now going to sentence us to death.'

The Lord Chief Justice answered: 'You must go to the place from whence you came, there to remain until ye shall be drawn through the open City of London upon hurdles to the place of execution, and there be hanged and let down alive, and your privy parts cut off, and your entrails taken out and burnt in your sight; then your heads to be cut off and your bodies divided into four parts, to be disposed of at her Majesty's pleasure. And God have mercy on your souls.'

As the Lord Chief Justice's final commendation sounded, with peculiar irony, through Westminster Hall, the condemned men broke into the words of the *Te Deum* and were led back in triumph to their several prisons.

Next day the remaining seven priests were tried on Burghley's indictment and – except for Collington, who could prove that he was in Gray's Inn in London when he was supposed to be at Rheims – condemned in the same way.

An alibi for Ford, similar to Collington's, was offered by a priest named Nicholson, but the judges ordered the witness to be committed to prison, where he came near to death from starvation.

Campion lay in irons for eleven days between his trial and his execution. Hitherto his family have made no appearance in the story; now a sister, of whom we know nothing, came to visit him, empowered to make him a last offer of freedom and a benefice, if he would renounce his Faith. There may have been other visitors – for certain details of his life in prison, such as his statement, quoted above, that in his last racking he thought they intended to kill him, can only have reached Bombinus through the report of friends – but the only one of whom we have record is George Eliot.

'If I had thought that you would have had to suffer aught but imprisonment through my accusing of you, I would never have done it,' he said, 'however I might have lost by it.'

'If that is the case,' replied Campion, 'I beseech you, in God's name, to do penance, and confess your crime, to God's glory and your own salvation.'

But it was fear for his life rather than for his soul that had brought the informer to the Tower; ever since the journey from Lyford, when the people had called him 'Judas', he had been haunted by the spectre of Catholic reprisal.

'You are much deceived,' said Campion, 'if you think the Catholics push their detestation and wrath as far as revenge; yet to make you quite safe, I will, if you please, recommend you to a Catholic duke in Germany, where you may live in perfect security.'

But it was another man who was saved by the offer. Eliot went back to his trade of spy; Delahays, Campion's gaoler, who was present at the interview, was so moved by Campion's generosity that he became a Catholic.

London was very gay that winter. Anjou was there with his suite and the Court was wholly given over to their entertainment. Sidney, out of favour with the Queen, was engaged with the *Apologie for Poetrie*. The 'little frog' was the man of the moment, and to him various friends of Campion resorted in the hope of gaining his intercession. They found him skipping about the tennis court. It was the day before Campion's execution and, by the aid of the French abbé who acted as the Duke's confessor, they were able to obtain an interview. The little man listened to what they had to say; he looked at them stupidly, as though he were just awakened from a deep sleep, scratched his beard and then, turning on his heel, with the one word 'Play', resumed the interrupted service.

Campion's last days were occupied entirely with his preparation for death; even in the cell he was able to practise mortifications; he fasted and remained sleepless on his knees for two nights in prayer and meditation.

Sherwin and Briant had been chosen as his companions at the scaffold. They met at the Coldharbour Tower, early in the morning of 1 December, and were left together while a search was made for the clothes in which Campion had been arrested; it had been decided to execute him in the buff leather jerkin and velvet venetians which had been so ridiculed at his trial. But the garments had already been misappropriated, and he was finally led out in the gown of Irish frieze which he had worn in prison.

It was raining; it had been raining for some days, and the roads of the city were foul with mud. A great crowd had collected at the gates. 'God save you all, gentlemen,' Campion greeted them. 'God bless you, and make you good Catholics.' There were two horses, each with a hurdle at his tail. Campion was bound to one of them, Briant and Sherwin together on the other.

Then they were slowly dragged through the mud and rain, up Cheapside, past St Martin le Grand and Newgate, along Holborn to Tyburn. Charke plodded along beside the hurdle, still eager to thrash out to the last word the question of Justification by Faith alone, but Campion seemed not to notice him; over Newgate Arch stood a figure of Our Lady which had so far survived the Anglican hammers. Campion saluted her as he passed. Here and there along the road a Catholic would push himself through the crowd and ask Campion's blessing. One witness, who supplied Bombinus with many details of this last morning, followed close at hand and stood by the scaffold. He records how one gentleman, 'either for pity or affection, most courteously wiped' Campion's 'face, all spattered with mire and dirt, as he was drawn most miserably through thick and thin; for which charity or haply some sudden moved affection, God reward him and bless him.'

The scene at Tyburn was tumultuous. Sir Thomas More had stepped out into the summer sunshine, to meet death quietly and politely at a single stroke of the axe. Every circumstance of Campion's execution was vile and gross.

Sir Frances Knollys, Lord Howard, Sir Henry Lee, and other gentlemen of fashion were already waiting beside the scaffold. When the procession arrived, they were disputing whether the motion of the sun from east to west was violent or natural; they postponed the discussion to watch Campion, bedraggled and mud-stoned, mount the cart which stood below the gallows. The noose was put over his neck. The noise of the crowd was continuous, and only those in his immediate neighbourhood could hear him as he began to speak. He had it in mind to make some religious exhortation.

'*Spectaculum facti sumus Deo, angelis et hominibus,*' he began. 'These are the words of St Paul, Englished thus, "We are made a spectacle unto God, unto His angels and unto men," verified this day in me, who am here a spectacle unto my Lord God, a spectacle unto His angels and unto you men.'

But he was not allowed to continue. Sir Francis Knollys interrupted, shouting up at him to confess his treason.

'As to the treasons which have been laid to my charge,' he said, 'and for which I am come here to suffer, I desire you all to bear witness with me that I am thereof altogether innocent.'

One of the Council cried it was too late to deny what had been proved in the court.

'Well, my Lord,' he replied. 'I am a Catholic man and a priest; in that faith have I lived and in that faith I intend to die. If you esteem my religion treason, then am I guilty; as for other treason I never committed any, God is my judge. But you have now what you desire. I beseech you to have patience, and suffer me to speak a word or two for discharge of my conscience.'

But the gentlemen round the gallows would not let him go forward; they still heckled him about his letter to Pounde, about the invasion by the Pope and the Duke of Florence.

In a few halting sentences he made himself heard above the clamour. He forgave the jury and asked forgiveness of any whose names he might have compromised during his examination; he addressed himself to Sir Francis Knollys on Richardson's behalf, saying that, to his knowledge, that man had never in his possession a copy of the book, which the informers declared they had found in his baggage.

Then a schoolmaster named Hearne stood forward and read a proclamation in the Queen's name, that the execution they were to witness that morning was for treason and not for religion. Campion stood in prayer. The Lords of the Council still shouted up questions to him about the Bull of Excommunication, but now Campion would not answer and stood with his head bowed and his hands folded on his breast. An Anglican clergyman attempted to direct his prayers, but he answered gently, 'Sir, you and I are not one in religion, wherefore I pray you content yourself. I bar none of prayer; but I only desire them that are of the household of faith to pray with me, and in mine agony to say one creed.'

They called to him to pray in English, but he replied with great mildness that 'he would pray God in a language which they both well understood'.

There was more noise; the Councillors demanded that he should ask the Queen's forgiveness.

'Wherein have I offended her? In this I am innocent. This is my last speech; in this give me credit – I have and do pray for her.'

Still the courtiers were not satisfied. Lord Howard demanded to know what Queen he prayed for.

'Yea, for Elizabeth your Queen and my Queen, unto whom I wish a long quiet reign with all prosperity.'

The cart was then driven from under him, the eager crowd swayed forward, and Campion was left hanging, until, unconscious, perhaps already dead, he was cut down and the butcher began his work.

When the spectacle was over the crowd dispersed. An emotional witness records that several thousand were turned to the Faith by the events of that day. Many thousands there have been, but they were not in that assembly. The Elizabethan mob dearly loved a bloody execution, and any felon was the hero of a few hours, whatever his crimes. If any felt uneasy about the Queen's justice, there were gentler pleasures to attract their minds; in particular two Dutchmen, who were the rage of the moment; the one was seven feet seven inches in height, 'comelie of person but lame of the legs (for he had broken them of lifting a barrel of beer)'; his companion was a midget who could walk between the giant's legs, wearing a feather in his cap; he had 'never a good foot nor any knee at all and yet could dance a galliard, no arm but a stump on which he could dance a cup and after toss it about three or four times and every time receive the same on the said stump'. With distractions of this kind the fate of the three priests was soon forgotten. One man, however, returned from Tyburn to Gray's Inn profoundly changed; Henry Walpole, Cambridge wit, minor poet, satirist, flâneur, a young man of birth, popular, intelligent, slightly romantic. He came of a Catholic family and occasionally expressed Catholic sentiments, but until that day had kept at a discreet distance from Gilbert and his circle, and was on good terms with authority. He was a typical member of that easygoing majority, on whom the success of the Elizabethan settlement depended, who would have preferred to live under a Catholic regime but accepted the change without very serious regret. He had an interest in theology and had attended Campion's conferences with the Anglican clergy. He secured a front place at Tyburn; so close that when Campion's entrails were torn out by the butcher and thrown into the cauldron of boiling water, a spot of blood splashed upon his coat. In that moment he was caught into a new life; he crossed the sea, became a priest, and, thirteen years later, after very terrible sufferings, died the same death as Campion's on the gallows at York.

And so the work of Campion continued; so it continues. He was one of a host of martyrs, each, in their several ways, gallant and venerable; some performed more sensational feats of adventure, some sacrificed more conspicuous positions in the world, many suffered crueller tortures, but to his own, and to each succeeding generation, Campion's fame has burned with unique warmth and brilliance; it was his genius to express, in sentences that have resounded across the centuries, the spirit of chivalry in which they suffered, to typify in his zeal, his innocence, his inflexible purpose, the pattern which they followed.

Years later, in the sombre, sceptical atmosphere of the eighteenth century, Bishop Challoner set himself to sift out and collect the English martyrology. The Catholic cause was very near to extinction in England. Families who had resisted the onset of persecution were quietly conforming under neglect. The Church survived here and there in scattered households, regarded by the world as, at the best, something Gothic and slightly absurd, like a ghost or a family curse. Emancipation still lay in the distant future; no career was open to the Catholics; their only ambition was to live quietly in their houses, send their children to school abroad, pay the double land taxes, and, as best they could, avoid antagonizing their neighbours. It was then, when the whole gallant sacrifice appeared to have been prodigal and vain, that the story of the martyrs lent them strength. We are the heirs of their conquest, and enjoy, at our ease, the plenty which they died to win.

Today a chapel stands by the site of Tyburn; in Oxford, the city he loved best, a noble college is rising dedicated in Campion's honour. 'There will never want in England men that will have care of their own salvation, nor such as shall advance other men's; neither shall this Church here ever fail so long as priests and pastors shall be found for their sheep, rage man or devil never so much.'

Mells – Belton – Newton Ferrers
October 1934 – May 1935

Appendix One

CAMPION'S BRAG

[To The Right Honourable, The Lords of Her Majestie's Privy Council]

RIGHT HONOURABLE

Whereas I have come out of Germanie and Boëmeland, being sent by my Superiours, and adventured myself into this noble Realm, my deare Countrie, for the glorie of God and benefit of souls, I thought it like enough that, in this busie, watchful and suspicious worlde, I should either sooner or later be intercepted and stopped of my course. Wherefore, providing for all events, and uncertaine what may become of me, when God shall haply deliver my body into durance, I supposed it needful to put this writing in a readiness, desiringe your good Lordships to give it y^r reading, for to know my cause. This doing, I trust I shall ease you of some labour. For that which otherwise you must have sought for by practice of wit, I do now lay into your hands by plaine confession. And to ye intent that the whole matter may be conceived in order, and so the better both understood and remembered, I make thereof these ix points or articles, directly, truly and resolutely opening my full enterprise and purpose.

i. I confess that I am (albeit unworthie) a priest of ye Catholike Church, and through ye great mercie of God vowed now these viii years into the Religion of the Societie of Jhesus. Hereby I have taken upon me a special kind of warfare under the banner of obedience, and eke resigned all my interest or possibilitie of wealth, honour, pleasure, and other worldlie felicitie.

ii. At the voice of our General Provost, which is to me a warrant from heaven, and Oracle of Christ, I tooke my voyage from Prage to Rome (where our said General Father is always resident) and from Rome to England, as I might and would have done joyously into any parse of Christendome or Heathenesse, had I been thereto assigned.

iii. My charge is, of free cost to preach the Gospel, to minister the Sacraments, to instruct the simple, to reforme sinners, to confute errors — in brief, to crie alarme spritual against foul vice and proud ignorance, wherewith many my dear Countrymen are abused.

iv. I never had mind, and am strictly forbidden by our Father that sent me, to deal in any respect with matter of State or Policy of this realm, as things which appertain not to my vocation, and from which I do gladly restrain and sequester my thoughts.

v. I do ask, to the glory of God, with all humility, and under your correction, iii sortes of indifferent and quiet audiences: *the first* before your Honours, wherein I will discourse of religion, so far as it toucheth the common weale and your nobilities: *the second*, whereof I make more account, before the Doctors and Masters and chosen men of both Universities, wherein I undertake to avow the faith of our Catholike Church by proofs innumerable, Scriptures, Councils, Fathers, History, natural and moral reasons: *the third* before the lawyers, spiritual and temporal, wherein I will justify the said faith by the common wisdom of the laws standing yet in force and practice.

vi. I would be loth to speak anything that might sound of any insolent brag or challenge, especially being now as a dead man to this world and willing to put my head under every man's foot, and to kiss the ground they tread upon. Yet have I such a courage in avouching the Majesty of Jhesus my King, and such affiance in his gracious favour, and such assurance in my quarrel, and my evidence so impregnable, and because I know perfectly that no one Protestant, nor all the Protestants living, nor any sect of our adversaries (howsoever they face men down in pulpits, and overrule us in their kingdom of grammarians and unlearned ears) can maintain their doctrine in disputation. I am to sue most humbly and instantly for the combat with all and every of them, and the most principal that may be found: protesting that in this trial the better furnished they come, the better welcome they shall be.

vii. And because it hath pleased God to enrich the Queen my Sovereign Ladye with notable gifts of nature, learning, and princely education, I do verily trust that – if her Highness would vouchsafe her royal person and good attention to such a conference as, in the ii part of my fifth article I have motioned, or to a few sermons, which in her or your hearing I am to utter, – such manifest and fair light by good method and plain dealing may be cast upon these controversies, that possibly her zeal of truth and love of her people shall incline her noble Grace to disfavour some proceedings hurtful to the Realm, and procure towards us oppressed more equitie.

viii. Moreover I doubt not but you her Highness' Council being of such wisdom and discreet in cases most important, when you shall have heard these questions of religion opened faithfully, which many times by our adversaries are huddled up and confounded, will see upon what substantial grounds our Catholike Faith is builded, how feeble that side is which by sway of the time prevaileth against us, and so at last for your own souls, and for many thousand souls that depend upon your government, will discountenance error when it is bewrayed, and hearken to those who would spend the best blood in their bodies for your salvation. Many innocent hands are lifted up to heaven for you daily by those English students, whose posteritie shall never die, which beyond seas, gathering virtue and sufficient knowledge for the purpose, are determined never to give you over, but either to win you heaven, or to die upon your pikes. And touching our Societie, be it known to you that we have made a league – all the Jesuits in the world, whose succession and multitude must overreach all the practices of England – cheerfully to carry the cross you shall lay upon us, and never to despair your recovery, while we have a man left to enjoy your Tyburn, or to be racked with your torments, or consumed with your prisons. The expense is reckoned, the enterprise is begun; it is of God, it cannot be withstood. So the faith was planted: so it must be restored.

ix. If these my offers be refused, and my endeavours can take no place, and I, having run thousands of miles to do you good, shall be rewarded with rigour, I have no more to say but to recommend your case and mine to Almightie God, the Searcher of Hearts, who send us His grace, and set us at accord before the day of payment, to the end we may at last be friends in heaven, when all injuries shall be forgotten.

Appendix Two

The following list is not intended as a display of industry nor as a guarantee of good faith. They are the books which, while I was working on this subject, I found chiefly interesting and relevant; which I can commend to any reader who wishes to amplify details that I have stated too briefly, too vaguely, or too allusively. Simpson's *Life* is copiously annotated. I have not been to the trouble of verifying his references from their original sources; certain very learned men, who did not like Simpson, have been through his book with a fine comb. I have accepted what they left unchallenged.

E.W.

Edmund Campion, Richard Simpson. (Williams & Norgate, 1867.)

Martyrdom of Father Campion and His Companions, Cardinal Allen. (Burns & Oates, 1908.)

Ten Reasons, Edmund Campion. (Manresa Press.)

Histoy of Ireland, Edmund Campion. (Sir James Wares's edition. Dublin, 1633.)

On the Life and Martyrdom of Father Edmund Campion, R. Persons. (Manresa Press.)

An Answer to a Seditious Pamphlet lately cast abroad, Wm. Charke. (1580.)

A true report of the Disputation, A. Nowell and W. Daye. (1583.)

Trial of Campion and His Companions. (Cobbett's *State Trials*, 1809.)

The History and Antiquities of the University of Oxford, Anthony à Wood.

A Histoy of the University of Oxford, C. E. Mallet.

The Prayer Book of Queen Elizabeth. (Ancient and Modern Library of Theological Literature.)

The Publications of the Catholic Record Society, *passim*.

The Elizabethan Clergy and the settlement of religion, Henry Gee.

English Catholics in the Reign of Queen Elizabeth, J. H. Pollen. (Longmans, Green & Co.)

Letters and Memorials of William, Cardinal Allen, Thomas Knox.

An Elizabethan Cardinal, Martin Haile.

One Generation of a Norfolk House, A. Jessopp. (Fisher Unwin, 1913.)

The Celtic Peoples and Renaissance Europe, David Mathew. (Sheed & Ward.)

William Cecil, A. Gordon Smith. (Kegan Paul.)

How the Reformation Happened, Hilaire Belloc. (Cape.)
Queen Elizabeth, G. E. Neale.
History of the Popes, Pastor. (Kegan Paul.) Vols. xix, xx.
The Life and Reign of Elizabeth, John Stow. (1631.)
Chronicles, Ralph Holinshed.
Parish Life under Queen Elizabeth, W. P. M. Kennedy.
Elizabethan Life in Town and Country, M. St Clare Byrne.
Elizabethan England, W. Harrison. Ed. Wittington.
Social England, ed. H. D. Traill.
Tudor Tracts, ed. A. F. Pollard.
Political History of England, A. F. Pollard.
Bishop Challoner, Michael Trappes-Lomax, in *The English Way*.
Lives of the Elizabethan Bishops, Rev. F. O. White. (Skeffington.)
England and the Catholic Church under Elizabeth. A. D. Meyer. (Kegan Paul.)
Memoirs of the Missionary Priests, Bishop Challoner.
Annals of the Reformation in England, John Strype. (1736.)
Sir Francis Walsingham, Conyers Read.
History of England, John Lingard. 4th edition.
The Reformation and English Education, Norman Wood. (Routledge.)

THE LIFE OF
THE RIGHT REVEREND

RONALD KNOX

FELLOW OF TRINITY COLLEGE, OXFORD
AND
PRONOTARY APOSTOLIC
TO HIS HOLINESS POPE PIUS XII

compiled from the original sources

by

EVELYN WAUGH

CONTENTS

Preface   133

Book I
LAUGHTER AND THE LOVE OF FRIENDS
1. Heredity 1798–1888   139
2. Environment 1888–1900   153
3. Education 1900–1906   167
4. Performance 1906–1910   191
5. Accomplishment 1910–1914   213

Book II
KEEPING AN ARMAGEDDON   237

Book IIII
THE HIDDEN STREAM
1. Nova Conspersio 1917–1926   267
   Appendices to Chapter One   300
2. 'Chaplaincraft' 1926–1939   305
3. The Second Spring   337
4. Keeping Another Armageddon 1939–1947   362
5. Hortus Conclusus 1947–1957   389

Appendix   413
Bibliography   416

PREFACE

R onald Knox lacked only longevity to be a national figure. Had he lived to be eighty he would, most unwillingly, have found himself assumed into that odd circle of ancient savants and charlatans whom the Sovereign delights to honour and the popular press treats with some semblance of reverence. He died at sixty-nine still essentially a private person.

This book, I surmise, will prove to be the forerunner of many weightier studies of him. Its primary purpose is to tell the story of his exterior life, not to give a conspectus of his thought; still less to measure his spiritual achievements. His published works provide abundant material for research and criticism by specialists in many subjects. Here I have attempted to provide the essential biographical facts they will need.

How do I come to be writing it? the reader may ask. In 1950 Ronald asked if he might appoint me in his will as his sole literary executor. There was not much more than fifteen years between us; the clergy are notoriously longer lived than the laity; I did not think it likely my services would be needed. But he put my name down and left it there. One of my duties was to appoint his official biographer.

He was himself one of Hilaire Belloc's literary executors and, three years later, when we were discussing the choice of Belloc's biographer, I raised the question of his own. 'Yes, I suppose someone will want to write something,' he said without enthusiasm. He had grown up in a tradition by which everyone had some literary commemoration, even the men of twenty who were killed in battle, and he regarded the attention of a biographer as an inevitable concomitant of death like that of the coffin-maker and grave-digger. Later he spoke of writing his autobiography. Until the end of 1956 it did not occur to me that I should outlive him; early in 1957 it seemed probable that I would do so, and I conceived the ambition of attempting the portrait myself. At the end of June, when he knew he was dying, he gave me instructions about his papers. I then asked for his approval of my project. He gave it. He could hardly have refused. But next day he wrote to a friend reporting my suggestion in terms which leave me in no doubt that his acquiescence was not prompted by mere politeness. He was well aware of the limitations of our friendship. I knew him primarily as a man of letters rather than as a priest; that is to say, I never went to confession to him or asked him for spiritual or moral advice. He knew, also, my curiosity and lack of discretion. He knew the kind of book I was likely to write, and, I believe, this is what he wanted – or, rather, was prepared to tolerate – as distinct from what a sober scholar or edifying colleague might have written.

If the picture I have drawn seems sombre, it is not by inadvertence.

At Ronald's death the Roman Catholic Church in every English-speaking country lamented the loss of a rich ornament, and the story unfolded in pulpit and newspaper was one of the cherished and privileged survivor of a golden age.

The brilliantly precocious youth, cosseted from childhood; the wit and scholar marked out for popularity and fame; the boon companion of a generation of legendary heroes; the writer of effortless felicity and versatility; the priest who never bore the burden of a parish or a diocese, but always lived where he chose, in patrician country-houses and university common-rooms; who was always the 'special preacher' on great occasions; who never lost a friend or made an enemy; the man whose exquisite politeness put everyone at his ease; the translator who brought the Vulgate to life for his own generation and for the future; the author of numberless unrecorded, unforgotten quips – this, is it not? is rather the impression left by the obituaries. But genius and sanctity do not thrive except by suffering. If I have made too much of Ronald's tribulations, it is because he hid them, and they must be known to anyone who seeks to appraise his achievement.

My special thanks are due to Ronald's sister, Lady Peck, to Mr Laurence Eyres, to Lady Acton and to Mrs Raymond Asquith. As will be apparent in the following pages, I should have been helpless without their kindness.

I have made myself a nuisance to numerous friends of Ronald's and, for the love they bore him, they have always given more than I asked. I have met with none of the obstructions which biographers often suffer. There have been others who were not Ronald's friends or mine, but from simple goodwill have gone to the trouble to find information. My apologies are offered to any whom I have neglected to name in the following list: the Hon. John Addington, Mr Peter Anson, Lady Helen Asquith, the Master of Balliol, Mgr J. Barton, Mgr F. Bickford, Sir Nevile

Bland, Mr Thomas Burns, Father P. Bushell, Mgr Reginald Butcher, Father P. Caraman, S.J., Mr G. Kitson Clark, Miss Dorothy Collins, Mr J. J. Creaven, the Countess of Dalhousie, Mr Alfred Duggan, the Countess of Eldon, Mgr Valentine Elwes, the Hon. Mrs Hugh Fraser, Mrs Roger Fulford, Sir Ralph Furse, Mr Samuel Gurney, Father Michael Hanbury, Dr Robert Havard, Mr Haydon-Baillie, Father Edward Hickey, Mr Thomas Higham, Mr Geoffrey Hitchcock, Mr Christopher Hollis, Canon Hood, the Earl of Iddesleigh, Mr Peter Ingrams, Mgr Vernon Johnson, Mr Judah, Mr Robert Laffan, Miss Antoinette Lambert, Miss Joyce Lambert, the Bishop of Lancaster, Mr Philip Landon, Major-General J. C. Latter, Sir Shane Leslie, Bt., Rev. B. Lloyd-Oswell, Mrs Joly de Lotbinière, Laura Lady Lovat, Mr H. F. Macdonald, Mr John McDougall, the Hon. Mrs Marffy, Mother Margaret Mary of the Congregation of the Assumption, Mr Hugh Marsden, Mr George Marshall, Father C. C. Martindale, S.J., Father Gervase Mathew, O.P., Mr Charles Newman, Brother James Oakley, Mr J. B. Oldham, Mr George Painter, Mr Maurice Platnauer, Mr Arthur Pollen, Miss Dorothy Pratt, Mr F. E. Pritchard, Mr Philip Radcliffe, Mrs John Roberts, Father J. F. Rogers, S.J., Mr Frank Sheed, the Headmaster of Shrewsbury, Mgr G. D. Smith, Mr S. S. Sopwith, Mr J. M. Street, Mr Christopher Sykes, the President of Trinity, Mr Thomas Twidell, Mrs Villiers, Mr David Walker, Mr W. P. Watt, Mgr Gordon Wheeler, the Rev. W. de Lara Wilson, Mr and the Hon. Mrs J. D. Woodruff, Mgr Worlock, Dom Hubert van Zeller, Father Alfonso de Zulueta.

BOOK I

Laughter and the Love of Friends

———◆———

Oh dear friendship, what a gift of God it is. Speak no ill of it.

FR BEDE JARRETT, O.P.

Quoted p. 230

I doubt if we do laugh at anything in this sublunary world except when we think we see imperfection in it. Are we, then, to think of heaven as quite humourless, St Philip Neri and St Thomas More never smiling again?

RONALD KNOX TO MISS JOYCE LAMBERT, 1944

Chapter One

HEREDITY

1798–1888

R onald Arbuthnott Knox was the youngest of the family of four sons and two daughters born between 1880 and 1888 to the Rev. Edmund Arbuthnott Knox (later Bishop of Manchester), son of the Rev. George Knox, and Ellen Penelope, daughter of Thomas Valpy French, Bishop of Lahore.

Ronald had no memory of either grandfather. They died in the same year, 1891, when he was a child of three. Both were clergymen of the evangelical party in the Church of England; both served in India and had close connexions with the Church Missionary Society; they lived as neighbours for a short time in Surrey; but they were not friends. There was between them a profound difference of character which is apparent in their portraits.

A miniature painting of George Knox belonging to the family presents a plump complacent face, clean-shaven save for a wisp of side-whisker; the nose is large, the eyes small, the lips prim with a hint of cruelty; the hair is thin, long, and soft; baldness lends a spurious height to the smooth brow. He was the elder by eleven years.

Thomas Valpy French, in the last photograph taken of him, is an ascetic and a visionary; between the full Newgate fringe and the curling white hair the face is gaunt, the forehead massive; the mouth is resolute, the eyes deep-set and far-seeing. Intelligence, aspiration, and endurance are written in every deep line of the weathered skin. His story is full of significance for those who would assess the complex ingredients of Ronald's character and achievement.

Bishop French was the son of a well-born, well-to-do clergyman who was content to remain vicar of Holy Trinity, Burton-on-Trent, for forty-seven years. At Rugby he was a pupil of Arnold's but not one of those chosen for special training, whose young consciences were early burdened with the prospect of great responsibilities. All his life his spirit grew. As a boy he made little mark. Nor was he greatly impressed by the famous headmaster whose sermons in chapel were 'not the Gospel as he had been accustomed to receive it'.[1] He lacked the pride, he later said, to 'revel' in the independence of judgement which Arnold inculcated. Independence he had, but 'the exercise of it was often a very painful duty'.[2] At Oxford, where he went as a scholar of University College in 1843, he was known as a hard-reading man of very strict life, imperious, pure, earnest; one in whose presence 'frivolity itself was abashed'. He was elected fellow in 1848 and took Holy Orders in 1849. In 1850 he 'received the call' to India, in an appeal on behalf of the Church Missionary Society from an Old Rugbeian, Henry Fox. From then until death his life was consecrated to the East, a recurring cycle of prodigious effort, collapse, recuperation, and renewed effort. First he was sent to Agra to found a school. He saw his work there laid in ruins by the Mutiny, but in that year of alarm he made his reputation for intrepid devotion, working on quietly in his quarters far from the protection of the garrison, while panic spread round him and each day brought news of approaching disaster. At length he took refuge in the fort, but only on the condition that his native Christians should be admitted with him. Next he went north, first as Principal of St John's College, Lahore, later as Bishop, where his diocese stretched from Karachi to Peshawar and Delhi, including the unsettled territory of the North-West Frontier. He followed the Army to Kabul, preaching long, abstruse sermons at church parades, which the men forgave him when he visited them in their bivouacs and dressing-stations. He travelled through Cashmere and Persia, mastered several native tongues and made the acquaintance of many others, working early and late in the hot season and the rains.

In whatever language he preached, he rose to heights where few of his hearers could entirely follow him, but his earnestness was infectious, and in private conversation he charmed men of every race. He braved cholera and plague. He suffered all the discouragements common to missionaries among Hindus and Mohammedans. Not for him the exhilarating triumphs of his colleagues in Central Africa. He made few converts. He bore witness. That eventually became his obsession – simply to proclaim his Saviour and to tell the story of the Redemption to whoever would listen in places where it had never before been heard. Failing health made him resign his bishopric in 1887, but he set out, not for England, but for a tour of eleven months in the heart of the Turkish Empire, suffering greater

[1] Rev. Herbert Birks, *Life and Correspondence of Thomas Valpy French*, 1895. Vol. I, p. 8.
[2] Ibid., Vol. I, p. 11.

privations than he had known under the British flag, visiting the ancient heretical and schismatic Christian communities, which were little known to Anglicans of the period. He found no pristine simplicities among them, but superstitions darker than those of Rome itself. He did not seek to make Protestants of them as the American Baptists were doing. He believed that if they were brought the true word of God they would purify themselves as the English had done four centuries before. A Chaldean priest let him share his altar and he was grateful for the act of hospitality, but he did not attach any special significance to it. Thomas French was not concerned about the validity of his Orders; his religion was not sacramental. For him the Divine Presence in Holy Communion was a change worked in the heart of the recipient not in the hands of the priest. The Church of Rome was always an obstacle to him, blocking his way the more firmly the farther he travelled. It was also a mystery; an unaccountable mixture of good and evil.[1] Everywhere the work of the missionary nuns commanded his ungrudging admiration, and in his prayers it was to Catholic masters he continually and increasingly turned; not to the Fathers only, but to specifically popish guides, Lacordaire, St Francis de Sales, the Curé d'Ars, St Charles Borromeo, Fénelon, and such less wellknown names as Père Didon and Padre Montefeltro; even to Newman, whom he had rejected decisively in youth. At the end his spiritual life was fed almost entirely from Catholic sources.

At length in the spring of 1889 he returned to England for what was expected to be his final retirement with his wife, for in the course of his heroic career he had married and begotten eight children, the eldest of whom, Ellen, was already the mother of Ronald Knox. In a letter to his wife he once wrote of Oxford: 'It was there that I fixed for you and there, too, I fixed for India which you are almost disposed at times to think a rival in my affections, are you not?'[2]

'Almost'? 'at times'? Of the thirty-eight years of their married life an aggregate of seventeen was spent in separate continents. From time to time a home was established, but in England he was away five nights a week, preaching, raising funds, attending conferences; in India he was half his time in the saddle, toiling through remote districts to return to his wife in Lahore, prostrate always with fatigue, often injured and seriously ill, to resume immediately his ceaseless, blinding linguistic studies. Mrs French and his children suffered the common lot of the sundered families of the British Empire with an essential difference. There was no worldly reason

[1] Ibid., Vol. II, p. 276.   [2] Ibid., Vol. I, p. 14.

for the Bishop to remain in India. England was full of pleasant opportunities for a man of his quality. He remained by choice, obedient to his imperious vocation.

Now at last he was welcomed home in the fond belief that his remaining years would be spent in domestic tranquillity. His diary records the day of reunion as one of the happiest of his life. But his vocation would not let him rest. He called on the headquarters of the C.M.S., where, he thought, he was not quite as welcome as of old. He may have aroused the suspicions of the stricter evangelicals. At Lahore he had admitted Anglican nuns of High Church sympathies and had tolerated the controversial 'Eastward position' (of the clergyman at Holy Communion). His Urdu translation of the *Book of Common Prayer* had not been approved. Although he had the assistance of a committee, the work was essentially his own, and he was thought to have been too free and idiosyncratic. This opposition coming at a time when he was near success in shedding all personal vanity hurt him bitterly. He was confident of his finer sense of both languages than his critics; more than this, he felt that his own fervent use of the prayers had given him a special light on their character. The rebuff struck at his spirituality as well as at his scholarship. Sixty years later the incident was to be re-enacted in the life of his grandson with a curious similarity of detail.

As he felt he was being excluded from Indian affairs, his imagination was stirred by the Arab world, of which he had had a glimpse on his travels.

> The only home-work of any importance suggested [he wrote in September 1890],[1] was four months' locum tenancy for the Bishop of Exeter, in taking charge of his diocese during his absence in Japan. Were I ten years younger such a delay at home would be of no great moment. . . . I own I have been much perplexed. . . . I can but come to this, that when *full* light is not given one must accept the best light one has, and move slowly forward with *some* hesitancy but still more *trust*.

In fact, he had decided to go to North Africa for 'a few weeks, or months, or more, as God may appoint' to perfect himself in Arabic. As he pondered the matter further light seemed to come. England had lately acquired Zanzibar; the East African coast and the slave routes inland came under her influence. The key to all this Moslem world was the Sultanate of Muscat on the Persian Gulf, where he had once spent a few hours on

[1] Ibid., Vol. II, p. 323.

an earlier journey. Soon he was certain that his destiny lay there, and in November 1890 he set out without official commission, unpaid and alone. His last six months were the consummation of his singular quest.

From Tunis he moved to Kairowan. In that holy city of Islam where no Catholic priest had ventured, he proceeded to collect little audiences in the courts of the mosques and tell them the story of the Gospel. He was recognized as a holy man, and was not molested. Staying at the simplest inn, wearing what approximated to native dress, he spent his hours of physical rest in a scholarly examination of the teaching of Abd-ul-Kadir, the patron saint of the place. Thence for Christmas he moved to Egypt and in Cairo had the good fortune to meet a young friend, Alexander Maitland, whom he had himself ordained, returning to his post in Delhi. Maitland volunteered to accompany him as far as Muscat, and in January 1891 they set out together down the Red Sea in a small Turkish steamer.

No one at Muscat expected them. There was a British Agent in the Sultanate, but the Bishop refused to call on him until he had established himself, believing that official hospitality would compromise his mission. Throughout the stifling day the two clergymen sought lodging, at length finding temporary shelter in the dirty upper room of a Goanese grog-shop. Fortunately they had been fellow travellers with an American merchant who had consular authority on that coast. This chance acquaintance, a Presbyterian, offered them the use of an empty warehouse of his, not in Muscat, but in the town of Muttra, three miles distant by boat. After two days' vain search they were glad to accept.

Muttra contained a dozen mosques and seven buildings which would have passed for houses in India. The rest was a conglomeration of huts in wattle compounds. It was populated by Negroes, Hindus, Baluchis, and Persians, besides the predominant Arabs. There was no European or Christian of any kind. A Mahratta doctor, retired from the Indian Medical Department, was the sole reminder of the world they had inhabited. They had no servant and little furniture; a few pots and cups, two teaspoons, and a rusty knife. Sand-flies and mosquitoes infested the place. They had no nets. Dust storms often swept through the house. Now in the cool season the heat was oppressive; in summer it would be quite unsupportable. When at length they made themselves known to the British Agent he advised them to be gone.

Maitland remained with the Bishop for a month. He rose at dawn to find the Bishop already up and absorbed in prayer. He went to market and returned with eggs and milk and prepared breakfast. The Bishop worked at his Arabic till dinner, for which Maitland would collect dates and curry ready cooked from the bazaar. The two clergymen then held a service, praying together, reading the Bible and sometimes a sermon, and in the last two hours of light the Bishop would set out sometimes alone, sometimes taking Maitland with him, to mix with the people and visit neighbouring villages. They drank a cup of tea at sundown, sang evensong together, put out the lamp, and composed themselves for the night.

When their month was up, on March 9th, the old man was left quite alone. He lived from day to day by what he took for God's guidance. His diary for March records wanderings in Muttra and Muscat, conversations in doorways and at street corners, an occasional invitation to enter a private house. In the main mosque he was offered but refused the sheik's armchair, declaring significantly that he belonged to the fakir class. There he expounded the gospel to a receptive audience.

In April the hot weather set in and he had an attack of fever, At the beginning of May he learned that his son-in-law Edmund Arbuthnott Knox, Ronald's father, had decided to leave his pleasant country rectory and move to Birmingham.

> I think few, if any, missionary posts abroad are to be compared for utter and absolute self-devotion like that you are called to [he wrote]. I shall be glad if permitted in the coming kingdom to sit at the feet of very many of my toiling, suffering, impoverished and often well-nigh distracted brethren, charged with the spiritual care of such great masses. . . . At present I cannot tell which way the guiding hand is directing me. I have seldom experienced such baulkings of purpose. It is well deserved, I must believe. Day dawn may break on what is perplexed and rather overclouded.

This was written in solitude and under the waxing incandescent wind of summer. By the same mail he sent his last letter to Mrs French. He mentions preaching to lepers; during Ramadan the Arabs tend to be intolerant; he hopes to retire until the month is over to a village named Sib, twenty-eight miles distant on the coast. On May 6th he left Muttra for this retreat in an open fishing-boat. They sailed through the heat of the day and at evening found a straggle of huts, a palm grove, and some wells. The American who had befriended him before had a house here too, an open shed of wattle and thatched leaf. Two sheikhs had been deputed by the Sultan to keep an eye on him. Next day, Ascension Day, he walked three miles to call on the local headman, and on his return was sick. The house gave no shelter from the scorching wind; he lay in the open for some hours, then crept under the house among the piles on which it stood. There he became insensible and was revived by water poured on his head. The attendant sheikhs urged him to return to Muscat and hired a boat, but it was two days before he could move. When he did so, Ramadan was over, everything was shut. He took refuge in a room near the British Residency and charged his servant to keep his arrival secret. He remained there until May 13th, when the Indian doctor found him unconscious; he was moved to the Residency, where he died on the 14th. The emaciated body was prepared for burial by the Christian hands of a family he had never met, Goanese Catholics, who had revered him at a distance; the funeral took place that evening, the British Consul reading the service.

Maitland visited Sib to collect the details of his last days. One of the village elders remarked: 'He had put away this world and was entirely occupied with the things of eternity.'

No one followed him in the phantasmagorical Muscat mission. He had borne witness as his vocation led him – a Protestant Charles de Foucauld – far beyond the horizon of George Knox.

2

Ronald's father, writing of the two contemporary Scottish Archbishops of Canterbury and York, said, 'They had not in their bones the veneration for The Book of Common Prayer which I have inherited as a tradition of primary importance',[1] but in fact his own Anglicanism had no deep roots. From the sixteenth until the beginning of the nineteenth century the Knoxes were Presbyterian. They descended from the family who in the thirteenth century held lands in Renfrewshire which included Ranfurly, the name chosen for the earldom to which a branch was raised in 1831. These properties were sold in the seventeenth century when the family moved to colonize County Down. There they multiplied (Ronald Knox's great-grandfather was one of a family of twenty-six) and various members established themselves at Prehen, Rathmullan, Dungannon, Waringsford, and Moneymore. The original grants of land supported only the elder sons; younger sons went into professions and trades, with the result that in a hundred and fifty years the Knoxes, like other families of the Plantation, constituted a formidable tribe, implacably hostile to the remaining native

---

[1] The Right Revd. Edmund Arbuthnott Knox, *Reminiscences of an Octogenarian*, p. 306.

Irish, conscious of kinship, but varying in economic status from spacious landed gentry to small farmers and shopkeepers.

It was among these Protestants of moderate means that the United Irishmen of 1798 were first recruited. They were a secret society whose secrets were well known to the Government; they were republican in sentiment, taking the American colonists as their model and the Jacobins as their allies. Their meagre hopes of success depended on surprise, strong French help and the unqualified support of the Catholics. None of these conditions prevailed. The leaders were betrayed and captured before they took the field; there was no French invasion; the Catholic clergy refused to bless a movement whose origins had an apparent affinity with the Orange Lodges and the Peep O'Day Boys and whose ideas smacked of French atheism, and the peasant risings were local and uncoördinated. The small English regular forces were easily able to suppress the ill-organized Jacquerie, and the way was laid open for the Act of Union.

Ronald's immediate forebears, the Knoxes of Edentrellick, squireens and linen merchants, were deeply implicated in the business. The head of this branch, Alexander Knox, died in the year after the rebellion. Of his family of twenty-six three, Anne, George, and James, were children of his first marriage. Anne was married to James Porter, the Presbyterian minister at Grey Abbey near Dromore. A handsome popular man, whose religious views are said to have been more Arian than Calvinist, he had been a lecturer on the natural sciences and a fiery pamphleteer against Lord Londonderry. His name was on the list prepared by the informers, and a reward was offered for him at the first stir of trouble. He was betrayed, arrested, and hanged outside his own meeting-house on July 2nd. The charges against him were ill supported, but there can be little doubt of his guilt. His eldest son, then aged fourteen, carried the rebel standard at the 'battle' of Ballynahinch, where on June 12th General Nugent with a small force routed some 5,000 men of County Down. James Knox, Anne's brother, fought in this affray and received a sabre cut from which he never fully recovered.

Our concern is with Ronald's great-grandfather, George Knox the elder, and we do not know what part he played that day. Possibly he, too, was in the field. What is certain is that he left the country immediately afterwards and that his flight was in some way a consequence of the rebellion. Atrocities were committed by the troops in the countryside, but when men were brought to trial the sentences were in general rather lenient. Many who might have been hanged were sent into exile. There is no record of any legal process in George Knox's case. Perhaps the army of occupation connived at his escape. Mystery surrounds every aspect of his career; his son George, Ronald's grandfather, never spoke of him.

On leaving Ireland he went to Jamaica. He can have brought few resources with him from his family, but in a short time he had (according to family tradition) somehow acquired a plantation and a stock of slaves.

He had not been in the island two years when, by an odd turn of chance, General Nugent, the victor of Ballynahinch, came there too, as Lieutenant-Governor and Commander-in-Chief. Nugent made Knox his A.D.C.

It is pleasant to imagine the scene of recognition and reconciliation; to picture the magnanimous enemies at their ease on a wide veranda fighting again the campaign of 'ninety-eight over their rum and cheroots under the tropic stars; very pleasant – but there is another plausible though odious explanation of George Knox's rise to popularity and favour. It is possible that he was one of the many government agents in the United Irishmen and that he fled, not from the justice of the Crown, but from the vengeance of his kin, whose blood-money was the foundation of his fortune.

He returned once briefly to Ireland in 1805 and married Laetitia Greenfield, the daughter of a Church of Ireland clergyman. Immediately after the wedding he set out alone for Jamaica, settled his affairs there, and shortly afterwards sailed for England, where he set up house with his wife in Henrietta Street, London, as a West Indian merchant.

His son George, Ronald's grandfather, was born there (or by another account in Nottingham Street) in 1814 and another son, Alexander, soon after. Alexander succeeded to what little was left of his fortune after the abolition of slavery. No reason other than caprice has ever been given for this discrimination. Laetitia Knox died in 1818, leaving the unloved, disinherited elder son desolate and embittered.

The facts are few, and all is conjecture concerning the character of George Knox the elder. One may suppose that something more than mutual antipathy determined the son's grim silence; there must also have been a moral cause, but so many things excited the reprobation of George Knox the younger, that it is impossible to adduce from it any grave delinquency. The father may have been an easy-going, adventurous man of the world; he may have been a villain; George Knox the younger would hardly distinguish; both in his simple judgement were equally Hell-bent.

Certainly the son's Anglicanism cannot be derived from the father, who seems to have abandoned Presbyterianism without adopting any recognizable alternative.[1] Nor can it be ascribed to the mother who died when he was four. A place was found for him at St Paul's School when he was ten, and this may have been the occasion of his formally joining the Church of England.[2] It was by his own wish, and against his father's, that he became a clergyman. He was a man of more than average intelligence, with a good grounding in the classics and in French, but at Cambridge, where he was sent after failing for a scholarship at Trinity, Oxford, it was then impossible to read for Classical Honours until after taking Honours in Mathematics. No mathematics, he used to say, were taught at Dr Cleath's St Paul's. It is hard to reconcile this explanation with the list of Cambridge successes won by Paulines of the day. George Knox, at any rate, read for a pass and found himself in 1837 an ordained clergyman, unqualified for a fellowship or a college living and devoid of any influential connexions which might bring him preferment at home. India offered larger opportunities, and in 1838 he received a chaplaincy under the Company and sailed for Madras, where he remained seventeen years; long enough to earn his pension. His work there lay exclusively with the English community, among whom he was well respected.

In 1844 he married Frances Reynolds, one of two highly eligible sisters who were brought east in that year to find husbands. The younger sister married the fourth son of the eighth Viscount Arbuthnott, a connexion that was preserved in the Christian names of both Edmund and Ronald Knox, although all intercourse between the sisters ceased when the Arbuthnotts were first beguiled by the sermons of a High Church London preacher and later became Roman Catholic. The Reynoldses were a Quaker family, until lately rich London merchants with a large estate at Carshalton, now somewhat impoverished; their mother, recently dead, had been the daughter of a director of the East India Company. These antecedents won them an immediate welcome into the best society of Madras. Frances Reynolds was in every way a good match for George Knox, whom she long survived, to be a potent influence on his grandchildren.

Eleven years later he resigned his chaplaincy, and the whole family, which now comprised four sons and three daughters, moved to England. Two years followed of curacies and lodgings; finally, George Knox was

---

[1] The Church of England in Jamaica was by all accounts in a deplorable condition in his time. There was a Presbyterian minister in the island, but there is no evidence of George Knox having resorted to him.

[2] No information is available either from the authorities of St Paul's or from the Mercer's Company, which then controlled it, whether or no Anglicanism was a condition of entry.

appointed Central Association Secretary of the Church Missionary Society and a home was established at Waddon, then a rural hamlet, near Croydon. Here they remained for sixteen years under George Knox's stern and absolute rule. It was such a household, now, one may suppose, extinct, as has been rather often portrayed in English letters. His son, Edmund, left his own account of it[1] suppressing any hint of reproach and scrupulously setting out whatever could be honestly said in his father's honour.

The household comprised the parents, eight children, two servants, and a nanny. George Knox's gross income at this time was £665, narrow but far from penury. The austerity, which approximated to privation, of their life was imposed by the father's will rather than by necessity. They occupied the larger part of a house divided in two, with an empty stable, a prolific walled garden, and a small paddock which was the children's sole place of recreation. Indoors there was only work; no games, no novels, no easy-chairs, no visitors. They never stayed away or entertained other children. Ruskin's works were banned as frivolous. The halfpenny a week pocket money was devoted to the church plate; when moved to larger benefactions, as they were in the cause of the Lancashire cotton famine, they were allowed to subscribe threepence a week on condition of their subsisting on dry bread at breakfast and tea. At normal times they were given one slice with either butter or jam at each of these meals. Dry bread was always unlimited in quantity. At midday there was a solid dinner. Their clothes were home-made and seemingly indestructible, passing from one growing child to the next. They seldom suffered the humiliation of comparing them with other children's. Once or twice they were taken to a party in the neighbourhood, but always removed hungry at the start of the round dances which preceded the supper. They made no friends and caught no infectious diseases.

Mrs Knox was now an invalid and indulged to the extent of a deck-chair. She was dearly loved. She retained in private her Quaker habit of fervent extempore prayer. George Knox's devotions were lengthy but prosaic. His spirit determined the character of the home.

The appointment he held with the C.M.S. was one of more than a dozen secretaryships, some of which were filled by laymen. His duties, corresponding to those of a modern Public Relations Officer, were not precisely defined. They were in general to stimulate interest in foreign missions in his area. They should have taken him out and about the

---

[1] Edmund Knox, op. cit., pp. 24–34.

parishes, but he preferred to remain at home. He was not the man to shirk hard work, but he fancied himself as a writer, and was happiest in his own study writing, in a curiously illegible hand, appeals, reports, and pamphlets, which with age became increasingly argumentative and acrimonious. The hours he spared from these works were spent in instructing and chastising his children. George, the eldest boy, ran away and was later knighted for his services in India. Lindsey, the youngest, bit him so severely in the thumb during one of his floggings that he was persuaded to mitigate his discipline thereafter. He was altogether too much at home for the happiness of his family; perhaps too much, also, for the efficiency of his work. When he ceased to be secretary it was contrary to his wishes and in defiance of his bitter protests. 'I have been shamefully treated,' he wrote, denouncing 'Gedge, my relentless opponent' and 'the internal jobbery and manipulation in C.M.S. committees'. It is probable that by the late 'sixties his harsh Calvinism was ceasing to be an attraction to subscribers. Bishop French offended by the very slight inclination towards Tractarianism of his later life. George Knox adhered too faithfully to the principles of the Society's founders, but he was not left without compensation. A living was found for him in Rutland, and he was given the editorship of the *Church Missionary Intelligence*.

3

Edmund Arbuthnott Knox, Ronald's father, spent his formative years in the seclusion of Waddon. He was naturally clever and industrious. In spite of the multifarious drawbacks of his home, he grew up cheerful and pious, and in old age was able to say gratefully of his father, what he could not say of himself, that his children all remained steadfast in the faith of their schoolroom.

The only sum which his education ever cost his father was the customary shilling tip to the school porter on his first day at St Paul's, October 13th 1857. After that he not only supported himself by scholarships but also contributed towards the modest expenses of his younger brothers and sisters. St Paul's in his time was much as his father had known it; 153 boys, a clerical staff, a schoolroom, a yard; no dining-hall or playing-fields; a thorough classical grounding.

In 1865 he went to Corpus Christi, Oxford. It was already his firm desire to take Holy Orders. In his restricted field of observation everyone of any importance had been a clergyman, but his father was not entirely sympathetic. George Knox had no mystical regard for priesthood and he had a positive horror of curacies. There was no family living for Edmund. If he wished to be a parson, Edmund must become a don. If he failed to get a first in Mods, his father warned him, he must go down and make a career for himself as a layman in India. The warning was quite unnecessary. Edmund took three firsts and was elected Fellow of Merton. At the same time he had the offer of a tutorship at Addington Palace to the son of Archbishop Tait. The only tears recorded of George Knox were shed when he learned that Edmund had refused this unique opportunity. He need not have grieved. Without any unworthy self-seeking Edmund Knox followed a course of steady ecclesiastical advancement.

Merton when Edmund Knox went there was neither a pious nor a studious college. Alban Hall next door, which welcomed idle undergraduates, was an established temptation. As tutor and later dean of Merton Knox set himself to reform all this; statutes were enforced; prayer-meetings held for undergraduates, sermons preached to the servants, promising scholars recruited from the Public Schools; Alban Hall was acquired and incorporated by the college. At the same time he worked devotedly in the poor parishes of the city and took a vigorous part in theological controversy. He was denounced by Purey-Cust at the diocesan conference on the false charge of having taken a sacrilegious photograph of the altar at Cuddesdon College and of circulating it for partisan reasons among the evangelical clergy.

Edmund Knox's religious opinions were uncompromising and consistent. He eschewed the puritanism of his father and was a genial and humane man, fond of fishing and of Highland scenery, as fearless in opposition to the highly placed dissenters and agnostics who were increasingly influential in public life, as to his subordinate clergy who showed a taste for unseemly ornaments. Before his ordination Bishop Mackarness advised him to make a serious study of Church History.[1]

'My Lord,' he replied, 'I hope to make a study of the Reformation.'

The Bishop answered rather curtly: 'I did not mean that', but throughout his long and prosperous career Edmund Knox never wavered in his belief that the Church of England was the creation of the sixteenth century. In later life scientific and textual criticism of the Bible made him slightly modify the theory of verbal inspiration in which he had been educated, but he clung all the more tenaciously to the Prayer Book as being both the legal charter of the Church of England and the monument

[1] E. A. Knox, op. cit., p. 81.

of national liberation from the tyranny and corruption of Rome. He had no sympathy with colleagues or with members of his own family who preferred to regard it as the vehicle through which sacramental life was transmitted from earlier ages. In private he admitted that he did not regard episcopacy as an essential of catholicity. His devotions were not sacramental. It did not strike him as being at all incongruous that, in a college dedicated to Corpus Christi, Holy Communion should be held only twice a term; indeed, he was edified to remark that the pre-Reformation gold chalice and paten, which is the college's proudest possession, had been used by John Jewel, Richard Hooker, and John Reynolds.[1]

It was during his parochial work in Oxford that he renewed his acquaintance with Thomas French. They had met, briefly, when he was a small boy at Waddon. During his periods of recuperation from the Indian Mission French used to take temporary duty at various English churches. Thus he had come to Beddington, and there gave some instruction in Sanskrit to Edmund's elder brother, George. Now he appeared at St Ebbe's, Oxford, with his eight children, to the eldest of whom, Ellen, Knox became engaged when, in 1876, the statutes of Merton were amended to allow the marriage of four of its fellows.

Ellen Knox was a delicate girl, of whose life there is little record except in the distant, affectionate memories of her surviving children. The air of Oxford was thought to be deleterious to her. This and the appointment of Chavasse as Principal of Wycliffe Hall, which relieved Knox in his post as the sole effective champion of evangelicalism in Oxford, determined him to leave. When the college living of Kibworth in Leicestershire fell vacant in 1884 he accepted it, bringing with him two sons and two daughters; two more sons were born at Killworth, of whom the younger (born on February 17th 1888) was Ronald.

[1] Ibid., p. 77.

Chapter Two

ENVIRONMENT

1888–1900

Kibworth Rectory, with its pleasant gardens and large glebe, provided a more attractive home than any the Knoxes were to enjoy in any of their subsequent moves. The parish comprised the contrasted and antagonistic communities of Kibworth Harcourt and Kibworth Beauchamp; hunting-boxes and the villas of retired business-men on the one side, on the other the freehold cottages of the 'stockeners'. The church, in competition with three sects of dissent, was well attended. The previous rector had been active and happy at Kibworth for forty years, but there was no scope in this agreeable retreat for Edmund Knox's exceptional energies. He was a man of his age, drawn to the new, teeming industrial cities; he was a controversial man, and he liked to be in the thick of it, where contemporary issues were debated and decided. For all the political radicalism of Kibworth Beauchamp there was a conservatism, sprung of the heavy Leicestershire clay, which Edmund Knox, despite his political toryism, found oppressive. Nor was Mrs Knox happy. She, too, aspired to wider opportunities than the village Sunday School. The change of climate had not been for the healthier. She and the children were often ill. To her keen aesthetic sense the aspect of the countryside was insipid after the unique beauty of mid-Victorian Oxford; to both husband and wife the gossip of fox-hunters seemed inane after the sharp, informed conversation of the University, with its frequent incursions of eminent men from all quarters of Europe. Most important of all the disadvantages was the lack of a proper school for the elder children.

Edmund Knox had not grown up to regard boarding-schools as either normal or desirable. Later he was persuaded otherwise, but he never entirely overcame his prejudice against a process which seemed to him contrary to nature. Even when his sons were happy and conspicuously successful at Eton and Rugby, he felt ill at ease when called to give Confirmation at a Public School.[1] At this stage he aspired to give his

---

[1] E. A. Knox, op. cit., p. 173.

children, in a more humane form, the education he had himself received; efficient instruction at a day-school, moral and religious guidance at home; an arrangement that could only be contrived in a city.

The Deanery of Manchester fell vacant; this would have satisfied all his immediate needs, and he was assured that the Prime Minister, A. J. Balfour, had decided to offer it to him; but Manchester at the time was a battlefield of High and Low Churchmen, and Knox was a party man of plain colour. At the last minute his name was dropped in favour of a less provocative candidate's. Balfour, whose own religious observances alternated indifferently between the Churches of Scotland and England, remained conscious of Knox's qualifications for promotion and later recognized them. Meanwhile Knox did not repine. The decision having been taken to move from Kibworth, he applied in 1891 to the trustees who controlled evangelical appointments, and was offered the huge and forbidding parish of Aston-juxta-Birmingham. With many heart-searchings he accepted and moved to a vicarage which on his first visit he had difficulty in finding, so hidden was it in its mean street by the smoky mass of a brewery, so indifferent were the immediate neighbours to their vicar's presence among them.

Bishop French, it has been mentioned, wrote in admiration of his son-in-law's decision. When that last letter was read, there must have seemed an ironic contrast between the circumstances of the solitary old fakir on the Persian Gulf and the busy, hale, family-man in his Midland vicarage, but Edmund Knox, too, was destined to suffer heroic loneliness. On December 25th 1891, in spite of the sombre surroundings, he recorded the first entirely happy Christmas for some years. Winters at Kibworth had been seasons of family illness; now at last Mrs Knox seemed quite recovered, but early in the New Year she developed her last illness; all that spring and summer she weakened and sank, until in August she died at Brighton while Knox sorrowfully watched her. In a respite from her bedside he took the opportunity to refute an atheist who was addressing holiday-makers on the beach, and to usurp his pulpit. This was the moment of conception of the Blackpool Mission, which occupied the cheerful summers of his later life.

There followed two direful years of widowhood made tolerable only by incessant work. Emily Knox, his second sister, attempted to take Mrs Knox's place. Her health and abilities failed, and the children were dispersed. Knox lived alone with a single servant-housekeeper. He engaged seven curates, for whose stipends he was personally responsible;

he organized Sunday Schools for 5,000 children; he himself taught Bible Classes of 200 men and prepared all candidates for Confirmation; he raised and administered parish funds of £8,000 a year; he founded a Monday Luncheon Club for the evangelical incumbents of the city; he was a leading member of the Church Congress of 1893 at which a High Church demonstration was made against Charles (later Bishop) Gore; he enlarged the cemetery; he enhanced his fame as a preacher. So the dark period passed in a glow of work.

The bereaved children had no such distractions, and for the elder it was a time of barely mitigated woe. The two 'little boys' (as they were known in the family up to a ripe age), Wilfred and Ronald, alone escaped the burden of tragedy. They were sent to their Uncle Lindsey, at Creeton near Grantham, where they spent the greater part of four years in what Ronald remembered as untroubled happiness. He often emphasized this early contentment, partly from gratitude for the kindness shown him, partly from impatience with certain contemporaries who blamed their own irregularities on the rigours of an evangelical upbringing. He was apparently unconscious of anything lacking in the affection given him, but those who knew him best in later life, the mothers especially of the children in whom he delighted, discerned in his zest for spontaneous love and for the intimacies of a vicarious family life something of the uncertainty, loneliness, and persistent hunger of the heart which spring from a motherless childhood.

Lindsey Knox – he who bit his father – had grown into a bachelor clergyman of simple tastes, of placid temper, and of no ambitions. His parish was very small and his duties light. He was thus enabled to devote what energies he had, to his nephews' education. He was not a man of very deep learning; that was not required; he knew enough to keep the little boys busy, and he had two pupils of abnormal intelligence. They learned the Catechism, the Thirty-nine Articles, and the Bible; Latin very thoroughly; some Greek, French, and Mathematics. At the age of six Ronald subscribed a letter to his father: '*Ton amans* υἱός *Ronald Arbuthnott Knox*'. It is related, with rather doubtful authenticity, that when the two little boys, aged seven and six, were taken to the sea, Wilfred asked: 'Ronnie, do you consider that Xenophon's men cried "θάλαττα" or "θάλασσα"?' and Ronald answered: 'The latter.'

The Gender Rhymes were so deeply embedded in their minds by Uncle Lindsey that years later when a friend, composing an inscription, telephoned to ask Ronald the gender of *calix*, he immediately turned to:

Masculines are found in – ix
Fornix, phoenix, and calix . . .

oblivious of the fact that every day of his life he was saying: 'Hic est calix meus.

But Uncle Lindsey's influence was reserved to the schoolroom. Creeton Vicarage, unlike Waddon, was ruled by women; indeed, it was often referred to as 'grandmother's house', for Mrs George Knox had moved there after her husband's death, occupied the two best rooms, and kept her own maid and carriage. She dressed and spoke in the old Quaker style; her spirit expanded in widowhood and permeated the household; to her may be attributed some of the scrupulous precision of expression and abhorrence of ostentation which characterized Ronald in all his vicissitudes. There were also three maiden aunts, the greatest of whom, Fan (Frances Laetitia), exercised direct control over all the household. Her rule was strict and even then antiquated, her piety serene. None of the aunts had ever mixed in any sort of society outside their own home, or heard any other opinion than their father's.[1] No doubt a large range of subjects was unmentionable at Creeton. Perhaps it was this early influence which, all his life, made Ronald so peculiarly reluctant to mention any question of sex even in its most impersonal aspect and so rigidly incurious and incredulous of the sexual delinquencies of others.[2]

Creeton was in no way a repressive home, as Waddon had been. There were no terrors of Hell fire – rather, an emphasis on the adequacy and applicability of the Redemption – no deliberate exclusion of what little outside intercourse was available. There were picnics with neighbouring children, but the little boys were perfectly content with one another's company. Outside school hours, every day except Sunday, they were free to play games of their own invention in the vicarage grounds. The village can be seen from the main railway-line and, so surveying it, Ronald later recorded in a newspaper article[3] fond, quite commonplace memories of paddock, pony, beehives, a swing, a damson-tree, the stone where he sharpened his slate pencil, the peculiar delight of plucking the 'night-caps' off the eschscholtzias (a plant which early fascinated him by the complexity

---

[1] Aunt Ellen was quite another woman; she had been to Oxford and made a career for herself which ended as Principal of Havergal College, Toronto.

[2] Wilfred Knox was always absurdly shy of women. Ronald, as will appear, found among women most of the happiest friendships of his middle and later life.

[3] Reprinted in *On Getting There* (Methuen, 1929).

of its spelling); the drama of a man gored to death by a bull and of the inquest held in the village school after a railway accident.

In the blighted summer of 1893 and again the next year Edmund Knox collected his children at Port Erin, then a village, in the Isle of Man. George Knox had never indulged in a seaside holiday, still less taken his family for one, but the August migration was now a recognized part of the routine of middle-off English people, and heavy at heart Knox conscientiously conformed. The children enjoyed themselves in their way. For the father the second visit, lacking all novelty, was harder to bear than the first. A young and disagreeable nursery-maid accompanied them – the old nanny had left. They lived in lodgings with a single sitting-room and ate whatever the landlady cared to send up; by day they walked, bathed, and played games; in the evening Knox read aloud from *Peveril of the Peak*. There was no adult company for him; the elder children were sickly, still chilled by the grief of their loss. The two senior brothers were now at second-rate boarding-schools which they disliked; they had their sad little secrets, which the sisters, taking the tone of their urban day-school, pried into and reported; there were frequent violent quarrels and, for the father, a dismal sense of inadequacy. It may have been during this August that he decided that he must find a second wife.

Ronald remained sunny and self-sufficient, occupied in his own imaginative pursuits, enchanted by Scott. His elders remember him once entering into a game of theirs. They were playing 'Buried Names', a pastime that has since become generally familiar in cross-word clues. A sentence had to be composed by each in turn, which concealed a proper noun.

'Buried town,' the father began: ' "That ship goes well in tonnage." '

'Linton,' cried the children, evading the trap of 'Wellington'. 'Hidden man – "The Turks show their crude nature in their treatment of the Armenians." '

And so on.

Ronald seemed busy with his toys. Suddenly he piped up from the floor: 'Buried town – "If you please, my gentle madam, as custard is very yellow, so rum is very red." '

On examination 'Damascus' appeared, but Ronald was challenged to give a plausible explanation of how his sentence could be used. It was, he gravely told them, the respectful remonstrance of an old butler to his mistress, who was drinking too much and not eating her wholesome pudding.[1]

---

[1] Winifred Peck, *Home for the Holidays* (1955), p. 86.

The holidays ended and the children dispersed, the elders to their hated schools, the little boys to chase the falling leaves at Creeton. Knox returned to his empty, sunless vicarage and the anodyne of unceasing benefaction. For him the winter loomed as dingy as the Birmingham blight, but, though he did not then know it, his future was radiant.

J. J. S. Perowne, the newly appointed Bishop of Worcester, was the brother of Knox's friend, the fellow of Corpus who later became Master; he had as his domestic chaplain Canon Gell, another old friend of Knox's. These connexions and his own obvious merits assured him of the Bishop's interest. In the autumn of 1894 he was offered the Rectory of the most important parish in Birmingham, St Philip's, the rank of Suffragan Bishop of Coventry, and the Archdeaconry of Birmingham; offices to be held simultaneously.

Birmingham had then an inadequate ecclesiastical status. It had been transferred from the diocese of Coventry to Lichfield, thence to Worcester, outgrowing all these ancient towns in wealth and importance. Its civic government was in the hands of Unitarians, Wesleyans, and agnostics; a large part of its poor were Catholic. Until Knox's appointment the archdeaconry was rather negligently exercised from Coventry. Bishop Perowne was happy among the rural charms of Hartlebury Palace and his own fine Cathedral, which still sported on its door the skin flayed from a Danish raider. Thus Knox found himself in the next six years endowed with all the influence and most of the authority which was later conferred on Gore when Parliament constituted Birmingham an episcopal see.

More important than these honours and responsibilities for Ronald and his siblings was the activity of Bishop Perowne and Canon Gell in finding their protégé a wife.

There was in the diocese a rather unusual clergyman named Canon Newton, Vicar of Redditch; unusual in that he had a very large inherited fortune. He had, too, a taste for building; at his first living near York he had found the vicarage inadequate and left behind him a mansion which was embarrassingly large even to his immediate successors in that ample age; he also built an extensive summer residence on a loch in the West of Scotland, where he owned a deer forest. Now he commemorated his arrival at Redditch by erecting a minor county seat at some distance from his parishioners and from his church. He had one small son, on whom all his hopes were centred, and six daughters, the eldest of whom, Ethel, was now twenty-seven years of age and unmarried. She was handsome, cultivated, pious, and lighthearted; Knox was forty-seven, threatened by premature middle-age, gloom, exhaustion, and corpulence. He had succeeded in everything he had undertaken; there was a career before him. No doubt the matter was debated between Canon Gell and Canon Newton. Perhaps the proposition was put bluntly to Knox. He merely records that he invited Ethel to attend his consecration at St Paul's Cathedral and that he took her presence there as the acceptance of the duties of a wife.

Material advantages were the least of what she brought him. She was not a particularly good housekeeper; her dinner-table was avoided by delicate feeders. She had no dot; the Newtons were generous in hospitality and in present-giving; they did not believe in diminishing the family capital for their daughters' benefit. Indeed, they did rather little for daughters apart from providing spacious and varied surroundings. Ethel and her sisters, though highly intelligent, were given no formal education. They picked up French from their mother's maid, history from their father's library. They taught themselves Latin and Greek; but Ethel never failed the Bishop either in dealing with his correspondence or in capping his quotations. (The diary for her wedding day has the entry: 'Finished the Antigone. Married Bip.') The Newtons gave Knox his annual fishing; they gave him the confidence that, should he die, his children would not be left destitute. These were the only direct benefits of the Newton fortune. What Ethel brought was of another order. She brought the fresh air of loch and moor, Liberty silks and Morris wallpapers, the sense of gaiety and humour where before then had been only recreation and wit. She swept away the last cobwebs of Waddon.

For the New Year of 1895, between the Bishop's consecration and his marriage, he took his whole family to stay at Holmwood, the house mentioned above, which Temple Moore had built for Canon Newton. The great-aunt on whom Winifred Knox had been quartered announced the engagement by bidding the girl kneel and pray to be spared from the worldliness inseparable from wealth. It was not the world but fairyland she found at Holmwood; an enchantress's palace full of ethereal beings, hot-house plants, expanses of carpet and parquet, abundant well-conducted servants, roaring fires, glittering leather bindings, laughter, and music; things at that time far from unique and less than Babylonian in luxury but deliciously exciting to the open, eager minds of children reared in narrower circumstances. If this were worldly, Winifred Knox remarked, she asked nothing better than to be worldly too.[1] For the little boys upstairs on that first evening there was magic too; something they had

[1] Winifred Peck, *A Little Learning* (1952), pp. 93–110.

never seen before; the electric light. They were not conscious, as their sisters were, of being sadly dressed. They were not awed by the splendours about them. They bounced on their unusually springy beds and turned the light on and off, on and off, ecstatically, tirelessly.

That night, when the Knoxes had retired, each of her sisters visited Ethel's room and warned her in varying tones of urgency that she could not possibly face that family. But Ethel had made up her mind. With no air of duty or self-sacrifice – just for the fun of the thing it seemed – she took over the whole daunting family and transformed their lives.

The first thing was to get them into good schools. This did not immediately affect Ronald, who was not yet of an age to enjoy the new regime. He, however, played his part in furthering his stepmother's plans. His brother Dillwyn, rising eleven, was top of his school at Eastbourne and had learned all they were likely to teach him there. He was clearly a potential scholar. Summer Fields, near Oxford, then, as now, was one of the leading preparatory schools of the country, with a particular aptitude for getting boys into College at Eton. It was at that time still managed by Mrs McLaren.

This remarkable woman, the wife of a gymnastic instructor, had begun by taking a few pupils, to whom she disclosed a genius for teaching and rapidly founded a large school. She married her daughter to a clergyman, Dr E. C. Williams, who succeeded her as headmaster before Ronald entered. The Bishop went to see her and was met with the seemingly inflexible ruling that no boy was ever admitted before the age of eight or over ten.

'A pity,' said the Bishop, rising to leave. 'For he will be joined, wherever he goes, by my youngest son, and he is an unusually brilliant child – only six and reading Virgil already.'

'Did you say six?' Mrs McLaren's voice called him back from the threshold. 'We will discuss your plan again.'[1]

Dillwyn was admitted to a year's coaching and, like Ronald later, was first in his election to College at Eton.

The Bishop returned from his honeymoon and installed his bride at St Philip's shortly before Ash Wednesday 1895. They never went abroad again; both preferred the English and Scottish countryside for their future excursions, but it was a little time before Mrs Knox was able to reform

---

[1] Ibid., p. 100. Lady peck mistakenly describes Mrs McLaren – whom she names 'Mrs W.' – as the widow of the headmaster.

the habit of summer holidays. She had grown up in happy ignorance of seaside lodgings; she knew nothing of the needs of schoolboys; the Bishop at first persuaded her that these unaccountable creatures required the outlandish routine of high teas and family cricket. For two Augusts she endured long hours in which the Bishop and his elder sons, Eddie and Dillwyn, batted and bowled while the rest fielded. Ronald, in the deep, happily collected wild flowers; Mrs Knox and the girls and Wilfred pursued the ball. In 1897 she introduced what then became their custom, the taking of a rural rectory. She also introduced the bicycle, or rather persuaded the Bishop to accept the present of a machine from the Coventry manufacturers. One bicycle was clearly useless. Mrs Newton supplied six more, and from then on they regularly rode in a party about the lanes of Devonshire, visiting churches and ruins.

Easter and Christmas were spent in Birmingham. The Bishop enumer-ated the conveniences of his new rectory; it was in the very centre of the city; near the municipal offices, both railway-stations, the trams, and a cab-rank; its double drawing-room could accommodate a meeting of two hundred. It should, he always maintained, have been the seat of the Bishop of the diocese.[1] it was altogether better than Aston, and Mrs Knox did her best to enliven it with chintzes and flowered wallpapers. But there was no garden; that had been sold and built over by the Bank of England. There was a small yard, just big enough to kick a football in; apart from that, there was nowhere for the children except the schoolroom.

Mrs Knox later described her first impressions of this stronghold in an article in the *Daily Chronicle*.[2]

Eddie Knox occupied the single shabby armchair, reading aloud with ribald comments Smiles's *Self Help*. Dillwyn sat lost in a Greek lexicon, Wilfred manipulated a toy train, the girls played a duet on the piano, Ronald lay before the fire with Wood's *Natural History*. They greeted her politely and continued with their pleasures. She withdrew and said to the Bishop: 'They really are clever children. They can occupy themselves.'

Five minutes later the scared face of Winifred appeared at the study door. 'You must come up. The boys are murdering one another.'

She found the little boys cowering in corners; the furniture was

---

[1] E. A. Knox, op. cit., p. 161. The Rectory has now been demolished after sustaining damage in an air-raid. On its site stands a six-story building let for commercial purposes except for the two top floors, which are the Lodge of the Provost of the Cathedral. Bishop Knox would not repine at this change. He had no sentimental objections to architectural 'improvements'.

[2] May 12th 1930.

overturned; *Self Help* had gone out of the window, and Eddie and Dillwyn were locked in what seemed a death grapple.

Gradually, as she won their affection, she tamed them. They took to frequenting the morning-room, where she read them her own favourites, Stevenson, Charlotte Yonge, Kipling, Jane Austen, and all the normal treasury of childhood which had never reached them, Lear's *Nonsense Rhymes*, *Uncle Remus*, *Alice in Wonderland*. She imposed no hush. If they liked to play halma and patience while she read, they were free to do so, and the new world of light reading was the sweeter to them for the casual form of its introduction.

Eddie – as he was known at home, 'Evoe' as he was later known to the world – produced a family magazine, the *Bolliday Bango*. He transcribed and illustrated it himself, but all his brothers and sisters were compelled to contribute. It was a parody of the popular weeklies of the day, with all the normal features – editorial, gossip, news, sport, fiction, jokes, correspondence, nature notes; a presage of his highly successful editorial career on *Punch*, but the allusions are now forgotten and the fugitive humour irrecapturable. Ronald's contribution is, it must be admitted, seldom anything but ineffably tedious – a serial drama in Latin, *Publius et Amilla*, which ran through many issues, growing in complexity of plot with his mastery of the language. The crossed loves of the eponymous hero and heroine are obscured by sword-play, impersonation, banishments, and assassinations, but the dialogue drags lamely behind the action.

Later Ronald set up as an editor on his own, naming his paper *The Gluttonous Grampoid*. He then continued *Publius et Amilla*, with the Prefatory note: 'This came out in the Bolliday Bango, and as it was contributed by instalments the former parts are less pure than the latter. This will account for the impurity and even incorrectness in the style of the former scenes.'

The work was never finished, but when at the age of ten he addressed a farewell ode to a visitor of his sisters', Miss Florence James, he signed it, 'By the author of Publius et Amilla.' This poem, also in Latin, is much more readable.

> *Florens Jacobi* [it begins] *cara sororibus*
> *Fortuna qualis mobilis, hinc abis,*
> *Hic affuisti quinque soles*
> *Tempus et esse breve en videtur.*

and so continues for several stanzas.

Bribed with chocolates, he reluctantly and laboriously produced an English version:

O Florence James to both my sisters dear
Like fickle fortune hence you go away
You here were present during five long days
And lo! the time doth seem to be right short.

These early accomplishments, and others even more striking which cluster in Ronald's adolescence, might suggest an unhealthy precocity and conceit. He himself wrote:[1] 'I cannot resist the impression that I was rather a horrid little boy', but nothing can be further from the witness of all who knew him; they agree in representing him as singularly sweet-tempered, merry, modest, affectionate, and open. He wrote in Latin because he enjoyed it, and if this uncommon amusement caused pride to his father, he enjoyed that too. When in 1896 he went to Summer Fields he was at once welcomed on his own frank and friendly terms by boys very ready to detect and punish any hint of the prig.

There were at that time 125 in the school, all boarders. Many of them went with him later to Eton and Oxford; three in particular, Julian and Billy Grenfell and Edward Horner,[2] were among his intimate friends for the whole of their short lives.

Summer Fields stands far up the Banbury Road in what was then open country. Beyond the playing-fields the meadows run down to the Cherwell, where the boys bathe. The buildings have been augmented and modernized since Ronald's time, but their nucleus remains little changed.

Ronald's life there was happy and uneventful. There were only two features of school life of which he ever complained; one, the daily distribution by the matron of three sheets of lavatory paper to each boy, a practice which he found niggardly and indelicate; the other, the presence of a loutish little boy called Hugh Dalton.[3]

In his last year Ronald was head of the school and a prefect. He was never good at cricket or football, but his incapacity was not of a kind to cause ridicule. He was delicate, agile, and plucky; happy in the water. He had an acrobatic gift of balance which later made him an expert at the delicate arts of punting a canoe, walking on a garden roller, going upstairs on a pogo stick, and holding the attention of a class of seminarists while he tilted his chair, raised his feet from the ground, and, gravely addressing them, remained poised for minutes at a time on its back legs. Scholarship was respected at Summer Fields. Dr Williams was then in early middle

[1] R. A. Knox, *A Spiritual Aenid* (1918), p. 11.
[2] The two elder sons of Lord Desborough and the elder son of Sir John Horner of Mells.
[3] Chancellor of the Exchequer 1945.

age. His rivals spoke jealously of him as a 'crammer'. When he died forty-three years later Ronald wrote to *The Times*[1] to refute this charge. 'He was an amazingly successful educationist,' Ronald said, 'with a genius for spotting. . . . But I never persuaded myself that we only got a shop-window education. I believe we had an admirable grounding, that steeping of the mind in the first elements without which education never seems to "take".'

Dr Williams had an enviable insight into examiners' minds. Ronald recalled how after breakfast at the White Hart at Windsor, where he was conducting his scholarship boys, he said: 'Let's see, what have you got this morning? History and Geography. Of course there's been all this talk of federating Australia. I suppose you all know the provinces of Australia and their capitals, but we'll just pass it once round.' 'So,' Ronald continued, 'we passed it once round and it was the first question on the sheet that faced us in Upper School.'

Ronald's letters from Summer Fields lack the naïvety that gives charm to the correspondence of some less competent children. With correct spelling and grammar he records the events of the week, his place in form, the amount of the Sunday offertory, his intention of writing a play in Greek – 'please excuse my not putting in accents'. In one letter he describes the presentation of a wedding present to an assistant master: 'One of us made a little address made up by me' – the first blade in a lush field of vicarious oratory. In later years how many flower-shows were opened, how many healths proposed, how many prizes distributed by Ronald's friends in the elegant speeches he wrote for them!

The South African War, which broke out at the beginning of his last year at Summer Fields, was a keen excitement to Ronald. He had no scruples about the morality or political wisdom of the undertaking. Here was something more vivid than the remote misadventures of Publius and Amilla; something as actual as Troy and Philippi. As the flags were moved on the schoolroom war-map he celebrated the campaign of 1900 in a variety of manners and metres:

> *Prepare all honours known in History*
> *And sing the paean of our noble French!*
> *For he has freed the town of Kimberley*
> *Where countless dazzling diamonds lie hid . . .*

And:

[1] March 15th 1941.

> Now every English heart beats high
> Exulting in its ecstasy
> And throbbing fast with glee
> For Ladysmith has been relieved
> The great attempt has been achieved
> And White's brave men are free . . .

And:

> Est a militibus jam capta Pretoria nostris
> Nec minus hinc longe denique Kruger abest
> Oribus Anglorum laudentur nomina Bobbis . . .

And:

> Mafeking relieved! The lost are found again
> The fourth great link in the relieving chain . . .

And:

> 'Charge! Forward' cried the Colonel. Up he sprang
> And pierced by hostile bullets fell again
> But through our very souls the order rang
> And we were charging up the slope amain . . .

And:

> Thou art taken, Thou art taken,
> Such proud city is thy doom.
> Buller ever presses round thee
> Taken, taken Wakkerstroom . . .

No doubt there was a strong infection of the genuine patriotic sentiment then rampant in the school, but there is nothing artless about these imitative and versatile juvenilia. It is thus that the creative artist first makes himself known more often than in moods of inarticulate emotion. They were exercises. He was learning the might and scope of the English language. All his life he found it easiest to express his thoughts in parody and needed special exertion and discipline to write *in propria persona* (a form of reticence he had in common with the very different boy who was to become his particular rival and friend at Eton, Patrick Shaw-Stewart). Until his last years he had the itch, when confronted with any literary form, to have a shot at doing the same thing better. Now at the age of twelve, it is painful to record, he included in his war poems an ode to Lord Roberts which began:

Dear old Bobby! once again
You begin a fresh campaign
(Bobby you're a good 'un)
Once again your skill comes in
Once again you go and win
(Bobby you're a good 'un.)

By such shameless and inept experiments is the mastery of a very difficult language achieved.

There is no reason to think that at this age Ronald had any intention to become a clergyman. It was in his blood but of his brothers, Wilfred went into the Civil Service before becoming the devout and clever theologian of his later years, Dillwyn lived and died an agnostic, and Eddie was a layman of conventional observances and open mind. Ronald was not drawn to the Anglican ministry as he saw it at Creeton and Birmingham; the attraction quickened only when the first light of Anglo-Catholicism gave him a glimpse of priesthood. As a small boy he certainly was not aware of anything that could be called 'a religious vocation'. His ancestry and upbringing made the Church seem a natural profession, but not an attractive one. He was taught Divinity as a school subject and excelled in it as in all school subjects. He enjoyed the hymns in chapel and, like many Anglicans, derived from them much of his earliest devotional and theological grounding. He was naturally docile, truthful,[1] and industrious. He composed a prayer for himself and said it daily: 'O God, I thank thee that thou hast heard all my prayers and I pray thee that thou wilt forgive me for all my sins and that the hymns may be nice, and that I may attend today, and ever hereafter. Amen.'[2] He had little to accuse himself of except day-dreaming, but he records that at that age, if ever, he experienced full contrition for his small faults. 'I do not think,' he wrote,[3] 'people with long memories and candid minds will find this description unnatural; the age of reason brings a sense of responsibility, before adolescence overlays it with the temptation to spiritual carelessness.

In September 1900 Ronald entered College at Eton.

---

[1] In the year 1897, he recorded in the *Universe*, October 15th 1926, he told a lie; the last 'real crash lie, *locutio contra mentem*', of his life.

[2] R. A. Knox, *A Spiritual Aeneid*, p. 12. [3] Ibid.

Chapter Three

EDUCATION

1900–1906

Ronald's first letter to his father from Eton, written on September 30th 1900, begins: 'Dear Father, I like Eton awfully.' His first letter to his stepmother, written a week earlier, had ended: '*P.S. Floreat Etona.*' It was a life-long love.

In 1917 he wrote in *A Spiritual Aeneid*: 'Leaving Eton I felt definitely as a tragedy; Oxford, in spite of its comparative freedom and historic tradition, was always a very poor second best.'

In July 1919, speaking at a Catholic Old Etonian Dinner[1] he said:

> The sentiment we feel towards Eton and the sentiment we feel towards the Church have something of a causal connexion.
>
> Those who were Catholic at school owe a special debt of gratitude to Eton because, in her infinite variety, she let them go their way, not fearing that, just because they worshipped apart from Henry's Chapel, they would be any the less Etonian for that.
>
> In the Church, as at Eton, it is the silent conspiracy of thousands of free human wills that secures unity and, for the sake of unity, uniformity . . .
>
> If she [the Church] did show something of that haphazard and almost wilful heterogeneity which is the mark of spontaneous growth, instead of the jerry-built monotony which others seemed to expect of their religion, we did not for that reason suppose that she was a ruin, to be visited only in the spirit of the tourist . . . and if some of that knowledge in us did not date from Eton, I can only say that in our Eton days we must have been very slow to learn.

Eton was the scene of Ronald's brilliant intellectual development and of his ardent and undying friendships. Most candid Englishmen recognize

---

[1] The Old Etonian Catholic Association holds dinners in London during Lord's week, when Ronald was often an honoured guest. But though he was delighted to take part in it as a social event and sometimes spoke anxiously of the dearth of Old Etonian priests to carry on the tradition of saying Mass for the members, he refused in 1953 to join in the project to endow a Catholic chaplaincy for the school.

it as a school *sui generis* which marks the majority of its sons with a peculiar Englishry, genial, confident, humorous, and reticent; which gives to each as little or as much learning as his abilities and tastes demand; which while correcting affectation allows the genuine eccentric to go his own way unmolested; which nourishes its rare favourites – among whom Ronald was immediately numbered – in a rich and humane traditional culture which admits no rival. The fact that it was the training ground of Edwardian plutocracy, that it afforded early intimacy with the sons of the powerful and opened the ranks of privilege to the ambitious, meant nothing to Ronald. The only specific ambition which he briefly entertained was not an exorbitant one – to become one of the 'conducts' or chaplains who sang the services in chapel – not exorbitant, that is to say, for anyone but Ronald, whose musical talents were meagre. This ambition sprang from his wish to spend all his days at Eton.

The illustrious historical associations of the school counted for much, but he saw the arcadia of Gray and the battle-school of Wellington transfigured by the medieval past. Our Lady's lilies were blazoned on the arms; her Assumption was exalted in the roof. It was the pious foundation of the 'Sorrowful King', Henry VI, with whom in his Anglican days he divided a romantic attachment to King Charles I. In his years at Ware – the farthest he ever travelled from Eton – when he knew little of the complicated processes of the Congregation of Rites, he spent much time in collaboration with Sir Shane Leslie in preparing and translating the evidence of Henry's miracles, in the hope that the Cause of Canonization, abandoned at the Reformation, might be reopened.[1] When he knew more of the bureaucracy of the Church he realized that, humanly speaking, the project was doomed to fail for lack of powerful support, but he never cooled in devotion to the patron of his boyhood.

Many years later, when he had seen a great deal of men from other schools, he was more than once consulted by Old Etonian Catholic converts about the education of their sons. His answers read almost as a palinode of the speech of 1919:

> The Catholics I tried to look after between 1926 and 1939 [he wrote to one father], seemed to me to practise all right if they came from good homes (not always otherwise) and, of course, they were very nice and easy for me to get on with, but they seemed neither to have nor to acquire a Catholic atmosphere. . . . In all my time there I never suggested one of them as suitable candidates for office in the Newman Society, because I

---

[1] *The Miracles of King Henry the Sixth*, 1923.

didn't think they'd take to it. . . . It did seem to me that for want of a Catholic background they were specially liable to get into trouble over their marriage arrangements. . . . I don't know if you would agree, but it seems to me that the Chapel and all that went with it were an integral part of the formation Eton gave me, and I would have felt hopelessly lopsided if I'd had to go off and worship somewhere else.

And in the same sense to another inquirer:

I've known a lot of O.K. Catholics and liked most of them; but I don't really think they are ever quite satisfactory as Catholics – or even as Etonians. They fall between two stools; as Catholics, timid and unin-structed; as Etonians, unintegrated.

But these letters should be read with the remembrance that the Catholic Hierarchy were engaged in an exhausting campaign to preserve the Church Schools from absorption by the State. In loyalty to them Ronald could hardly encourage the rich to observe different precepts from the poor.

Before Ronald went to Oxford as chaplain, there was a tentative suggestion by some Catholic parents that a Catholic House should be founded at Eton. Ronald was spoken of as the obvious Housemaster. Certainly no formal application was ever made either to Eton or to the Hierarchy. It is not known how the school would have responded. Such members of the Hierarchy as were unofficially consulted made it plain that they would regard the innovation as an intolerable injustice to the existing Catholic Public Schools. There is no evidence that the matter was ever broached to Ronald. It may be assumed that his answer would have been that of the Bishops. When sentiment and principle were in conflict, sentiment was always ignored.

For him to live, not exclusively, with people who were 'very nice and easy to get on with' was an innocent and necessary mitigation of the scholar's lonely life; something of the same order as his pipe of tobacco.

I am not going to decide [he once wrote to Sir Arnold Lunn] whether the average Catholic Mexican is what you call 'a better man' than the average Protestant Englishman. I do not know – I know which I would rather go for a walking tour with, but that is not the same thing. I prefer Englishmen to the natives of any other country in the world, but that is not going to do them much good, poor dears, at the Day of Judgment.[1]

---

[1] Ronald Knox and Arnold Lunn, *Difficulties* (1932), p. 229.

That expresses his final, mature verdict on his school; Etonians were not 'better men' than others, but he preferred them to any on earth.

When he entered the Catholic priesthood, he left the world where Etonians are generally preferred for one where they are slightly suspect. But his love of his school remained as strong and deep as ever.

2

By the end of the nineteenth century Eton had assumed its present form. J. J. Hornby was Provost and Edmond Warre Headmaster. They had ruled successively for forty-two years, during which the changes proposed by the Royal Commission of 1861 had been fully effected. During their time the school grew greatly in numbers, the curriculum was somewhat modernized, many new buildings were erected, and Agar's Plough was planted. By 1900 Warre's great powers were failing. He lived to be eighty-three, but he resigned from the headmastership during Ronald's time. The voice of neither man was distinctly audible in chapel – the one for its softness, the other for its resonance. They were figures of awe rather than of direct influence. Ronald's high gifts of mimicry were employed on their sermons; particularly on Warre's famous dictum: 'Dere's an evil elephant ("Element") come into de school. Nobody saw it come in. It came in bit by bit. But we must stamp on it and destroy it. It's de elephant of bettin' and gambling.'[1] The Master in College was very much more important. In Ronald's third year Cyril Alington[2] succeeded Goodhart in this office. He had been brought to Eton at the instigation of Donaldson,[3] Ford,[4] and Bowlby[5] with the express purpose of stimulating the religious life of the school. His sermons were refreshingly original in tone and highly popular. He professed a rather vague form of doctrine and wrote that Ronald in his last years at school had 'an excess of Faith',[6] but they became friends for life. Ronald dedicated his first book, *Signa Severa*, to Alington in stanzas which conclude:

[1] L. E. Jones, *A Victorian Boyhood* (1955), p. 177. Sir Lawrence Jones was an Oppidan, senior to Ronald. No doubt this version of Warre's sermon was much quoted, and Ronald later excelled in verisimilitude.

[2] Headmaster of Shrewsbury 1908, Headmaster of Eton 1916, Dean of Durham 1933.

[3] Rev. Stuart Donaldson, D.D., later Master of Magdalene, Cambridge.

[4] Rev. Lionel Ford. Headmaster of Harrow 1910, Dean of York 1925.

[5] Rev. Henry Bowlby. Headmaster of Lancing 1909, Canon of Chichester 1925.

[6] C. A. Alington, *A Dean's Apology* (1952).

Yet since I cannot choose but own
Some master on my primal page
Since somebody must needs atone
For spurring on my tender age,
I ask myself the question; 'Who
Could be more suitable than you?'

You, in whose first connubial bliss[1]
My verses were the only jar,
Who half incited me to this,
Will surely let me go so far
As write three letters none can blame –
The three initials of your name.

A multitude of Etonian memoirs have left vivid accounts of the masters of this period. Lyttelton, who succeeded Warre in 1905, was not a scholar of the calibre of the best of his staff, and commanded little respect from VI Form. A. C. Benson did not take in Ronald, who wrote in a letter that he 'distrusted' him 'profoundly'. For all the other masters with whom he came into touch he had respect and affection, and they rejoiced in the most ready mind they had ever met. Another Eton name must be added to those who influenced him; that of Miss Ward, the Matron in College. Ronald was a delicate boy and often in need of her attention. She was also a High Churchwoman and Ronald's first confidante in his religious adventures. Bowlby prepared Ronald for Confirmation and was able to do so without suggesting any of the Tractarian ideas which he later exemplified as Headmaster at Lancing. In his first half Ronald was 'up to' Ford in the lower division of V Form. 'Select Divisions', the system by which classes in each 'Block' were graded according to performance in the previous Trials, were introduced at the end of Ronald's second year, with the result that he was brought into successful competition with the scholars of the 1899 election. He was on the 'Newcastle Select' in 1903, two years and two halves after his entry into the school; an exceptional promotion into company with his brother Dillwyn, Daniel Macmillan, and others three years his senior. In 1904 he was *proxime accessit* to Macmillan for the Newcastle.

In his last two years he carried off the Harvey Verse Prize, the Latin Essay, and the Davies Scholarship; he was editor of the *Chronicle*, President

---

[1] Cyril Alington married while he was Master in College. Ronald wrote *A Prospective Epithalamium* for the occasion. *Signa Severa*, p. 7.

of the Essay Society and of the Shakespeare Society, and Secretary of College Debating Society.

The Newcastle Scholarship was the single notable reverse in Ronald's otherwise almost uninterrupted course of success at Eton.

There came to College in the election of 1901 a boy who differed from Ronald in almost every respect except intellectual brilliance, Patrick Shaw-Stewart, the younger son of a Major-General of small private means. He came to Eton from a day-school and was keenly aware of the lack of the friends already made at schools like Summer Fields, who surrounded Ronald among Collegers and Oppidans. For his first two years at Eton he was by his own account lonely and homesick, a failure at cricket, a pale, insignificant, rather bitter boy. He referred in a letter of November 10th 1903 to Henry VI as 'that eminently uninteresting monarch'.[1] A. C. Benson softened him slightly – later, at Balliol, when he showed signs of 'mellowing', Julian Grenfell remarked that he preferred Patrick 'pure mandrill' – and Hugh Macnaughten sharpened his wits and enlarged his appreciation of the classics. At Christmas 1903 he scored a record of 1,290 marks out of a possible 1,450 in Trials. This should have put him into First Hundred and established his order so as to make him, when his time came, Captain of the School. His promotion was, however, deferred, and next half he was second. This seemed to nullify his hopes of the captaincy – the only way by which an unathletic and not very popular Colleger could hope to enter 'Pop', the self-elected Eton Society of twenty-four in which all privilege and glory culminates. Shaw-Stewart was consumed with ambition. Those who knew him only superficially were inclined to regard him merely as a 'Scotchman on the make'. As will appear, he had other, endearing qualities which he hid from all but his intimates. He set grimly to work, and in the summer of 1904 won the Reynolds Scholarship over the heads of Macmillan and Ronald, but no one considered him a serious rival for the Newcastle. It was a tradition that the Newcastle Scholar, if not in VI Form at the time, was immediately promoted. Only thus could he disturb the order established on his promotion to First Hundred and put himself in the lead for the captaincy. The classical papers were part of the general curriculum and not susceptible of special cramming. The Divinity papers dealt with specific books. Already an avowed agnostic, he worked feverishly at the Scriptures and at Church History; so feverishly that his hair fell out (it grew again); so feverishly that he decisively defeated Ronald, who was leading in classics, and carried off the

[1] Ronald Knox, *Patrick Shaw-Stewart* (1920), p. 26.

prize. On hearing the result, Ronald sat down and read the *Book of Job* straight through; Shaw-Stewart gave up work for the next four years.

That autumn both boys sat for the Balliol scholarship; Ronald won the first and Shaw-Stewart the third. Strachan-Davidson, writing from Balliol in the absence of the Master, Caird, to announce Ronald's scholarship said: 'His knowledge is so remarkable that we feel he should do little work after he has got the Newcastle – in fact one of my colleagues suggests that he had better go a voyage round the world and forget it all.' But when Ronald was a certainty for the Newcastle he was struck ill and unable to sit. It was then that Shaw-Stewart revealed a glimpse of the chivalrous soldier who, in the Hood Battalion, was to emerge from his heavy, deliberately assumed disguise of the ambitious cynic. He went privately to the Provost and proposed that he should resign the Newcastle in favour of last year's *proxime accessit*, Ronald, and himself sit again without preparation. The offer was refused. No one, least of all Ronald, knew of it until after his death. This action illustrates what it was besides wit which endeared him to the most generous souls of his generation.

The Newcastle result, though promoting Shaw-Stewart, did not affect Ronald's place in the school, and he became Captain in due course for his last two halves. He had already, without a colour, been elected to 'Pop' by force of his personal charm. At no stage of his life did he seek friends; they sought him. The courtships and lobbying that preceded many elections to 'Pop' were totally foreign to Ronald's habits and aims. Things did not move quite so smoothly for Shaw-Stewart. A boy senior to him, who was expected to leave after the summer of 1906, decided to stay on, depriving him of the captaincy. He could no longer enter 'Pop' *ex officio*. It was, as he expressed it,[1] 'a matter of vital anxiety'. 'Pop' varies a little in character from year to year. In 1906, under the influence of Ronald, Edward Homer, Julian Grenfell, and Charles Lister,[2] it ceased to be exclusively athletic and enjoyed a leavening of what Shaw-Stewart scrupulously spelt 'intelligentzya'. He had two colours and a rather limited popularity among Oppidans. He set to work making friends as assiduously as he had crammed his Divinity – and as successfully. He had an engaging smile (which showed much of his gums). All that half he smiled continuously. He was elected. Ronald and his friends went up to the university. Shaw-Stewart remained to enjoy his Olympian ease, but his predominant feeling was one of disappointment. Now that 'the giants' had departed,

[1] *Patrick Shaw-Stewart* (1920), p. 20.
[2] Second son of the fourth and last Baron Ribblesdale.

success had lost its lustre. His idleness became conspicuous, and after one half he left, at his tutor's suggestion, to take up his Balliol scholarship in a bye-term and to rejoin his friends.

3

Ronald's father seems never to have visited him at Eton, and his stepmother once only, but they followed his career with attention and pride. His letters home – all at any rate which have been preserved – are rather cool in tone; and often humorous in intent, alternating a parody of nursery speech with an extravagant pedantry.

The following extracts indicate their character and Ronald's changing interests:

Undated (probably September 1901). To his sister Ethel –

I am dying to know how your photograph of me gracefully propped like a belated noctivagous reveller against the corrugated lithological specimen in the garden of our delightful country residence [one of the houses taken for the family summer holidays] so exquisitely named in the sonorous nomenclature of our somewhat verbose Cymric neighbours Glan Gwynnant, has come out in printing.

February 17th 1902. To Mrs Knox –

I have counted my tickets [a collection of railway tickets] and find I have 201 English ones.

February 23rd 1902. To Mrs Knox –

I went round Windsor Castle without seeing a single chair I should like to sit on. A throne there had a sort of chevaux de frise to stick into the back of one's knees. One might make a rhyme out of that.

March 7th 1902. To Mrs Knox –

I think it was very unkind of you to refer to dental ablutions. My chilblains are utterly perished off the face of my hands . . . the weather has been so mild that no further objectionable congelations have resulted.

June 6th 1902. To Mrs Knox (end of War in South Africa) –

I was upstairs emptying my bath when I heard from tearoom the noise of an 'oragger' (Oration) caused by the juxtaposition of knees with tables, feet with floors and other vociferous combinations of sound. I instantly exclaimed to myself 'There is war in the camp' and then rushed downstairs and asked someone 'Is it peace, Jehu?' . . . Someone hung out a Boer flag from one of Mr Broadbent's windows and a crowd collected round it breaking 7 panes of glass. . . . I assembled in Mozley's room and sang, together with other more or less unmusical associates God Save the King and a verse of British Grenadiers.

Undated. To Mrs Knox. (For the Eton–Harrow match at Lords 1902 he stayed with his friend Merton – his first recorded visit to London.) –

Merton's house is an extremely high but rather narrow place with a very imposing interior. Their meals are a sort of succession of entrées. I'm sure I was very polite. Our first dinner (late) there was a motorist, Mr White, who had been going 60 miles an hour in a motor-car of his. I rather pity Merton, his mother is so very particular about what he eats. When he eats something he oughtn't to his mother jabbers in French so I shan't hear; so Merton talked to Mr White in Latin of a peculiar form, quite his own.

I did look so smart siding about in a white waistcoat, carefully arranged blue tie with a carnation for a button hole and a stick with a blue tassel.

October 13th 1902. To Bishop Knox –

I was stricken by a disease (not very fell) . . . and amused myself in bed doing other people's construes for them. But I didn't confine myself to that; I read about 40 chapters of the Halicarnassian, 3 cantos of the Inferno, and a little Petrarch without a dictionary. . . . I have about 330 tickets, costing in all about 28 or 29£ (that is they cost that when new).

February 14th 1903. To Bishop and Mrs Knox –

Thank you very much for your (Father's) MS notes on The Romans. Dilly uses them more than I do. . . . In fact (but this is in strictest confidence) Dilly copied down a large splodge of one in his own Sunday Questions without acknowledging it.

He describes in detail, with a plan, the arrangement of his room 'a very nice reddy-brown print of Rembrandt, an Indian idol, a potted palm'.

I have been very bold. Having heard Marie Corelli run down by everyone I have met . . . I read one. . . . It did sort of leave my eyes watery at the end but then it was in front of a very hot fire. Besides, it was about a little boy who was neglected by his parents, a subject which always attracts my warmest sympathy.

October 5th 1903. To Mrs Knox –

Could you please send in addition to the Aristotle and the Welsh Grammar, my very nice clean pretty thick pair of brown gloves with fluffy bluey grey softitude inside which comes off on your hands. Mr Luxmore gave me a tea like this (1) lovely salad with fish in it (2) cold chicken and ham (3) rich pudding and (4) equally rich cake! . . . I am going to University Extension lectures by Prof. Churton Collins on Tennyson, Browning and Matthew Arnold; my tutor is paying instead of giving me a prize for work last year.

In that autumn Bishop Knox was appointed to the see of Manchester. He received A. J. Balfour's letter on September 20th and in his own words[1]

answered in the affirmative by return of post. No doubt some will think that I ought to have taken at least a week for consulting friends and for prayer and meditation. . . . Mr Balfour's position, at the moment, was extremely hazardous. The King at Marienbad was already coquetting with Campbell-Bannerman. I felt, and still feel, no compunction over the promptness of my answer.

The official announcement, however, was delayed until October 8th, when Ronald first heard the news from *The Times*. He was delighted and lapsed into nursery speech in his letter of congratulation with 'I s'pose', ''cos', 'I don't feel hardly as if it was all right', and other evidences of euphoria.

October 14th 1903. To Mrs Knox –

I spent almost 2 hours on Monday finding out facts about Manchester in School Library. . . . I judge [the Cathedral] there is much nicer inside than out. I wish there was a Close though.

I am afraid I also looked up in Whitaker to see something else. But then you see Hamilton is always very keen to know how far the fatal opulence of bishops really extends. (1) When do we move? (2) Where shall we then be living? (3) Shall we keep the same servants and all the same household so to speak?

I hope you don't think me snobbish and Mrs Proudieish for asking these questions, but I am so impatient somehow I hardly know how I shall last out the half without seeing what it's like.

[1] E. A. Knox, op. cit., p. 207.

October 21st 1903. To Bishop Knox –

I didn't really think you'd be much better off, only I looked up to see, just to see how much bishops were supposed to have. But I know once before I asked Mother some sort of question about if you were made an unsuffragan bishop, and she said it wouldn't make much difference; it would make much more if we got scholarships. But this time Hamilton was really anxious to know and I think a little disappointed when I told him of your answer. . . . I can't help taking an interest in bishoprics generally. But if you're too busy to tell me, or don't like to talk about it, or don't like me to talk about it, I won't write any more; only your explanation only wuddled me deeper. Do you mean to say that . . . if, when Bishop Grantly died, Mr Crawley of Hogglestock had been offered the bishopric of Barchester, would he have had to refuse 'cos he was too poor? . . . I don't mind about your being better off, but I can't see why any bishop should be worse off. . . .

November 2nd 1903. To Bishop Knox –

Thank you very much for your reassuring letter. You speak as if keeping a carriage was a necessary expense without any remuneration; but if we have a carriage, we save cab fares. Again, if we keep a garden, no more need to buy vegetables. Even extra hospitality has always its remains. . . . So we are practically better off. About the house sounds more serious. . . . I shall be ready to say *Sperabam meliora sed et pejora timebam* (a line of my own).

After the move to Manchester the series of Eton letters comes to an end. Four only have survived.

There is an undated letter to his father presumably belonging to that winter which shows a keen interest in diocesan affairs:

I am very sorry to hear that there is anyone so despicable as to disapprove of Mr Wright[1] being Canon. . . . The Dean and Chapter haven't any reason to object if they know nothing of Mr Wright; and if they know anything of him much less. . . . I have 4 reasons for taking this view (1) because you would be sure to get a suitable person anyhow (2) because I am sure Mr Wright is a suitable person (3) because I should be inclined to back a Bishop anyhow and (4) legally, because I'm quite sure your arguments are right. It is very grand getting a letter from the Athenaeum. I didn't know you belonged to it . . . believe me.

Though all Manchester should rise in arms against you,
Ever your very loving little son.
R. Arbuthnott Knox

---

[1] Bishop Knox's former pupil and curate, later Archbishop of Sydney.

March 27th 1904. To Mrs Knox –

I went up for leave to Hamilton yesterday. . . . I went into the new R.C. Cathedral at Westminster, and wasn't shocked.

July 1st 1904. To Mrs Knox –

They spelt Arbuthnott as Arbuthnot round the edge of the [Newcastle, proxime accessit] medal.

November 11th 1904. To Mrs Knox –

I should like books for presents; obscurer English poets, esp. before and just after the Revolution. Prose people like Landor and de Quincey, French books, Italian books, Classical books of almost any kind, for instance there is a new life of D. G. Rossetti for 7s. 6d. . . . or modern poetry . . . the only objection to such books being this that my principles rather disapprove of the tendency of books to grow smaller for fear that at some time they may disappear, and so I would rather have octavo books than duodecimos. . . .

4

There was no reminiscence of Barchester in Bishopscourt, the Knoxes' new and final home.[1] It stood two miles from the centre of the city in three acres of sooty gardens behind pretentious gates, lodges, and a short sweep of drive. Bishop Fraser, the second Bishop of Manchester, had bought it in the 'sixties in place of the more remote and more palatial Mauldeth Hall which his predecessor had occupied. It had been designed as the villa of a commercial magnate uncertain about his style of living. It had a chapel but no larder. No room faced south. There was one bath in an attic. The chaplain had to use a passageroom next to the butler's pantry. There were rats everywhere. 'Outside like a prison, inside like a nunnery,' one of the servants remarked. Having enumerated the disadvantages, Bishop Knox concludes his description: 'I do not know that any better home for a bishop's work could have been procured in or near Manchester.[2] Mrs Knox did what she could, but the structure defied the decorator. It remained an excessively ugly and inconvenient house, but one into which the Knoxes fitted very happily; they had a native toughness.

Ethel lived for the most part at home; Winifred was at Lady Margaret

---

[1] The house was badly damaged by bombs in 1942 and is now used for offices.
[2] E. A. Knox, op. cit., p. 221.

Hall, Oxford; Edmund, already showing signs of frivolity and extravagance, at Corpus; Dillwyn at King's College, Cambridge; Wilfred at Rugby. There was a sort of dank smoking-room off a passage at Bishopscourt which was given over to the boys; ordinands who strayed there were not made welcome. It was in this room that most of Ronald's holiday life centred.

The family were alone very seldom now, except on their summer holidays. There was a continual round of official hospitality, clerical and lay, the Judges of Assize, Examining Chaplains, diocesan clergy, town councillors. To all these Mrs Knox dispensed half-cooked mutton and sour claret with an informal grace which never failed to charm, while the sons, no longer prone to fisticuffs, enjoyed vehement argument and competition. Whatever friends they were making elsewhere, they remained not only affectionate but also deeply interested in one another.

Ronald was naturally hospitable. There had been little room for visitors at St Philip's Rectory and an uncertain welcome in that compact and critical young family, but by the time of the move to Manchester, where the elder Knoxes were tamed and mature and the Bishop's rather sombre hospitality was unstinted, Ronald began asking his friends to stay and visiting them in return. One of the first to come was Charles Lister, whose home at Gisburne was not far distant in miles but worlds apart in character. To Lister, who was indifferent to physical comfort, life at Bishopcourt was bizarre and exhilarating. On his first visit he disgraced himself and the Bishop by leaping the barrier at the Hippodrome and mounting a giant turtle in a tank. He was sent home, but he came again and often. Ronald was a frequent visitor at Gisburne. All the Listers were very tall and very beautiful, like their father, the last Lord Ribblesdale, whose portrait by Sargent jauntily dominates its room in the National Gallery. It is unlikely that Ronald ever met the elder son, Tommy, who served as a soldier first in South Africa, then in India, and was killed in January 1904 in Somaliland. Laura, a child at the time of Ronald's first visit, was to become an important figure in his middle years. She remembers him at this time as seeming almost *chétif* in their robust and carefree circle; so small and frail as he waved them off to the meet on hunting days and slipped back alone to the library; so quiet at table among the flashing, fashionable chatter of the visiting Tennants; so uncertain of his future among these heirs of power and privilege; an unlikely friend for Charles, but a very close one and a strong influence.

Soon Ronald's Christmas and Easter holidays were full of engagements. The summer remained for some years dedicated to family union. The question of its location was broached at Christmas and debated at Easter. Every year with their eight bicycles, their golf clubs, book-boxes, fishing-rods, and tennis rackets they migrated for six weeks to some large, remote, inexpensive house; private school or rectory, often a combination of the two. 'Everyone seemed in any holidays either to be reading for an examination or a scholarship,' Winifred Peck records. She remembers Ronald on the advice of his tutor ploughing through Meredith with far greater effort than through a Greek text, remarking gloomily at luncheon that he had 'done up to' page 61 of *The Egoist*.

> We ourselves [she writes] were only united in the holidays and however precarious that union might be with daily bickerings we presented a solid front against intruders. . . . we imagined that other people might think we were peculiar and yet we were quite sure that our family stand-point on almost any question was absolutely and unquestionably right.

There were callers, but Mrs Knox solved the problem of social relations by allowing the cards to collect until the last day of the holidays and then driving out in white gloves and a large hat to return them all in a single round.

It is worthy of note that the last surviving letter for many years from Ronald to his father should be that quoted above in which they were in complete sympathy on a matter of ecclesiastical policy. Family papers are often destroyed in a move, particularly in a move to a smaller house, but the Knoxes were moving into a larger. Ronald's letters to his father up till Christmas 1903 were carefully preserved; after that there are none. Posterity must regret this break in a series coming just at the time when Ronald was emerging from boyhood, when his powers of expression and observation were developing, his humour maturing, his wit being pol-ished; when he had so much to record of real importance to the student of his history. No doubt he did record it week by week in ever more felicitous language. He had no secrets from his father, no problems he was not eager to discuss, but his development was in a direction which his father deplored and came to regard as disastrous. In later years the Bishop reproached himself that he had been unable to keep his children in his own theological system. Ronald's defection from the Church of England, as will be seen, was a deep personal sorrow to him. It may well be that the Bishop looked back on those last years at Eton as the source of his failure; when Ronald's mind was pliable and his senses tingling with every new impression; when there was complete confidence between them both, the Bishop had been too busy with his new duties to shield him from the dangers to which he eventually succumbed. It may be that Ronald's letters in those years made unendurably painful reading. Sympathy is due to him if he decided to destroy the evidence, for Ronald himself designates Christmas Day 1903 as the birth of his Catholicism.

The processes of change in Ronald's religious opinions have been so precisely set out in *A Spiritual Aeneid* that the biographer need only follow the autobiographer.

Ronald, who was so very far from being an aesthete, who all his life distrusted and suppressed the emotional attractions of his religion, was first drawn to Catholicism by a work quite empty of polemics, that was compounded of aesthetic and emotional appeal of a kind which most Catholics would condemn as second-rate; R. H. Benson's *The Light Invisible*. Benson had lately become a Roman Catholic, but the book was written while he was still an Anglican. The tone is occult rather than genuinely mystical, but it presented Ronald for the first time with the ideas of the Virgin Mary as a central figure of devotion and of the priesthood as a peculiar state whose function was not primarily administrative, exhortatory, or exemplary, but sacramental. The ideas came to him in picturesque trappings and (he was not yet sixteen) fired his imagination.

Next half he was sitting for the Newcastle Scholarship for the first time. One of the set books was Wakeman's *History of the Church of England*, a book culminating in the narrative of the early Tractarian controversies and very slightly tinged by its author's Tractarian sympathies. To Etonians of Ronald's generation the estimable George Augustus Selwyn (a less romantic character than Ronald's own grandfather Thomas French) had become a joke. Wakeman provided new heroes for his worship and stirred his sympathies for the many unkindnesses suffered in the Oxford Movement by intractable clergymen.

There was much genuine, unobtrusive piety among certain Etonians of that time – Julian Grenfell regularly read *The Imitation of Christ* from the age of thirteen. There was also a distinct High Church set of boys who came from ritualistic homes. In the summer of 1904 Ronald began to seek them out. One lent him *The Ritual Reason Why*, a 'severely didactic book' comprising 'elaborate explanations of the mystical meaning symbolized by amices, incense, the sign of the Cross'. 'Every symbol', he wrote,[1] 'was sacred to me; long before I had ever seen a ritualistic service I became a Ritualist.' He took in the *Church Times* and learned the names of those

---

[1] R. A. Knox, *A Spiritual Aeneid*, p. 38.

remote figures whom he already looked to as his leaders. The Matron in College was sympathetic. 'At home my views were known, and doubtless regretted, but never led to the smallest discontinuance of kindness on one side nor (I hope) of respect on the other – certainly not of affection on either.'[1] The expression 'doubtless regretted' seems to exclude any definite expostulation and to confirm the suggestion made above that the Bishop had not appreciated the force of Ronald's tendencies or exerted himself fully to deflect them.

Ronald became a weekly communicant, on alternate Sundays in chapel and 'the church down town'. This church was quite free of ritualistic innovations, but when there Ronald adopted a few of the gestures he had read about; in chapel he behaved precisely as the other boys. He did not haunt congenial churches in the holidays, especially not in Manchester. Only once before going up to Oxford did he attend a fully elaborated Anglo-Catholic service. When he went with his brother for a fortnight to Germany and Belgium he rejoiced in the architecture of the churches and studied them thoroughly, but he never attended a High Mass. The eccentricities of the local religion affected him no more than the eccentricities of the local diet.[2]

The fire which in 1903 destroyed Mr Kindersley's house, killing two small boys in particularly poignant circumstances, affected Ronald little. It left the Headmaster and House-master quite overcome with grief and many of the older boys shocked and sobered, but Ronald merely reflected that if he was to become a clergyman he would prefer a post which did not entail attendance at death-beds. Next year, however, in his newly-found piety, the long fatal illness of his friend Hugh Merton moved him to private ascetic exercises which cannot be attributed to any book he had read.

Ronald wrote a sonnet at this time which Alan Parsons[3] kept in his common-place book.[4]

> *I have an errand on a stony way,*
> *That rises darkly to the mountain height,*

---

[1] Ibid., p. 41.   [2] Ibid., p. 44.

[3] A friend from Summer Fields who was with Ronald at Eton and Oxford and an intimate member of the circle which formed round Julian Grenfell and Charles Lister. He was unfit for military service and survived the War. He married Viola Tree, niece of Sir Max Beerbohm and daughter of Sir Herbert Beerbohm Tree, the actor.

[4] *Alan Parsons' Book. A Story in anthology 1937*, p. 3. In October 1937 Ronald wrote to Lady Acton: 'Viola Parsons is asking my leave to publish a sonnet of mine in a book about her husband: it says I wrote it in 1904 but I can't make head or tail of it now – I suppose I must have written it.'

And, from that zenith, stretching thro' the night
Sinks to the valleys of eternal day.
And yet I weary not; for God, my Stay
Hath ever set before my straining sight
Some earthly beacon, whose celestial light
Tempts the numb-hearted traveller to delay.
And here I meet old friends, whom I have tried
Beneath the shadow of the chastening Sword,
And quaff sweet draughts of Memory; or abide
By the great gulf of Silence overawed,
And worship, falling on my knees beside
The everlighted beacons of the Lord.

It is plain why on literary grounds Ronald rejected these lines from *Signa Severa*,[1] but they are deeply interesting to the biographer. How much was the sixteen-year-old sonneteer seduced from his intention by the demands of rhyme? How much did he consciously define a spiritual predicament? For the meaning, though obscure, can only be this: Ronald had a hard road ahead and he was taking it easy, preferring to loiter among friends and sentimental memories, which offered mere reflections of the light that was his true goal. But these distractions came from God, and he was content to remain by the wayside, 'numbhearted' worshipping as the 'everlighted beacons of the Lord' what he in fact knew to be 'earthly beacons'.

These stilted lines give an exact description of the state which an unsympathetic critic might have ascribed to Ronald in the years 1910–15.

At about this time he made a resolution which he recorded in words which have aroused some curiosity:[2]

> I think I could still point to the precise place on 'Chamber Stairs' where I knelt down at the age of seventeen one evening and bound myself to a vow of celibacy. The uppermost thought in my mind was not that of virginity. I was not fleeing from the wickedness of the world I saw round me. . . . But at this time (as in common, I suppose, with many people) I was just beginning to form close and intimate friendships. I was just beginning also to realize that in many cases such friendships were likely to be dissolved through circumstances of separation after leaving school. And, conscious for the first time how much my nature craved for human sympathy and support, I thought it my obvious duty to deny myself that tenderest sympathy and support which a happy marriage would bring. I must have 'power to attend upon the Lord without impediment'.

[1] See below, p. 185.   [2] *A Spiritual Aeneid*, p. 48.

Of these 'close and intimate friendships' one may be identified as especially prompting this vow. There were two brothers in College, both of them junior to Ronald, who exercised a particular fascination over their seniors. They were high-minded boys who, perhaps, were unaware of the depth of the affection they aroused; their cult was pure and romantic; but a cult it was, which spread beyond College to a heterogeneous and infatuated group. A year after the event Charles Lister wrote to a friend at Cambridge that the day when the elder was 'pilled for Pop' was the saddest he ever spent and of the younger that he had 'lost all sense of proportion' about him. It was this younger brother whom Ronald loved, and he was successful in establishing his primacy in the little court of troubadours. It was not in chagrin that he made his drastic resolve; nor did he fear in this innocent adolescent love any threat of adult passion. But he saw in his very success in the half-humorous competition of the coterie, something which, if fully indulged, might be a distraction. Often in his life he was to inspire ardent devotion in men and women younger than himself; a devotion which he was by nature disposed to reciprocate. And he knew, without direction, that such affections, lawful and normal in others, would in his case be an obstruction of his spiritual life.

His illness in the Lent half of 1906 always stood very large in Ronald's Eton memories. He delighted to recall that he was 'prayed for in chapel'. When he was Captain of the School, liked by all, loved by his large circle of elected friends, spoken of in London as the cleverest Etonian in human memory, he was struck with peritonitis. Appendicitis was then in fashion and no longer regarded as particularly dangerous. Charles Lister had it at this time. But in Ronald's case the surgeon was doubtful whether he could safely operate. He was taken by ambulance to a London nursing-home and for several days was in great danger. A letter of condolence and good wishes was signed by forty Eton friends. Telegrams of inquiry came in from old Etonians at Oxford and Cambridge. The Bishop of London celebrated Holy Communion for him in his nursing-home on Easter Day. There are countless historic instances of light-hearted young men being dramatically sobered by the sudden aspect of death; Ronald, rather, was inebriated by this draught of fame. He would remark in later life that if he had died then it would have been at the apogee of his earthly glory.

A more important event for his future development was a visit from the vicar of St Mary Magdalen's, Munster Square, a centre of Anglo-Catholicism which many of the nurses attended. Ronald was thus for the first time brought into direct contact with the movement with which he was to identify himself for the next ten years.

He had been near death, but he made what was in that day a swift recovery. He was never robust, and for the rest of his life he suffered from a weak stomach; any change of diet, for richer or for poorer, was always liable to bring indigestion; he was twice operated on for rupture, and in his later years wore an abdominal belt. But he returned late to Eton to luxuriate in the last six weeks of the summer half.

They constituted the period of highest natural happiness in his life.

Power had no attraction for him. As a member of Sixth Form he had long had the authority to beat anyone in College; he never did so. He had twice been beaten during his first year at Eton and accepted it cheerfully. He had no doctrinaire disapproval of corporal punishment; a personal distaste, rather, for violence in himself and pain in others. College Sixth Form had supper together after night prayers, and it was then that boys who had fallen foul of a particular member were summoned for chastisement. Ronald always left the room on these occasions. There were certain general offences which it was the duty of the Captain of the School to punish. These Ronald delegated to the second boy. He was always entirely free from the desire to impose his will, but he enjoyed his popularity and prestige at Eton to the full.

He had now done everything possible in school work. In this last half he began his literary career. Before he became editor of the *Eton Chronicle* he had written for it, doing editorials for Nevile Bland[1] at five shillings each and contributing light verse. Lately he had had verses accepted by the *Cornhill*. In the summer of 1906 he issued his first book, *Signa Severa*,[2] bound in Eton blue and published by Spottiswoode, a collection of verses in English, Latin, and Greek, dating from July 1903 to May 1906. The little volume ran into six editions, but copies are jealously guarded by their owners and seldom come into the market. He continued to write verses during his last half and published a selection of them four years later in his Oxford book, *Juxta Salices*. His facility and ingenuity were dazzling. The best known and most quoted of these verses is 'The Wilderness', which appeared in the *Eton Poetry Book* and was learned by many generations of Etonians. It was written when he was sixteen, under the spur, it is said, of finding a neat rhyme for hollyhock. It is a fanciful plea for the planting of a garden in Schoolyard.

---

[1] Sir Nevile Bland, K.C.V.O.

[2] The title derives from Lucretius V l. 1190. '*luna dies et nox et noctis signa severa*', rendered by Cyril Bailey 'the stern signs of night'. Apart from the obvious pun on '*nox*' there seems little significance in a title which Ronald always refused to explain.

> *Powers of the Bursary* [it begins] *who on a cursory*
> *Glance at the ruinous state of Schoolyard,*
> *Made us to travel securely on gravel,* –
> *Is not that gravel a little too hard?*
> *Does not the scenery call for some greenery?*
> *Call for a garden, in which we might lop*
> *Calceolarias of suitable areas,*
> Worthy to rest on the bosoms of Pop?

and contains the lines:

> *Look you where Gaffney* [the School Clerk] *is tending the Daphne!*
> *Idly the pedagogues murmur and fret,*
> *Clamouring* 'Tolle hoc improbum hollyhock!'
> Quid est absentiae cum mignonette?

Allusive, ingenious, dandified, esoteric, almost the last flowering of the art of Praed and Calverley, the verses were at the time of writing already a little old-fashioned. English humour was taking another direction in the merrier, more droll, more whimsical, more slap-dash style of Chesterton, Belloc and Harry Graham; a style which can only be worn by the light of heart, which in a sadder and duller generation has diminished and almost run out in the no-man's-land where Grub Street and the nursery meet. It may well be that after fifty years these exquisite achievements will find new enthusiasts.

'During my last half,' Ronald wrote in *A Spiritual Aeneid*, 'I am afraid I was something of a nuisance to the authorities.'

Such misdemeanours as are remembered would not trouble any but a very delicate conscience. He annoyed the Headmaster by a joke at Hugh Dalton's expense. 'Sunday Questions' are an institution at Eton. Boys are required to write a short essay for their division masters on a set biblical theme. The Sixth Form do this for the Headmaster. The questions were sent to College, and Oppidan Sixth Formers sent fags to collect them. One Sunday Lyttelton asked: 'What are the oldest parts of the book of Exodus?' Ronald intercepted Dalton's copy and changed 'oldest' to 'oddest'. The astute young politician quoted the grosser texts from the book and attached to his paper the question in the form in which he had received it. Next day inquiries were made and Ronald confessed. Lyttelton, a humourless man, thought this conduct unbecoming to the Captain of the School.

Charles Lister led Ronald into two escapades. He had joined the Independent Labour Party and was an enthusiastic propagandist. Lord

Ribblesdale accepted this eccentricity calmly. He consulted Mr Balfour, who remarked that it was better than keeping selling-platers or actresses. He procured a number of Marxist treatises, but Lister was not seen to study them. He engaged himself, instead, in raising money for a man calling himself 'Father Gapon',[1] who had arrived in England and attained a newspaper notoriety by claiming to be an Orthodox priest exiled from Russia for unorthodox opinions, who was mysteriously able to distribute funds for the relief of distressed prisoners in Siberia. Lister collected £75 from College. More than this he hired a hall in the town and with Ronald's help organized a meeting at which Gapon was to speak. On the day Gapon failed to turn up, and the audience instead heard Viola Tree singing airs from *The Tempest*.

In the previous half Lister had shown a paradoxical respect for tradition by composing a petition to the Provost and Fellows expressing the –

> general desire throughout the School that the successor of the late Miss Evans should be a member of the Evans family and that the name should be preserved on the roll of House-masters. . . . Up till today the House has been handed down from generation to generation. Its position as an heirloom of the Evans family has been legally sanctioned by successive Governing bodies.
>
> . . . We do not pretend [the document concludes] to have any voice in School appointments. . . . we only claim to represent the general opinion of the School that Mr Evans would be the fittest person to hold a post of such responsibility.

It fell to Ronald, as Captain of the School, to present this petition, handsomely printed on a folio sheet of handmade paper and subscribed by 'Pop', the Sixth Form, and representatives of every House.

Mr Evans was not appointed.

In the paragraph quoted above, Ronald continues: 'My literary efforts tended to scurrility – I mean, to "personalities" which were not everywhere appreciated.'

He is referring to *The Outsider*, the magazine he founded, which appeared on June 16th and ran for six numbers until July 31st and sold briskly at sixpence a copy. The magazine was not suppressed by authority, but the fourth issue was prefaced by the note:

---

[1] He is said to have gambled away the proceeds of his tour and to have enlisted in the Imperial secret police.

The Editors of *The Outsider* wish to apologise unreservedly to the Head Master for the unauthorised use made of his name in their last issue. They regret that any exception should have been taken in other quarters to certain items, which, as they hasten to take this opportunity of emphasizing, were never intended to convey any offence.

The paragraph about the Headmaster was written by Ronald himself: 'The Head Master has acquitted himself from the charge of employing detectives at Eton, but Marsden, K. S., has as yet made no similar avowal.' The other offensive items were written by Charles Lister under the heading 'Hard Cases (*with apologies to "Vanity Fair"*)', the parody of a column dealing with social predicaments in which some good-natured satire is devoted to masters' hospitality. Of this mild row Patrick Shaw-Stewart wrote:[1]

> No one was fuller of the rather misdirected but not wholly deplorable spirit of levity and mischief which animated that paper than Julian [Grenfell]. He and Ronald Knox were peculiarly able to gauge and enjoy, with perhaps a little regret, its effect on the mind and attitude of an Authority that had always singled them out (as it never had me) for petting and intensive culture. Indeed, in their two cases, I think Authority never wholly despaired, but took advantage of the anonymity of the contributions to impute to other editors all that struck its sensitive soul as outrageous.

Individual contributors to *The Outsider* were anonymous, but the editors were not. Their photograph as a comic group is on the cover of each issue. They are Patrick Shaw-Stewart, Ronald Knox, Robin Laffan, C. A. Gold, Edward Homer, Julian Grenfell, and Charles Lister.

Most of these names have appeared before. Gold was an athlete with a gift for acting. He and Ronald played Weller and Buzfuz in the trial scene from *Pickwick* at Speeches. All seven went up to Oxford together. All except Ronald and Mr Laffan, now the bursar of Queens', Cambridge, who became a clergyman (and later a Roman Catholic layman), were killed in the First World War.

The Outsider consists mainly of parody and of jokes *à clef*. It is the *Bolliday Bango* writ large. Of Ronald's contributions he reprinted only two, 'A Paraclausithyron' and 'Little Victims'. The latter, misdated in *Juxta Salices*, is an ode to the scholarship candidates which reveals how very superficial was the pose of cynicism with which *The Outsider* was charged.

---

[1] Anon. (Lady Desborough), *Pages from a Family Journal*, p. 312.

There in hay harvest weather they sit by fifties together,
  Inconsolably sit under the statue of Pitt –
. . . All for a cumbrous guerdon, distinctly akin to a burden,
  Weighing the shoulders down, known to the world as a GOWN:
All for Remove to hustle, as out of the passage they bustle,
  All for the dirtiest scug loudly to designate 'Tug!'
. . . All to compete for prizes of various labour and sizes,
  Which, however they sweat, Oppidans probably get;
All to live in a warren, with practices utterly foreign,
  Customs skilfully furled up from the rest of the world,
All to court a seclusion, in which, for fear of confusion,
  Oppidans none may know till they are ready to go . . .
Yes I am poor as a scoffer; and if you gave me the offer
  Six more years to remain – well, I would do it again.

However individuals might be ridiculed, all the pages of *The Outsider*
are alight with genuine good humour; there is no malice, no hint of
disloyalty to the school. The compunction which Ronald felt for his share
in the publication was primarily sentimental; a regret that anything taken
amiss should have clouded even momentarily that shining summer. It was
customary for boys to mope during their last days at school. Ronald's
sorrow was deeper. He felt he was going into exile.

Masters, farewell! Yet when I come,
  You will be here to know.
Farewell, my friends! Yet surely some
  Will follow where I go.
Masters and friends are not the care
  That racks my anguished mind;
One numbing thought alone is there –
  I leave myself behind.
. . . No more amid the scent of rose
  To tell my numbers o'er
In gardens where the water flows
  Along a flowery shore!
. . . Upon the willows, lone and drear,
  By Isis' banks that spring,
The harp that Thames rejoiced to hear
  Shall hush her jocund string;
Or if the alien children still
  Desire a song of glee,
In every thoughtless word shall thrill
  A heart that breaks for thee.[1]

[1] R. A. Knox, *Juxta Salices* (1910), pp. 13–14.

Ronald had no desire to grow up. Adolescence, for him, was not a process of liberation or of adventure. Manhood threatened him with tedious duties and grave decisions. His mind had flourished and matured while his heart was still a child's. He grew up slowly. Each stage of his growth imposed a burden; each enlargement of spirit, the loss of something fond. Perhaps some instinctive foreboding of the heaviness of the coming years tinctured his love of Eton and sharpened his longing to delay.

The path ahead looked smooth enough and flowery, but his line, 'I have an errand on a stony way', still haunted him and persisted in an undertone far into his future, when the 'earthly beacons' would lose their fire.

Chapter Four

PERFORMANCE

1906–1910

At eighteen, and for many years later, Ronald looked less than his age and rather less than his moderate height. He appeared in Oxford as a frail, slightly drooping figure with a prominent nose, a heavy under-lip which his pipe accentuated, an unobtrusive chin, large eyes.

He was highly susceptible to good looks in others and always nurtured a fond, half whimsical hope that he might be thought good-looking himself. 'Surely front view I'm not so bad?' he once said.

A freshman of 1912 writing to his mother[1] thus described him at the Union as a young don; except for the clerical collar his appearance had changed little since he was an undergraduate:

> . . . an ascetic-looking pale-faced hollow-chested shrivelled up young man
> with a clerical collar, a person with a hideous face, dull eyes, sensual lips
> and a weak chin – a figure whose sole significance lay in its frailty and its
> ugliness. . . . This puny figure, supporting itself carelessly against a table,
> without any apparent effort, without seeming to arouse itself for an instant
> from a sort of habitual lethargic condition, held the large house composed
> of the most varied elements spellbound as long as the unbroken flow of
> words poured forth from the unfaltering, but scarcely moving, lips.

In contrast to this description is a snapshot taken at Caldey the year before. It portrays him sitting on the beach beside (Mgr) Vernon Johnson, in an absurd and unidentifiable cap, tousled and grinning like an urchin.

Time added the lines of fatigue and perseverance. In repose his mouth tended to lapse sadly at the corners and his eyes to fill with melancholy, but in those early years he was seldom caught in repose; his face was always seen alight with humour, affection, and flashing intelligence.

Balliol welcomed him as one of the most promising scholars in the memory of the college. He came up in a throng of friends who had

[1] Ronald preserved this letter with the note in his hand 'Received from an anonymous source April 25, 1955'.

known one another since the age of thirteen at Eton (and many since the age of eight at Summer Fields), most of whom were content to live together undiluted for the whole of their Oxford lives. From the first Ronald looked farther afield.

In 1906 Balliol was at the slack water of its Victorian floodtide. Ignominious in its early history, heterogeneous in composition, inhabiting buildings of the most joyless architecture in the University, with scant cellar and mediocre kitchen, it still professed 'a tranquil consciousness of effortless superiority' which Ronald's generation was the last to justify.

Balliol was the creation of its nineteenth-century tutors. For that one period in English History scholarship was regarded as a necessary qualification for power, and in that period the teaching at Balliol was the finest in the country. The dons believed themselves called, not, as in the eighteenth century, to a life of leisure nor, as in the twentieth, to private research and public performance, but to the domestic task of training their pupils. The grim little group of rather elderly Snell Exhibitioners from Glasgow set a standard of industry and ambition which men from the Public Schools were persuaded to follow. At the end of the nineteenth century Balliol men were everywhere in positions of eminence and authority quite disproportionate to their numbers. It was said that there were three institutions for higher education in the country, Oxford, Cambridge, and Balliol. The prestige of the College attracted the ambitious from all quarters of the world. The sons of eminent Victorians came there as young men born to the purple; Public Schools reckoned their status by the numbers of their Balliol scholars. It was fondly supposed that these dissimilar elements would fuse into a harmonious microcosm of an ideal enlightened society. In fact, they split into a number of mutually exclusive sets.

Jowett had accepted the existence of an aristocracy. It was his achievement to train selected members of it for their responsibilities and to reinforce them with recruits from other classes. His successor, Caird, who was still Master when Ronald came up, added to Jowett's agnosticism a Radicalism which was to characterize the college for fifty years. He sought to create the prototype of what the University has become since the Education Act of 1944. Strachan-Davidson succeeded him in Ronald's second year. He had been Jowett's particular colleague. Many who loved Balliol regretted that he was not his immediate successor. By 1907 he was a man of exhausted energies. Almost the last of the celibate Life-Fellows, he had a certain antiquated elegance, took horse-exercise, forgot men's names, and connived at the high spirits of the young bloods. But he was too old to undo the work of Caird.

The dons, few of whom were Public School men, noticed and deplored the divisions of the College. The Chaplain preached against them, infelicitously raising the laughter of golfers by his denunciation of 'cliques and small clubs'.

A. L. Smith, the Dean (and later Master), thought the cure should be found in football. 'Sligger' (F. F.) Urquhart, himself an old Stonyhurst boy, wrote[1] in 1905:

> I have been trying to think out 'what we mean by the College' as you say. My ideal is that we should get the best men (in several ways) from the Public Schools and let them mix up with intelligent men from Birmingham etc. That will be the best for both sets. At present we seem to have too many of the latter. The result is that they don't mix, partly because they can form a world of their own, partly because the Public Schoolboys feel themselves rather in a minority and crowd together and because they have not enough grown-up interests to link them to the others.

The entry from Eton in 1906 was of unprecedented size – seventeen. If this was part of the policy recommended by Sligger, it was a total failure in its object.

These Balliol Etonians did not mix with 'the intelligent men from Birmingham etc.'; they did not mix with men from other Public Schools; they did not mix much with Etonians at other colleges, insisting at the Oxford Old Boy dinner in having a table to themselves. They formed yet another set in Balliol, an especially flamboyant and rumbustious one. They took possession of the Anna (the Annandale Society, a dining club), and after their dinners took possession of the College, sending 'waterfalls' of crockery down XIV staircase, serenading Gordouli of Trinity, and chasing nonentities out of the quad. When they came up, Balliol had only one man in the Bullingdon, and he was so little regarded that his hunting-breeches were hung in a tree. By their third year almost all the 'Anna' were members, and no one in the College disputed their pre-eminence. They were arrogant, rowdy, and exclusive, but unlike their counterparts at Magdalen and the House, they were not mere sprigs of fashion. They were prize-winners, both athletic and academic. When they referred to the rest of the College (as without rancour they did) as 'the plebs',[2] they

---

[1] Cyril Bailey, *Francis Fortescue Urquhart* (1936), p. 32.

[2] Charles Lister wrote in 1910: 'The new "Anna" does not seem to manage the Balliol democracy half as well as in the old days. They have neither Julian to suppress the plebs nor a

were not making a conventional distinction of social class. There were perfectly well-born men excluded from the 'Anna' while two Rhodes Scholars were boon companions. This coterie was a self-appointed aristocracy. They had standards of behaviour; they were often 'buffy', never sottish. They paid for the damage they did. They talked well. All of them loved poetry, and many of them wrote it. Several had outstanding good looks. They were fiercely hostile to the cult of decadence. Many of them, in their different ways, were religious. Strachan-Davidson could not find it in him to disapprove strongly. A. L. Smith disapproved. but was outmatched. Young Lindsay bided his time.[1]

The archetype of this unique set was Ronald's old friend Julian Grenfell, best remembered today as a war-poet. His 'Into Battle' is in many anthologies of the 1920s –

> *And Life is Colour and Warmth and Light,*
> *And a striving evermore for these;*
> *And he is dead who will not fight;*
> *And who dies fighting has increase.*

These lines contrast – unfavourably to modern taste – with Patrick Shaw-Stewart's less famous –

> *I saw a man this morning*
> *Who did not wish to die:*
> *I ask, and cannot answer,*
> *If otherwise wish I.*

Patrick Shaw-Stewart, for all his brilliance, was a very much simpler character. Julian Grenfell, in an exuberant, impersonal way, disliked everyone he did not know and loved all he knew constantly and tenderly. He was never a scholar like his brother, Billy; he read too widely and too erratically for success in the Schools. A fine horseman and shot, a ferocious boxer, exulting in wild and natural things, he overtrained and overtaxed himself, moved by a passion to perfect his magnificent physique, and so sometimes fell ill and moody. Born in the heart of the governing aristocracy to a mother who lived in a circle of devotees, he resented her occupations in the fashionable world and the endless, elegant house-parties at Taplow and Panshanger. He alone of his set chose the Army as a career

---

good fellow like me to keep them in a good temper. Things worked very well when I was there to cover up Julian's tracks, and Julian was there to make fresh tracks, as it were, and overawe the rebellious.' Lord Ribblesdale, *Charles Lister* (1917), p. 242.

[1] Alexander, first Baron Lindsay of Birker, Master of Balliol 1924–50.

and went to war with professional zest. His last letter to his father, written from Flanders a few days before his death, is about his new Gibb's rifle with its telescopic sight – 'It will be just the thing for loophole shooting, waiting till the face appears and drawing a bead.'[1]

After Julian's death, and a few months before his own, Charles Lister wrote of him:

> He was rather Franciscan in his love of all things that are, in his absence of fear of all God's creatures, – death included. He stood for something very precious to me – for an England of my dreams, made of honest, brave and tender men; and his life and death have surely done something towards the realization of that England.[2]

At the time and for many years after their deaths the two Grenfells, Charles Lister, and their fellows represented 'something very precious' to the whole Kingdom. If in time their memory grew clouded, it was not by doubt – the meanest natures only have been tempted to disparagement – but by a sense of unworthiness in their survivors and successors. Their sacrifice seemed, more plainly every year, to have been quite vain in realizing 'the England of their dreams'. Their brief lives are recorded in many books of memoirs. Ronald's name very frequently appears among theirs. They loved him and he them, but it is a misconception that he 'belonged' to their set in any exclusive sense. He was always welcome at Taplow and sometimes went with the parties which drove out from Oxford to spend Sunday there. As often he stayed in college with his own P.S.A. (Pleasant Sunday Afternoon) Club, when men from other schools and colleges met in his rooms to play parlour-games, the liveliest of which was 'Nebuchadnezzar', a kind of charade in which one group select the name of a historical or literary character and act in dumb show but in improvised costume a character whose name begins with each letter in turn. In summer Ronald shared a punt with Edward Homer and Patrick Shaw-Stewart, but he spent countless days on the river with Wilfred's friends from Rugby and Trinity; he knew men in every college and of every party. And these less illustrious young men also fell in battle. At no stage in his life did Ronald 'belong' to a set. No group or individual, male or female, clerical or lay, was ever able to establish proprietary rights in him, and often friends who thought themselves particularly privileged, were disconcerted to find how close he was to others whose very names were strange to them.

---

[1] *Pages from a Family Journal*, p. 542.   [2] Ibid., p. 567.

Ronald's tutor for Honour Mods was Cyril Bailey; Sandy Lindsay for Greats. He also went to de Paravicini and Strachan-Davidson and probably to Pickard-Cambridge. With one exception he formed no close friendships in the Balliol Senior Common-room. The exception was Sligger Urquhart.

Sligger was twenty years older than Ronald, but he had a youthful spirit which endeared him to a circle of undergraduates which generation after generation changed little in its essential character. Sligger was the first Roman Catholic since the Reformation to be elected Fellow of an Oxford college, and he made it a point of honour to refrain from any suggestion of proselytism. In its original draft *A Spiritual Aeneid* was dedicated to him in a letter which began:

> This book will have to be dedicated to you; because if it were to be dedicated to an Anglican, I should be accused of trying to convert him, and if I dedicated it to any other Catholic, he would be accused of having converted me. So N—— and M—— mustn't mind. And you mustn't mind either; because nobody yet ever did 'convert' anybody, and my admiration for the Catholic Church was none the less for your never worrying me or laughing at me all the time you saw me hunting shadows.

Sligger was Junior Dean when Ronald came up; an office he did not greatly like (though later he became Dean) because the obligations of maintaining discipline interfered with his freedom of intercourse with undergraduates. In 1907 he became Junior Bursar. He had private means and was never a professional scholar but rather a man of wide general culture. He was not a wit; nor an Oxford 'character' of whom people treasure and embellish memorable sayings. He drew people to him by his simple, unselfish affection. There were always a half dozen or more in his rooms every evening talking among themselves as much as to their host; and there were always people outside his circle who derided what they took to be its cosiness and softness.

Sligger owned a chalet which his father had built in 1864 in the valley of Chamonix. There every summer, except during the First World War, he took a reading party of his particular intimates. Ronald went once only, in 1908, and then not to *the* Chalet, for it had been burned down and was rebuilding, but to the neighbouring Chalet des Rochers, where was continued the traditional regime which exemplified Sligger's conception of the good life. It was not at all a luxurious regime, and addicts of the Chalet relished its austerities and restrictions. Some industry, some physical exertion, and a high standard of courtesy were expected. For

Ronald there must have been a flavour of Creeton Vicarage; with the great difference that the religion which permeated their host was invisible to those who were not members of his Church. He was Ronald's first Roman Catholic friend.

Perhaps because of his association with the Anna and his numberless activities outside the College, the Balliol dons never made quite the pet of Ronald that he had been at Eton, nor had he even that romantic loyalty to the college (apart from his individual friends there) that Hilaire Belloc had conceived thirteen years earlier and sung in 'To the Balliol men still in Africa'.

> *Balliol made me, Balliol fed me*
> *Whatever I had she gave me again*

was never Ronald's refrain.

Balliol for him was a place of passage.

2

During his first four terms Ronald kept a diary, a thing he never did at any other time except when abroad. For all the warmth of his reception and of the familiars who surrounded him, he felt himself at first an exile in Oxford, and even at the end he named his little book of collected undergraduate writing *Juxta Salices* (after the lament of the Jews in Babylon) and the Oxford section 'Bowings to Rimmon'.

The diary is laconic; little more than a list of engagements.

A few extracts may be taken as typical:

> Nov. 7 1906. Lunch with Raper[1] full of formidable ladies. Tea with Julian. Unsuccessful attempt to find Canning Club at the House 10.0.

> Nov. 10th. Battels 2.15.4. In afternoon bicycled with Charles to Dorchester and Wallingford, which has no Castle and no Roman remains.

> Nov. 12th. Rode with Charles and Laff to Godstow. Tea with Charles, Gold and Dicky Gibbs. Second meeting of Socialistic club – to be called in future the Orthodox Club. 9 members present. 5–4 majority in favour of secularism.

> Nov. 14th. Bought cards for Orthodox Club and had my hair cut.

---

[1] Fellow of Trinity whose friendship was largely responsible for Ronald's election in 1910.

Fr Waggett at P. H. [Pusey House]. Canning at the House: Old Age Pensions.

Nov. 15th. Rode to Cuddesdon [Theological College]. Tea with Watt.[1] Dinner with Wolmer.[2] Union – Whether social reform or Imperial policy more important; Wolmer telling. Spoke for first time, very ill.

Friday, Nov. 30th. Served at early celebration in Chapel. Went down in afternoon to Rugby and did some Tory canvassing, for no specific object, as there is no election on.

Thursday, December 6th. S. Nicholas. FOUNDER'S DAY at Eton. Corporate communion of O.U.C.U. in S. Mary's. Gave breakfast to Charles, Strachey and Finlay. Had to go away early on account of the Ireland.[3] Lunch with huge push, including Furse and H. T. Bowlby. Ireland again till 5 and solitary tea. Motion at Union that the Egotism of modern Life is a menace to the British Empire. Father Vaughan the draw of the evening. I spoke 3rd on the paper. Father V. spoke rather too solemnly and loud and there were few funny stories but some liked it.

Nov. (sic) 7th. Breakfast with Maclehose, Watt and one Hugh Jones, up for scholarship. Ireland. Lunch with Charlie[4] but could not eat much owing to horrible influence of Ireland hours. Tea [with five unidentified names]. Meeting of the Orthodox Club in my room, very large and a lot of food. Sat up till 4 – Heaven knows why – talking to Jack and Laff.[5]

Nov. (sic) 8th. Ireland.

These days of Ronald's first term are typical of all his four years as an undergraduate.

There is the continually widening circle of friends. The rare entry of 'solitary tea' marks a sociability that he was never entirely to lose. In later life he lacked the zest for new acquaintances, but he could not happily be left alone for a meal, and to live alone he found unendurable. At Oxford breakfast, luncheon, tea, and dinner were almost always in company, usually in a party.

The intense vitality of his undergraduate years was of brief duration.

---

[1] Mr W. P. Watt, a lifelong friend who later acted as his literary agent, a Rugbeian.

[2] Later third Earl of Selborne. A Wykehamist.

[3] The Ireland Scholarship. Ronald was treating the examination as a 'trial run'. He took it seriously and successfully two years later.

[4] Presumably Charles Lister. During his first term at Balliol new nicknames were briefly adopted for several of his friends. Cf. 'Jack' below.

[5] Edward Horner and Mr Robin Laffan. A few of Horner's friends called Horner 'Jack' for a short time; a name derived from the nursery rhyme.

To lunch with a 'huge push', to speak for the first time on paper at the Union, to stay up talking till four, while sitting for the Ireland – these were the feats of youth which read strangely to those who knew him only in maturity.

The expeditions by bicycle were a continuation of the family habit. Sight-seeing seemed a normal occupation to him, but it may be doubted how much he ever really enjoyed it. In later life he would say petulantly: 'I *won't* be shown things.' As his High Church sympathies waxed, his visits to churches lost their aesthetic and archaeological interest. He and his friends made a hobby of collecting evidence of the theological views of various incumbents. There were clues to be found in the furniture and decoration of the edifice, in the notices in the porch, in the garments hanging in the vestry, which afforded a highly specialized pleasure to the young sleuths.

Ronald always kept an eye on his weekly battels. During the time of which he kept a record they never rose above £4 0s. 8d. Or fell below £1 9s. 0d. It seems that his father expected him to support himself as he had done. To the open Balliol Scholarship and the Davies Scholarship from Eton, Ronald added in 1908 the Ireland and the Craven, worth, respectively, £30 a year for four years and £40 for two. The Hertford, which he took in 1907, the Gaisford in 1908, and the Chancellor's Latin Verse in 1910 were single prizes of £45, £20, and £20 each, which were spent on books. Occasionally, with his stepmother as intermediary, he asked for, and received, small sums from his father for specific, extraordinary expenses. He could not, had he wished to, have led the lavish life of some of the Anna; he gave tea and breakfast parties and asked men in for port or mulled claret after Hall rather than entertaining to luncheon or dinner, but there is never the smallest hint that he ever felt at a disadvantage with his richer friends.

Almost every evening of term was spent at the meetings – sometimes at two or three meetings consecutively – of the various clubs which Ronald joined with engaging impartiality; smart and sombre, Tory, Liberal, and Labour, pious and convivial. Ronald joined them all, the O.U.D.S. alone excepted. It was an expensive club, looked at askance by the Grenfell set, whose amenities were excelled by the Grid. The business of rehearsal and grease-paint was not to Ronald's taste. He did his best theatrical turns impromptu, inspired by the gaiety of a group of friends. Undergraduates of the period were less interested than their successors in public figures and more interested in one another. They met at these clubs purely for their own amusement and for the winning of a local prestige, which glittered in their eyes more attractively than any eminence in the adult world. Even at the Union guests from outside the University were rare; there was none during Ronald's term as President. From 1926 to 1939, his years at the Chaplaincy, Ronald spoke regularly in Eights Week; there is therefore no haze of the legend which distorts so much of the years before the First World War, about his Union performances. He was the paragon. Though he recorded that he spoke 'ill' on his first appearance, he won immediate popularity. He had the unique distinction, that a speech he delivered as an undergraduate at the Union was quoted a few days later in a leading article of *The Times*. 'The honourable gentlemen,' he had said, 'have turned their backs upon their country and now have the effrontery to say they have their country behind them.'[1] In Hilary Term 1908 he was Secretary, Junior Librarian in Trinity and President in Hilary Term 1909. Elections then were decided by the candidates' abilities in debate. No one voted for a political party. Ronald at this time described himself as a 'Tory-Socialist' or as a 'Socialist-Tory', by which he meant primarily that he abhorred equally the materialist Liberalism dominant in the country and the Jingoism professed by the thrusting young Conservatives who were typified by F. E. Smith and Carson. His Toryism was that of the Canning Club, a small and select group who met to read and discuss papers on political questions to the antiquated accompaniment of snuff-box, silver punch bowl, and church-warden pipes. His Socialism was that of the Orthodox Club referred to above. It, too, was highly exclusive and had a red voting urn and red balls for the election of members.[2]

Ronald was no economist. Although a Fabian by membership, he was entirely out of sympathy with the bureaucracy the Webbs were planning. It was chiefly from his brother, Wilfred, that he caught his slight and transient infection of Socialism.

Wilfred at Oxford was not an Anglo-Catholic – indeed, he passed through a phase of scepticism – but he was a 'Christian Socialist' when that movement was largely in the control of High Churchmen. This was an old-established liaison. Mid-Victorian caricaturists delighted to present ritualistic curates as the pampered pets of silly, pretty women. They were far wide of the mark. The company of proletarian youths mitigated the hard living conditions of those they satirized. In the drab working-class

---

[1] *The Box and the Puppets*, Nathaniel Micklem (1957), pp. 34–35.

[2] In later life Ronald used to speak of this as a whim of Charles Lister's which he was amused to indulge, but a letter survives written by Lister to Nevile Bland in November 1906 which reads: 'I am founding in a secondary position to Bros Knox a new Society – Socialist in character.'

areas of the industrial cities the Anglo-Catholic parishes formed bright little islands of pageantry; gymnasiums and reading-rooms were linked with altar-societies. Rags were briefly changed for cassocks and cottas. Here were no squire-patrons or retired naval officers to object to innovations. Here the missionaries had a prestige and authority which fitted their priestly office, and they brought back to the Universities and Public Schools authentic accounts of destitution and injustice. The Community of the Resurrection, Mirfield, where Ronald was a visitor, took an open share in party politics, conferring with Keir Hardie and appearing on Labour platforms. Though widely enterprising in his choice of acquaintances, Ronald was never, like Lister, at his ease in Ruskin College or with trade unionists from the town. Once, in a moment of high spirits, he helped agitate a paper-box factory at Banbury, but when Lister fomented a strike inside the University confines among the girls at the Clarendon Press, he held back. He had no wish to get sent down.[1] He was a young man of the University clubs with their panelled rooms and mulled claret and insatiable appetite for paradox, rather than of the draughty public hall and the Party slogan.

Lister's Socialism was more deeply felt if less ingeniously expounded. It lasted him through Oxford and faded only with his loss of confidence in the personalities and methods of contemporary politics, not with any desertion of principle. He combined his revolutionary ideas with an unembarrassed enjoyment of the delights of privileged society, which Ronald commemorated in the *Isis* with a parody of Gilbert:

> *Conceive me if you can*
> *A crème-de-la-crème young man;*
> *A fervid Etonian*
> *Anti-Gladstonian*
> *Down-with-the-rich young man.*
>
> *A rescue-the-poor young man,*
> *A waiter-look-sharp young man,*
> *A ride-in-a-motory*

---

[1] Lister was, in fact, sent down for a term because entering Trinity after Tommy (Sir Alan) Lascelles' twenty-firster, he greeted with excessive familiarity a man who proved to be the Dean, and fell prostrate before him. He was given a mock funeral, Shaw-Stewart pronouncing the panegyric and Ronald inscribing the epitaph: 'I wist not, brethren, that he was the high priest' (Acts xxiii. 5). This stone was removed and put back face inwards. Its precise position, in or near XIV staircase, is not known. Next term in reparation Raper asked Lister to dine at High Table in Trinity. The Dean then greeted him: 'You won't remember me. I am the High Priest.'

Keep-to-your-coterie
Friend-of-the-world young man.

A fight-the-police young man,
A don't-go-to-war young man;
An early-Tractarian
Take-in-the-Clarion
Dine-at-the-Ritz young man

A Magdalen-push young man,
A camel's-hair-coat young man;
A shout-in-the-quadrangle
Nature-of-God-wrangle
Snip-for-a-first young man.

Politics were never a primary interest to Ronald. Of the 1909 General Election he wrote: 'I am thinking of contributing (slightly) to the election expenses of George Lansbury, who's standing for Bow and Bromley. He's a good Socialist and a good Catholic, and several chalks cleverer than the average Labour M.P. Otherwise I take no interest in the election.' In later years he became an unenthusiastic Conservative. As an undergraduate he would argue any case with anyone, the more fantastic the better.

> I was [he wrote] early marked down for a speaker who could be depended upon to support any view in a debating society. . . . I must have acquired an unenviable reputation for defending the indefensible. . . . I have once, owing to a shortage of speakers, opened and opposed the same motion.

His slight, schoolboy figure popped up everywhere. His appearance always meant a quickening of interest that was seldom disappointed. Once, when the Arnold, a grave political club, was meeting in his rooms a dull paper was read about Egyptian affairs. Four desultory speeches followed. Everyone looked to Ronald to enliven the evening. He rose, recited five, pointed, impromptu limericks about the previous speakers and closed the evening.

He was later rather doubtful of the value of those debates. They trained a man, he thought, to leave the obvious unsaid even to the detriment of truth; to prefer the ingenious and extravagant to the sound argument; to compromise with reason. They removed rhetoric from its true function as the art of persuasion, and made it the art of entertaining conversation. Ronald said of his brother Wilfred that he 'was too clever to find his way easily into the Church and too simple to feel the need of it' and of himself that his submission to Rome was delayed, partly, because 'it seemed so obvious'. But the effect on Ronald as an artist of all these unrecorded, unremembered displays of verbal brilliance was to turn him temporarily from the written to the spoken word and so give his prose style, when he turned seriously to writing, that idiosyncratic lucidity in which his speaking voice is always audible. Ronald never wrote a sentence, however subtle the meaning, in which the reader loses his way and has to turn back to recover the thread of its construction. He never perpetuated the cacophanies which look at first glance inoffensive in print but confound the tongue when pronounced.

He wrote little as an undergraduate beyond some articles and light verse for the *Isis*, which he edited for a term at the beginning of his third year. *Juxta Salices*, in which he collected his undergraduate *jeux d'esprit*, does not, except in the very clever 'The Visitors' Book, Hartland Quay' quite fulfil the promise of *Signa Severa*. Ronald was too restless, too much engrossed in the dead languages, too quick to snatch the opportunity of the moment, to settle down to painstaking English composition. The Symposium written for the Decalogue – a Balliol literary society, 'so called because there were nineteen members' – was thought very amusing when performed but, like *The Outsider*, it falls flat when deprived of topicality. The book was never a success; it sold a few hundred copies and left Ronald with a small debt to Alden's, the printers. In 1910 he submitted a poem for the Newdigate Prize, without success.

The diary quoted above shows how lightly Ronald took the Ireland in his first trial run. He made no preparation for Mods. Shaw-Stewart shut himself up for some weeks and read hard. Ronald entered for the examination with a nonchalance that approached hubris. His papers were finished an hour or more before the prescribed time, and he sauntered out of the Schools, leaving the rest diligently writing and revising. To qualify for a first it was necessary to get alphas in seven papers out of the fourteen (or an optional fifteen). Ronald was rightly confident of his ability to get these. A gamma cancelled an alpha. Betas were neutral. Ronald had read the set books at school and remembered them well. It did not occur to him that he could fall below beta. He did not trouble to re-read them, and the texts he knew were not those from which the papers were set. This omission was evident in the Theocritus paper, where a German text by Wilamowitz was used in which the iotas subscript were printed adscript. Not merely translation but a commentary on textual variations was required. Ronald's commentary, though ingenious, betrayed that he had never heard of Wilamowitz.[1] That paper, certainly, and possibly others on the set books, were marked gamma, with the result that Ronald took a second. It has been suggested that the examiners thought it salutary to take him down a peg, but his academic reputation suffered so little that he was offered a Fellowship at Trinity before he finished his Final Schools (in which he took an easy first) and was there set to work as tutor in Honour Mods.

3

There is, surprisingly, no definite date given in the *Spiritual Aeneid* for Ronald's decision to take Holy Orders. It was made, perhaps over a long period, during his four years as an undergraduate. Through all the time when his eager, questing, sceptical mind was exploring and experimenting he remained steadfast in his religious practices and increasingly obsessed by the minutiae of ritual and theology. By his last year his intention was generally recognized.

Balliol Chapel in 1906 was still stark new, its ugliness as yet unsweetened by the faint flavour of 'period' which modern connoisseurs claim to discern. Sociological and ethical precepts were uttered from its pulpit, but it was not a place of prayer. Ronald kept the compulsory chapels which were the alternative to 'rollers', but went elsewhere for his devotions. In his first term he became, and remained, an habitué of Pusey House.

He was expected there. He had met one of the Librarians in the Summer of 1905 and had made an impression. A senior contemporary (now Mgr) Vernon Johnson, records[2] that in the summer of 1906 he was told at Pusey House: 'By the way, an extremely brilliant boy who has taken the first scholarship at Balliol is coming up from Eton next term. He has leanings in our direction. Pray that he may not lose his faith at Oxford.'

The 'direction' of Pusey House was the high, severe Anglicanism of the Tractarian whom it commemorated. The building housed Canon Pusey's fine theological library, and the Librarians, numbering originally three, five in Ronald's time, were learned clergymen engaged on research, the defence and propagation of Pusey's theological opinions and the

---

[1] The authority for this statement is Mr Thomas Higham of Trinity, the Public Orator, 1939–58. Other scholars have doubted its plausibility.

[2] *Pax*, Winter 1957.

spiritual welfare of undergraduates who found their College chapels uncongenial. The genius of the house was donnish rather than monastic. Its religious services eschewed all Roman decorations. It attracted a small, regular congregation who in that city of cliques tended to become a distinct society with its own gossip and allusive humour. Ronald made neither a secret nor a display of his devotions. He went to Holy Communion at Pusey House twice a week during term. His more worldly friends were aware of his peculiar habits and respected them, while his fellow-worshippers were edified to find him kneeling humbly beside them in the early morning after an evening of paradox and applause at the Union. Friendships sprang from these meetings in St Giles', and through them Ronald began to meet many of the prominent Anglo-Catholic clergy of the day, who often passed through Oxford; men who indulged more luxurious ritualistic tastes and taught a doctrine more exotic than Pusey's. But Pusey House remained his spiritual home.

On Sundays he always went to the High Celebration of the Cowley Fathers – popularly spoken of at that time as the 'Cowley papas' or 'Guv'nors' – often taking friends with him in the hope that the plainsong choir, Father Waggett's lively sermons and the restrained ritual – slightly more sumptuous than Pusey House but still in strong contrast to the profusion of St Barnabas – might seduce them into his own school of churchmanship. He used also to go there four times a year to make his Confession.

By the end of his undergraduate time Ronald had collected a group of friends who met regularly for tea on Fridays to discuss Anglo-Catholic policies.

These 'spikes', as they were dubbed, came mostly from homes untouched by Anglo-Catholicism; often strongly opposed to it. There was an element of domestic rebellion in their new-found beliefs and practices which gave relish to some; for Ronald it was purely a sorrow. Bishop Knox had established himself as the leader of the Evangelical Party, and in his own diocese cheerfully persecuted ritualistic clergymen, some of whom had contumaciously erected curtains round their altars (in accordance with the 'Sarum Use') which made it impossible to conduct the Communion Service from the North side as the Bishop ordained.

In Manchester Ronald felt himself in conscience bound to attend one of the churches which his father found particularly obnoxious. He made no secret at home of his ecclesiastical adventures. Bishop Knox knew that he went to confession and did not attempt to forbid him; the practice was not contrary to the Prayer Book, and Bishop Gore had given his approval;

but much which Ronald now believed and did seemed to his father plain treason to the Church of their upbringing. It was discouraging to the Bishop to return from his sorties against his clergy only to find their cause cleverly championed at his own table. While Ronald was still an undergraduate and a layman his extravagances were mildly vexatious. Later they were to become something very grievous.

The collector's interest in Anglo-Catholic parishes and communities was a staple of conversation at Ronald's Friday teas. Of these places of interest there was no more notable specimen than Caldey Island, where Ronald went for the first time in the Long Vacation of 1909. Here flourished an Anglican Benedictine Abbey. Ronald and his friends, on this occasion, stayed in the Guest House; it was a reading party, not a retreat; but he attended many of the monastic Offices and was enchanted by the spectacle.

After his submission to Rome Ronald was scrupulously respectful of the *bona fide* errors and cherished eccentricities of his former fellow-churchmen. In the case of Caldey, with its subsequent history well known, he allowed himself a few rare expressions of criticism:[1]

> There was a faint air of make-believe about the old Caldey; this I think contributed something to its charm. The island itself was a fairy-story island; those caves, those little combes, those wide beaches. The buildings – I wonder if Mr Anson[2] quite does justice to the buildings? Perhaps 'Hollywood Cinema' is a pardonable hit at their style; they do not look altogether real. But how well that fitted the dreamworld Caldey was!

And of the founder and Abbot he wrote:[3]

> . . . Extreme Anglicanism was badly in want of a leader. . . . It might have been supposed that Dom Aelred was the answer to our difficulty. . . . Here was the Abbot, a man of dynamic energy, but when the Caldey community made its submission neither I nor any of my friends were tempted, for a moment, to follow their example. We had been under the spell of Dom Aelred, but not under his influence. . . . What held you was the brightness of his eyes. They were not (as I then saw them) the eyes of a mystic. . . . It was rather some trick of hypnotism they had.

This singular man, Benjamin Carlyle, who in after years as a Roman Catholic secular priest won a good name in Canada by his work among criminals, was in 1909 just emerging into prominence. Caldey Abbey was

---

[1] *Pax*, Summer 1940.
[2] Peter F. Anson, *The Benedictines of Caldey* (1940).   [3] *Pax*, Spring 1956.

his creation. As a young medical student he was fired with the passion of forming and leading a Benedictine community. A cursory visit to Buckfast was his only direct acquaintance with monasticism. He taught himself theology and liturgiology. He had no money and no influential friends. For the first six years of his struggle against every discouragement he was a layman. In 1904 he was ordained in America and allowed by the Archbishop of Canterbury to call himself a 'priest in Colonial Orders', but his name was never admitted to *Crockford's Directory*. Lord Halifax early befriended him. Gradually he won the support of other powerful laymen, and in 1906 purchased Caldey Island, which is outside Anglican diocesan jurisdiction, and began building. He went on building throughout his time there in the fanciful style mentioned above, embellishing his estate with turrets and pergolas, crazy-pavements, gold-fish, and peacocks. In the seven years of the Abbey's existence as an Anglican institution he raised and spent more than £68,000. Postulants came to him from all quarters, but mostly from the ill-educated. They and the professed brothers lived a withdrawn life, but meanwhile the island became a resort, not only for those seeking guidance in contemplative prayer but also for sight-seers of all sorts, pious or merely curious, who delighted in the *trompe l'œil* reproduction of Roman Catholic ceremonies. Here was something entirely unique in the Church of England.[1] Thirty or more monks cowled and tonsured, singing 'not as Angli sed ut Angeli'[2] and in Latin; living by strict Cistercian-Benedictine Rule of mortification and obedience. It seemed the consummation of seventy years striving to undo the Reformation and achieve full Catholic life inside the national Church. Mr Athelstan Riley wrote of Caldey exultantly as 'the greatest phenomenon in the Anglican Communion, founded by one of the strongest of the successors of St Augustine'.[3]

Ronald and his friends were certainly titillated by the complete Romanism of the regime. There is a nuance of naughtiness in many of the Anglo-

---

[1] Father Ignatius Leycester Lyne of Llanthony called himself an 'Anglo-Benedictine Abbot', but his propensities were those of Savonarola or Wesley rather than of a contemplative monk, and his shifting, often neglected little band of adherents never made a satisfactory 'show-piece'. Nor can Father Ignatius properly be regarded as a member of the Church of England – though in defiance of his bishops he claimed to be one – since he derived his priestly Orders from a curious prelate named Mar Timotheus, who arrived uninvited at Llanthony and ordained him, validly enough, into a Church of his own. Mar Timotheus was a North American of French extraction who had been consecrated Archbishop in Ceylon on the authority of the heretical and schismatic Jacobite Patriarch of Antioch. In the year after this ordination Mar Timotheus obligingly offered to consecrate Father Ignatius Primate of England.

[2] *Athelstan Riley, Pax*, June 1910.   [3] Ibid.

Catholic expressions of the time. What to the monks was simply the Opus Dei was also, to the undergraduates, a splendid tease of the bench of Bishops. Ronald wrote from Caldey to his sister, in a phrase which would later be abhorrent to him, of 'a most wonderful Mariolatrous hymn'.[1] But he was also genuinely moved by what seemed 'in microcosm a vision of a revived pre-Reformation church',[2] and his habits of devotion were enriched.

4

Ronald's diary omits all records of his vacations. These were spent mainly in working for Schools, at home or in reading parties. At Eastertide 1907 he went to Rome with his brothers, followed the customary round of classical sight-seeing, was unimpressed by the baroque or by papal magnificence, and complained in his letters home of the difficulty of procuring *Punch*.

In January 1909 he and Patrick Shaw-Stewart went to stay with Edward Homer at Mells. The Homers had lately moved from the large Soanesque house in the Park, to the surviving wing of the Manor-house, which had been their original Tudor home. After many vicissitudes this lovely old house had been adapted to Lady Homer's fine taste and the gardens terraced and planted. Edward Homer was less studious than Ronald and Shaw-Stewart. They had the house to themselves, and kept late hours and enjoyed Sir John's cellar. For his devotions Ronald bicycled to Frome, where, he wrote to Shuttleworth,[3] there was 'a very jolly church which is very old and most Catholic. They had High Mass and Procession before breakfast.' Shaw-Stewart read the lesson at Mattins in Mells parish church.

Edward's sister Katherine had just been married. Ronald had met her once in his first year at Balliol. He records: 'Raymond Asquith to lunch with fiancé' (sic); the first mention of one of his most intimate friends. 'V. jolly old house with a church (gorgeous Somersetshire tower) in the garden' is Ronald's comment in a letter to his elder sister on this first acquaintance with the house where he was to spend the last years of his life and the church in the shadow of which he was to be buried.

---

[1] The *Salve Mater misericordiae*. Mr Gurney records that on first hearing it, Ronald though it 'going a little too far'.

[2] *A Spiritual Aenid*, p. 86.   [3] See footnote, p. 210.

Juxta Salices includes some ingenious verses commemorating other reading parties.

In his last year Ronald moved into lodgings at the old Parsonage, St Giles.

Julian Grenfell, Edward Homer, and Patrick Shaw-Stewart moved out of College together to Longwall. Ronald shared with W. G. Fletcher, R. D. Furse, H. K. Marsden, and D. R. Brandt. He was the common link between them. Mr Hugh Marsden, now the chief repository and recognized authority of Eton lore, was the 'Marsden K.S.' mentioned in *The Outsider*. He was at Merton. The others were at Balliol and members of the Anna. Fletcher, known as 'Hôj' (a derivative of 'Hodge', the name given him because of his stolid Englishry) and (now Sir) Ralph Furse were also Etonians. In the ante-chapel at Eton there hangs the French flag recaptured single-handed from the Germans by Fletcher, shortly before his death. Brandt was a Harrovian, a cricket blue and all-round athlete, a first in Mods, and a 'snip-for-a-first' in Greats (though in the event he was obliged to take an 'aegrotat'); he had played Charles II in the 'Decalogue Symposium'.[1] His letters[2] show that Ronald did not lead quite such a subdued life during his last year as the reader of *A Spiritual Aeneid* might suppose:

> Our digs have been a large and satisfactory success so far. But late hours are bad for Greats. . . . There's a Keble fellow who sleeps next to my room. Name − Stock or Stocks, but we always speak of him as Mr Stork or Mr Sparks. He must be rather mouldy about us. We have been known to sing (this includes Ronnie − think of the poor man!) from 11 to 12 and the night Ralph Furse left us, we broached a bottle of port (me auctore, I confess) at 12 and sang loudly and vinously till 2!
>
> Ronnie is full as ever of Catholicity. Has a Spike tea on Thursdays, [Fridays?] when mysterious men creep past my door. There is an Etonian tea too on Tuesdays.[3]

None of his fellow lodgers came to the Friday teas. Brandt was losing his belief in institutional religion. The others were conventional in their observances. None of them took advantage of what was, for Ronald, the chief attraction of the Old Parsonage; its proximity to Pusey House.

Visits from Longwall were frequent. Patrick Shaw-Stewart and Ronald sometimes met to take their minds off Greats by reading Aristophanes together. Ronald's chief concession to Schools was to give up debating.

---

[1] *Juxta Salices*, pp. 58−88.   [2] *D. R. Brandt*, Ed. Charles Clay (1920).
[3] Op. cit., pp. 36, 37.

In his last year he made a new friend and a new kind of friendship. Ted Shuttleworth[1] was two years his junior at Balliol, good-looking – Ronald described him once as 'languidly dangerous' – light hearted, popular, fond of cards and horses and guns. He was Ronald's first 'convert', the forerunner of the group who two years later made a cult of him as a spiritual leader. He and Shuttleworth wrote to one another weekly during vacations in terms of frank endearments, exchanging fashionable gossip for ecclesiastical, posing and answering questions of theology. Shuttleworth required instruction both in the niceties of ritual and in the fundamentals of the creed. In one letter he mocks the Low Church habits of a local clergyman, in the next he expresses doubts of the divinity of our Lord and the freedom of the will. Neither Shuttleworth nor any of Ronald's early friends seems to have been troubled by problems of ethics. Whatever their temptations and shortcomings, all accepted the moral law. They sometimes questioned whether an institutional religion was required to sanction it, and, if so, what religion, but it was not until his return to Oxford in 1926 that Ronald was confronted with a generation who doubted the traditional conceptions of right and wrong. Ronald made a sound and devout Anglican of Shuttleworth. In this, as in the other loving friendships of Ronald's youth, there was nothing possessive. He wished his friends to love one another, in this case Shuttleworth and Alan Parsons, as later Guy Lawrence and 'C'.

At the end of the Summer Term, 1910, Ronald's generation went down; Julian Grenfell to the Army, Edward Homer to read law in F. E. Smith's chambers, Charles Lister to the Diplomatic Service, Marsden and 'Hôj' Fletcher to be schoolmasters, Furse to the Colonial Office, Alan Parsons to the Civil Service and an early marriage. Brandt took a Fellowship at Brasenose, but his interests lay outside Oxford, and after two years he devoted the short remainder of his civilian life to social work in Bermondsey. Only one of the circle showed an interest in money. Patrick Shaw-Stewart, fortified by an All Souls fellowship, went into Baring's Bank, where he was, as always, brilliantly successful. It was a great parting of friends; for Ronald the severance from nearly all his secular connexions. From now on he became a churchman.

After taking his Schools he went abroad with Mr Samuel Gurney, a munificent young Anglo-Catholic whom Ronald had known slightly at Eton and Oxford, with whom friendship had developed after he had gone

---

[1] The Hon. Edward Kay-Shuttleworth, 1890–1917; second son of first Baron Shuttleworth; father of fourth and present Baron.

down. Mr Gurney's hospitable rooms in Albemarle Street became Ronald's *pied-à-terre* in London.[1] They went to hear the Abbot of Caldey preach at All Saints', Margaret Street in November 1908, and in July 1909 were together at the Guest House on the reading party mentioned above. Mr Gurney presented the Abbey with its bells.

Now, in June 1910, he invited Ronald to travel as his guest to Oberammergau for the Passion Play. They went in the mood of pilgrims. Ronald threw out of the train window the *Winning Post Annual*, which Mr Gurney had inappropriatley bought at the bookstall. Ronald was, in Mr Gurney's words, 'conspicuously impressed' by the portrayal of the crucifixion at Oberammergau. He bought his first rosary there and began to learn its use, but while his host went to Mass at the Catholic church, Ronald sought and found an Anglican service. They said Compline together in their lodgings.

They went on, in a holiday mood now, to Belgium, where at the Grand Hotel, Bruges, they met, by arrangement, a party of 'spikes' headed by the Rev. Maurice Child.

He was four years older than Ronald and had been ordained the month before, but wore secular dress – straw hat and flannels. They were not strangers. Ronald had heard him preach when he was a deacon at Plymouth, had met him and enjoyed his company. It is from the Belgium visit that the friendship properly dates, which was to be of great importance in Ronald's next seven years.

They made an irresistibly amusing pair. Child lacked Ronald's scholarship and literary genius. He suffered none of the restraints which Ronald's academic position and tender conscience imposed. He was immensely more daring; a versatile man, without shyness or conventionality, with a relish for humanity in all its varieties; the fearless associate, and often the salvation, of riff-raff; a practical joker and wit; a highly readable journalist, an attractive preacher, an adventurous traveller, something of an epicure, something of a sportsman; an advertiser, an *enfant terrible*; a pastor, to those who met him in that capacity, of wisdom and tact and patience. These two had much to give one another, and together they flashed meteorically across the summer skies of their Church. It is impossible now to distinguish exactly between their several parts in the high jinks of the time. Much that is generally attributed to Ronald is, probably, attributable to Child, and vice versa.

---

[1] He also stayed with the Bishop of London in St James's Square. The Bishop was slightly scandalized to hear Ronald on the telephone arranging to 'hear Mass'.

The meeting at Bruges was decisive. Ronald there first felt fully at home in a Catholic country. Flemish quaintness moved him where Roman magnificence had failed. He had been to Bruges before in August 1903 with his brother Wilfred and had kept a journal in which were conscientiously noted all the chief sights. But he was a very English boy at the time, derisive of foreigners and hungry for porridge and bacon and marmalade; quite without interest in continental devotional habits. The little town now became his Holy City; something he could comprehend and emulate; a City of God which, by Grace, might be recreated in England. He had his rosary blessed at the shrine of the Precious Blood. He and his friends, prayer and laughter alternating, travelled round the small kingdom. Ronald was resolving a problem. There were three choices open to him: that of an ordinary parochial Anglican life; a Greats tutorship at Balliol; the Fellowship and chaplaincy at Trinity. This last offered none of the High Church amenities on which he had come to depend. But Mr Gurney was a Trinity man; Child, with the tactical sense of a party organizer, liked to place supporters in posts as diverse as possible. With their advice, at the Hotel Harscamp at Namur, among jolly barnyard imitations, Ronald wrote his acceptance to the President of Trinity.

Chapter Five

ACCOMPLISHMENT

1910–1914

The core of the *Spiritual Aeneid* is the period from the summer of 1910 to the summer of 1915, during which Ronald prepared for ordination, became deacon and priest of the Church of England, served as Chaplain at Trinity, collected a brilliant circle of undergraduate disciples, and made himself known throughout the country as the leading writer and preacher of the extreme Anglo-Catholic Party; the period in which he brought to its highest polish one of his literary skills.

He spent those five years in an almost exclusively ecclesiastical circle. It was natural for him to regard its interests as paramount; he sometimes wrote as though the whole nation were similarly preoccupied and had no other subjects of discussion than Lord Halifax's attempt to reissue the first Prayer Book of Edward VI and the collaboration of Protestant missionaries in East Africa. There was much else being talked about in England at that time – Post-Impressionism, woman's suffrage, the Russian ballet, Home Rule for Ireland, the Marconi scandal – but church affairs *were* talked about with vehemence and in detail to an extent entirely foreign to the modern age.

The Church of England was the religion of a governing class which then ruled a great part of the world. Her roots spread deep and wide in the established order, holding it together and drawing strength from it. Her fortunes were the concern of statesmen and journalists. The two older universities, despite all the secularism of the late nineteenth century, were still centres of theological energy.

The Chaplain of Trinity was due to retire in 1912. The Bishop of Oxford agreed that there was no need for Ronald to attend a theological college or to spend the year of his diaconate, as was usual, in parochial work. He was left to prepare himself for the Anglican priesthood in his own way and with his own chosen guides. His tutorial work at Trinity – Logic, Homer, Virgil, and 'Divvers' – was to begin in Hilary Term 1911. For

Michaelmas Term 1910 he had leave of absence and took what should have been the highly congenial post of private tutor to the brother of one of his friends at Eton, who was preparing at home for an Oxford scholarship. The boy, who is referred to in the *Spiritual Aeneid* as 'C', became his lifelong friend, but there was an early brief rupture of their connexion.

It was inevitable that besides coaching him in the Classics, Ronald should speak of what lay much nearer his heart. Indeed he regarded it as his duty. In answer to an inquiry from Ted Shuttleworth whether he was 'making C a Catholic', he wrote on October 10th: 'I'm not making him anything yet, but biding my time. I trust I may be sent some opportunity.'

The opportunity came that month. Ronald's kind of churchmanship was new to C, and he was attracted by the services at a neighbouring High Church to which Ronald led him, but it was Ronald's character which enthralled the boy. It was the first time in his life that he had glimpsed holiness. C's parents were of Nonconformist stock and were less impressionable. Ronald described the incident in a letter to his sister:

> *S. Charles Borromeo* [November 4th] 1910
>
> I'm not conscious at present of any particular leanings of the kind you think [towards Romanism]. . . . No, my dear, it isn't that, it's Mrs C. She (having made certain discoveries) wanted me to promise not to mention anything connected with religion in private conversation to her son. Of course I refused; from Thursday the 27th to Tuesday 1st we were arguing almost continuously. On All Souls Day I went and saw my Director, and, fortified by his authority, finally refused. So I left yesterday: they may want me to come back, but I can't do it under any promises whatsoever. The only thing which complicates the situation is that I'm by now extremely (and not quite unreturnedly) fond of the boy, and it's been a horrid wrench to go without saying a word to him of what I wanted to say. At present I lurk here [a house in Eaton Place] with a rich and Catholic bachelor who prides himself on providing rest cures for nerves and hearts jarred like mine.[1]

It happens to countless young men at the start of their careers to take a job and to lose it in more or less ignominious circumstances, but this incident affected Ronald so painfully that seven years later he set it down as one of his formative experiences. This more than normal tenderness

---

[1] Stuart Johnson, a cousin of Mgr Vernon Johnson, who died in his old house in Eaton Place at the age of eighty-eight in the same week as Ronald; he remained an Anglican to the end, and spoke much of Ronald on the last day of his life.

was the inseparable companion of his genius. When, once or twice, his youthful high spirits incurred rebuke he was disproportionately dismayed, lacking, as he did, both Child's impervious cheek and the *plaisir aristocratique de déplaire* of the Anna. He was solicitous of the dignity of others, almost morbidly diffident in making any claim to gratitude or applause, courteous to strangers, ingeniously inventive in his kindness to friends, constant in his loyalties, and these manifestations of charity usually found their reflection in the treatment he received. But on the rare occasions when he met unkindness, he was, in proportion, so much the more bitterly hurt.

Temporarily homeless, Ronald was taken in at Pusey House, and there he spent the remaining weeks of the term beginning the biblical studies which were to occupy so much of his later years. The chief danger to religion then seemed to be the destructive work of the German textual critics and the historical speculations of Dr Schweitzer. Ronald turned his sceptical mind on these sceptics and on the 'handbooks' which uncritically popularized their often self-contradictory conclusions. Early in 1911 he moved into college at Trinity and, having at first little contact with undergraduates, began to associate with the leading theologians of the University and with the vigorous young men, slightly older than himself, who were aspiring to take their places. This latter group he found to be much infected with German habits of thought, habits which to him seemed to endanger Faith itself. In preparation for the diaconate he equipped himself to meet them on their chosen ground. He, who suspended judgement in so many less important matters and in practical affairs often shrank painfully from a decision (in July 1949 he – need it be said? humorously – wrote to a priest of a Catholic writer whose work was causing dispute: ' – I haven't read and was hoping I needn't have any view about it. I've now reached the stage of being in two minds about whether one ought to be in two minds about things or not; and an infinite regress threatens') never for a moment doubted that Catholicism was, and must be, the historic Faith of Christendom. Such temptations against the Faith as he suffered – and he was near despair in the year before his reception into the Catholic Church – were total. Either the whole deposit of Faith was divinely inspired and protected and developed under divine guidance, or it was false. He never saw it, as did many of the contemporaries with whom he now took issue, as an agglomeration of history and fable, of hints and shadows of Truth, of vestigial philosophic notions and dark superstitions from which anyone could pick at will whatever he found agreeable, and discard the rest. He was for some years uncertain where he could find the authority which guarded and administered the Faith, but he always recognized it as a single, indivisible whole.

The Long Vacation of 1911 Ronald spent at Caldey – his fourth visit – living in the monastery, following, as far as a visitor could, the monastic rule and acquiring the habit of mental prayer. He was ordained deacon in the Cathedral at Oxford before the beginning of term, and adopted the additional name of Hilary, which now, for some years, figures on the title pages of his books.

On the eve of his ordination he wrote to Sligger:

> I don't really see my way beyond Anglican orders at present. At the same time I can't feel that the Church of England is an ultimate solution: in 50 years or a hundred I believe we Romanizers will either have got the Church or been turned out of it. I may not live to see it, but I hope never to live so long as to cease praying for it.

His view of the Church of England remained constant as long as he preached from her pulpits. He expressed it many times with ingenuity and eloquence. She was a true branch of the Latin Church of the West, which through an accident of history had been partly severed from the trunk. She was feloniously held in bondage by the State. She was justly entitled to all the privileges that had been hers in 1500, and to all the developments of the Council of Trent. It was her manifest destiny in God's own good time to return rejoicing to her proper obedience. He accepted the validity of her Orders on the *a priori* reasoning that it could not be God's will to leave so many excellent people, who in good faith sought them, deprived of the sacramental graces. There is a sentimental note – a note indeed which Ronald, when he turned in disgust from *A Spiritual Aeneid*, may have condemned as luxurious self-pity – in the terms in which he bemoaned the separation:

> Sorrowing she [Rome] calls us like that Mother of old, who sought her Son and could not find him, as he sat refuting the doctors in the Temple; but we too must be about our Father's business, though we meet our Mother again only after a Gethsemane, it may be, a Calvary. And surely we dare not doubt that Jesus will be our Shepherd, till the time when he gathers his fold together; and that though we do not live to see it, England will once again become the dowry of Mary, and the Church of England will once again be builded on the rock she was hewn from, and find a place, although it be a place of penitence and tears, in the eternal purposes of God.[1]

---

[1] *A Sermon Preached on the Feast of S. Charles, K.M. 1912 at S. Cuthbert's Church, Philbeach Gardens*, published by the Society of King Charles the Martyr.

And later:

It is not for us, the glamour of the Seven Hills, and the consciousness of membership, living and actual, in the Church of the Ages; we cannot set our feet upon the rock of Peter, but only watch the shadow of Peter passing by, and hope that it may fall on us and heal us. . . . And yet, even now, we are not left without hope . . . Mary . . . has not forgotten her children just because they have run away from their schoolmaster, and unlearnt their lessons, and are trying to find their way home again, humbled and terrified in the darkness.[1]

The greater part of the Long, 1912, was again spent at Caldey – his last visit until, in very different circumstances, 1935. On September 22nd Ronald was ordained priest in St Giles's Church, Reading, and said his first Anglican Mass on September 24th at St Mary's, Graham Street, London. A card from the Rue St Sulpice with a steel engraving of languorous piety and paper-lace edges was printed to commemorate the occasion. On it, as on his Newcastle medal, Arbuthnott is spelt incorrectly.

Since his diaconate Ronald had adopted an ecclesiastical costume in Oxford, and sometimes in London, as near as could be got to those he had seen in the streets of Bruges; cassock, silk stockings, and buckled shoes; to these he now added what he described in a letter as 'a quite new sartorial outrage by the name of a mantelletta'.[2] Those who knew him only in later life, when his clothes were barely respectable, will learn with surprise that there was a touch of the dandy about him in those days. 'Slig dear,' he wrote from Manchester to F. F. Urquhart, 'do you happen to know or can you find out for me, whether there is a Catholic laundry in Oxford that would iron surplices properly, i.e. in accordion pleats? If so, I hope to trade with them. My sister thinks ordinary wash people won't do it.'

These surplices were worn not only in the pulpit but also, in Trinity chapel, at the altar where he celebrated on alternate Sundays with the President, who occupied the 'northward position' as preferred by Bishop Knox. At Graham Street in London and at the other places where Ronald officiated in Oxford – St Stephen's House and an Anglican sisterhood – he wore a chasuble and said much of the service in the words and form of the Latin Missal. Many of his friends took a particular delight in continental church manners, and Ronald made considerable fun of old-fashioned

---

[1] *Naboth's Vineyard in Pawn* (SS. Peter and Paul, 1913). Sermons preached at St James's, Plymouth, in August 1913.

[2] It has been suggested that Ronald meant a 'Ferraiuolo'.

evangelical observances, but the externals of religion were never of great importance to him. He loved the Catholic Church and, because of her, such ornaments and ceremonies as he took to be her especial marks. He lived to see the Roman Church abandon many of the features he emulated as an Anglican. He saw the relaxation of the eucharistic fast and the irruption of the laity into the liturgy; he saw ecclesiastical architects turn their backs on the Mediterranean and follow the stark, proletarian fashions of the north. Some of his later sermons (particularly the Corpus Christi series at Maiden Lane) are rebukes addressed to himself for his sentimental regret at the changing face of the Church.

'The baby doesn't understand English,' he once said with unusual vehemence, when asked to perform a baptism in the vernacular, 'and the Devil knows Latin.' But his vexation was merely part of the general conservatism of his tastes. It had nothing to do with his religion, which was founded on biblical scholarship, theological orthodoxy, and mental prayer.

As an Anglican Ronald's mind was possessed by an ideal of the Church of England; he believed she had an essential personality which was often obscured but never obliterated; he ascribed the graces that came to him in prayer to his participation in that personality; he saw his group of friends, in communion with the saints in heaven, as constituting the real Church of England whose eventual triumph was guaranteed by God. His prayers were so easy and his association with his friends so congenial that he was able to live for some years in a hallowed world of his own. Only now and then did some event in the world outside shock him into doubt. Such an event was the break with C. He had come to regard his father's views as the absurd survival of an unhappy era; he was now sharply reminded, in a case where his personal affections were involved, that a great part of the governing class regarded his deepest beliefs as exotic and deleterious. Only an immediate withdrawal into sympathetic surroundings cured him then of the malaise which his set called 'Roman fever'. Another such event was the case of two Brighton vicars who in the summer of 1910 resigned their livings because their bishop forbade them to reserve the Blessed Sacrament.

> Ever since I went to Caldey [he wrote to Ted Shuttleworth], and more since the last time I went abroad, I've felt that Reservation and adoration in general of the Blessed sacrament is what we ought to have been fighting for all along, more than incense, possibly more than vestments. I suppose Chichester can't help it – trained in a rich Mod-High London Church and a Northern Deanery. It's enough to make one try to be a Bishop.

His personal affections were not involved in that case, and his response was one of hopeful defiance. But this mood was not constant. A few days later he is writing to Shuttleworth: 'The Vicar here is a member of the E.C.U.,[1] yet he went through all the silly antics of Choral Matins with a self-satisfied air. I never felt so doubtful about the Anglican Church as now, when I mean to get my bread and butter by it. Oh for Caldey.' But Caldey was there, eager to welcome and potent to comfort him. Human sympathy, at this time, was a necessary safeguard of his Faith. The two years of doubt which preceded his reception into the Catholic Church were also a process of emancipation from the bonds of friendship.

In questions of intellect, untroubled by emotion, Ronald was ready for a scrap. In 1911 his close association with Anglican theologians of different schools convinced him that the prime danger to his Church was not Protestantism but Modernism. He foresaw that in a short time the Anglican Hierarchy would allow all the disputed ritualistic practices which congregations wanted. He feared that their tolerance would be extended to doctrinal aberrations. The youngish men, mentioned above, who in the event did rise to positions of authority (one to the Archbishopric of Canterbury) seemed to be drifting into a fog of scepticism from which it might be his vocation to rescue them. They were preparing a book (it was no secret) to be entitled *Foundations*, in which to set out their far from homogeneous doctrine. Ronald knew them all well, liked them, and appreciated their idiosyncracies. Before their book appeared he published in the *Oxford Magazine* his most famous lampoon *Absolute and Abitofhell*, a poem in the manner of Dryden, which summarized the weaknesses of each of them. This appeared in Michaelmas Term 1912 when Ronald was newly ordained priest. It was an immediate success. *The Oxford Magazine* sold out and reprinted; a very elegant *edition de luxe*, now a rarity, was issued by the Society of SS. Peter and Paul;[2] it is still in print, delighting by its literary brilliance a generation of readers who have never opened *Foundations*.[3] The victims took the poem in good part. Dr Temple, the future Archbishop, who appeared under the name of 'Og', sent a post-card: 'Ta for puff. Og.' But the churchmen of Ronald's own school recognized in it the germ of a more serious purpose. Stuckey Coles, the Principal of Pusey House, and J. C. Howell, the vicar of St Mary's,

[1] English Church Union; an Anglo-Catholic association.
[2] See below, p. 220.
[3] Ronald Knox, *Essays in Satire* (1928), pp. 81–88. *In Three Tongues*, ed. Laurence Eyres (1959).

Graham Street, urged Ronald to write a serious refutation of *Foundations*. This he did in 1913 in *Some Loose Stones*. It was partly an assertion that 'the speculations of critics are *hypotheses*, based on *a posteriori* evidence, and, as such, in their very nature uncertain'[1] and partly a detailed exposure of the inconsistencies of the authors of *Foundations*, addressed to readers who accepted the same authorities as they. This, the first serious work of Ronald's, sold remarkably well for a book of its kind – some 4,000 copies – and was received everywhere with respect and, in many quarters, with enthusiasm. Ronald appeared for the first time as something more than an *enfant terrible* of the company of Maurice Child; as a sober academic theologian and a champion of orthodoxy whose career might influence the future history of the Church of England. There were still dioceses where his indiscretions had made him suspect, but he was increasingly in demand in pulpits and on platforms all over the country, where he was welcomed not only as the attractive spokesman of a party but also as a devotional preacher of delicate emotional appeal.

But he also greatly enjoyed himself with Maurice Child. 'It was easy to say of us at this time,' he wrote, 'that we thought what we thought, did what we did, for fun. I repudiate the accusation entirely, but no one shall persuade me that it was not fun doing it.'

Child always kept a flat or house in London which, whatever the address, was the centre of an exuberant hospitality which Ronald often enjoyed. He was a curate first at St Silas, Kentish Town, notorious as a centre of defiance to episcopal authority; later he went to Holy Trinity, Sloane Street, almost, it has been suggested, as a 'cover' to associate himself with respectable High Anglicanism. He and his set fully indulged their extravagant Romanism during the summer holidays, when they were lent a mission church of St James-the-Less, Plymouth.

The Society of SS. Peter and Paul was primarily Child's creation. This firm began modestly in the premises of the Medici Society, with which Mr Samuel Gurney was connected, as the producers of Lord Halifax's *Mass Book of Edward VI*. In 1911 it became a properly constituted company, with Mr Gurney as unpaid secretary and offices in Margaret Street in deliberately chosen proximity to a staid Anglican emporium. Over their shop-window they provocatively announced themselves as 'Publishers to the Church of England'. Mr Gurney had the leisure and taste to achieve the fine technical standards for which their publications

---

[1] *A Spiritual Aeneid*, p. 152.

soon became noted. 'Nip' Williams[1] and Cyril Howell provided theological weight; the Duke of Argyll added social prestige; but Child was the *animateur*. It was he who devised the advertisements in the *Church Times* for 'Lambeth Frankincense' and 'Latimer and Ridley Votive-candle stands', and sent curates to scour the back-streets of Soho for rococo ecclesiastical ornaments.

For one of the aims of the Society of SS. Peter and Paul was to revolutionize Anglican taste. Until then the Alcuin Club and Percy Dearmer[2] had represented, to Ronald as to others, the height of aestheticism and archaeological propriety. In Child's eyes only the baroque at its most luxuriant could express the assertion that the Church of England was not a survival of the second year of Edward VI but a living part of the Catholic Church of Italy, Spain, and Latin America. The 'Sarum' riddle posts which Bishop Knox was felling in Manchester were equally abhorrent to Maurice Child. The Society of SS. Peter and Paul was soon doing a brisk trade in gaudy objects, bought or looted from foreign convents; things until then quite out of favour, which ten years later appeared profusely in the show-rooms of fashionable, secular decorators.

The Society of SS. Peter and Paul was a shop and a publishing business, but it delighted Child to mystify. He borrowed a church near Regent Street for the Feast of SS. Peter and Paul and widely advertised a High Mass to be sung there at which 'members of the Order need not wear their insignia'. A large congregation was rewarded by an elaborate ceremony, replete with innovations and revivals.

A full generation after the days of mob violence and penal prosecutions there still lingered about Anglo-Catholicism a faint whiff of the spices of danger. Child revelled in conspiracy. A handful of London curates were known to be meeting under his auspices, calling themselves facetiously 'the Band of Hope'. Vicars who did not know what they were up to, became alarmed. Child liked it to be thought that they were plotting all manner of outrage. In fact. they met mainly to make jokes.

Ronald held slightly aloof from the full flamboyance of these pranks, but he was in general sympathy with the objects of the Society of SS. Peter and Paul, and he shared its laughter. There was, and still is, a distinctive *genre* of Anglo-Catholic humour very different from the jocosity

---

[1] The Rev. N. P. Williams, Chaplain of Exeter College, Oxford; later Lady Margaret Professor of Divinity and Canon of Christ Church.

[2] The Rev. Percy Dearmer, then Vicar of St Mary the Virgin, Primrose Hill; author of the *Parsons' Handbook*, first published in 1899, later Professor of Ecclesiastical Art, King's College, London.

of Roman Catholic presbyteries. It has its own school of light verse which began, perhaps, in the Parish Magazine of St Alban's, Holborn, when in 1901 the Rev. Gabriel Gillett published *The Rector Explains his Position*, and more than fifty years later still flourishes for a far wider audience in the works of Mr John Betjeman. Ronald added to this esoteric corpus several parodies of Anglican hymns, which changed hands in manuscript, were copied into commonplace books, and sung at parties, but were never printed.

His reputation today is in no danger of the charge of flippancy, and no one is likely to be at all scandalized (or greatly amused) by this typical production of the period:

> We love S. Botolph's Church
> A late Victorian pile:
> All England you may search,
> Nor find such Gothic style.
>
> We love the pitch-pine pews,
> On which our coat-tails bend,
> Designed to make us muse
> Upon our latter end.
>
> We love the alms-dish, which
> Between the vases stands,
> It helps us to enrich
> The poor in heathen lands.
>
> We love the windows bright
> With red and yellow paints,
> Presenting to our sight
> The better class of Saints.
>
> We love the Vicar's pram,
> In which, with tender care,
> He wheels his one ewe lamb
> To join in Evening Prayer.
>
> We love to feel that we,
> Renowned for moderation,
> Shall come off well at the
> Archdeacon's Visitation.

He helped translate the Roman liturgy of Holy Week (which he lived to see curtailed and, in his view, impoverished by Papal decree). Nearly forty years later he made another translation for Messrs Burns, Oates, and

Washbourne, a version designed to be read alongside the Latin, not to be sung in its stead. How free and full-hearted he had become in the intervening years! The *Exultet* of 1911 is a pastiche of Cranmer:

> Rejoice now all ye heavenly legions of Angels: all things that pass understanding: for the King that cometh with victory, let the trumpet proclaim salvation . . .
>
> . . . I pray and beseech you therefore, dearly beloved, that all ye who are present seeking this heavenly brightness, make your supplication with me to the Almighty that he would shew forth his mercy toward me.

In 1950 he rendered it:

> Joy for all heaven's angel citizens, joy in the secret council-chambers of God! In praise of this royal Conqueror, let the trumpet sound deliverance. . . . Brethren well-beloved, by the strange glow of this holy light drawn together [*Astantes vos, fratres carissimi ad tam miram hujus sancti luminis claritatem*], pray you, in my company cry to Almighty God for mercy.

As has been mentioned above, he gave the Society of SS. Peter and Paul his Plymouth sermons to publish. More important, he gave them *Reunion All Round*.[1] This pasquinade, in the manner of Swift, was written in four days at Eastertide 1914. It satirized the impulse prevalent among certain Anglicans to sink doctrinal differences with the Nonconformist sects in the interests of Christian good fellowship; an impulse which had lately caused scandal when Bishop Weston of Zanzibar condemned (and sought authority for his condemnation) an inter-denominational service held in the neighbouring diocese of East Africa. This – 'the Kikuyu incident' – proved decisive to some hesitating members of the Anglo-Catholic party who, in the language of the set, 'poped'. To Ronald it was merely the provocation for one of his most accomplished essays. Mr Gurney took immense pains to produce the replica of a late seventeenth-century pamphlet and made it the masterpiece of the Society of SS. Peter and Paul. Its success was wider than that of *Absolute and Abitofhell*. G. K. Chesterton, whom Ronald had long admired, reviewed it with enthusiasm. The Prime Minister had it read aloud as he basked on the river-bank at Sutton Courtenay. Anglican bishops, who had hitherto looked askance,

---

[1] *Naboth's Vineyard in Pawn* (1913) comprises three sermons. *The Church in Bondage* (1914) contains these sermons and nine more. It is possible that *Absolute and Abitofhell* appeared, as a SS. Peter and Paul publication, just before *Naboth*. It is probable that *Reunion all Round* came out after *Naboth*.

gave their approval. For Ronald it was the last flowering of his precocious youth; the perfect culmination of the golden summer of 1914.

That Long Vacation he began to collaborate with 'Nip' Williams on a work of theology which was never finished; he preached at the annual festival of St Margaret's Sisterhood, East Grinstead, 'an unimpeachable bulwark of Tractarian tradition'.[1] Stuckey Coles commended his address to the Oxford E.C.U. The slight peevishness which had troubled Ronald from time to time, which he had sometimes impetuously expressed, gave place to euphoria. He was supremely at his ease in the Church of England.

War transformed his life as completely as any recruit's in Kitchener's Army, but the impetus of his success still carried him forward another year in the public life of the Church of England, and his performances during that year may conveniently be mentioned here, out of their chronological order. He had longstanding engagements to fulfil. That autumn he preached at York, Southampton, London, Worcester, Reading. In December he was with 'Nip' Williams principal speaker at a clerical conference in Birmingham. In Lent he preached twice in London churches, at Shrewsbury, and in the University Church at Oxford. In Holy Week he gave a course of addresses at both St Mary's, Graham Street, and All Saints, Margaret Street, carried by taxi from one crowded congregation to another, just as of an evening in his first years at Oxford he had sped from college to college and club to club. The Society of SS. Peter and Paul published these addresses (on impetrative prayer) under the title *Bread or Stone*. They also issued anonymously in their series of 'York Books' his Birmingham lecture on 'Authority'.

In the Easter vacation occurred the conference which Ronald commemorates in the *Spiritual Aeneid*[2] with the quotation: '*Miseri, quibus ultimus esset ille dies*' ('That day of feasting – O misery – our last'). A letter survives in which he set down his account of the evening before the taste had turned sour:

> April 29th 1915
>
> I have to tell you, if only I may be the first to tell you, of the meeting between Mackay's 12 incumbents, and 30 or so very forward curates, which was organized by Howell and came off last Monday. Oh that you had been there!
>
> There was a dinner beforehand at Pagani's – Maurice and Roscow and Underhill and Humphrey and Magnus and Holland and my brother and Shaw of S. Matthew's and myself and two more you wouldn't know: we

---

[1] *A Spiritual Aeneid*, p. 171.   [2] p. 189.

got into the right frame of mind there. I've put texts to the pictures in a new Vanheems' [the clerical outfitter] catalogue, which was handed round at dinner. The incumbents, or several of them, dine in cassocks, so we were all in long frock coats.

῎Εσπετε νῦν μοι Μοῦσαι. How shall I describe that gathering? The incumbents, people like Tracy and Giraud, and all the fiercest curates – Fynes-Clinton, Butterworth, Harvey of St Edwards, et hoc genus omne: Kilburn and Scott (of Sunbury) gave us one or two elder extremists. Only Gamier and Blofeld looked as if Anglicanism had survived 1900. Underhill led off, putting the case for open reservation, communion from the tabernacle, and exposition, pleading the needs of the laity. Scott made the first of a series of gloriously pithy speeches about episcopal authority, he's wonderfully sound. Then Fynes-Clinton arose and we thought we were to have nothing but accounts of the antics of Hippopotamus Copronymus and the Liturgy of Prmysl for the rest of the evening: I had to hold Magnus down, he was getting so restive. Then I got up and said I'd been asked in to witness a dog-fight and wasn't satisfied with the sport shown hitherto; would an incumbent tell us whether they refrained from these things through (a) disapproval, (b) reverence for Bishops, or (c) fear of the congregation? And if a church were attacked for exposition, would he back it up? (That was St Saviour's, and they knew it.) Boyd of Knightsbridge took up the challenge and said it was a matter of policy. . . . Then we rammed St Saviour's down their throats – Humphrey and Maurice and Howell did. . . . I spoke again quite late, but I hardly know what I said, I was so excited: you must get it from Humphrey. In the end, of course, we got no further and finished up with considerations about Randall's 'pronouncement' which is taken very seriously at Margaret Street.

Here I could tell you more, but the Church has her secrets, Basil, as well as the Navy. . . . My hand aches: I've written 50 sheets in two days!

This exuberant letter was addressed to a naval chaplain at sea. In what mood was it read, wistfully or with impatience? How did the balmy airs of Caldey blend with the tang of the North Sea? The holocaust of Ronald's friends lay in the future. They went to their deaths with the sense of sacrifice. Few of their causes prospered. One identifiable achievement, infinitesimal by one measure, infinite by another, was that they brought an excited young clergyman to his senses.

2

Ronald's life as an Oxford don was complementary to, and to some extent distinct from, his life as a leading churchman. He lectured in Logic,

Homer, and Virgil to candidates for Honour Mods. Few of his pupils survive. One has preserved the text of his Virgil lectures. Forty-five years after they were given, in the full light of all the subsequent innovations in educational methods, they still appear fresh, witty, and original. At the time there was no other Mods tutor so lively. It was probably to help in delivering his lectures that he bought a typewriter, a 'Brick' model with an ink-well instead of a ribbon, which was later replaced by a neater apparatus. There can have been few dons of his time so equipped, and it may well be imagined with what disdain he would have regarded its intrusion into the University had it been the invention of a later decade. As time went on he became increasingly at one with it. He wrote a good hand, but he was not a neat-fingered man and he took no pleasure, as many writers have done, in the use of the pen. Most of his private letters are in holograph, but when he had something to say which required close thought, he found the keys of the typewriter in some way an aid to precision. There is a letter of his to Mr Laurence Eyres written in 1927 in which he began to type halfway through with the words: 'I'm sorry, but I can't think properly with a pen.'

The typewritten sheet became an adjunct of all his sermons. His undergraduate speeches when not entirely unpremeditated had been from notes, but as early as December 1914, at the Birmingham Conference on 'Authority', he apologized for 'departing from three principles which usually govern my conduct in these matters. The first is never to speak without having what I propose to say written down.'[1] The reasons for this habit, which was never obtrusive to his audience, were partly of prudence to safeguard himself from being carried away into exaggeration or indiscretion; partly artistic – there was one, and only one, proper expression for his thoughts, which had to be sought with care, not left to the mood of the moment; and partly psychological – his mind had a trick of working simultaneously in more than one way. Thus when it was most intently engaged in a verbal problem he would keep distractions at a distance by playing patience. He required the paper in his hands and the words under his eyes to keep his thoughts from wandering in the pulpit. In fact, he was usually fully rehearsed and word perfect in his part. The manuscript satisfied a nervous need. 'I tried a very good piece of bluff this morning at Mass,' he wrote many years later in a letter, 'by putting on my spectacles to read the notices and then taking them off for the Conference,

---

[1] '*Authority in the Church*. For Private circulation only. Printed by request of the Conference.' 47 Temple Row, Birmingham, p. 12.

so that people wouldn't see I was cribbing from my ms. But nobody noticed.'[1]

Among his candidates for 'Divvers' – the now extinct Divinity Examination which had to be passed some time before Final Schools and which, postponed, hung heavy over many a man's last year – he met duller minds than he was used to. Rising to the challenge, he evinced for the first time the peculiar ingenuity in mnemonics that was to endear him to his forms at Shrewsbury and Ware and leave them for life with an ineradicable deposit of superfluous information. Among other *memoriae technicae* he designed a game on the model of Snakes and Ladders, played with dice on a board illustrating the missionary journeys of St Paul; the foot of a ladder stood at Beroea, where 'the Jews were more noble than those of Thessalonica'; Ephesus, where there was a riot, was a snake's head leading back several throws.

Now, as later, Ronald was constantly invited to entertain club meetings. He learned to be economical in this matter. When he composed a paper he kept it in a drawer and brought it out on demand, repeating it at different colleges and to different generations until he himself tired of it – his audiences never did so – when he would issue it in print. He came to regret the precipitate publication in the *Blue Book 1912* of his paper (originally read to the Gryphon Club at Trinity in 1911), *Studies in the Literature of Sherlock Holmes*,[2] not only because it prematurely impoverished his repertory but also because it brought him a form of fame which he found tedious. 'I can't BEAR books about Sherlock Holmes,' he wrote some thirty years later to an editor who had asked him to review one. 'It is so depressing that my one permanent achievement is to have started a bad joke. If I did start it.'

In fact, he was not the first to make a textual examination of the Holmes stories. Frank Sidgwick[3] had done this in Cambridge ten years earlier, but Ronald never saw it; few did; certainly not Conan Doyle, who wrote to Ronald on July 5th 1912: 'I cannot help writing to tell you of the amusement – and also the amazement – with which I read your

[1] There is an anecdote of doubtful authenticity which relates that on one of the first occasions when as a Catholic he preached *coram episcopo*, the Bishop said: 'An interesting sermon, Father, but it was a pity you had to read it.' To which Ronald answered: 'I am bitterly conscious of my disability, my lord. Only the other day a friend remarked, "When I saw you go into the pulpit with a sheaf of papers I thought we were in for another of those dreadful Pastorals."'

[2] *Essays in Satire*, pp. 145–78.

[3] Frank Sidgwick was the son of a Fellow of Corpus Christi, Oxford. Born 1879, educated Rugby and Trinity, Cambridge. He published a book of verses in 1916. Founder of the publishing firm, Sidgwick and Jackson.

article on Sherlock Holmes. That anyone should spend such pains on such material was what surprised me. Certainly you know a great deal more about it than I do,' and he continued for four pages to discuss the criticisms in detail.

It was the cult started by Ronald's paper which disinterred Sidgwick's original essay. Enthusiasts on both sides of the Atlantic bound themselves together – and are still so bound – to make an intensive, light-hearted but sometimes rather heavy-handed, study of the stories. This was far from Ronald's intention. He had merely chosen Sherlock Holmes and his chronicler as being widely known literary figures in order to satirize the German critics whose biblical speculations he was then reading (just as later he satirized the Baconians by finding a cryptogram in Tennyson's 'In Memoriam').[1] It was natural to his mind to note the discrepancies in whatever he read. The analogy between Conan Doyle and the Evangelists was not complete, but it provided a topical and telling construction with which to expose the pundits.

At about the same time he wrote a paper on the theology of Ella Wheeler Wilcox, which combined a deliciously funny reading of that poet's literary infelicities with a more sombre exposure of the fatuous, contemporary 'uplift' to which he returned more directly in *Caliban in Grub Street* and *Broadcast Minds*.

In 1911 there appeared '*A Still More Sporting Adventure*, by Lavinia and Priscilla Daisyfield. Humbly dedicated to the authoresses of "An Adventure"', published by Basil Blackwell. It is a skit on the account, then causing a sensation which has not yet abated, of the vision enjoyed by Miss Moberly and Miss Jourdain in the gardens at Versailles; it purports to be the translation of a Latin manuscript describing a vision of Dido and is full of recondite delicacies for the Latinist. Fletcher of Magdalen was the originator of the work. Ronald completed and embellished it with an ingenious symposium (pp. 44–76) – a literary form which fascinated him until the end of his life. Neither author acknowledged the work at the time, and it had small success. It was a great delight to Ronald when, forty years later, Mr Painter of the British Museum identified him as part-author; not for any personal vanity, but because such a precise and unrewarding piece of literary detection restored his confidence in the survival of scholarship.

★

---

[1] *Essays in Satire*, pp. 223–38.

Ronald's first two terms in his new college were rather lonely. Ted Shuttleworth was still up; otherwise he had few undergraduate friends, but in Michaelmas Term 1911, a deacon in his noticeable clerical dress, he quickly attracted the new generation of Trinity men. He took to being 'at home' on Wednesday evenings after hall, dispensing port and bananas to all the most amusing junior members of the college. The company selected itself: men knew without formal invitation whether they would be welcome, rather as they did in Sligger's rooms in Balliol or at 'Veneer's' in Sir Compton Mackenzie's 'St Mary's',[1] with the difference that the host was young, scintillating, and a jump ahead of them in every joke. It was known as 'Ronnie's bar' and was frequented by athletes as much as by scholars, and by men without any particular religious interests.

The 'Spike Teas' went on as before. Not only undergraduates but dons, visiting clergymen, and theological students from outside the University attended in fluctuating numbers. An elderly London vicar still recalls the pride with which he sometimes found himself deputed to pour out tea. There were always honey sandwiches, and Ronald usually stood in his soutane leaning on the chimney-piece, pipe in hand, with a lock of hair drooping over his forehead while the party listened to the latest squib and to the gossip from Graham Street and the Society of SS. Peter and Paul.

By the end of 1912 a third circle, of whom Ted Shuttleworth had been the forerunner, was beginning to form round Ronald, some from Trinity, more from Magdalen and Balliol; cleverer than the 'banana eaters', grander and gayer than the Friday afternoon 'spikes'. 'It is hard to give a definition or even a description of them,' he wrote,[2] 'except perhaps to say that in a rather varied experience I have never met conversation so brilliant – with the brilliance of humour, not of wit. It was among these that I first began to make proselytes.' It was an apostolate of laughter and the love of friends.

But behind the merriment lay deep personal affection, much eager concern with ecclesiastical politics and, in some cases, a striving for real piety. Many of the freshmen of 1912 had heard at school and at home of the golden age of the Grenfells, Charles Lister, and Patrick Shaw-Stewart. Legends fructified in Oxford, and Ronald, as their sole survivor in the university, had the lustre of these heroes. The younger generation tasted in his rooms at Trinity the brilliance and warmth of the Anna without its arrogance; its wit and romanticism turned towards religion. C, coming up

[1] Compton Mackenzie, *Sinister Street*, Vol. II, passim.
[2] *A Spiritual Aeneid*, p. 117.

to Balliol in 1912, found Ronald's court already forming and joyfully took his place there. Another freshman of that year was Guy Lawrence, whom Ronald called 'B' in the *Spiritual Aeneid*. His friendship was the strongest human affection of Ronald's early manhood.

Father Bede Jarrett, the wise and holy Provincial of the English Dominicans, thus counselled a monk whose conscience was troubled by the intensity of human love and the fear that it might obscure his spiritual life:[1]

> Then as for the point you mention, I would only say this, that I am exceedingly glad. I am glad because I think your temptation has always been towards Puritanism, narrowness, a certain inhumanity. . . . You were afraid of life because you wanted to be a saint and because you knew you were an artist. . . .
>
> . . . Now evil is overcome by good, by God, by love of God, by reaching for him everywhere. You must not be afraid of looking for Him in the eyes of a friend. He is there. You can at least be sure of that. To love others is not to lose Him but if possible to find Him in them. He is in them. You will miss finding Him only if you merely love yourself in them. That is the blinding nature of passion; it is self-love masquerading under a very noble disguise . . .
>
> . . . I agree that to say that your desire to bring God to Y. is sufficient justification for your friendship is all bunkum. . . . You love Y. because you love him, neither more nor less, because he's lovable. You won't find any other sincere reason however hard you try. . . . Enjoy your friendship, pay the price of the following pain for it, and remember it in your Mass and let Him be a third in it. The opening of The Spiritual Friendship: 'Here We are, thou and I and I hope that between us Christ is a third.' Oh dear friendship, what a gift of God it is. Speak no ill of it.

Those words might have been addressed to Ronald in 1912, He loved Guy Lawrence simply because he was lovable; the love was returned; each guided the other to the love of God.

Little is recorded or remembered of this rare spirit. At Winchester he had been Prefect of Chapel and Captain of VIs, summits of Wykehamist ambition. He came up to Trinity as senior classical scholar and seemed more mature than his contemporaries, taking more trouble in furnishing his rooms and dressing better; there had been a change of fashion since 1906. Smart undergraduates no longer wore flannel trousers and shooting-coats, but dressed in term as they did during the vacation. Illness – he was

[1] Kenneth Wykeham George, O.P., and Gervase Mathew, O.P., *Bede Jarrett* (1952), pp. 117–19.

perhaps consumptive – and the War prevented his taking Schools. He played Soccer for the University and was President of the O.U.D.S. He was tall, fair, intelligent, very fastidious, impulsive, affectionate, and highly strung. When he came up, he had a half-formed intention of taking Holy Orders; sometimes he spoke of becoming a clerical don like Ronald. Later, after his reception into the Roman Church, he decided to try his vocation as an Oratorian.

Oxford – the little world where 'the sun rose over Wadham and set over Worcester' – was more than the background of the friendship. It was an integral and determining part of it; a place so hallowed that when war separated them, Lawrence could not bring himself to revisit it on leave; nor could Ronald long remain in his memory-haunted rooms.

In July 1914 Lawrence wrote from a house-party in Scotland: 'Every day I see more clearly that unless one is totally independent of others one ought never to go to Oxford: it makes life unbearable in the long vac. by contrast.' A few months later from camp he thanked Ronald for the gift of *Sinister Street*, Vol. II. 'The Oxford part is singularly good to my mind. The absence of incident is especially good and clever. Really I don't think there was a single incident in my two years which wd. have been the least interesting to anyone but ourselves.'

One incident stands out, Lawrence's sudden, grave illness during his second term, which necessitated his removal to San Remo. It was then that Ronald heard an anxious voice on the telephone from Pusey House telling him of the defection to Rome of the Caldey community. At any other time the news would have been highly disturbing. That morning Ronald had no thought for anything but his friend.

That was the only shadow on their two years of happiness. Ronald showed Lawrence and his friends the Catholic Church as he then conceived it. He introduced them to Child and his set. They served him at the altar (at St Stephen's House and St Thomas's Convent, where they could follow 'extreme' practices forbidden in Trinity. Ronald himself prayed in Latin but lapsed into English for his dialogue with the server) and went to him for confession. They spoke of him as their 'director'. Very few of them lived through the War. They achieved nothing, consummated no love, left no posterity, no published word, no university honours even. The men of Ronald's own year enjoyed a short lease of full manhood; these went straight to death without any other memorial than the multitude of disembodied Christian names in the letters which Ronald preserved in cardboard boxes among his files of sermons. All they took with them to war was what Ronald had taught them of God. One survivor, who was taken prisoner by the Turks at the capitulation of Kut, is Mr Laurence Eyres. His name will occur often in the following pages. He was Ronald's early disciple at Trinity; a member both of the athletic and of the scholarly sets, he frequented the 'bar' and the 'spike teas'. He later followed Ronald into the Church and to St Edmund's,[1] formed the best existing collection of Ronald's writings, and edited the posthumous book of his *jeux d'esprit*. He was more than a disciple. Ronald consulted him often on questions of Greek translation and in many of the decisions of his personal career.

During these years everyone close to Ronald – his family, his colleagues, his followers – watched him anxiously, expecting him at each crisis – the Caldey conversions, the 'Kikuyu Incident' – to make his submission to Rome. He alone was quite unconscious of the fate which all foresaw for him. His acute logical mind, which would have seemed to lead him in only that one direction, was delighted to exercise itself in ingenious justifications of his position. The happiness of his Oxford friendships seemed to lack nothing for completeness.

In the vacations Ronald assembled reading parties. Middlecott, near Bovey Tracey in Devon, where at Ilsington there was a sympathetic parish church, took the place of Caldey. It was convenient for Plymouth, where Ronald often preached. These parties never developed the stable character of Sligger's chalet. Their membership varied among Ronald's various circles of friends.

For part of the Long, 1914, he was lent More Hall, a fine old house in the Stroud valley, the property of an eccentric Anglican clergyman named Charles Edward Sharpe,[2] who was trying to found a religious community there from the wreck of Caldey.

That August promised to be a month of delight. The party were all members of Guy Lawrence's coterie. Ronald chose the white wine. Lawrence found the cook – 'in art as well as in body she is good and plain'. C was an uncertain starter, fearing his mother's disapproval. 'Why should C give any reason whatever for his whereabouts?' Lawrence wrote. 'It's all silly nonsense this buckling to the old-fashioned ignorance of his

---

[1] See below, p. 273.

[2] He later became a Roman Catholic, but not a priest; nevertheless he continued to wear a cassock and liked to be addressed as 'Father Sharpe'. During his last illness he was nursed by Blue Nuns in Bristol. He left them the property, which is now a home for the aged under their care.

parents and hanging onto his mother's apron strings. I should like 5 minutes conversation with her on the point.

'I think we shall all have a priceless time,' he added.

None of them, in the event, came.

The first intimation of change was from a Trinity man who had just gone down, Kenneth Mackenzie, who was one of the first of Ronald's friends to be killed. He wrote: 'Alas – I fear I shall not be able to come to Stroud owing to this ridiculous war as I have applied for a commission with a view to "keeping" an Armageddon.'

It was the voice of them all.

BOOK II

Keeping an Armageddon

KEEPING AN ARMAGEDDON

1914–1917

Not even momentarily was Ronald touched by the zest for battle which inebriated the country in August 1914.

He was not a pacifist in the popular sense. He believed the War was just and that it was his country's duty to achieve a victorious peace; that is to say, to right the wrong which had provoked the War. He had no sympathy with the politicians, who in the end succeeded in imposing their ambition to destroy the German and Austrian Empires.

On August 28th 1915 he wrote to (now Major-General) John Latter, then on active service:

> As to what people in England think about the war, which you say is not to be what the papers say, I find it hard to draw the distinction – not because the papers reflect the views of the people but vice versa. I haven't any doubt what *I* think of it – so long as we could secure the restoration of Belgium, I think we ought to want peace at every moment and with all possible personal sacrifices. Eat this if you're taken prisoner.

He did not at once recognize – who did? – the monstrous physical catastrophe that impended, but while his countrymen were singing and waving flags, he stood back aghast at the gross dislocation in the moral order, which kept him on his knees, alone, six hours a day for the last three weeks of the month, in the house where he and Guy Lawrence had planned their reading party.

The German Army moved across Belgium with what, then, seemed outrageous brutality; the little towns, daily reported sacked and gutted, were peculiarly dear to Ronald; he had few friends in the Regular Army; casualty lists were not yet what they became, a roll of irreparable personal losses, but every letter brought news of young lives turned off their course. The swift and decisive campaigns of Bismarck were the measure of modern war. Pundits spoke of victory before Christmas. Enthusiasts feared that they would miss the shooting match. In that false perspective Ronald resented the disruption of everyone's plans; he who liked to know where he would be and what he would be doing on any particular day three months ahead; just as, entering the pulpit, he liked to know precisely what he would be saying in ten minutes time, once remarked: 'A man's first duty is to his plans,' and here was everyone going down before his Schools, leaving his chosen calling for the entirely unsuitable profession of arms.

Ronald never had much regard for military prowess. In both World Wars friends of his distinguished themselves without impressing Ronald. Gallantry he considered an attractive physical quality, like good looks; something very remotely connected with the Christian virtue of fortitude. (He was himself unreasonably timid in the presence of such creatures as mice and moths.) The acts of heroism which he admired were acts of self-sacrifice.

He did what he could to prevent the dissipation of the coterie. On August 14th he wrote to Mr Laurence Eyres:

> Is it too much, I wonder, to hope that you've resisted the temptation to be patriotic, and are going to do your duty instead, by taking Greats at the ordinary time? Heaps of Oxford people, even very unmilitary ones like Guy Lawrence, seem to be enlisting, and I think it's awfully fine, but I do think it's rather a waste for people who are really receiving an education – I suppose that means less than 2000 people in the British Isles – to break it off in the middle like this. . . . The sort of questions one was asking, and things one was anticipating are such a mockery to read now. Write to tell me if you're going to do anything rash: but don't do it.

And on August 20th to the same friend:

> I think you're quite right about people who mean to be priests. In the case of a person who certainly meant to be, I should always advise (as a director) that he shouldn't take arms. My reason would be, not that a future priest ought not to risk being killed, but that he ought not to risk killing anybody. . . . He ought never to have known that blood lust which I suppose everybody more or less gets in battle.
>
> I only gave Guy my advice as a Don; that he ought to hold on because of schools; he wasn't taking any of that. Though he's meant for a long time to be a priest, I don't think he's yet definitely considered his vocation, and I told him that I wouldn't like to give him my advice as his confessor, because I don't think he's sufficient spirit of obedience to feel *absolutely* at rest in his conscience in acting on a director's advice: and anything in the world is better than a bad conscience.
>
> . . . What I should be afraid of with him is that if I said 'Either you

oughtn't to go to war or you oughtn't to be a priest', he would begin to wonder whether he wasn't really using his vocation as a cloak for cowardice and slackness.

The Blessed Curé d'Ars whose life is (I think) the most heroic of any which is described to us in any detail after Our Saviour's, ran away when a seminarist to escape the conscription of 1810.

None of the young men who, a month before, had hung on Ronald's words, now heeded him. All competed feverishly for admission to the New Army. Guy Lawrence, finding official channels congested, resorted to the curious expedient of demanding and getting an interview with the Lord Chancellor[1] and persuaded him to write personally to Kitchener on his behalf, with the result that some weeks before his friends, he was growing a moustache as an infantry subaltern in Belton Park Camp.

'They seem to say,' he wrote, 'that Germany will retire fairly soon into their impregnable Rhine fortresses. France will do the same. Kitchener's Army will go out by degrees starting soon after Christmas and in April the most gigantic struggle ever known will begin.'

There was very little explicit patriotism about the mood of 'joining-up'. It was a fashionable craze with, behind it, a sense of private honour; of a debt on demand that had been incurred by privilege. To this was added within two years, for those who survived so long, a sense of doom, clearly discernible in almost all their letters; an intuition that they were lagging behind their friends and had no proper place among the living. Meanwhile Ronald, heavy at heart, received cheerful letters announcing one after another the transformation of all his coterie. The reading party at More Hall became a solitary retreat, the first he had made since his ordination; even then he had had the monastic community round him. This was the first time in his life that he had lived quite alone.

The direction of his prayers may be seen in the little book of meditations which resulted from them. *An Hour at the Front* was published at a penny by the Society of SS. Peter and Paul and sold over 70,000 copies. The proceeds went to the Prince of Wales' Relief Fund.

> These devotions [Ronald wrote] are intended for those who either find the repetition of long vocal prayers wearying, or who, being accustomed rather to that inward prayer, which is not formed with the lips, are

---

[1] Lord Haldane, soon to be driven from office by a disreputable campaign in the newspapers, had been responsible, as Liberal Minister for War, for the organization of the British Expeditionary Force, and was trusted by Kitchener.

nevertheless conscious of some difficulty in adapting that method to the exigencies of a great national affliction.

There are twelve sections of two pages each; each headed by the drawing of a clock face marking the passage of five minutes. Ronald records that he spent six hours daily in prayer at More Hall. It is probable that these were the subjects of half hours of his meditation.

> Pray for Victory for the arms of the country.
> *Suggestions* – Commend your country to the care of God *simply because it is your country*; and you are therefore bound to intercede on its behalf.
> Then remember in the sight of God the justice of our cause. . . . Pray to God that he will pardon our sins, which cry to him for vengeance; and, since he has seen fit to use us, unworthy as we are, as champions of his justice and pity, pray that he will exalt his holy Name before the whole world by giving us the Victory, if it be his Will.

Prayers follow for Peace; for soldiers and sailors – ' . . . the untried whose hearts fail them at the moment of battle: that those who are tried by long waiting and suspense may have confidence and quietness . . . that in the hour of victory they may preserve the fame of England and their own purity in the sight of God'; for friends and relations at the front; for 'the honour of God; . . . that Churches may be spared, that Church worship may be unhindered'; for all in deadly sin 'on whom death may come suddenly'; for noncombatants; for the bereaved – 'that God will keep them from the slightest yielding to that terrible despair, in which man turns and curses God'; for sick and wounded; for the dying – 'Picture to yourself that even now as you pray, there are probably numbers of souls enduring the terrible agony of parting from their bodies and few of them able to face the next world with sure confidence'; and for the dead – 'Think of the poor souls in Purgatory, seeing now, as they could not see, and we cannot see on earth, the enormity even of their lesser sins. . . . Grant them, O Lord, eternal rest, and let everlasting light shine upon them.'

These, we may be sure, were the occupations of Ronald's mind, while beyond the Stroud valley the bands were everywhere playing the recruits into camp.

He never doubted that he was precluded from bearing arms; nor did he think it possible that he would be accepted as a chaplain. Maurice Child's application was refused on the grounds, it was said, that in his interview with the Chaplain-General he was asked what he would do for a dying man, and answered: 'Hear his confession and give him absolution.' The correct answer was: 'Give him a cigarette and take any last message he may have for his family.'

One typically quixotic service occurred to Ronald; might he not go into voluntary captivity so that Anglican prisoners of war should not be left without religious ministrations? His proposal was forwarded to the Foreign Office but rejected on the grounds that any such arrangement through a neutral agency was tantamount to collusion with the enemy.

He returned at the beginning of October to be chaplain of Trinity.

> If you and I, Sligger [Ronald wrote in the unpublished preface to *A Spiritual Aeneid*], had to earn our living, and took on a job as one of those guides who hang about outside the Bodleian and St Mary's, what a much better account we could give of it than they do! We shouldn't worry our traveller with the old Bocardo and the Octagon House and where Prince Rupert slept at St John's and where Addison walked (if he did walk in Addison's Walk), and where Cecil Rhodes first dreamed of Empire. 'All that,' we should tell him, 'is prehistoric; it belongs to the stone age. History begins in 1914.' We should recount to him the names, and show him the haunts, of our dead. . . . 'History' we should tell him 'is deeds, not achievements', and he would go his way to lecture in the provinces on Reconstruction, not understanding how much he had missed in not knowing all these, and all those others who shared with us Oxford and the countryside and the river and the sun that rises over Wadham and sets over Worcester.

The last Oxford generation whom Ronald was to know for fourteen years came up that autumn. They found themselves greatly reduced from their normal numbers in an almost deserted city. Ronald now gave his lectures on the Odyssey in his own rooms, so few were his pupils. He was able to smoke and stop to relight his pipe again and again while he ruefully regarded the little group and regaled them with the humour and courtesy of the year before; examining *Eric or Little by Little* in a parody of the German critics of Homer; expounding Nausicaa's instructions to her maiden to 'wash' Odysseus:

> It is not clear whether she meant them to take their guest into the bathroom, supervise his undressing, dip their fingers into the water to see if the temperature was right, invite him to get in and then scrub him with one of those nasty things one's nurse used to use, often filling one's eyes with soapsuds − or whether they were just to take him to the bathroom door and say: 'Here it is; there's plenty of hot water; there's clean towel on the rail and soap in the tray; and if you want anything, you'll find a bell just over your head':

telling a pupil (Major-General J. C. Latter) one day that his Latin style 'if I may say so, still resembles that of the official communiqué rather than that of the official correspondent' and later when he had tried to achieve Augustan rotundity: 'No. This time, if one may be pardoned the observation, it looks as if you had had considerable difficulty in filling up a reply-paid telegram.'

It was the old technique, now reduced to rigmarole.

Ronald was trying, in the catch phrases of the time, to 'carry on' with 'business as usual', but he was sick at heart in the empty quadrangles and the full Common-rooms of dons, some of whom seemed to welcome the war as the dons of Zuleika Dobson welcomed the mass-suicide of the undergraduates as the removal of what had always been a disturbing element in academic life. Most of all, Ronald felt the futility of his position as chaplain. His little flock were scattered. It was to them, wherever they were, that he owed his first duty. So for two terms he devoted his lonely and now ample leisure to keeping in touch.

He wrote hundreds of letters, very few of which have survived. The answers are here, all letters of gratitude; thanks for hospitality, for prayers, for news of friends, for presents of tobacco and compasses and pipes, for loans of money, for new books, for counsel; for visits to camps and barracks, undertaken all that bleak winter in the discomfort and dislocation of wartime travel. All his resources were devoted to keeping the coterie together.

But in many of the letters more is expressed than gratitude and the regret for good times that have passed.

> When I enlisted in the Inns of Court, when they asked my religion, I said 'Catholic' and they put me down 'R.C.'.

> I was yesterday constrained for the first time to attend the Chaplain's Mass – 4 officers and 1 man – Y.M.C.A. tent, portable altar 2' 6" × 10" – Priest vested in hood etc. Northern position . . . the Regimental Doctor is a Catholic – but I haven't so much as smelt another anywhere – except the Romans in my platoon.

> I don't think Rome produces a particularly fine character in men of the army. Many R.C.s believe and know precious little. But the system . . . reduces misunderstanding to a minimum. Also no one ever shows the least surprise at a R.C. being truly devout.

These extracts from the letters of three of the coterie illustrate the spiritual discomfort which most of them suffered. Guy Lawrence was more fortunate.

'Great news!' he wrote from Belton, 'The Chaplain reveals unknown heights of Catholicism ... showed me with pride a pyx in which he intends reserving the Blessed Sacrament in the trenches,' but it was a precarious consolation. A change of posting could deprive him of the sacraments in his greatest need.

That was the heart of the matter. A young man who could be upset by the spectacle of a portable altar-stone merely needed to be shaken into a sense of what was essential. To be given a cigarette as viaticum outraged a different order. Most of Ronald's delicately nursed coterie now found themselves dependent on the spiritual ministrations of good-natured brother-officers who had never heard a confession and disdained all pretensions to offering the sacrifice of the Mass. All the delicate shades of the Anglican spectrum – 'Prot.', 'Mod.', 'High', 'Catholic', 'Extreme' – were merged in khaki. The plain alternatives were 'C. of E.' and 'R.C.'.

The predicament was not new. 'Poping' and 'verting' had been staples of gossip for years. A curate at Margaret Street, who was a friend of all the coterie, decided to 'pope' in protest at the Kikuyu incident. Ronald defined the decision of the Archbishop's Committee on that affair as: 'the service at Kikuyu was eminently pleasing to God and must on no account be repeated', but, examined logically, it was not more flagrant than many similar incidents in Anglican history, all of which had produced a storm of talk, one or two lonely defections, and in the long run a slight strengthening of the Anglo-Catholic position. What was new was the urgency of decision.

Rome had always been regarded as a last resort; a threat to restrain their opponents. If such and such a policy prevailed there would be an Anglican schism. A puritan national Church would remain, while all that had arisen from the Oxford Movement would in a body seek reconciliation with Rome. But as things turned out no particular scandal, dispassionately considered, seemed quite to justify such drastic action. Time would tell. The Anglo-Catholics would leaven the lump until eventually the whole Church of England, complete with her historic buildings and titles, retaining perhaps her own vernacular liturgy, would joyfully return to her natural obedience. There was a whole lifetime ahead in which this gracious consummation could gently be brought about. And now, suddenly, a lifetime meant a few months.

As the period of military training came to an end and the New Army was reported fit for service, Ronald's disciples turned to him for advice. He could not advise them to face death with troubled consciences. Tom

Bischoff of Trinity, an elegant sidesman at Margaret Street, who survived the War and lived until 1951 a pious layman, was the first to go.

Within a few days Guy Lawrence and C came to Ronald and told him they were going too. It was a day of revelation for Ronald, for he suddenly found that where his heart was most deeply committed, his ratiocinations were meaningless. There was nothing he could say, and nothing he wanted to say, to keep them at his side. They left to think it over and on May 28th Lawrence wrote:

> You told me to act on my own judgement and I've done so. My mind was made up for me this morning. God made it clear to me and I went straight to Farm St., asked for Father St John and explained all to him. He took me through the faith for a little and then baptised me and received me and heard my confession. It was all done in under one hour. . . . I know I am happy and I only long for you to be happy with me. Come and be happy. C will, I think, follow very soon. I am to see him this afternoon. You've been and still are my best friend, Ron: there is no shadow between you and me.

The news went round and elicited varying comments.
One friend wrote:

> Well, well, C and Guy have certainly scored off you. I'm sorry to be flippant about it but at present I can only see a whole new field opened up where we can devise things to make Guy writhe. I think we shall be able to twit him most fearfully. We must certainly try. . . . I really and truly wish I could say, think or do something which wasn't absolutely futile but what can one do if Guy and C both think they ought to be Popes? We can't stop them. . . . Oh Lord, what a mess.

Another wrote:

> I can quite understand that C and Guy make things harder for you and I shan't forget you or them. . . . It is quite obvious to start with that if you want someone you love more than yourself to accept a position which is not yours, there can be no real sacrifice of truth in their doing so or in your remaining as you were. If by taking this step it meant the denial of the truth of certain things you believed to be true, you could not possibly allow it on any grounds because your love for your friend will oblige you to try and make him believe what you hold to be the truth. . . . I am assuming all the time that you are not dissatisfied with your own position . . . the difference is a difference of detail and not the truth itself and you wish it for your friend because his expression of the truth is an *easier* one and you want your friend to have content rather than worry, a time of peace rather

than the life of difficult struggle you are having. . . . Guy's and C's position is easier because it is more logical and so more simple and direct and less conflicting and controversial . . . I do not think one is justified in trying to hold a position in a system which is fundamentally conflicting with that system even if one is led to believe that one's own position may change the whole system. It is no good playing Rugby fives in an Eton fives court because you want the other three players to see what a much better game Rugby fives is and what a nuisance a pepper box is. The only way to show the superiority of Rugby fives would be to play Rugby fives in a Rugby fives court with 3 other people playing Rugby fives; then if it was played well it might be acceptable and the other might be rejected.

Though I have a sort of feeling that you ought to take the step too yet I hope you won't because I think you have a special message for the C. of E., one of prayer and of faith but more particularly of reverence and worship some idea of which I claim to have got from you and you alone, but if the lines you were going on were not quite and just exactly the lines you are going on I feel that I and others would get so much more from you – you have so much to give, Ronnie, we are all wasting you.

'I am assuming all the time that you are not dissatisfied with your own position.' This assumption had ceased to be valid. When Ronald wrote *A Spiritual Aeneid*, Guy Lawrence was still alive and Ronald was in the first confidence of his new-found faith. For both these reasons he understated the human, proximate cause of his unrest in the spring of 1915.

He drew up, as he records, a list of thirty-one opposed propositions, for and against his submitting to the Church of Rome. The first of these is, 'If you don't, you'll lose Guy and C', and the retort, 'If you do, you'll lose pretty well all your other friends.'

The document is headed '*Diabolus Loquitur*'; its intention is to dispose of the selfish and frivolous elements that might affect a decision.

If you go now, you can avoid fuss and publicity, with this war on: if you go now you won't raise any Cain in the C. of E., with this war on.

You'll have the religion you like without trouble: yes, but you'll have it without excitement.

You'll no longer be thought dishonest: you'll no longer be thought original.

You won't be able to pray properly till you do: you oughtn't to take any decision while you aren't praying properly.

You'll get rid of all this indecision: you'll be burning your boats.

You'll no longer feel you ought to be edifying your friends more: you'll no longer be able to work among the kind of people you like.

Your fellow-priests won't be married: but they'll be much more vulgar.

And so on.

The document ends: 'Vade retro Satanas.'

The crucial question is not stated: what sort of faith had he in a Church which, however ingeniously he defended it, he could not confidently commend to those he loved, when they were in danger of death? That was the question which nagged Ronald for two years.

Ronald dated his doubts from St Augustine's Day, May 26th, two days before Lawrence's reception. His brother Wilfred was the closest to him of all his family. He once described him as 'just like me only more so'. In the years since the founding of the Orthodox Club, Wilfred had taken a post under the Board of Education and given it up to work at the Trinity Mission in London. He had come to accept all Ronald's faith and to enjoy his religious practices. Finally, he was ordained an Anglican priest. When Ronald attended Wilfred's first Mass at St Mary's, Graham Street, he was struck cold by the fear that this was not a real Mass, nor his brother a real priest.

On July 22nd he wrote to Ted Shuttleworth:

> Now I come to my own position – or rather complete absence of position. I didn't pay any attention to the thing [the report of the Archbishop's Commission on the Kikuyu incident] at all – being of the ultra-Graham St. way of thinking [that Bishops were 'confirming machines', whose prohibitions had no force] until Guy Lawrence and C took the line they did. It wasn't simply my two best converts doing it – or rather preparing to do it, for C hasn't been received yet: it was more that when they consulted me, I suddenly found that I wanted them to go, didn't in any way dissuade them, if anything encouraged them to go. Ever since I've been wondering why, and what's happening to me: I've simply lost all interest in the Forward Movement, and, without feeling the smallest attraction *towards* Rome, have conceived appalling doubts as to whether my own position isn't as illogical or dishonest as people have told me all these last 3 years, and been laughed at for their pains. I've somehow got quite off the rails and I don't know if I'm going to jolt back into them or break away completely. What I've done is to refuse all preaching invitations received during the last two months, so as to think it all over quietly in the Vac. I daresay nothing will come of it all: if it does it will mean complete eating of my words from the very time of my ordination.

A few days later he received the following letter from C:[1]

---

[1] This letter is, in fact, undated, but it seems clear that it must have been received after Ronald wrote to Shuttleworth on July 22nd.

I'm going to be rather odd. I'm *not* going to 'Pope' until after the war (if I'm alive).

1) My people. Not at all a good reason, which weighs . . . [The two following words are illegible. C's normally fine handwriting is much agitated in this letter.]

2) My whole brain is in a whirl. I don't think God will mind. I mean I've felt at last after a lot of thought and prayer that it would be wrong to go now. Because I can't think things calmly now. And I think somehow now that with my mind as it is, it would be almost sacrilege. If I get through I'll go away from home and you and everything and try and find God's guidance. But I believe now that I may have to *relearn* everything. I felt a kind of inspiration that this was right – lately.

It's so dreadful about Guy. Will you advise me? We go to France Sunday.

This was very different from Lawrence's exultant 'Come and be happy'. Nor was it a simple acceptance of Ronald's own position. It was rather a repudiation; a declaration of independence of both Ronald and Lawrence. He was going to 'relearn everything' away from them.

2

Ronald, meanwhile, oppressed by the futility of war-time Oxford and haunted by the memories of peace, had gone down from Trinity with leave of absence to become a temporary schoolmaster.

This was something which many dons were doing. Those who were at a Public School during the First World War will remember the elderly scientists of international repute and the ripe classical scholars who vicariously 'did their bit' by 'freeing' younger men for the Army. Some of them were unendurably tormented; others brought into their form-rooms, for some at least of their pupils, a grateful hint of adult culture.[1]

Ronald went to Shrewsbury, where Cyril Alington, his old Master in College at Eton, had gone as Headmaster in 1908.

Salopians could then say: 'the headmaster before last was appointed the century before last'.[2] The school was founded by a charter of Edward VI and numbered among its early alumni Sir Philip Sidney, Father Humphrey

---

[1] 'Brilliant Arcturus' of *Absolute and Abitofhell* introduced Dr Schweitzer's teaching to his Divinity class at Lancing and unwittingly succeeded in making an agnostic of at least one impressionable boy.

[2] J. Basil Oldham, *A History of Shrewsbury School* (1952), p. 201.

Leech, Lord Halifax 'the Trimmer', and many other men of note. In the eighteenth century it sank to a dozen sons of local tradesmen and was near extinction. Three remarkable Headmasters, Samuel Butler, the grandfather of the author of *The Way of all Flesh*, Benjamin Hall Kennedy, the originator of the famous Latin Grammar, and Henry Whitehead Moss raised it to a great Public School, and it was so specified, together with Eton, Winchester, Harrow, Charterhouse, Westminster, and Rugby, in the Public Schools Act of 1868. Boys came not only from Shropshire, Wales, and the new neighbouring cities in the Midlands but from all over the Empire. It moved from its picturesque but narrow quarters in the town to a new estate on what Ronald called 'the adorable curve' of the Severn. Boys were no longer flogged for boating, as they had been by Butler; they took their places in the crews of both Universities. But, until Alington's appointment, for the whole of the school's history the head-masters had come from Cambridge, and all but one had been themselves Salopians.

Alington was younger than most of his assistant masters. After Moss's prosperous but very long reign the school was ready for change, and he at once introduced new, young masters, many from Eton and Oxford. Hôj Fletcher, with whom Ronald had shared digs, was one of these, before he went on to Eton. Another, and a close friend of his, was Evelyn Southwell. Hôj was killed in March, the first of Ronald's intimates to fall, and Southwell took his death as his own summons to fill his place. Ronald stepped in for Southwell, who with Malcolm White is still fondly remembered at Shrewsbury. Both came as masters in the same term, joined the Rifle Brigade together, and fell within a few weeks of one another in the summer of 1916 at the Battle of the Somme. A joint memoir of them, *Two Men*, was privately printed in 1919.

Southwell was two years older than Ronald. They had been in College together at Eton and had seen something of one another at Oxford, where Southwell had rowed for the University in 1907 and 1908. He was a dedicated schoolmaster who handed over his form, Vb, as a sacred trust and wrote constantly of it from the trenches; a devotee of the classics and of the river, of French literature and of Hilaire Belloc. Ronald took his place not only in the school but also in the New House, the lodging for young bachelor masters which Southwell and White had endowed with their own peculiar enthusiasm and poetic spirit, and made the reconstruction of undergraduate digs, a place of hospitality, disputation, song, and friendship, which persisted after their departure.

It was in this atmosphere, beguiled and consoled by it, that Ronald endured a year and a half of superficial happiness and interior distress. It was from here that he travelled to Wilfred Knox's first Mass and there he returned in dejection. It was there that he received the letters quoted above. It was there that he read the casualty lists, which throughout his time there brought with grim monotony the news of agonizing losses.

In *A Spiritual Aeneid* he pays full tribute to his affection and gratitude for Shrewsbury. He barely hints at the school's debt to him. He came without wages and he worked devotedly. When first he made the arrangement with Alington he stipulated that he should be free at week-ends to go for his devotions to Oxford or London and should say a mid-week Mass in a private chapel in the School House.[1] No doubt originally, before Easter, when the matter was discussed and settled, Ronald also had the intention of using his week-ends for the occasional sermons for which he was in constant demand. These privileges were of little avail in his new mood of doubt.

At the beginning of the holidays he wrote to Ted Shuttleworth from Hickleton, 'I never celebrate without wondering whether anything's happening, and I don't think I could hear a confession now. Perhaps it's just a sort of brain-storm and will wear off,' and four days later from Maurice Child's house in Plymouth:

> I can't entertain the slightest doubt as to whether the Roman view of us, as a whole, may not be the right one, without feeling the same doubt about every detail of devotion and practice. I have to set my teeth in order to consecrate, and make my thanksgiving after communion or confession with a mental reservation – simply because I see so clearly that IF the Roman view should be the right one, our orders and still more our jurisdiction become matters of such uncertainty that the probabilities of there being anything in them are hardly worth considering.
>
> I don't mean, if I'm given the grace to hold out, to be dislodged from my position merely by the worry of this continual double-mindedness. I don't want anything less than complete conviction to justify a change. . . . I can only go on saying my prayers and trying to resist the unworthy motives on both sides [those itemized in the document *Diabolus loquitur* quoted above] which threaten to influence me.

Ronald does not mention in these letters the incident at Hickleton which he records in *A Spiritual Aeneid*,[2] his chance meeting with Father Martindale. This Jesuit, himself a convert while still a boy at Harrow, was

---

[1] No longer existing.   [2] Pp. 200, 201.

there in connexion with the biography of R. H. Benson,[1] which he was writing. Ronald had come with Maurice Child to lay his troubles before Lord Halifax, the recognized lay leader of the Anglo-Catholic movement. Fr Martindale's memories of the incident, set down forty-three years later, differ considerably from Ronald's set down after two years. Fr Martindale writes:

> I forget what he said in his Aeneid about our meeting at Ld Halifax's but I feel he slightly softened down its abruptness. On the eve of my departure he and Mr James [?] arrived just as we were crossing the hall to dinner. . . . He rushed up to me and said: 'Can I speak to you?' I said: 'Not now, obviously; but come up later when I shall be packing.' He came and said: 'Will you receive me into the Church?' I said: 'Why?' He said: 'Because I don't believe the Church of England has a leg to stand on.' I said: 'But that's only a negative consideration. Why do you think that the RC Church has legs?' I remember this clearly and being amazed that so logical a man didn't see that *not* being C of E did not necessarily mean being an RC. I couldn't repeat textually how the talk went on, but he seemed quite aghast, and ended by agreeing that he must produce something positive before he could be 'received'.

Ronald's version reads:

> We came down to dinner in the fading light of the August evening, both dressed in cassock and ferraiuolo, priests, it was impossible not to feel, in a Catholic household. The first figure I saw in the hall was a familiar one; it was Father Martindale. . . . To meet in this way one of the very few Catholic priests I knew, one for whose powers I had already the utmost respect, seemed too good to be a coincidence. I went and talked to him in his room while he packed. . . . I did not come to him for actual direction but for advice as to whether, in his view, such a state of mind made it right for me, or a duty to me, to shut my eyes and take a plunge. His answer was the last thing I expected: 'Of course, you couldn't be received like that' . . . I caught my breath.

The shock of that meeting, whatever precisely was said, was one of the determining processes of Ronald's development.

Maurice Child, J. C. Howell of Graham Street, and one or two others of his close associates were completely in Ronald's confidence. They

---

[1] Ronald always felt an affinity for R. H. Benson; perhaps because there was a physical resemblance between them and because both were the sons of Anglican bishops and both Etonians. To the observer their differences of temperament and of accomplishment seem enormously wider than their similarities.

inclined to explain his troubles as a 'brainstorm'; as 'war-nerves'. He also dutifully reported to his father and to Cyril Alington. The former was struck with horror at this confirmation of his own forebodings. The latter urged him, so long as he did not take the final step, to continue his work at Shrewsbury. And into this work Ronald engrossed himself as an anodyne to his tortured mind.

His form consisted partly of bright, small boys, who might be expected to escape the War and go to the Universities in the first years of peace, and partly of athletes of eighteen or nineteen whose immediate, and often final, prospect was the trenches. It was hopeless to try to interest these in Latin verses. Ronald left them to lounge at the back of the classroom, and they, liking him and sensing that he was not fair game for ragging, left him undisturbed to amuse and, in a few cases, to inspire their juniors.

Vb was used to Southwell's unconventional methods, which the older masters, who had been at Shrewsbury before Alington, deprecated. Southwell made them all write English verse and read them Homer with tears in his eyes. Ronald was bizarre even by these standards. He wore clerical dress – for it was embarrassing for a young man to appear in plain clothes – but no longer with any panache. He was invariably late for early school and arrived nonchalantly as the last of his form slipped into their places.[1] He strolled about the room discoursing easily on a wide range of barely relevant subjects. He discarded the text-books and with great labour composed all his own exercises. He treated the boys, not as immature undergraduates, but as children. His exercises soon became known as 'Ronnie's games'.

Nothing was further from Ronald's aim than to found a new, experimental system of education. It was rather that, at a very sad time, he threw all his energies and ingenuity into making his form happy by keeping them constantly surprised.

One of his clever young pupils, Mr G. Kitson Clark, now of Trinity, Cambridge, writes:

> I have sometimes wondered since then whether some of this was not wasted on us, and whether in contrast to it there was not something to be said for those masters whose methods were duller, but whose discipline was stricter. What I believe was of value beyond calculation was our contact with the depth and riches and critical powers of his fine scholarly mind. . . .

[1] There were good precedents for unpunctuality at Shrewsbury. Two famous Headmasters, B. H. Kennedy and H. W. Moss, were almost always late. J. Basil Oldham, *A History of Shrewsbury School* (1952), pp. 115 and 152.

When I speak of gratitude I believe I speak for other Old Salopians, particularly those who passed in his time through Vb. We would not wish this episode in his career to slip from the record.

Many Old Salopians, indeed, after forty years still treasure relics of his regime. He worked long into the night in the New House with hekto-graph and coloured inks preparing the 'games' for next day.

He taught vocabulary by preparing lists of English words and loose slips of the corresponding Greek; many of them words that had not been encountered in reading. The class had to fit the slips to the list, often by guesswork.

He would issue to each boy a sheet of paper written in green ink with a story which represented an episode in Ancient History; a large number of the proper names would be fictional and written in blue ink. The form had to supply the correct names.

He would teach Greek and Latin simultaneously by giving out two parallel, incomplete texts to complete from one another.

He composed his own rhymes, in the manner of Kennedy, for inculcating syntax.

> *Si pupillum exsecrer*
> *If a pupil were to err*
> *Huic detentiones dem.*
> *He'd stay in till 1 p.m.*

There is always an element of the jig-saw puzzle in schoolboys' Latin verses. Ronald emphasized this by giving each of his form an envelope individually addressed to him, containing hundreds of Latin words, typed on separate slips of paper, and a summary of the story which the words could be arranged to tell. The boys, the cleverer ones at any rate, 'beheld', in the words of one of them, 'Latin verse being created before our incredulous and fascinated eyes'.

Once he issued an unseen which was pure gibberish, containing no genuine Greek words at all except the particles and conjunctions, and watched his form struggling with it and producing wild versions for the whole of the hour.

He also took a small VI form set in Latin. These came to him in his rooms and, it is remembered, he was so sorry for their not being allowed, as he was, to smoke, that he provided sugar-biscuits. Those sessions occurred after 'lock-up' in the evening, and boys returning from them had to show a signed 'excuse' from the master to the Head of the House. Once Ronald wrote this *laissez-passer* on a biscuit. On another evening he handed a large sheet of paper with the 'excuse' written in circles, with at the end in a very small circle 'Look at your hands'; he had coated the underneath surface with burned cork. Another 'excuse' was an aluminium strip, typed out at a slot-machine at the railway station.

He composed for the bell at the New House the inscription: COEPIT GLISCERE CLASSIS DISCERE VERBA MAGISTRI: EXPERGISCERE: VANUM EST HISCERE: VOX DATA SISTRI.

He boiled newspapers in order to caulk the windows of rooms in winter. He dressed up a bust of Dante to represent the opposing General on a Corps field-day. He let a boy, whose birthday it was, take his form. He spoke several times in Chapel – not preaching from the pulpit on matters of doctrine, but following Alington's lead, who sometimes read extracts from Plato on Sunday evenings – always humorously; a few phrases have been remembered, such as his conclusion of a description of Balaam: 'Of course, Balaam was the ass.' He contributed to *The Salopian* many of the Latin translations of Belloc which have since been collected and edited by Mr Laurence Eyres.[1]

These fragments, and many like them, are remembered from Ronald's five terms at Shrewsbury. Some of his pupils recall that he walked about with a black book saying his office – 'learning a Latin Prayer Book by heart' one of them thought; some remember that he looked sad once or twice when he was alone. But to all those young eyes the spectacle was of someone essentially gay. They had no inkling of the darkening of spirit he was undergoing, nor, when he left, did any realize that his motive was to sever ties that were threatening to become too pleasant. Leaving the Anglican Church would mean cutting himself off from Oxford, Eton, and home. He did not want to add Shrewsbury to the list of places that made Anglicanism too dear to him.

In the holidays Ronald was left prey to all his anxieties. He no longer had his preaching engagements, conferences, or reading parties; there was nothing he wished to write; no cause to promote. The regiments he had visited in their training camps were now in France or the Dardanelles. Oxford was unendurable. Ronald wandered aimlessly between Ebury Street, Middlecott, and other haunts of his former associates, but he was not such good company as once he had been. Only with the boys at Shrewsbury, entirely outside his problems, could he assume his old gaiety; when he was with those who had his confidence, he fell into controversy,

[1] *In Three Tongues*, 1959.

and the more they loved him, the more distressing did they find his condition.

He left Shrewsbury in December 1916. Alington was going to Eton. Southwell had been killed. His obligations were over.

3

That Christmas at Manchester was a sorrowful one. The happy family circle at Bishopscourt was almost disbanded. E. V. Knox was in the Army. Dillwyn, having been elected Fellow of King's College, Cambridge, had moved to London and was working in the War Office, Wilfred was a curate at Graham Street; he now held theological views, shared by their sister Winifred, entirely unsympathetic to the Bishop, and Ronald, the favourite son, was barely on speaking terms with his father. There had been a time when their differences had taken the form of mild jokes – a composite photograph of the Bishop showing him in the canonical vestments he abhorred; a whiff of incense secretly introduced in his private chapel. Now with Ronald's defection in the balance there was nothing which this fond pair could say to one another that did not exacerbate deep feelings of dread and remorse. Each, in the love he bore the other, felt impelled to argument, often so painful that it had to be pursued by notes left on the hall table. Ronald explained his position to his father, and they parted in despair of reconciliation.

But the Bishop was now roused. His conscience would not let him rest until everything had been said which might have been said earlier, to deter Ronald from the course he saw more plainly than Ronald. In January and February he wrote three long letters of admonition; they are urgent and deeply affectionate. Ronald had explained to his father that his self-effacement of the last two years had been from respect to him.

> You will believe [the Bishop wrote] that our last conversation has been on my mind ever since we parted. The pathos of the sacrifice which your love for me has demanded has been constantly before me – the burying of your talent – the danger of your drifting into infidelity. Had you been far less dear to me than in fact you are, the thought of this surrender must have haunted me. Loving you as I do, I am oppressed with the sense of my unworthiness of such devotion on your part. If the question were simply that of releasing you from an almost intolerable position, I should have been obliged to say at once 'Let me bear my portion of the burden, and face my own sorrows, which my sins have well deserved.' I do hope, as far

as I can read my heart, that it is not through mere selfishness that I fight against your submission to Rome. Let me try to put down some of the considerations which weigh with me.

1. *The burying of your talent.* That Talent has been conspicuously the gift of exercising religious influence on young men of education. Charles Lister's memoir and the Grenfells' show you in a circle of the most brilliant boyhood of England.

Those two books, which had lately appeared, had given the father his first insight of Ronald's position at Oxford. Academically the Bishop's record was not far below his son's. Ronald had never talked at home about his friends, and the Bishop had been too much occupied with his own affairs to take notice of any activities of Ronald's except his publications and sermons, most of which he had deplored. Now he realized the nature of the unique private apostolate that was to be lost to the Church of England.

'Honestly I look upon the Roman priesthood as the grave of the talent that is especially yours.'

He reverts in all his letters to Lister and the Grenfells. But in stressing them he was unwittingly producing just those arguments which Ronald had itemized as *Diabolus loquitur* and answered with *Vade retro Satanas*.

In many closely reasoned pages the Bishop set out his view of the Church and of the religious life; a view so different from Ronald's that he might have been urging the claims of Mohammedanism or Mormonism for all the bearing it had on Ronald's problem. There was nothing by now that Ronald had not read and studied about the pros and cons of Anglicanism. Only when his father appealed to his heart and to the pain he was causing, was Ronald affected, and then strongly.

Finally, in July, the Bishop for the first time went too far in his reproaches. He accused Ronald of seeking 'calm' at the expense of others; of himself in particular, who would be obliged to resign his see if Ronald left the Church of England.

Ronald was stung to expostulation.

I don't think it's quite fair to say I am asking for 'calm', certainly not for *exterior* calm – I mean the absence of conflict with the world, with sin, with doubt, even with temptations against faith. And the only interior calm I hope for is the consciousness of serving God as he wants to be served, of taking my part in his work. . . . But as for you, Paw [the name by which his children all addressed the Bishop], I really don't think my decision ought to affect you in that way. As you know I haven't preached in the Manchester diocese these five years. As you know, I've done my best these last two years to drop out of sight altogether, simply in order to be able to stand alone and not compromise others. . . . And now, when I ask nothing better than to be allowed to follow what I feel is God's will, wherever it leads me, quietly and without fuss, it seems that you may feel called upon to resign the diocese, and Wilfred[1] sometimes talks as if he would leave his parish, so that the very publicity I fled from when it might have been flattering, is now to be forced upon me when it can only be embarrassing. Now I have written this, I'm afraid you will think I am accusing you (were such a thing possible) of want of considerateness: of course I don't mean that: of course I don't mean that I've any right to have a say in your decisions. What I do mean is, that whereas in 1915 people might have said 'What? The Chaplain of Trinity – the man who wrote Some Loose Stones' nowadays, except for a few people at Oxford and Shrewsbury, my name would hardly suggest more than 'Let's see, wasn't he President of the Union once?' If that is all – and honestly I think it is: I've twice been asked 'How's Ronnie?' by people who mistook me for Wilfred – then whatever your personal feelings, I don't see that your official position is compromised. . . . Please, please ask the advice of people who have the welfare of the Church of England at heart before you put your resignation in the hands of this (very temporary) Government. I daren't pretend that your affection for me won't make your work seem bitter for a time if such a parting has to happen: but honestly I don't think anyone will expect you to resign or have a right to be surprised if you don't.

Is it necessary to add, that *of course* as a Roman I should refuse to undertake any public activities of any kind within the limits of the Manchester diocese while you are in charge of it?

Please forgive me for writing so strongly: it isn't that I feel my decision, in a matter of conscience, ought to be influenced by the way in which others will take it, but simply that the parting from you, so far as it is a parting, is bad enough without the thought that I am involving you in temporal loss.

It may be mentioned here, out of its due order, that the Bishop did not carry out his threat, but remained in his see after Ronald's reception for another four years of unimpaired activity. He fought a successful action in the courts against the English Church Union, which sued him when he refused to institute a vicar convicted of a taste for incense. He took a conspicuous part in the Lambeth Conference of 1920, where he deplored the Anglican insistence on episcopacy as an essential of union with

---

[1] It has been stated on good authority that Ronald's conversion did, in fact, prevent Wilfred Knox's election to a college chaplaincy at Oxford. He took refuge in Cambridge and ended his days there.

Nonconformists. When he finally resigned from the labours of diocesan administration, he had abundant energies left to organize the opposition to the 'Deposited Prayer Book' of 1927; once again successfully. He was eighty years old when he received a letter from Rosslyn Mitchell, a Member of Parliament whose speech had moved many votes, saying: 'To you more than any man is due the decision of the House of Commons. The generalship of an octogenarian has resulted in a great victory.'

Whatever his private sorrows, his public prestige and success were totally unaffected by Ronald's change of communion.

4

In these months of hesitation Guy Lawrence maintained an insistent call to decision. In September 1915 he was invalided home from the Dardanelles; he had escaped the battle in which his regiment was almost obliterated, but he was very ill with dysentery and graver complications. Ronald visited him at his home in Lichfield, but there was a shadow between them. They agreed not to mention 'the Roman question', but it was in both their minds, and Lawrence found it impossible to keep his side of the bargain.

Sometime in November, he wrote:

> You and I haven't written to each other for weeks. I suppose you're being silly and thinking I don't have you in mind every day. It's just because I have you in mind so much that I've felt I can't write. You see, I'm very miserable about your condition. I think about it all so much. I can't make myself believe that you are really trying hard to make up your mind. And I don't want to hurt your feelings, or influence you. So that's why I haven't written. I can't write without mentioning it at all, can I?

In November the medical board found him unfit for active service, and in December he sailed for South Africa to act as A.D.C. to Lord Buxton the Governor-General. He wrote from the ship: 'Why ever didn't you come up just to see me off on Saturday? I thought you'd be sure to come and see the last of me. Perhaps you'll write: anyway, I'll be glad if you go and join poor old Wilfrid at the Beda next year.'[1]

★

---

[1] Wilfrid Moor, late of Margaret Street, had gone to the Beda College in Rome, which prepares men of late vocation for the priesthood.

He wrote regularly from the various official residences, and in all his letters, full for the most part of satirical accounts of local social life, there are reminders of the future he foresees for Ronald. Before sailing for the Dardanelles he had written: 'Tell me your good news soon.' That remained the refrain of all his letters until Ronald's reception.

In June 1916 he wrote from Livingstone:

> You seem a bit more settled, Ron, but it rather looks as if you were coming down on the wrong side of the fence! However, I'm afraid I am trespassing on forbidden ground. I have more or less definitely decided now that when peace is declared and I am free again I shall offer myself as a Postulant to the Oratory. I shall get there what I've wanted and missed ever since I became a Catholic, the opportunity, or rather the compulsion to work at nothing but religion.

This letter reached Ronald while he was making his decision to leave Shrewsbury. Its confidence and hope contrasted poignantly with his own despairing abandonment of religious work. Moreover, these letters from Lawrence show increasing impatience with the peace and luxury of his life, a determination to get back to the firing line. Ronald was deprived even of the comfort of knowing his friend safe.

Lawrence was praying for him, as were Sligger and Father Martindale, and, at the latter's request, a Convent of Poor Clares. Charles Lister's sister, now Lady Lovat, was a recent convert. Apart from these, Ronald knew very few Roman Catholics, and those he knew were far from being typical. Nothing in the Church attracted him save her divine authority. He had promised to do nothing hastily. He kept his word, but meanwhile his whole spiritual strength seemed to be draining away.

In the summer of 1916 he decided to take no holiday at all but to work instead at the War Office in Military Intelligence. Dillwyn had found a *métier*, the breaking of enemy ciphers, so exactly suited to his talents that he pursued it all his life. Ronald may have helped in this department, but the main task assigned to him was in M.I.7.D., a branch which had a small office in the Adelphi, where they studied the newspapers of neutral countries so as to trace the operations of enemy propaganda. To facilitate his work, Ronald, in a few weeks, acquired a working knowledge of Norwegian which, as far as can be known, was never of the smallest use to him in later life. He did his work to the satisfaction of his superiors, who, at the end of the summer, urged him to continue. He agreed to start again after Christmas and to serve there for the duration of the War.

For the first nine months of 1917, after a brief spell alone, he lived with

Maurice Child and Vincent Baker at 209 Ebury Street. He helped a little at Graham Street. He had to pray, and he still prayed best at the altar, even though haunted by doubts of his position there.

Child found him a depressing companion, and now began to urge him to make up his mind one way or the other. At first he deplored the thought of an unobtrusive defection, 'slipping away', as he described it, 'like a piece of soap going down the drain'. An act of that kind could be turned to party advantage, if it were made in protest against some episcopal judgement. As a private act of conscience it would have no force. But Child was not only a party organizer. He was also a diagnostician of sick souls, and he realized, better than Ronald, that he was in danger of total loss of faith. It has been claimed for him that he induced Ronald to go to Farnborough and himself took him there and introduced him to the Abbot. This is not borne out by Ronald's own account written immediately after the event, but undoubtedly he was using his influence that summer to make Ronald 'pope'.

The sequence of events is plainly set out in *A Spiritual Aeneid*. At the beginning of Lent Ronald saw Father Martindale at Oxford, who realized that his discontent was no passing mood and advised his immediate reception, but Ronald put off his decision until he had leisure to make a retreat. It was not so much that he doubted what his decision would be. It was rather that in London, in the office and the air-raids and the chatter of Ebury Street, he was too distraught to make any act of will. He must be alone. That opportunity would not come until his annual leave in September. Meanwhile in June he was notified that his Fellowship at Trinity would come up for reconfirmation next term; a pure formality. He wrote to the President saying he would not stand for re-election. He knew that his decision, whatever it was, would unfit him for the chaplaincy of the College. He might find himself an agnostic with Dillwyn; never an Anglican with Wilfred.

Father John Talbot, of the London Oratory, was one of the few Roman Catholic priests he knew; they had met at Sligger's. He was a convert, twenty years older than Ronald. Ronald wrote his obituary in *The Tablet* in March 1939 saying:

> . . . He was always there if you wanted him; and perhaps from long acquaintance you marked yourself as the sort of young man one meets in John Talbot's room. . . . If the comparison may still be used, the simplest thing to say of him is that he was the opposite number, in London, of Sligger at Oxford; his rooms had their characteristic *clientèle*, on Sunday mornings especially, which irresistibly carried your mind back to a don's

rooms in the garden quad at Balliol; and indeed there were many there who drifted on, as if predestined, from one *salon* to the other. . . . He had indisputably St Philip's own knack of making people come to see him by being always at home when they came; and his clients, like those of the Santo, were in great measure the young men of fashion who are commonly reproached with shunning clerical society . . . good Catholics, indifferent Catholics, semi-detached Catholics, enquirers on their way to the Church.

To him, a man very different from the normal product of the diocesan seminary, Ronald now had recourse. 'He suggested with penetrating wisdom that the most important thing was to get away from the atmosphere of controversy; I had better go to a French community who had never heard of the First Prayer Book or the Nag's Head Story – Farnborough was one of his suggestions.'[1]

Ronald had once met the Abbot of Fort Augustus, Sir David Hunter-Blair, and found him 'a jolly old bird'; a man rather different from the general run of monks; a much travelled, sociable, convert baronet with a passion for genealogy – Ronald was destined to find his way into the Church mainly by the guidance of eccentrics. The Abbot recommended him to the Abbot of Farnborough. Ronald delayed going until his leave fell due. Some time before he lunched with Vernon Johnson and said: 'It's Rome or nothing now.' His purpose at Farnborough was not to pray for guidance in choosing between two forms of Christianity, but to pray for the gift of Christian Faith.

There was no secret made of his visit or of its purpose. His name was posted for the monks' prayers at Fort Augustus. Perhaps Ronald was the only person who had any doubts about the outcome.

The rest is simply told in the guest-master's diary.

> Sept. 8th Rev. Mr Knox arrived during Vespers to make a week's Retreat . . .
>
> 11th Took the Rev. Mr Knox for a walk. He is an exceedingly nice young fellow, very modest and unassuming. He is a fellow of Trinity College, Oxford, as I discovered by chance today. we met D. Sibley in Deepcut Church.
>
> 19th Mr Knox has made up his mind to become a Catholic. Fr Abbot is going to receive him in a day or two.
>
> 22nd Mr Knox was received into the Church by Fr Abbot after the Conventual Mass.

[1] *Spiritual Aeneid*, p. 237.

23rd After Vespers I took Mr Long and Mr Knox to Hillside[1] for
     Benediction. The singing today was remarkably good.

24th Mr Knox left us today after Mass. I quite miss him.

5

From Farnborough Ronald wrote to his sister Winifred:

> Just for yesterday I allowed myself to be happy, because it is nice to have
> come to a determination, but between now and Saturday (when I'm to be
> received) I'll be having to write a very unhappy series of letters. Most of
> the time I've prayed in the chapel here, I've been kneeling under a statue
> of St Louis, who holds a crown of thorns. . . . It's so hard now to think of
> anybody but Paw. . . . It's so hideous to feel I'm not in the least worth all
> the trouble I'm causing.

Ronald wrote dutifully to the Bishop of Oxford, to Lord Halifax, and
to the President of Trinity and with deep affection to his family and to all
his close old associates. It is clear from the answers, which he preserved,
that he had expected some breaches of friendship; all are uniformly kind.
No one imputed caprice or impetuosity, all attributed the highest motives
to him.

His father was his chief concern. The Bishop did not dissemble his
sorrow, but the subject had been worn thin between them during the
preceding year. All he said now was:

> First I must acknowledge gratefully the affectionate spirit in which your
> letter was written, and express my satisfaction that you will not be required
> to repudiate your baptism.
>
> Next I will say what I said to both the Clergy from this diocese who
> went over, that when the time came for their return they might be sure of
> a most hearty welcome. In both cases the desire to return has been
> expressed, but the correspondence has never gone beyond my letter in
> reply. I need not say what your return would be to me though I am
> conscious that my hopes of it must reckon with difficulties almost insur-
> mountable. Still it is only on this side that I shall dwell in writing to you. I
> am enclosing a copy of the prayer which I have been offering and shall
> continue to offer on your behalf. There is little, if anything, in it which
> you could not use. The day will come when we shall know as we are
> known.

---

[1] The convent now domiciled in the former house of the Empress Eugénie.

I suppose that I must address my letters to you as a layman. You cannot know what that means to a father.

But Fiat Voluntas Tua.

The Bishop of Oxford, Charles Gore, with whom he had been on affectionate terms, wrote:

Thank you for telling me. I should have many things to say, if I were once to begin reflecting on your step. But I have decided to say nothing at all except that I commend you to God and the power of His Grace and the guidance of His Spirit: and that I hope we shall be together at last, if not on earth, then in paradise.

One of his comrades in the 'Band of Hope' asked for the gift of his Anglican Missal and uses it to this day.

Wilfred Knox wrote:

Of course it won't make any difference; why should it? After all our views are far closer than they were when we were at Oxford, when I never believed in anything, and it never made any difference there; certainly I've no intention of coming the heavy Anglican, merely because you have adopted the other of the only two views possible for a Christian. I can't say how sorry I am, but it certainly won't make any difference as far as I'm concerned.

C wrote:

It seems that, for the moment at least, the end of the journey has been reached – reached that is by you and Guy, while I am still lagging, timid, cowardly and faint. I feel sure you are right. I hope God will bless you and that you will be very happy. I am certain you'll be happier than you have been for years.

From a personal point of view, though, it's rather sad. 3 years ago we were a happy party and all agreeing and ready to continue together. I feel horribly now like a deserter. Only I do hope you and Guy think of me at any rate as an honest 'conscientious objector' – for the moment. . . . I suppose you were right, and that for a time we shall have to let our ways part, according to the hand of Fate. . . . Honestly, I don't believe it's all been useless. There is left in me at any rate a memory; an experience never forgotten or, I hope, a turn of mind, which but for you I should never have had, remains to me – 'for information and necessary action' if God wills.

Guy Lawrence wrote:

My Dearest Ron,

I am so glad. That's rather platitudinous, isn't it? I don't know quite what else to say. It is a tremendous relief – to you of course, but also to me. Now you and I are in the same boat, Ron; before we were hailing each other vaguely across a wintry sort of sea. You must be quick and become a priest. . . . After 3 weeks I'll be passed fit for General Service, and then – who knows?

When the news of Ronald's reception was published in the papers there was a further batch of letters, one from an old college servant at Trinity who had known Newman and recalled how 'tears rolled down his venerable face as taking my hand he said, Oxford turned me away for becoming a Catholic. Thank God now Trinity retains a Catholic servant.'

Miss Ward, his old friend at Eton, wrote: 'It was not a surprise. . . . I may even say I had a premonition of it long ago in those happy days of 1906, when you lay ill in bed and I sat and studied the strong resemblance of your profile to Newman's.'

There were many letters of congratulation from Catholics, mostly recent converts, whom Ronald had never met. The editors of two or three Catholic papers solicited contributions. But of his real friends there were fewer than half a dozen Catholics to welcome him among them.

BOOK III

The Hidden Stream

———•———

Sitientes ibimus Afros

Chapter One

NOVA CONSPERSIO[1]

1917–1926

Ronald did not go back to Ebury Street. He went instead to stay with a Balliol acquaintance and his wife in Alexander Square, near the Brompton Oratory.

He was exhilarated by little of the proselytizing zeal commonly attributed to converts. He had found what he sought, interior peace. He had stepped into a totally strange world which he must cautiously explore before he could find his place in it. He had no immediate wish to lead anyone else. All his polemical energy was for the time exhausted, but he owed a debt of honour to his former associates, to explain how and why he had abandoned them. He issued a brief statement announcing his dissociation from the Society of SS. Peter and Paul. He completed a dry, logical essay which he had begun in 1915, and issued it through the Catholic Truth Society under the title of *The Essentials of Spiritual Unity*. Then he addressed himself to his friends in *A Spiritual Aeneid*.

In the dark and hungry winter of 1917, when there was no good news from any front, he worked calmly. As soon as he decided that he was not validly ordained, he had offered himself for military service, but the colonel in command of his department refused to release him; he was told he might, if he wished, continue the same work in uniform. He preferred to wear lay dress until he took the tonsure, and to serve for the duration of the War as a civilian. His hours at the War Office were from 9 a.m. to 3.30 p.m. His afternoons and evenings were free for writing, and the book was finished by Christmas.

Thirty-three years later he wrote of it to the publisher who wished to produce a new edition: 'I feel sick when I try to read it, and can't imagine anybody having a different reaction. If I really tried to do a new edition, there's hardly a sentence I'd leave unaltered.' A revised version might

[1] I Cor. v. 7.

make the public 'think this is me saying something I want to say – and it isn't. To me it's simply a period piece.'

He did, however, consent to its reissue, and beyond translating the Latin quotations for the benefit of a generation educated differently from his own, made no changes. In the new preface he compared the book to 'the pad at your bed-side, villainously scribbled over in pencil, upon which you recorded, at the very moment of waking, last night's dream'. He had hard things to say about his literary style; criticisms to which the most fastidious reader will hardly subscribe. His distaste had deeper roots than the aesthetic. In the intervening years his mind had so widened that the problems of his youth seemed trivial. He had travelled so far in wisdom and holiness that he shrank shamefully from the exact portrait of his former self.

A Spiritual Aeneid is a 'period piece' as far as Ronald's later development is concerned; a 'period piece', too, in its *dramatis personae* of Anglican divines whose problems and preoccupations have ceased to be those of their successors; whose fame, with a few exceptions, has become the property of specialists only. It might well have borne Mr Robert Graves's title, *Goodbye to All That*. It was the last important book he was to write for several years.

Meanwhile he had to make some plan for his immediate future; or rather to put himself in the hands of those who would do so for him.

He had no doubts of his vocation to the secular priesthood.

Early in October he was received by Cardinal Bourne. He was not a man with whom Ronald had any natural sympathies. Devout, industrious, well-instructed, the Cardinal was quite devoid of anything which would have passed for scholarship, taste, or humour in Ronald's Anglican circle. He had no felicity of expression in speech or writing. His upbringing had been peculiarly narrow. His predecessor had been an aristocrat, his successor was the son of a village carpenter, each with the generous candour of his origin. Bourne came from a home of genteel poverty; indeed barely from a home at all. In her widowhood his mother could seldom afford to have him with her in his holidays, and after his brother's premature death – with the doctors forecasting his own – she went abroad as a governess to earn his school fees. He knew no life except that of religious institutions; he had no acquaintance that was not professional and official. Moreover, he combined a genuine personal humility with an exceedingly lofty conception of the dignity of his position and with an absolute confidence in all his opinions (which he believed to have been revealed to him in prayer). He was thus singularly disqualified from normal social intercourse.

From beginning to end of my relations with Cardinal Bourne [Ronald wrote years later in a private letter] I never found it possible to take a conversational initiative. More than once I completely failed to get across what I wanted to say (even on important matters), because he always ran the conversation himself. I never failed, in his presence, to feel like a fag taking a note round to some tremendous blood at school.[1]

The Cardinal, who had been twenty-one years a bishop, and fourteen years Archbishop at the time of Ronald's reception, was well experienced in ecclesiastical education. He was not capable of appreciating Ronald's potentialities, still less of directing his elusive temperament, but he accepted the plain facts of his intellectual achievements and realized that there was little which a seminary could teach him. What Ronald needed was to accustom himself to Catholic habits. The Cardinal decided that two years would be enough for that; meanwhile he left him, as the Bishop of Oxford had done, to devise his own course of study. While Ronald's war-service held him in London, the Cardinal recommended that he should live at the Oratory, read in the library there, and share the life of a Catholic community.

It was a humane and, in many ways, a wise decision. There are those who have said that Ronald subsequently suffered from the lack of a full, formal theological training. Certainly, to the end of his life, he tended to refer theological problems to others, but that was in accordance with his temperament. His weary and hypersensitive condition in 1917 might well have made life insupportable even at the Beda with its long experience of unusual students. The Oratory was the ideal half-way house between Trinity and St Edmund's, where, as will be seen, he subsequently settled.

Ronald moved to the Oratory on November 26th and was put down in the books as 'an ecclesiastical student paying his own pension'. There was never any question of his entering the Oratorian noviciate. He was a lodger, pure and simple, but for thirteen months he kept, as far as was possible, the rule of the house, hearing Mass daily, leaving at eight-thirty, returning directly his work was done, attending Benediction, sharing the community's recreation, and going to bed at ten. It was a period of sorely

[1] A particular interest attaches to this confession. An official of Ronald's time at St Edmund's was removed from his post as the result of a complaint to the Cardinal made by one of the staff on behalf of most of his colleagues. The official believed (and apparently was encouraged to believe it by Bourne's faulty memory) that Ronald had sought the interview and made the complaint. Ronald was aware that it was made, and sympathized with it, but he did not make it himself. This misunderstanding troubled Ronald in his last months and he specifically charged his biographer to state these facts.

needed 'cool repose, light and peace', to which he always looked back with fond gratitude.

It was a period of particular happiness in prayer.

He had made his first Communion at Farnborough on September 23rd. On October 6th he was confirmed at Westminster by Cardinal Bourne.[1] Sligger Urquhart arrived unexpectedly in the chapel and stood beside him as *patrinus*. Confirmation is a sacrament which Catholics are inclined to receive in a somewhat perfunctory way. Much less is commonly made of it than of a first communion.[2] Ronald went to Westminster with no expectation of any extraordinary experience. His first thought was to contrast the matter-of-fact preparations with the solemnity of his Confirmation as an Anglican. Pentecostal Grace took him quite unawares. Twenty years later he told Lady Acton that he then experienced an exaltation in the Divine Presence and a nearness to God analogous to breathing and to a physical perception of the flutter of wings.[3]

He was very reticent about his spiritual life.

In 1926 he wrote to a lady who had consulted him about her dryness in prayer: 'It is only by his [God's] mercy, I think, that religious practices ever become easy for us, now and again, for a few months at a time. We must expect always to have to set our teeth.' And to the same correspondent thirty years later: 'You are always praying for consolations [the technical term used by spiritual writers for ease and emotional fervour; it has no connexion with the answers to impetrative prayer]. I don't think it's wrong to ask for them (though it is a thing I should never dare to do myself).' And in another letter: 'To be dry in Lent when our Lord fasted, to be feeling irreligious on Good Friday, when our Lord suffered dereliction – all that is quite correct and liturgical. . . . When you do "get any kind of satisfaction out of one's prayer" say "I'm such a feeble creature God has to give me sweetmeats".'

These extracts from private letters, together with hints to be found in his published work, suggest that Ronald's prayer, throughout most of his life, was very often dry and laborious. He rather seldom experienced in the Catholic Church the easy sweetness he had known among the summer breezes of Caldey. Mystical writers agree that it is a common, if not universal, sign of advance in the spiritual life when 'consolations' are withdrawn, and the soul is left without any sensible delights often for very

[1] This was, perhaps, the occasion of the interview mentioned above.
[2] Cf. Thérèse of Lisieux, *Autobiography of a Saint*, tr. R. A. Knox (1958), p. 109.
[3] See Appendix I, p. 300.

long periods. But at the first step on his stony way, he, who lately had been so near despair and was in after years to display so eminently the gifts of the Holy Ghost, was given unmistakable confirmation of the choice he had made.

He told a friend that in his first months as a Catholic he received the 'consolations' he needed and often ran to church in his impatience to begin his prayers. He looked forward to his meditations as periods of pure joy. And at St Edmund's it was his radiant devotion which most impressed his more discerning colleagues.

The present Bishop of Lancaster, Dr Flynn, writes:

> My most outstanding memory of him [at St Edmund's] is his absorption in prayer before the Blessed Sacrament. That made so profound an impression on me that one day, years after, preaching in the North on the Love of God as an act of the will, which would not involve the emotions, I said: 'Don't tell me that this is all the love of God means. I have *seen* people in love with God.'

2

Across the Channel the slaughter went on. Ronald now had few friends left to lose. On November 21st Edward Homer died of wounds. Patrick Shaw-Stewart heard the news while on home-leave from Salonika. His object in coming to England was to get himself posted from a safe staff-appointment to his old battalion in the Naval Division. The brilliant and beguiling youth who had never failed in anything, for whom all life's prizes seemed to wait his taking, had little wish to outlive his friends. He now used all his charm and influence in high places to get into the firing line. He was killed on December 30th commanding his battalion with exemplary courage.

> *Was it so hard, Achilles,*
> *So very hard to die?*
> *Thou knowest and I know not —*
> *So much the happier I.*

At the end of August Ronald heard the heaviest news of all, Guy Lawrence's death.

No letters from Lawrence to Ronald are extant after the first note of congratulation on his reception into the Church. He had joined the Grenadiers, and in the spring of 1918 was on a course at Chelsea Barracks.

The old intimacy was once more resumed. 'I always felt I was still getting to know him better each time I saw him,' Ronald wrote.

Lawrence's death completed the annihilation of all the human happiness Ronald had found for himself. He was now a stranger in the world, but in his new-found spiritual strength he was able to accept the wreck of his human affections with a submission which surprised himself. 'John Talbot says he's gone straight to heaven,' he wrote to Sligger, 'and I expect he knows.'

Writing to Mr Laurence Eyres, some five months later, to condole with him on the death of a deeply loved brother, he wrote:

> When I heard about Guy Lawrence I was completely numbed to all feeling for three or four days, but expecting all the time that when I became unnumbed I should simply break down. As a matter of fact when the numbed feeling did go off, it was as if I'd had an operation – a sore wound there which I'd never felt as a fresh wound. . . . I expect God saw I wasn't fit to bear the real smart, being the creature I am. Perhaps you'll be privileged to suffer more acutely on your loss, but if you are in that sort of numbed state, don't think it's a loss of faith. One's prayers are very bad then and don't feel real at all; but then nothing else does either. One's simply 'under the cloud', anaesthetized by Providence for fear (I suppose) one should be tempted to rebellion. I think I murmured to Providence over two dozen or so of my friends, but not over Guy.

When this letter was written Mr Eyres was not yet a Roman Catholic. Ronald could not decently say that since his reception he had a livelier faith in the over-riding wisdom and mercy of God than in the days when he had 'murmured against Providence', and a surer sense of the impermanence of human loss.

To Sligger he wrote: 'There must be bits of one's heart which can't carry a strong current of emotion and simply fuse (like an electric light). Or there might be a more spiritual reason. But the fact is I simply haven't been worried about Guy at all. My thoughts don't travel to him unless I want them to.'

He was being prepared for his new vocation by the severance of every early association, and he was strengthened to accept God's will for him.

On November 11th 1918, while the crowds were singing and drinking and embracing in the streets, Ronald sat alone in his quiet room in the Oratory. 'There is a rumour here that they have signed an armistice,' he wrote wryly to a boy at Shrewsbury.

3

Ronald's duties at the War Office ceased in December 1918. His future had already been decided by Cardinal Bourne. He was to go to St Edmund's, Old Hall, in Hertfordshire. The alternative had been one or other of the colleges abroad. The Cardinal himself had been trained at St Sulpice in Paris; most convert clergymen go to the Beda in Rome. There was also the suggestion, never officially formulated, of the United States. (Sir) Shane Leslie,[1] an Eton contemporary and a convert, proposed this to Ronald, who replied on October 29th:

> Your idea of an American University sounds at once very seductive and rather alarming. You will have to reckon with Westrninster. When he gave me the first two minor orders (be seated, I beg!) – when he gave me the first two minor orders, I took a blood curdling oath to remain tied to the soil of the Home Counties. A formality, I hear you say – but you'd have to settle with him. Personally, if I had to choose between Rome and America for three years, I believe I'd rather do the latter – what a horrible confession.

Ronald was much relieved when the Cardinal decided on St Edmund's. The College was particularly dear to the Cardinal's heart; it was there he had spent his last terms as a schoolboy and there had recognized his vocation to the priesthood. It lies in a large, well-planted park, amid agricultural country, bleak in winter but agreeable in summer, seven miles from the little town of Ware (Edmundians dislike the popular appellation 'St Edmund's, Ware'), and its history, like its buildings, presents a microcosm of two centuries of Catholic vicissitudes. The property has belonged to the Church since 1769, when it was bought by Bishop Talbot to accommodate the illicit private school formerly existing at Standon Lordship. At that time Catholic education was absolutely forbidden in England, but breaches of the law were connived at, and an average of twenty-five boys, drawn from all parts of the country, were housed and taught in the small Caroline house which is now used as the infirmary. By the Relief Act of 1791 the penalty for keeping a Catholic school was reduced from life imprisonment to one year's and (a more valuable concession) informers were deprived of their rewards.[2] This measure

---

[1] Sir John Randolph Shane Leslie, 3rd Baronet of Castle Lesley, b. 1885, the author of numerous works of fiction and biography.

[2] Except in the case of sending boys abroad for their schooling; informers could still claim £200 for them.

inflamed riots in London, but in Hertfordshire the school was openly known as 'Old Hall Green Academy'.

The French revolutionaries expelled the English colleges from the Low Countries and took possession of their properties.[1] Catholics were now recognized as allies against the Jacobins, and refugees, both French and English, were kindly received. From the English refugees all but one of the leading Catholic schools in England directly descend. To Old Hall came the comparatively recent offshoot of Douay, the Secular College of St Omer. For them was erected the large, plain, brick house which remains the central feature of the present buildings. By the accident of the date of occupation the newly constituted college for both lay-boys and seminarists was dedicated to St Edmund. The lay school did not immediately prosper; in fact, it declined gravely as the Jesuits and Benedictines, established at Downside and Stonyhurst, drew away the sons of the old Catholic squirearchy. Pugin described the place as a 'priest-factory' and designed an audacious chapel for it that was opened in 1853. The Ward family greatly befriended the College, but it was always short of money. In 1869 Cardinal Manning removed the seminarists to Hammersmith; Cardinal Vaughan sent them to Oscott; Cardinal Bourne restored them to St Edmund's.

In 1918 the College comprised, as it does today, two distinct bodies under one President. There was the seminary for men of university age preparing for priesthood in the archdiocese of Westminster, known as 'Divines', and there was the school for boys of Preparatory School and Public School age, who consisted partly of ordinary 'lay boys', destined for the professions and business, whose parents paid their fees, and partly of the 'church boys' preparing, it was hoped, to enter the seminary; these were supported mainly by the archdiocese. The boys lived, worked, and played together without distinction, save that the 'church boys' rose earlier and made a meditation in chapel before Mass.

Cardinal Bourne brooded and prayed much about the future of St Edmund's. It was, he considered, one of the four main works God had placed before him.[2] Within sixteen weeks of his enthronement building was begun on a new wing. School was home for the Cardinal. He felt the need for an important educational institution under his own direction. Wonersh, the seminary of the Southwark diocese, which as a young man

---

[1] The compensation paid by the French in 1825 was confiscated on Lord Gifford's order and used to build the Marble Arch in London.

[2] Ernest Oldmeadow, *Francis, Cardinal Bourne* (1944), Vol. II, p. 168.

he had founded, was closed to his attentions by Bishop Amigo, the greater part of whose diocese he had unsuccessfully attempted to absorb into his own. The English Public Schools were at the height of their prestige and were being augmented by the Protestant foundation of the Stowe group. Downside, Stonyhurst, and the other leading Catholic schools had long adapted themselves in most external features to the prevailing model. The limited number of English Catholics who desired, and could afford, this type of education had established ties of loyalty to them. One of their concerns was to preserve their English character in the influx of applications from Latin America. There was always a place in them for an English boy. The Cardinal had no hostility to them, but no doubt he recognized that the quality of the secular clergy, and consequently of the hierarchy, was somewhat impoverished by the monopoly enjoyed by the Jesuits and Benedictines, who tended to recruit potential priests into their own ranks.

'It was in the years 1917-1920,' he wrote,[1] 'that the solution gradually broke in on me.' He would create a new Public School, to whose size he set no limits, under the management of the secular clergy. The 'church boys' should live apart like Collegers at Eton and Winchester, and round them should be grouped a collection of Oppidan houses, some of them with married lay Housemasters. A generous but quite inadequate legacy confirmed him in the opinion that the plan was inspired. Suitable boys were to be attracted by a policy of occasional conspicuous hospitality and judicious indirect advertisement. But parents were not to be so easily changed from their allegiance. One lady of an old Catholic family, after an interview with the Cardinal, remarked in frank bewilderment: 'His Eminence seemed almost to be suggesting that *we* should send *our* boys to St Edmund's.' There was no place for the school which Cardinal Bourne conceived, nor was he the man to make a place for it, but in 1918 the plan was taking a broad shape in his mind, and the accession of Ronald to Westminster seemed, like the legacy, a broad hint of divine approval.

The Cardinal's immediate proposal was that Ronald should make his headquarters at the College for the two years before his ordination as priest, should help in the school, be free to carry on his theological studies and his own writing and go away at week-ends. He did not then disclose his larger ambitions for the place, nor the part which he expected Ronald to play in them.

★

[1] Ibid.

Ronald spent seven and a half years at St Edmund's. Some of his friends have regarded them as a time of exile from his proper field. Certainly he was kept there too long. Certainly the work given him was greatly below his capacity. Certainly in his last years there he was eager for a change; this not from any ambition for a place of greater prominence or influence, but from distress at the internal state of the College. There was an irreconcilable personal dissension, in which Ronald's sympathies were keenly involved. What to more robust members of the staff was the cause of exasperation and contempt was for Ronald destructive of his whole social happiness and a gross impediment to his intellectual activity. He would have been content to remain, under orders, in a lowly office, but he was at St Edmund's in a brief, unhappy period when it did not afford a peaceful retreat. His affection for his pupils and for most of his colleagues and his loyalty to the College were unaffected by the experience. He was a frequent and happy visitor there until the end of his life. It was, perhaps, as well that he should thus sharply encounter, early in his life in the Church, something of the many anomalies in the economics of Grace. It was one of the lessons he went to St Edmund's to learn.

'I came to St Edmund's as such a raw recruit,' he wrote,[1] 'still needing to learn, by contact, the ethos of the Catholic mind.'

There is no shadow of affectation in this expression of ignorance. One of the entries in the list[2] which he made in 1915 of the pros and cons of submission, reads: 'You'll be a more important person – but in a less important show.'

These propositions, both so dead contrary to all reason and observation, make the baffled reader suspect that there has been a transposition; but they stand plain, each in its column, in Ronald's precise hand and give some measure of his conspectus of the Church he was entering. He was complacently insular, and in many respects remained so all his life. His travels were meagre and superficial; he had a gently humorous distrust of everything foreign; he had been brought up in an age when 'Land of Hope and Glory' had no undertone of irony and the stability and expansion of the British Empire, and with it the Church of England, seemed to follow a law of nature. Even so, when all these limitations are considered, the two propositions still seem preposterous.

In the four years since they were set down, Ronald had lost all wish to be 'an important person' nor did he ever repine at the lack of adequate official honours. Did he by 1919 recognize the Church as 'an important

---

[1] *The Edmundian*, July 1937.   [2] See above, pp. 245–6.

show'? He would not have loved her the more in that aspect. With his pleasure in paradox, his leaning towards lost causes, his desolation among the fruits of victory in the War, it is probable that he rather cherished R. H. Benson's vision in the *Lord of the World*, of the universal Church reduced to a fugitive Pope bearing solitary witness to the truth which all mankind else had abandoned. Neither in 1915, 1917, nor at any later date did Ronald find any satisfaction, or indeed plausibility, in the image of the Church as an institution of world power. He became a Catholic in violation of all his tastes and human sympathies, in obedience to his reason and in submission to what he recognized as the will of God. He asked from the Church only priestly orders and the right to do her bidding, but in many ways he knew less than the average well-informed Protestant layman of her physical life.

The only secular priest he had met was Father Maturin, the chaplain to the Catholic undergraduates at Oxford, who had gone down in the *Lusitania*, and Father Maturin was a convert from the Cowley Fathers. He was under no illusion that all priests were like the London Oratorians, the Farnborough Benedictines, or Father Martindale, S.J. He had grown up to believe with his Anglican friends that, except for a few illustrious converts, the Roman clergy were a rough and rather tricky lot. He now sought to identify himself with them completely, eschewing all religious dandyism. St Edmund's, with its stalwart virtues and incidental imperfections, embodied the spirit which infused the parishes and controlled the policy of the Church in England. There he set himself to learn her language and her habits of life, to love, and be loved by, her typical members. The lessons he learned and the friendships he made there were as formative as those of Eton, Balliol, and Trinity. During his time some sixty or seventy priests passed through the seminary as students and lecturers, some of them on the way to bishoprics, and these formed a solid company who in his later years never failed him in respect and affection, welcoming and supporting him in his vicissitudes, accepting him without reservation as one of themselves, and, in very many cases, taking him as their model. He was never to be, as R. H. Benson had been, an exotic; at St Edmund's he was given a view deep into the human heart of the Church and an intimation of how he could best serve her.

He first went to St Edmund's in February 1918 as a week-end visitor. The President, Canon (later Archbishop) Myers, was a bland, learned, dilatory man to whose kindness of heart Ronald later paid tribute. He had been brought up in Belgium and was often employed when a French-speaking churchman was needed. During these absences and also when in residence he was content to leave the effective management of the College to a subordinate.

On the occasion of this visit Ronald impressed the staff, who had been expecting a formidable pundit, by his youth and modesty. The fact that he sometimes contributed to *Punch* particularly impressed them, but they had been at pains to study the only book of his immediately available, *Signa Severa*, and their polite references to it convinced Ronald that they had known it since its publication.

An anecdote illustrates Ronald's mood that day. He was taken for a walk by one of the priests on the staff, and as they went down the avenue of bare chestnuts, his companion felt moved to remark: 'Come on ye buds, bust. There's a fine line for a *Punch* poem.'

Ronald appeared to be a little depressed by this sally. They walked for an hour through dismal lanes and footpaths, talking of general matters. Ronald seemed preoccupied. At length they returned in chill twilight up the avenue. Ronald then said:

> 'Come on ye buds, bust.
> 'You really must
> 'And show this unfortunate new-comer
> 'How beautiful this place can be in summer.'

In his hour of need he had summoned to his aid the Muse of the *Bolliday Bango*. It was his first essay in presbytery humour.

Early in February 1919 Ronald took up his post in the school; his duties to teach Latin, his wages £30 a year. The payment of the clerical staff, who were drafted there with little consultation of their own preferences, was not lavish. The President received £100 a year and priests £70 or £80. There were five priests and three laymen on the staff. The total number of souls in the College, which rose slightly in the following years, was about 130. The standard of education was lower than in the leading Public Schools. A Higher Certificate was the height of aspiration. There was an unmistakable touch of irony when in 1924 Ronald published at the Clarendon Press his edition of *Aeneid vii–ix*, a school-book of alternate passages of text and translation, with a preface and notes full of discreet wit, and described himself on the title page as 'Assistant Master at St Edmund's, Old Hall, sometime Fellow of Trinity College, Oxford'. There was not the same tradition of easy social intercourse with the boys as exists at Eton and Shrewsbury. Masters, called 'Professors', each had a pair of rooms. There were two common-rooms, one with a billiard table. They ate in Hall, where the food was copious but coarse. The water was peculiarly hard. Ronald suffered severely from indigestion throughout his time there, but none but a very few friends were aware of this continual discomfort.

The time of Ronald's arrival was not a fortunate one. Some three-quarters of the College were down with Spanish 'flu, and he was given the rooms of a convert clergyman who had just died. The work of the school was disorganized, and Ronald found himself improvising in many departments. When normal routine was resumed Ronald's syllabus was not unduly heavy. His particular concern, which made no demands except on his patience, was with the Latin of Higher Certificate candidates. He continued with this task and with others in the school even after he had been made, in 1922, 'Professor of New Testament' in the seminary; a post which, for a man as conscientious as Ronald, demanded much labour in the composition of new lectures. He is remembered as recommending the Greek Testament as a 'useful crib to the Douay version'.

His way as a schoolmaster was a restrained and limited continuation of his way at Shrewsbury. He introduced in a modified form some of his peculiar mnemonics. He was no longer late for school. He no longer wrote official notes on biscuits or on aluminium tape. He no longer let boys, on their birthdays, take the form. Some of the boys at St Edmund's lacked perception of the distinction between friendliness and familiarity and had to be kept at a little distance.

One scene of his form room is memorable. During his early years the school was 'inspected' by the Joint Oxford and Cambridge Board, an inquest which often caused uneasiness in schools of uncertain position. One of the inspectors proved to be his old friend Mr Thomas Higham of Trinity. The meeting was a complete surprise to both. Ronald was taking his form in *Aeneid*. He gave no sign of recognition, but quietly said: 'Pay no attention to this gentleman. He's stone deaf.' Mr Higham played up, sat blankly cupping his hand on his ear while a boy construed, then rose, said, 'I have not been able to hear anything you have said, but I perceive by the intelligent look on your faces that you have fully mastered the text', and left them.

A few minor eccentricities – such as a habit of lighting his pipe outside the cricket pavilion with a burning-glass – impressed his pupils, but his high spirits were on the whole hidden from them and kept for his colleagues, who were barely aware that he had known, and still knew when he was away from St Edmund's, a wider world than theirs. The conception of him as a resigned and dyspeptic exile may be dispelled by the following extracts from a letter written by Mr J. J. Creaven, which has the full tang of the common-room at St Edmund's.

I went to St Edmund's, Ware, in Jan. 1920 from Galway to teach, in the school, a mixed syllabus of many subjects only one of which I was really qualified to teach – Logic for London University Inter-Arts. This was being taught by Fr Knox and he was anxious to be rid of it. From the first he showed me the greatest kindness and I came to love and almost reverence him for such friendliness and humility in one of his genius were quite beyond my expectation. He was vivacious, full of good humour, always up to some prank or other. I was sometimes the victim as when I was playing billiards one afternoon and found myself being hunted for my 'brush' – I wore my hair long and thick until I was ridiculed out of it – by a clerical pack led by Knox on all fours.

He did a regular 'turn' in Common Room and school concerts – a little girl reciting 'Queen of the May' at a village concert breaking down and rushing off the stage in tears. The Vicar appears, apologises for the little girl and then himself reads the rest of the poem with expression, and much unctuous emphasis. This was a very successful turn, his Vicar particularly good burlesque. He and I combined in a small act at a school concert. When the curtain rose Knox was standing beside the piano with a piece of music in his hand. This was surprising for every boy in the school knew that Fr Knox had no music in him. He claimed to be able to distinguish 'God Save the King' from 'The Minstrel Boy' but no more. So they waited with keen expectation for him to begin. The pianist played the introduction and Knox began to sing in a high tenor the popular sentimental ballad 'Because'. The facial expressions of the 'singer' caused a near-riot – I could not see them for I was the singer crouching down in the cover of his Cappa Magna. At the end I stood up and we took our bow – but did not give an encore.

He was a good performer at billiards but greatly preferred Billiards Fives in which you hit the ball with hand and more often than not send it flying off the table.

He held the College record for the Pogo Stick – a heavy pole about 5 ft. long and tipped with iron. It had two foot rests on springs one on either side set about 2 ft. from the ground. You grasped the pole, stood on the foot-rests and bounded up and down with the pole. Whoever had the largest number of bounds without falling off was the winner. Knox, I believe, held the record and might have reached a much higher score if he had not rashly held his trial in the stone-flagged Ambulacrum, his cassock tucked up to his waist, biretta on head and the pogo stick with iron tip smiting the stone flags and sending the reverberations throughout the whole

College. And reached the ears of the President – Canon Myers, who was supposed to be in London.

Ronald was ordained sub-deacon on June 22nd 1919 and deacon shortly afterwards. On October 5th he was ordained priest at Westminster.[1] At the end of the War Bishop Knox distributed among his children the money left by their mother. Each received £3,000. This legacy, together with his earning power and the facts that he had cost the Church nothing for his education and was willing to acquit his superiors of the obligation of supporting him in old age, were taken as satisfying the conditions for an ordination 'on his own patrimony'. This absolved him of the 'blood curdling oath' tying him to the soil of the Home Counties. He was now free to go where he liked provided the responsible bishop agreed. Wherever a priest is, he comes under the jurisdiction of a bishop; like a soldier, he always has a commanding officer; but Ronald was entitled to post himself and cross-post himself more or less as he pleased.

It was not in his character to insist on privilege, and no hint was given by the Cardinal that there was other work for him. At the time of his ordination Ronald had not quite finished the course of Moral Theology he had set himself, and he spent most of the school holidays December 1919–January 1920 at St Edmund's reading. That complete, he was ready to accept engagements to preach outside the College. These soon became very numerous. No hindrance was made by the authorities, who were glad to see his fame established and enhanced. He led a double life, spending holidays and week-ends travelling all over the country winning in his new Communion something of the lustre he had enjoyed in his old, while on the weekdays of term he followed the humble routine of a schoolmaster.

The Editorial of *The Edmundian* for February 1927, commenting on his departure, said:

> As was suggested by Canon Myers, life at St Edmund's was a kind of corrective for Father Knox for what he found outside. . . . Now quite probably all this never occurred to the mind of Father Knox; or, if this statement be untrue, then it is undeniable that no one would ever suspect that there was ever anything in the life of 'one of the masters' that was being taken as one takes nasty tasting medicines, as a corrective to what would else be harmful. He was so completely one of the crowd, enjoying

---

[1] His Catholic First Mass card is a very much more modest document than the Anglican but is equally misprinted; the reference for the text being given as 1 Cor. iv. 7, instead of 2 Cor.

to the full the company of his colleagues and finding real satisfaction in devoting his time and work to the students under his care.

Ronald went far beyond his strict teaching duties in his attempts to infuse St Edmund's with his spirit. He took charge of the Debating Society, and in his summings-up gave the boys, accustomed to the exposition of trite opinions, a glimpse of the polish and invention of his undergraduate days. To other societies he read several papers, some new, some old favourites, new to them, such as the *Studies in the Literature of Sherlock Holmes* which he had written in 1911. An example of his humanizing effect may be discerned from the programme of what was ostensibly the 'Literary Society'. In one term they heard: 'Some of the Motives of Schism in Bohemia', by the Vice-President; 'The Condition of the Church in France', by the President; 'The Catholic Church in America', by the Rev. A. J. Hogan, S.J.; 'The Conversion of the Norse Peoples', by the Rev. H. Harrington; Ronald's was the sole literary topic discussed, 'Humour and Satire', the paper which forms the Introduction to *Essays on Satire*.

The pages of *The Edmundian* sparkle with his contributions. No signature was needed for a review which began:

> The fabled clergyman who gave out from his pulpit, 'Today is Easter Day; last Friday was Good Friday, but as it was overlooked it will be kept next Friday,' might have saved himself from these embarrassments if he had possessed a copy of the unpretentious but tastefully produced booklet that reaches us from Burns, Oates & Washbourne, entitled *Ordo Recitandi Divini Officii*, etc., etc., etc., (1/6 net). The author modestly preserves anonymity, nor does he betray his identity by any marked individuality of treatment; but his colleagues will be glad to welcome a piece of solid work from his pen, and will not fail to recognize his painstaking attention to detail and his terse, nervous Latinity.[1]

In April 1920 he composed an ingenious verse epitaph for Bishop Ward, the initial letters of each line forming the words 'Bernardus Episcopus'. In July 1922 he contributed to *The Edmundian* some English verses on the smell of the pigsties. In 1924 he wrote songs in the manner of Gilbert for the school pantomime.

But it was not primarily for his attempts to lighten the rather sombre internal life of the College that Ronald was valued by his superiors. He was needed for the new campaign of publicity. It was an avowed aim of

[1] *The Edmundian*, April 1st 1923.

the authorities to make the annual speech day a 'feature of the London season' – a phrase which struck many at St Edmund's as worse than fatuous – comparable to the Eton and Harrow match at Lord's. Invitations were sent to a wide selection of fashionable and important people, some of whom accepted. It was rather naïvely supposed that these guests would be amused by a Latin play. Ronald was accordingly put to work, and in 1924 produced *Thesauropolemopompus* on the topical comic theme of the war-profiteer. The character best enjoyed by those of the audience who enjoyed it at all, was a British slave who talked dog-Latin – 'Bene ego nunquam!' rendering the exclamation 'Well, I never!' Next year saw *Londinium Defensum*, a more ambitious play, full of ingenious Latin neologisms such as delight the Public Orators of Oxford; it refers to the Wembley Exhibition, American tourists, and other topics of the day. Some of the visiting clergy are said to have picked up part of the meaning, and many of them, reading it at leisure, have come to treasure the printed edition; parents accepted it with resignation as part of the general tribulation inevitable on such festivities; the spectators most to be pitied were the guests of especial honour, the Lord Mayor of London and his Sheriffs, who on a very hot afternoon and after a heavy luncheon were obliged to sit through the abstruse drama in their robes of office. After Ronald's departure the 'tradition', as it was briefly dubbed, of the Latin play was allowed to lapse.

The authorities were solicitous that Ronald should spread the fame of the College by inviting there at other times some of his more influential acquaintances. This he sometimes did without much enthusiasm, but a use to which he readily lent himself was the recruitment of lay-masters. These were better paid than the clergy; £250 a year and their keep, which, if they wished it, lasted all the year round. It was not an unattractive proposition, especially for a young convert, and as early as May 1919 Ronald wrote the first of a series of letters to Sligger Urquahart asking him to suggest suitable undergraduates in their last term at Oxford. One of the men far above the normal standard of St Edmund's masters who were thus introduced was the precise classical scholar, Ronald's old friend Mr Laurence Eyres.

Mr Eyres had returned to Trinity after the War to take his Final Schools. All that year he fretted about his religious position, and in July 1920 Ronald, drawing on his own recent experience, wrote to him:

> I should have thought you ought to precipitate a mental crisis before next September, i.e. before you take up any definite job. If you take up

fresh work with an old wound, as it were, still open – with a question at the back of your mind still undecided, it seems to me it must result in either (*a*) your burying the question away, insincerely, amid a crowd of new duties and interests, stifling the spirit of enquiry, or (*b*) doing your new work half-heartedly with the feeling that after all the whole thing is provisional [for it was at the back of Mr Eyres's mind that if he became a Catholic he should also become a priest]. . . . Surely what you want to do is to take yourself by the scruff of the neck and say '. . . I mean by such and such a date, after prayer and reading what I can, and thinking the thing out (not just brooding on it) when I can, to reach a DECISION. . . .' I do really think it's important because if you stifle the appeal of Grace it's hard to expect you'll be given a second chance.

In August he wrote from Farnborough Abbey:

The mistake is to suppose that, having such a conviction as that as to the truth of the Gospels, the meaning of Our Lord's words, and so on, it should still be necessary to wait for an extraordinary flood of illumination on the top of that before making one's submission. That may be vouchsafed to some, but is certainly not vouchsafed to most people; they have to proceed, in taking the step, on a strong human conviction and it is only in the taking of it that it becomes the strongest certitude of their lives.

Ronald wrote often and at length to Mr Eyres during this period. In one of his letters he says: 'One of my first reflexions when I was converted was "now I belong to the same Church as Judas Iscariot".'

Ronald knew Mr Eyres's character intimately, and he is, perhaps, the only person whom he frankly urged into the Church. He did not give him his formal instruction or receive him, but Mr Eyres was, if the phrase is tolerable, 'Ronald's convert'. He was at length received, not as soon as Ronald proposed, in March 1921, In September of that year he came to St Edmund's, where Ronald enjoyed the inestimable comfort of his companionship for more than four years. Mr Eyres made out Ronald's Income Tax returns and acted as almoner for some of his charities. They walked together every afternoon of term, rigorously refraining from grumbling, and imposing on one another a fine for any mention of the feature in their lives they particularly disliked. Most evenings Ronald spent with Father Healy, the Headmaster of St Hugh's, the Preparatory School, a priest whom Ronald took as his guide in practical affairs of the priesthood, submitting every sermon to him before preaching it.[1] These and Father (now Canon) George Smith and Father Harrington, an

---

[1] There is a conflict of opinion as to whether he did this under orders from his superiors.

impetuous Stonyhurst man of Ronald's own seniority, who died prematurely, were Ronald's closest associates on the staff.

In 1922 Cardinal Boume made the change (since abandoned) which he had long pondered. The 'church boys' were separated from the 'lay boys'. Ronald was offered the post of Housemaster to the 'lay boys', but he declined it on the grounds of his dislike of inflicting corporal punishment. On his suggestion they were divided into two houses; Mr Eyres was given charge of one. From that term more of Ronald's work was among 'the divines' of the seminary, and less with the school.

4

It has been said above that Ronald at this time led a double life. Outside St Edmund's he preached often. In 1922 he was already prominent enough to be chosen by Harold Begbie as the only Catholic in a superficial and vulgar survey of various leading churchmen, entitled *Painted Windows* and published under the inappropriate *nom de guerre*, 'A Gentleman with a Duster'. Except for the occasional sermons, which are easily dated, Ronald's preaching requires, and will no doubt in good time receive, the attention of a team of research-workers. It was his habit to use the same sermon often. He kept the typescripts filed and when invited to a new congregation drew out whatever seemed most suitable, but he seldom repeated exactly the same sermon. His mind played on them, adapting, combining, enriching, and rejecting; and eventually, when enough of them had been collected to admit of coherent arrangement, he published them in books. There is no certitude that any particular sermon survives in its precise, original form. What is known is that the books comprise his final revised versions, as he would now wish them to be read.

In 1920 there appeared a spurious book of Horace Odes V[1] which hoaxed some critics. Ronald contributed Odes 3, 4, 5, 7, 14, 15 and Appendices 1, 8, 9, 10, 11, 12, 13γ to this. These verses were presumably written at various times before his reception into the Church. His collaborators were J. U. Powell, A. B. Ramsay, and A. D. Godley, all Oxford dons.

By 1921 he was engaged in ephemeral writing which occupied part of his restless intelligence and supplemented his salary, which on his ordina-

---

[1] *Q. Horati Flacci Carminum Liber Quintus a Rudyardo Kipling et Carolo Graves Anglice Redditus* (Basil Blackwell, 1920).

tion had been raised to £70 a year. E. V. Lucas was a frequent guest at Beaufort.[1] He encouraged Ronald in writing (what has lately, it seems, become a term of opprobrium) *belles lettres*. There still survived in the popular Press of the time a corner for light essays of the kind which Ronald could produce effortlessly. During the next seven years he wrote many columns for the *Daily News*, the *Evening Standard*, the *Universe*, the *Morning Post*, and other papers, a few of which he reprinted,[2] but most of which he was content to leave forgotten.

In 1923 he published *Memories of the Future: being memoirs of the years 1915–1972 written in the Year of Grace 1988 by Opal, Lady Porstock*, in part a parody of the current autobiographies of women of fashion, in part a gentle satire on current whims – educational, medical, political, and theological. Occasionally for several pages, as when Lady Porstock turns to the Church, irony disappears totally. There is no attempt to make the flesh creep as in R. H. Benson's *Lord of the World* or in the subsequent prophetic books of Mr Aldous Huxley and George Orwell. Science is not going to achieve any revolution; existing foibles and aberrations will be slightly accentuated, but England will continue to be a plutocracy; Society will continue to amuse itself; what is most out of date at the time of writing will be rediscovered and welcomed as the height of modernity; the Church of England will lose a little more Faith; the Roman Catholic Church will gain a few more members; human folly and human sentiment will remain the same; the next World War (of 1972) will be no Armageddon; as things were, so they will continue, with the Grace of God silently working on individual souls.

The book was enjoyed by a fair number of cultivated readers; it made no popular sensation, nor was it designed to do so.

In the same year appeared *The Miracles of King Henry VI*,[3] the joint work of Ronald and Sir Shane Leslie, the fruit of much research and correspondence between the two editors; a handsome memorial to Etonian *pietas*.

In 1924 appeared *Sanctions: a frivolity*. Mallock's *New Republic* was an essential book to Ronald, perhaps his favourite work of secular literature outside the Classics. The form of it attracted him throughout his life, and he considered its use in the projected work of apologetics which was in his mind up to the time of his last illness. *Sanctions* is a highly elegant essay

---

[1] See below, p. 292.
[2] R. A. Knox, *An Open Air Pulpit* (1926); *On Getting There* (1929).
[3] Cambridge, at the University Press.

in this manner; a heterogeneous and unnaturally lucid house-party find all their conversations turning towards the question: what are the ultimate sanctions, social, intellectual, supernatural, which determine man's behaviour and destiny? 'A frivolity' is not an entirely apt sub-title. As might be expected, Ronald does not, like Mallock, leave the question unresolved; a very delicate final hint gives the decision to the unobtrusive Catholic priest.

In the same year he published *A Book of Acrostics*. These puzzles were enjoying a brief return to favour. Ronald's exceptional facility enabled him at the expense of a few minutes work a week to earn £3 for a regular feature from a now defunct periodical named *The Illustrated Review*.

In 1925 he published the first of his six[1] detective stories, *The Viaduct Murder*.

Ronald regarded these books, as he did his acrostics, as intellectual exercises; a game between writer and reader in which a problem was precisely stated and elaborately disguised. He was not seeking to write novels. He had no concern with the passions of the murderer, the terror of the victim, or the moral enormity of the crime. He eschewed psychology, violence, the occult, and the macabre. He provided a pure distillation for a few addicts. As his brother, Dillwyn, had systematized and regulated the haphazard games of the Birmingham schoolroom, so Ronald observed and sought to impose a code of rules, which he later set out in his Introduction to *The Best Detective Stories of the Year (1928)*.[2]

At the time there was a limited but eager public for these puzzles. Fashion has turned from them, as from acrostics. When they come back into fashion, Ronald's stories, because of their austerity, may seem less dated than those of his more romantic and more dramatic rivals. None was more ingenious than he, more scrupulous in the provision of clues, more logically complete in his solutions. Very few women have ever enjoyed them.

In 1926 he published *Other Eyes than Ours*, the story of a hoax played on a circle of spiritualists; there is a highly satisfactory denouement and much incidental parody and satire, but in this book, for the only time in his life, he has been reasonably accused of 'padding'. Twenty years later

---

[1] *The Three Taps* (1927); *Footsteps at the Lock* (1928); *The Body in the Silo* (1933); *Still Dead* (1934); *Double Cross Purposes* (1937).

[2] They were later adapted to form the initiation oath of the Detection Club, a society founded in 1929, which included G. K. Chesterton, Dorothy Sayers, Mrs Agatha Christie, and all the leading detective-story writers of the day. See Maisie Ward, *Gilbert Keith Chesterton* (1944), p. 457.

short novels became the fashion. Ronald then regretfully remarked that his publishers had always insisted on 75,000 words. *Other Eyes than Ours* would be more enjoyable at half the length.

The common-room at St Edmund's was not equipped with wireless but Ronald often listened with mixed irritation and fascination during his holidays. Broadcasting, it might have been thought, was a medium particularly suited to his talents, but neither then nor later did he often engage in it. The aim of the British Broadcasting Company, not yet a Corporation, was to avoid definition and dispute. In its religious programmes it sought to give opportunities to the clergy of all denominations, but to provide services which should exclude and offend none. The Catholic Hierarchy were reluctant to co-operate with what in those days threatened to become a diluted and synthetic 'B.B.C. Church'. Later when dogmatic and controversial assertions were welcome, Ronald found, as did many others, that except for those living in easy reach of a headquarters, the hire was not worth the labour. A sermon preached into the microphone could be used once only, and then without the personal encounters which he valued in his exploration of the Church; moreover, he was too polite to disregard the tedious correspondence which a broadcast invariably provoked. In secular subjects his humour was at first too recondite and later too racy of an earlier period to be widely popular.

It was sometimes convenient to him in his journeys to and from Scotland to speak at Edinburgh, where in the 1920, a friend, Mr George Marshall, was Station Director. On November 25th 1923 he gave a religious address, no copy of which has survived.

On Saturday, January 15th 1926 he gave a performance from Edinburgh which was relayed to England and Ireland under the title 'Broadcasting from the Barricades'. It was prefaced by an explicit statement that it was a work of humour and imagination, enlivened by realistic 'sound effects', which were still a novelty.

The script is printed in *Essays in Satire* under the title 'A Forgotten Interlude'. Read today, it seems barely credible that it could have caused a tremor of alarm in the most timid listener. He had no idea of imposing on anyone. The intention was broad parody.

He began with an imitation of a don commending the French Revolution. He proceeded to the 'News' in palpable exaggeration of what was then the official manner:

> The Unemployed Demonstration. The crowd in Trafalgar Square is now assuming threatening dimensions. Threatening dimensions are now

being assumed by the crowd which has collected in Trafalgar Square to voice the grievances of the unemployed. Mr Popplebury, the Secretary of the National Movement for Abolishing Theatre Queues, has been urging the crowd to sack the National Gallery. The desirability of sacking the National Gallery is being urged by Mr Popplebury, secretary of the National Movement for Abolishing Theatre Queues. One moment please. London calling; continuation of news bulletin from reports which have just come to hand. The crowd in Trafalgar Square is now proceeding at the instigation of Mr Popplebury, Secretary of the National Movement for Abolishing Theatre Queues, to sack the National Gallery. The National Gallery was first erected in 1838 to house the famous Angerstein collection. . . . It is now being sacked by the crowd on the advice of Mr Popplebury [and so on].

. . . Sir Theophilus Gooch, well known for his many philanthropic schemes, will now address you on the Housing of the Poor. . . . One moment please. From reports which have just come to hand it appears that Sir Theophilus Gooch, who was on his way to this station, has been intercepted by remnants of the crowd still collected in Trafalgar Square, and is being roasted alive.

After enumerating various other fantastic outrages he concluded:

A threatening demeanour is being exhibited by the crowd which is now approaching the B.B.C.'s London station. One moment please. Mr Popplebury, Secretary of the National Movement for Abolishing Theatre Queues, with several other members of the crowd, is now in the waiting room. They are reading copies of the *Radio Times*. Goodnight everybody; goodnight.

The script had not been sent to London for previous examination. Twenty minutes after the end, while Ronald and Mr Marshall were at supper at the Caledonian Hotel, Lord (then Mr) Reith was on the telephone saying that the staff at Savoy Hill were being annoyed by anxious inquiries. The excitement was not quickly abated, although reassuring bulletins were issued by the B.B.C. On Monday the Managing Director, as he was then entitled, asked for a full transcript by telegraph. Ronald left that night for Dublin, where he was due to speak, and so escaped the reporters, who harassed Mr Marshall throughout the weekend. On Monday every paper gave large attention to the incident with various degrees of reprobation.[1]

---

[1] In the United States this broadcast was imitated some ten years later in more fantastic terms with even more fantastic results.

The Tablet, which at that time spoke with the voice of Cardinal Bourne, took Ronald heavily to task. 'Frankly', the editor wrote, 'we wish that Father Knox had not done this . . . Few literary deeds are more facile and more tiresome than the shoving of serious things into a droll context. And a Red Revolution is a very serious thing indeed . . . There are in England groups of hireling Communists who must have been enormously encouraged by the fact that many Britons were badly scared last Saturday.'

It is not true, as has sometimes been stated, that as a result Ronald was 'black-listed' by the B.B.C. Lord Reith uttered no rebuke. A few months later, when Mr Marshall had been promoted to Glasgow, Ronald spoke from there during the congress of the British Association in parody of a popular scientific talk illustrating the sounds, now made audible to the learned, of vegetables in pain. He was invited to debate in 1927 and 1928. It was by his own choice that he did not again speak on the wireless until 1930.

But the incident had wider importance. It was the first revelation to politicians of the gullibility of simple people by this new apparatus; a quality which was to be largely exploited in the years to come.

Ronald himself was not much cast down by his reception. His conscience was perfectly clear of any malicious intention, and he could not take seriously the annoyance of people so egregiously lacking in humour. He had outgrown the phase of extreme sensitiveness when he had shrunk from the imputation of frivolity. A colleague at St Edmund's remembers his unaffected delight in hearing himself roundly abused over their beer by two men in a fishing inn. But some of the doubts of his complete suitability which, as will appear, afflicted the Universities' Catholic Education Board during that spring, may be attributed to this little scandal at the microphone.

Such were Ronald's literary activities at this period. He was fortunate in having his old Balliol friend, Mr W. P. Watt, as literary agent. Mr Watt's father had the best practice in London. Ronald made none of the bad bargains which have embittered some literary men.

His later years at St Edmund's were financially prosperous. Apart from the sales of his books, his fees for preaching and lecturing, his stipend at the College and the interest on his mother's legacy, he edited a weekly acrostic, wrote occasionally for many newspapers and regularly for the *Evening Standard*. In 1976 he recorded that he received from all sources £1,300 a year. He had no expenses of board or lodging, either during term or holidays. In accordance with his undertaking not to become a charge on the archdiocese, he began to save for his old age. Except during his thirteen years at the Oxford chaplaincy, he was able to put by something every year. He was well advised in his investments, interest accumulated. At his death he left a little over £22,000. There are no accounts to show how much of this sum was directly saved out of his income, how much represents the appreciation of shares. What he saved for himself and what he spent on himself were, throughout most of his working life, a small part of his earnings. What he gave away can only be guessed from the chance hints that fall in the biographer's way. It is now known, because to preserve his anonymity he had to employ an almoner, that while at St Edmund's he paid the school fees of two boys whose parents could not afford them.[1] Throughout his life he subscribed suitable sums to organized charities and institutions of the kind which publish the names of their supporters – he wrote to the secretary of one such fund: 'I find the most agreeable letters to answer are appeals for money' – but his main benefactions were to individuals, especially to individuals, priests for example who fell into disgrace, for whom there is little general sympathy. He was not an impetuous man liable to sudden accesses of emotional generosity. It is certain that deliberately and secretly year after year he dispensed large sums of which there is no record except in the grateful hearts of their recipients.

5

While, during term and in his visits as preacher to parishes in all parts of the country, Ronald was establishing himself with the Catholic clergy, he was in his holidays getting to know the laity.

As has been said, he was at first almost friendless in his new Church. One of the few letters he received from Catholics on his reception was from Charles Lister's sister, Laura, who had become a Catholic in 1910 shortly before her marriage to Lord Lovat, a handsome and much loved Highland chieftain who had kept his twenty-first birthday and taken over his heavily encumbered property of some 250,000 acres before his bride was born.

In the South African War Lord Lovat had raised, trained, and led a regiment of his own clansmen, the Lovat Scouts.[2] In the House of Lords

---

[1] Laurence Eyres, 'Some Edmundian Memories', *The Edmundian*, Autumn 1957.
[2] In this he was following family tradition. Simon Fraser, the son of the Lord Lovat beheaded for treason in 1745, raised 4,000 men to fight for George II in Portugal and Canada. Archibald

and on public platforms he was a respected exponent of Scottish interests and of the ideals of Empire. He was a fine shot and all-round sportsman and the highest authority on the habits and health of grouse. His boundless friendships included King George V, politicians of both parties, men of fashion, Canadians and Australians, crofters, and racing touts. He was also, through the Catholic marriage and early death of his grandfather (who would have tried to bring up his heir a Protestant), what was very rare in the Scottish aristocracy, a Catholic.

His seat, Beaufort Castle, in Inverness, since much reduced by fire, stands in a position of great beauty above the River Beauly. When Ronald first went there at Christmas 1918 it was a very large Victorian-baronial pile. Here for nearly twenty years Lady Lovat gave him his holiday home. There was always a room for him in the bachelors' wing; there was always a table for his work in the library; there was unfailing sympathy and humour for him in the boudoir; and in the great gallery and dining-hall a tumultuous succession of every kind of guest. It was here Ronald first met Maurice Baring,[1] who was a visitor nearly as frequent as he. They were united in the Faith, in their love of language, in unfading mourning for their host of common friends (for Maurice made no distinctions of age, and though ten years older had been close to the Grenfells and their set), and in their solicitous devotion to their hostess. They became fast friends. Day after day they sat opposite one another in the library, each with his typewriter at work on his own book.

At the time of Ronald's first visit to Beaufort there were three children, aged from seven years to one; two more were born while he was at St Edmund's. Till then he had known very few children. It is improbable that he had ever been alone with one. His life had been lived among bachelor dons and clergymen, undergraduates, elder brothers and sisters, maiden aunts, schoolboys. In later life he delighted the children and grandchildren of many friends, but it was an art he had to learn. He learned it on the young Frasers, and there was a certain meticulosity about him that did not at once appeal to those wild, barefooted creatures of the moors. His delicate English humour did not easily penetrate their little

---

Fraser, his brother, raised the Fraser Fencibles for service in Ireland. The barony attainted in 1745 was revived in 1857, in favour of Thomas Fraser, who had already been created a peer of the United Kingdom in 1837. See Francis Lindley, *Lord Lovat* (N.D. *circa* 1934). Simon, Lord Lovat, who married Laura Lister, was the fourteenth Baron.

[1] The Hon. Maurice Baring, poet and novelist, 1874–1945, fourth son of first Lord Revelstoke. See Ethel Smyth, *Maurice Baring* (1938); Laura Lovat, *Maurice Baring* (1947).

Scottish skulls. They greatly preferred Maurice Baring's spontaneous, infectious hilarity. Ronald played their games too intently. They resented the prescriptive rights he claimed over the decoration of the Christmas-tree. Now and then he let himself go, chased them round the house in the dark, and quite frightened them; then they loved him. Once when one of the children had to open a concert and complained that she was unable to make a speech or sing anything other than 'God save the King' he composed these verses for her to sing to that tune:

> *Since neither my Papa*
> *Nor my beloved Mamma*
> *   Hopes to be present*
> *And open this bazaar –*
> *Or rather concert – far*
> *Be it from me to bar*
> *   This duty pleasant.*
>
> *Although I wish I were*
> *At Beaufort Castle, where*
> *   Just now I'm stoppin',*
> *Yet it's my duty, ere*
> *I can resume my chair*
> *Graciously to declare*
> *   This concert open.*

But in their youth he was essentially a grown-up to them, a rather crotchety familiar of their mother's, an accepted part of the household, not so intelligible as the men who came to shoot and fish, not so fascinating as Sir Compton Mackenzie, not such fun as Maurice Baring. It was left to other children to make a playmate of him.

In August 1919, while a deacon, Ronald preached his first sermon as a Catholic – a distinction mistakenly claimed by more than one English church – at Eskadale, the parish church of Beaufort, to a mixed congregation of crofters and visitors at the castle. In the summer of 1922 he went to Lourdes with Lady Lovat.

Lord Lovat's finances were liable to fluctuate. Sometimes he was obliged to let his shooting. For two years, 1923 and 1924, he let the castle with it. Lady Lovat then took a house at Rottingdean, where Ronald settled as one of the family. It is impossible to estimate the debt he owed her in those years; what Father Healy was doing at St Edmund's, she was completing in the world, showing him the way, giving him confidence, and receiving in exchange his full affection.

Lord Lovat's sister was married to Archibald Stirling of Keir. This household became one where Ronald stayed regularly on his journeys to Beaufort. He said the first Mass in the chapel there after the famous Anrep mosaics were completed, and the Stirling children grew up in his confidence.

His acceptance by one highly exclusive section of the laity was formally recognized in 1922, when he was appointed Chaplain of Magisterial Obedience in the Knights of Malta. He was at the same time meeting and endearing himself to the organizers of parish bazaars and the secretaries of Catholic societies all over the country and to the schoolboys who would later form the centre of his chaplaincy at Oxford.

He first visited Ampleforth to give the boys' retreat in the autumn of 1922. He used to recall how on that occasion the community slightly disconcerted him by their attentions. When he wanted to be alone and pray, they tried to divert him with sightseeing. Irresistible courtesy carried him off into every corner of school and monastery, until on his last morning he wished to cash a cheque. The Assistant-Procurator was pointed out to him. Ronald accosted him with his request. The monk turned in absolute silence and led him, three paces ahead, to the office, opened the cash-box, and counted the notes, still without a word. At last, Ronald thought, he had found a monk of admirable rigour. He bowed silently and made to leave. 'You have just time,' said the Assistant-Procurator, 'for me to show you the new boiler.'

The variety of his new connexions is illustrated by the contrast that at Christmas 1920 he stayed at Arundel with the Duchess of Norfolk and at Christmas 1921 at Kingsland with Hilaire Belloc.

He and Belloc had met often at Oxford and debated together at the Union. In temperament they were the whole width of the Church apart; each appreciated the other's singularity and respected his genius. Belloc had 'blown in' on him, as Ronald reported to his sister, when he was at the Oratory and exuberantly congratulated him on his conversion. The friendship of Maurice Baring made a new strong bond between them, as it did between Ronald and G. K. Chesterton.

He and Chesterton had met several times on public occasions and had written to, and of, one another with enthusiasm, but each lived in a separate milieu, and neither would have claimed the other's personal friendship in 1922. Their influence on one another was literary. Writing to condole with Mrs Chesterton on her husband's death in 1936, Ronald wrote, with a touch of the hyperbole appropriate to the occasion:

He has been my idol since I read the Napoleon of Notting Hill as a schoolboy; I'll only hope that you, who know as no one else does what we have lost, will find it easy to imagine as well as believe that he is alive and unchanged. Thank God for that faith; that I have it when so many of my friends lost it was due, I think, under God to him. May he be pardoned all that remains to pardon; I don't think he can be long for Purgatory.

Ronald played an unobtrusive but important part in Chesterton's conversion.

Since 1915 or earlier Chesterton had been so near the Church that his friends had begun to wonder whether he would ever enter it. Intellectually he accepted the full Catholic Faith; but he was as slow to action as he was quick in thought. Various considerations, practical and sentimental, held him back. At length in 1922, after visiting Jerusalem and Rome, he made his decision. He did not, like Ronald, seek Authority but, surprisingly in a man of such transparent innocence, Absolution. Ronald's was naturally one of the names that occurred to him and to his friends as a priest suitable to instruct and receive him. During the summer of 1922 they exchanged a series of letters, mostly concerned with the difficulty two busy men found in arranging a meeting; a difficulty which in Chesterton's case was complicated by his father's death, his wife's illness, and a change of house. Ronald's letters have not survived; Chesterton's, with one exception, are printed in the biography.[1] The exception was given to a friend as a keepsake and forgotten when Mrs Maisie Ward was collecting her material. It illustrates Chesterton's life, rather than Ronald's, but is here appended so that the series may be complete.[2]

Mrs Chesterton was not then a Catholic. She had one old and trusted friend in the priesthood, Fr (later Mgr) John O'Connor, whose appearance and manner suggested 'Father Brown'. Chesterton was anxious to avoid any unnecessary element of strangeness in the ceremony of his reception which might disturb his wife. On July 17th 1922 Ronald wrote:

> I'm awfully glad to hear that you've sent for Father O'Connor and that you think he's likely to be available. I must say that, in the story, Father Brown's powers of neglecting his parish always seemed to me even more admirable than Dr Watson's powers of neglecting his practice; so I hope this trait was drawn from life.

Chesterton was received by Fr O'Connor that month. He wrote that Maurice Baring and Ronald had done most in his time of uncertainty to

[1] Maisie Ward, op. cit., pp. 391–5.   [2] See Appendix II at end of chapter.

help him into the Church. 'You could fluster Gilbert but not hustle him,' said Fr O'Connor.[1] All these had shown patience and delicacy, which was rewarded four years later by the reception of Mrs Chesterton.

At about that date Chesterton wrote the well-known quatrain:[2]

NAMESAKE

Mary of Holyrood may smile indeed,
Knowing what grim historic shade it shocks
To see wit, laughter and the Popish creed
Cluster and sparkle in the name of Knox.

It was partly Chesterton's conversion, much publicized by others, not by himself, which prompted (Sir) Arnold Lunn to write in 1924 a series of hostile biographical studies entitled *Roman Converts*. Ronald was one of the subjects, and his own estimation of his position in relation to Chesterton's is expressed in a letter to (Sir) Shane Leslie, who asked him to reply to Sir Arnold in the *Dublin Review*: 'It's all very well for G.K.C. because he's "arrived" but I can't do that kind of thing without being accused of self advertisement. Chesterton has only to refute an attack on Chestertonism; I shall have to refute an attack, not on Knoxianism, but on Knox.'

He was tempted to send a sharp letter to Sir Arnold, but forbore and wrote instead in a light and conciliatory manner: 'Thank you for the compliment, for it is, I suppose, a compliment of sorts, like the crocodile pursuing Captain Hook.'

> I remember thinking at the time [Sir Arnold writes][3] that there must be unsuspected reserves in that strange religion of his, if he could reply with such humour to so hostile a study of himself. . . .

Ronald said later:

> You narrowly escaped receiving the most terrific snorter. I had just drafted it out. Instead, with a real effort, I sat down and wrote a reasonably polite reply. This would seem to be one of the few occasions when doing the right thing has had the right results. It was clearly right not to send you a snorter, and I'm glad that for once doing the right thing did not have disastrous consequences.

---

[1] Maisie Ward,. op. cit., p. 387.
[2] *Collected Poems of G. K. Chesterton* (1927), p. 15.
[3] Arnold Lunn, *And Yet so New* (1958), p. 3–4.

Thus, outside St Edmund's, Ronald's career prospered, while at the college he grew increasingly ill at ease.

In January 1926, when Mr Eyres left to try his vocation at Ampleforth, he was deprived of the daily companionship which had done much to reconcile him to his troubled conditions. It was by then clear that the Cardinal's hopes for the college were not to be realized. The internal dissension had become more acute. Few, if any, of Ronald's friends outside the College knew of the particular cause of his distress, but many saw he was unhappy, and all deplored the waste of his genius; if not in his own interests, in those of the Church. As early as Christmas 1923 Belloc had written to him:[1]

> It is of importance to England today that every testimony should be given [Belloc is writing of the paramount importance of 'bearing witness to the Faith'] and I cannot but think that if all your time and energies were free . . . they would be spent to the country's good . . . In a school, with people already Catholic and with work which another might do, the full effect is lacking. . . . Half a dozen talents change the whole of a society – but used at pressure and in the open. It is the unseen force of many prayers, and, more, of accepted sufferings, which furnishes the power: but the power must be exercised by an active and continuous direct and open appeal. You can give this. I do think that now, in your maturity, it would be of decisive effect, and that all occupation uncongenial to that principal affair may well be – or rather *ought* to be abandoned. It is a waste.
>
> I have no business to write thus, and no excuse save my very strong conviction.
>
> '*Etre Catholique, c'est tout.*' To remake Europe is our intense and urgent call. Of the higher things I know nothing. I was not called to them. But I know *that*: and I know that very few men can so act anywhere: in England but a dozen, and that you are one of them.

Belloc did not know Ronald very well; he appreciated neither the weakness nor the strength which made him unsuitable for the role assigned to him; neither the diffidence which held him back from controversy and his constitutional dependence on orders; nor the sanctity which placed him among those whose prayers and accepted sufferings generated rather than exercised power. Ronald sometimes divided people into the Greek categories of 'drastic' and 'pathetic'. He was, in that sense, pathetic; Belloc eminently drastic. Belloc was obsessed by the unrecognized crisis of the times; he saw a great void in the human government of the Church, a fog

---

[1] *Letters from Hilaire Belloc*, ed. Robert Speaight (1958), pp. 147–8.

of mediocrity in high places. It was the moment, it seemed, when Divine Providence should raise a champion. The spectacle of Ronald's enormous gifts being frittered away on light literature and routine schoolmastering moved him to indignation. It is said, on no first-hand authority which the biographer has been able to trace, that finding himself in Cardinal Bourne's company at some function, he raised the question with him. If he did, the Cardinal gave no sign of being impressed. He found Ronald very useful to St Edmund's.

Meanwhile other friends, led by Sligger Urquhart, were working to find a solution of Ronald's difficulty. Mgr ('Mugger') Barnes, the chaplain to the Catholic undergraduates at Oxford, was of an age to retire; a situation more evident to others than to himself. The appointment of a successor was then, as now, in the hands of the Universities' Catholic Education Board, a body of twenty-one members drawn from the hierarchy and the two Universities, the majority of them laymen. Sligger had been elected in 1898 and was a munificent and active member. Cardinal Bourne was a member *ex officio*.

In 1925, if not earlier, Ronald's name was being canvassed for the succession; Mugger Barnes supported him, but had fixed no date for his retirement. Another candidate was the Oratorian Fr Pollen, a man of great holiness but of the same age as Mugger Barnes; there was no certainty that the Oratory would release him.

On March 21st 1926 Ronald wrote to Mr Eyres:

> Sligger tells me that Barnes probably does mean to retire this summer but that as soon as my name was mentioned at the Board meeting, the Cardinal said he was v. anxious I should not leave St Edmund's yet, 'while the experiment was still so new'! though of course he would not in any way wish to hamper the decision of the Board. . . . I'm rather annoyed, because when Cambridge was vacant [in 1922] H.E. talked to me about it, and said he didn't see it was much good my name being put up, because I hadn't enough money. Now that I have enough money, he doesn't mention it to me at all; he's rather like Pooh-Bah (is it?) in the Mikado; as Chairman of the Universities' Board[1] he expresses the hope that it will not be necessary for him as Patron of St Edmund's to recommend himself as Archbishop of Westminster not to let me go. If I am to stay here till the 'experiment' succeeds, I fancy I shall be here for the rest of my lifetime or his.
>
> Nobody [he added glumly] will get a H.C. this term.

[1] In fact, Cardinal Bourne was not Chairman. The Archbishop of Birmingham held that office.

On March 24th James Hope,[1] an influential member of the Board, wrote to Sligger: 'With regard to Knox. I take no strong view personally as I do not know him well enough, but I am satisfied that many people think him very unsuitable, and I am more than doubtful as to whether he could be carried at the meeting.'

Ronald was ill with jaundice and nervously distraught that spring. On April 20th he wrote to Sligger:

> I think it's quite possible that some of the parsons in Oxford would not be best pleased at my return . . . I think there are millions of points of view from which it would be quite unsuitable to send me there. But I'm getting such a frightful complex about leaving this place that I can't see straight at all and must leave it in other hands than my own.

Sligger's were the right hands. At the beginning of May he had an interview with Cardinal Bourne and persuaded him to withdraw his opposition. He represented to Mugger Barnes that if he did not retire at once, Ronald would in desperation find some other post and be lost to the chaplaincy. He also worked gently and persistently on the members of the Board, and at their meeting in July the appointment was finally made.

Ronald telegraphed the news to Mr Eyres at Ampleforth and later wrote to describe its reception at St Edmund's: 'Myers; "Well, er, I congratulate you, but personally, well I think you're going into a hornet's nest." I refrained from pointing out that in some ways I had been excellently trained for the experience.'

Later he amply acknowledged his debt to St Edmund's. At the moment of leaving his emotion was one of pure relief.

---

[1] Later first Lord Rankeillour.

Appendix I

In elaboration of the conversation referred to on p. 270, Lady Acton writes:

My question to Ronnie was, whether the 'breathing' mentioned by St John of the Cross[1] was something actually experienced. And he said it was, and that he'd experienced it at his Confirmation. I suppose Ronnie must have been provided with the necessary mystical faculties for experiencing it. Anyhow I understood him to mean that he had an experience like extra-breathing being added to his own – not an intellectual conviction of any kind.

He was reluctant to talk about it, but I pressed on (though not on the same day) and asked: 'Is that the breathing of the Holy Spirit?' He said it was. I said: 'You wrote that our bread is not real bread. God created it as an analogy to help us understand the Bread of Life. Is our breathing, similarly, an analogy to help us understand real breathing; the Holy Spirit? Is He Real Breathing?' He hesitated a bit. Then he said: 'I think so. Earthly fatherhood is an analogy for the Father, and earthly sonship for the Son, so it would be incongruous if the Holy Spirit didn't have His earthly analogy.'

Is it possible to make it clear that it (this experience) was of the highest order? I understand that anything from the 'Prayer of Quiet' onwards comes under the heading of 'infused prayer', whereas this appears to be a temporary experience of the State of Union.

The passage referred to from St John of the Cross reads:

The breathing of the air is a property of the Holy Spirit, for which the soul here prays so that she may love God perfectly. She calls it the breathing of the air, because it is a most delicate touch and feeling of love which habitually in this estate is caused in the soul by the communication of the Holy Spirit. Breathing with that His Divine breath, He raises the soul most sublimely, and informs her, that she may breathe in God the same breath of

---

[1] *Spiritual Canticle.* Stanza XXXVIII. E. Allison Peers's translation 1934.

love that the Father breathes in the Son and the Son in the Father, which is the same Holy Spirit that they breathe into her in the said transformation. For it would not be a true transformation if the soul were not united and transformed in the Holy Spirit as well as in the other two Divine Persons, albeit not in a degree revealed and manifest, by reason of the lowliness and the condition of this life. And this is for the soul so high a glory, and so profound and sublime a delight, that it cannot be described by mortal tongue, nor can human understanding, as such, attain to any conception of it.

A theologian comments on Lady Acton's letter as follows:

There is no means of telling whether this grace 'was of the highest order' without any further evidence of mystical prayer in R.'s life. If there *is* such evidence, then this is obviously crucial (or perhaps I'd better say 'might be' crucial). A *single* experience of the highest order would be almost unthinkable.

Again, 'analogy' is a very broad term. The relationship between the human father and son is real, a real fatherhood. R. is implicitly referring to Ephesians 3, and to his own translation of St Paul – i.e., when we consider the relationship between human and divine fatherhood, it is the divine and not the human which is the *term* of the analogy; i.e., the first and infinitely greater reality is the relationship between the First and Second Persons. Now the question of bread is different – bread, in the context, being a figure for food or sustenance. And Our Lord in the Holy Eucharist as the sustenance of the supernatural life is a higher reality than food of natural life. But the analogy between the first analogy (Fatherhood) and the second (Bread) is not perfect; for in the second case we are dealing with a sacramental sign. It is an exaggeration to say (simply) that God created bread as an analogy; He created it as a means of sustenance. Now when R. said all this (and it is important to remember that he said it on 'another day'), he is speaking, not against a background of mystical experience necessarily, but as a theologian of the O.T. (Breath of life, spiritus vitae, natural breath – the Hebrew concept of the soul; and the Holy Spirit communicating supernatural life.) Hence, when he says 'real breath' he means that the Holy Spirit, in Hebraic terms breathes supernatural life into us. Now all this is intelligible outside of mystical experience – the Holy Spirit, the living indwelling breath of the supernatural life, the expression the 'breath' of the life of the Trinity. I think that what one could say would be that R. was *aware*, at the time of his confirmation, of his sharing the Divine Life, of the Divine Life being communicated, of the vital union which every soul in grace has – without, normally, being thus aware of it – with the Blessed Trinity. What perhaps he wished to say by using the comparison and the reference to John was that as we are aware of the life in us (natural) through the muscular action, etc. which accompanies breathing – sense-awareness of vital movement (especially deep-breathing, mountain- and seaside-air, etc.) so he was aware, in that moment, of the supernatural life being communicated. To press the analogy any farther would verge on the silly. Nor does the analogy give us any insight as to the particular *level* of this mystical experience. It does not of itself indicate transforming union in the traditional sense (it was above the graces given in the prayer of quiet, since those are not perceptible supernaturally). But neither is there any evidence to show that it was of the highest order (I would say not, myself). However, it is an incident in his life that is of the greatest interest, and should be recorded.

Appendix II

Dear Father Knox,

I had meant to make some attempt to finish the fuller reply I had actually begun to the very kind letter you sent me, I am ashamed to think how long ago, before my recent trouble; and though the trail and tangle of those troubles will still, I fear, make this very inadequate, there were two things in your letter I feel I ought to acknowledge even so late.

I cannot tell you how much I was pleased and honoured even by the suggestion that you might possibly deal with the instruction yourself; it is something that I should value more vividly and personally than I can possibly express. But as this was so long ago, before so many delays and interruptions, I fear your margin of Sundays in London must now be very much narrowed. But I think there must be a Sunday or two left on your list; and with your permission, I propose to come up next Sunday, if I could have the pleasure of seeing you then. I have no doubt it could be arranged through Maurice Baring or somebody, supposing you have no arrangements of your own which you would prefer. Then we could see what could be done with that possibility, or finally make some arrangement about another one. I rather feel I should like to talk to you once more in either case: I hope it would not be an inconvenience.

For the other matter, I hope you do not really feel any need to apologise for what you said about private troubles dismounting a man from public platforms; for it is exactly what I am feeling most intensely myself. I am in a state now when I feel a monstrous charlatan, as if I wore a mask and were stuffed with cushions, whenever I see anything about the public G.K.C.; it hurts me; for though the views I express are real, the image is horribly unreal compared with the real person who needs help just now. I have as much vanity as anybody about any of these superficial successes while they are going on; but I never feel for a moment that they affect the reality of whether I am utterly rotten or not; so that any public comments on my religious position seem like a wind on the other side of the world; as if they were about somebody else – as indeed they are. I am not troubled about a great fat man who appears on platforms and in caricatures, even when he enjoys controversies on what I believe to be the right side. I am concerned about what has become of a little boy whose father showed him a toy theatre, and a schoolboy whom nobody ever heard of, with his brooding on doubts and dirt and daydreams of crude conscientiousness so inconsistent as to [be] near to hypocrisy; and all the morbid life of the lonely mind of a living person with whom I have lived. It is that story, that so often came near to ending badly, that I want to end well. Forgive this scrawl; I think you will understand me.

Yours very sincerely,
G. K. Chesterton.

P.S. Forgive the disreputable haste of this letter; my normal chaos is increased by moving into a new house, which is still like a wastepaper basket. I am coming up to town tomorrow, and will try to fix something up with Maurice or somebody.

Chapter Two

'CHAPLAINCRAFT'

1926–1939

A t Oxford, for thirteen years and for the only time in his life Ronald had a house of his own and a cure of souls.

The house stands at the corner of Rose Place and St Aldate's and bears the traditional but deceptive name of the Old Palace. Even today, after large sums have been spent, there is nothing palatial about the gabled building, part Tudor, part Caroline, with its narrow entrances, steep little stairs, and low ceilings. When it first caught Mugger Barnes's fancy, it was a ramshackle congeries hemmed in by slums, comprising two dwellings, two shops, a yard, and various outbuildings. It had (and has) what house agents describe as 'a wealth of old oak' and some handsome plaster work; centuries of vicissitude were recorded in many quaint features grateful to the tastes of the Edwardian era. The freehold was bought by the Newman Trustees for £3,000, and a further £2,500 were spent on necessary repairs and adaptations. There were two sizeable rooms, one of which served as chapel.

Four generations of Oxford men remember Ronald seated most of the day either at the writing-table or on the fender of the long room on the first floor. When he came, this room was almost derelict; it housed a miscellaneous collection of books and was sometimes used for Newman Society meetings. Mugger Barnes had a study also on the first floor which Ronald converted into a bedroom. Ronald and the city authorities, who destroyed the surrounding houses which blocked its windows, made the present Chaplain's Room habitable and attractive. There was (and is) a dining-room on the first floor which serves also as a passage to the Chaplain's Room; on the second floor is the large room, originally used as the chapel, later, as will appear below, as the lodgers' common-room, three bedrooms, and a bathroom, which Ronald equipped with two baths. Some mature guests, accustomed to less Spartan intimacies, were disconcerted to find themselves bathing in company with undergraduates. The third floor had attic bedrooms and a bathroom for the servants. The ground floor was largely taken up by the shops. The remaining space was used as domestic offices.

Ronald was fascinated by every feature of his new home. Before leaving the chaplaincy he composed a report for his successor sixty-five pages long entitled: *The Whole Art of Chaplaincraft as practised in the University of Oxford between the year 1926–1927 and the year 1938–1939: digested under twenty headings*, the opening sections of which give both a detailed history of the building and household-hints which record many of the minor preoccupations of his tenancy.

> The wireless shop must not be allowed to burn a fire in the upstairs grate; if this happens, the smoke comes out between the floorboards of the chaplain's room.
>
> The floor should not be allowed to develop holes because rats wander round in the wall. The tap which turns on the gas-fire is a very loose one, and care should be taken to avoid switching it on inadvertently.
>
> The second-floor bed-room on the North was condemned by the delegacy as unsuitable accommodation for an undergraduate; I have therefore been compelled to sleep in it myself.
>
> If the cold taps are turned too far, they make a loud buzzing noise which is all too audible in the chapel.
>
> The harmonium has not been used since 1927, and might be the better for some tuning.
>
> In the old chapel stood a very imperfect list of Catholics who fell in the great war; I had to remove this because the quotation at the top, *Dulce et decorum est pro patria mori*, had been attributed, by an oversight, to Ovid.
>
> The larger sofa [in the Newman Room] was presented to the Society by Mgr Barnes, who assured me that it was the sofa on which his father proposed marriage to his mother.
>
> Who owns the library, in law, might be the subject of a very delicate legal enquiry.

During Ronald's time a new chapel was added, light and graceful and adequate in size for all foreseeable needs, with a club-room below, and the waste ground was laid out and planted as a garden where Ronald spent many not very effective hours with spade and hoe.

The admittance of women to the chaplaincy, which occurred during the Second World War, and the overcrowding of the University which followed the Butler Education Act, have made the chapel obsolete, and a large temporary structure, which Ronald described as 'a rococo tin tabernacle', has obliterated his garden. His Newman room is still in use. Some of the schemes, hotly debated in recent years, for deflecting traffic from the High Street have threatened the amenities of the chaplaincy, but it seems probable that the structure of the Old Palace is reasonably safe from demolition.

The property had in the Middle Ages belonged both to Dominicans and Franciscans, and Ronald, who knew and loved all the waterways of the neighbourhood, delighted to recall that they had used the Twill mill-stream which runs under Rose Place and emerges prettily into the Christ Church Memorial Garden. He himself had followed this 'true branch of Isis' from the turn close by the gas-works into the mill-pool under the Castle walls, through her subterranean course into the Meadow, and he later eloquently commemorated her in the title and preface of his second volume of Oxford Conferences, *The Hidden Stream* (1952).

Then at the Reformation Bishop King built there on the confiscated estate and gave his title to the palace.

The career of this first and last Catholic Bishop of Oxford (for Bishop Goldwell, who lived and died in exile, was elected but never confirmed in the see) is a microcosm of the Tudor clerical biography; he was an unheroic man who had the great good fortune to die a year before Queen Mary.

> I picture the old man [Ronald wrote][1] striding up and down this very room where I said office this morning, trying to adapt himself to the altered conditions of 1553 – saying goodbye for the nonce to *Dearly beloved brethren*, banging off the dust of five years from his neglected breviary and starting out again on *Aperi Domine*. What a retrospect was his. He had seen Wolsey fall, and Cromwell, and now Cranmer was going the same way. He had seen the monasteries dissolved and shared in their spoils, and now the loot was in danger. He had taken the Oath of Supremacy and now he saw the Supreme Head of the Church in England declaring she was nothing of the sort. The times were out of joint; surely it was not Robert King's province to set them right. . . . I confess I go to bed the more courageously for the knowledge that my predecessor made a good end.

Ronald was thrown into some agitation at the prospect of acquiring pots and pans. He stayed at Trinity in late September, and Lady Lovat came to supervise the move into the Old Palace. She chose the curtains and chair covers and the dining-room chairs. More than this, she provided Mrs Lyons, the old housekeeper from Beaufort, an inestimable boon who for eleven years devoted herself to Ronald's service, serenely adapting herself from the spacious and varied regime of a great house to his narrow

---

[1] *The Universe*, December 10th 1926.

and regular habits, doing the cooking herself, directing the two maid-servants, and assuring for him the physical conditions essential to his cure of souls.

He was the fifth Catholic Chaplain at Oxford since the Reformation. Each of his predecessors styled himself 'Catholic Chaplain to the University'. Since the post was not officially recognized, Ronald insisted that he was 'Chaplain to the Catholic undergraduates'.

Anglican control of the University had been gradually surrendered during the nineteenth century, but the admission of Nonconformists was not immediately welcomed by the Roman Catholic hierarchy, who feared the prevalent agnostic atmosphere. In 1867 Cardinal Manning, a Balliol man, obtained a formal prohibition from Rome to the entry of Catholics to either of the Universities, and for nearly thirty years the only 'higher education' officially available for them in England was in the upper forms of the Catholic schools, at many of which there were rather unruly groups of men of university age, inappropriately named 'Philosophers', who were allowed to graduate by examination in London. As it became recognized that the project of founding a Catholic University for the United Kingdom was chimerical, the decree was increasingly resented, particularly by the second generation of converts of the Oxford Movement. Some defied it. Many evaded it. In fact, the Newman Society, the club of the Oxford Catholic undergraduates,[1] was founded during Manning's life-time seven years before the chaplaincy. In 1894, after Manning's death, a petition was presented to the Pope, and in the following year the prohibition was rescinded, with the proviso that at both Universities special lecturers should be appointed to counteract the dangers to faith, and the Universities' Catholic Education Board was constituted, primarily to choose and pay these 'professors'. The Board decided that a resident priest at each university would best fulfil the Pope's intentions. There was a 'professor' at Cambridge for two years. At Oxford the two functions were from the first, 1897, combined in the same office. Half-hour didactic sermons, or 'conferences', on Sunday mornings, given either by the chaplain or a visiting priest, were accepted as satisfying the ordinance for apologetic lecturers. Thus the chaplain's original, essential duty was not merely to say Mass for the undergraduates and hear their confessions but to instruct them. The chaplaincy as originally constituted and as maintained by Ronald was for men only.

---

[1] 'Newman Societies' at other places are normally associations of university graduates.

If women turn up at the undergraduates' Mass [he wrote in the *Whole Art*] they should be made to sit close to the wall; no male will sit on either side of them for fear of looking responsible for them. If I find that a woman is making a habit of coming, I try after a time to choke her off as politely as I can, pointing out that I am not supposed to poach on the preserves of Cherwell Edge [a convent-hostel] or St Aloysius, the parish church.

The number of Catholic undergraduates rose during Ronald's time from about 130 to about 170, the increase being entirely made by men from overseas and scholars from secondary schools. The numbers from Public Schools fell slightly, but these remained the staple of his congregation.

Ronald had few illusions about these young men. It has been suggested that he returned to Oxford expecting to find the world of Julian Grenfell and Ted Shuttleworth and Guy Lawrence still as he had left it. In fact, he was disposed to overestimate the huge hiatus of the War. He and Sligger had often discussed the changed character of the young. He had stayed in Balliol, and in Sligger's rooms had seen the coming and going of the new generation. Mr Cyril Connolly remembers such an occasion. He and Sligger's other new friends expected a *revenant* from a world they grudgingly admired. Ronald expected nothing, sat with his pipe in his corner, and made no effort to impress. They were disappointed; he, in the days before he had any idea of returning to Oxford, had been incurious. When he found himself by profession once more among undergraduates, he learned that though language and habits and tastes had changed, English youth was not so utterly foreign as he had supposed. He made many friends among the young; no longer with the intensity of his own youth; but he was able still to find agreeable companions for the dinner-table and the river. The great difference lay in his new relationship of responsibility towards them.

Ronald was succeeding a man who was in many ways the antithesis of himself. Mugger Barnes had been chaplain at Cambridge from 1902 to 1914 and at Oxford from 1915 to 1926. In his obituary[1] Ronald said of him that his most memorable – and perhaps by implication his most enviable – quality was serenity. 'He never fussed.' In his long experience of undergraduates he had learned to accept their doubts and peccadillos with a detachment which Ronald never achieved. It was his experience, the Mugger said, that most men between the ages of eighteen and twenty-

---

[1] *The Tablet*, November 21st 1936.

one gave up the practice of their religion and that most came back to it later. One of his maxims was: 'undergraduates only last three years'.

Like Ronald (and unlike Fr Martindale), he was most at his ease in the society of his own class and was not assiduous, as Ronald was, in seeking out and attaching to himself men of different origins. He was a well-bred man with a discursive and curious mind that was full of antiquarian speculation and oddities of information. He was no scholar, as the University understood the term, and, perhaps for that reason, the more welcome at High Tables.

Ronald recorded that the Mugger made the chaplaincy recognized as an 'institution'; that was to say that he made himself well liked and his position respected in a limited but influential circle. He was not a spiritual or intellectual force. That position, in the early 'twenties at Oxford, was held, though not sought, by Fr C.C. Martindale, S.J., who at Campion Hall dazzled and stimulated the most various undergraduates by his restless zeal, incisive diction, and by his modernity. He went down as Ronald came up. They overlapped for one term only. Fr Martindale was loaded with academic distinctions, but he held aloof from High Tables. It was Ronald's achievement in a great measure to combine the positions of these two dissimilar priests.

The antagonism he had anticipated was barely discernible. Trinity at once elected him to Common-room rights. Mr Higham and Mr Philip Landon, among others of his old friends, made him specially welcome. Since 1915 clerical influence had still further declined in Oxford, and if anyone looked at him askance in any Senior Common-rooms, it was not as an Anglican apostate but as a Christian. It was a time when Marxism and Logical Positivism were in the ascendant. It would have suited many of the young dons better to see the Church still represented by a genial and picturesque anachronism than by a sounder scholar and sharper wit than themselves.

There is scant record of Ronald's first steps in the chaplaincy. They were impeded by the very fact that so little had come to be expected of Mugger Barnes. Speaking in June 1939, in his last conference as chaplain, Ronald said: 'I want you to treat my successor as the chaplain whom God has sent you, and make things easy for him, as far as possible, at the start; after that you won't need any encouragement from me. But just at the start, do try to make things easy for him. Go and see him, and let him make your acquaintance, as soon as he has had time to comb out the freshers; don't hang about waiting for an invitation to dinner. I remember so well, you see, how difficult it was starting on this job.'

He had felt rather isolated during his first term at Trinity when the life of the University was perfectly familiar and agreeable to him. He was now returning after eleven years' absence to a changed world. It did not take him long to establish himself, but for someone so constitutionally reluctant as Ronald to intrude on others and so constitutionally scrupulous to omit no duty, there must have been much anxiety and frustration during his first weeks, as day after day he sat alone among the tea-cups and sandwiches, waiting for men who never called.

That, at least, is how he was inclined to remember them thirteen years later, but there is a letter extant written to Mr Eyres on November 6th 1926, after five weeks of term, which gives a slightly different account:

> My flock. About 125 as far as I can gather; probably there are a few stray Hungarians etc. to be brought in. I ask freshers to a laborious series of dinner-parties. I am perhaps half way through them – and the older people on the whole have been very friendly about dropping in. Rather over ten per cent are from Ampleforth, and I wish to goodness it was 100. At least eight out of fourteen were at Communion on All Saints' Day – not bad for a Monday.[1] Oxford generally – Fuller than I thought with people I still know.

In the conference quoted above Ronald also said:

> I am leaving to my successor a document about six times as long as this sermon, explaining to him exactly how everything has been run while I have been here. I have left it to him in the certainty, and almost in the hope, that he will set to work on perfectly different lines as soon as he finds his feet here.

Few biographers have enjoyed the use of a document like the *Whole Art*, giving, as it does, so complete an account of the subject's habits of life during a long and important period. Was the expression of hope that it would be disregarded, entirely candid? In the event it at once became a document of historic interest only, but had there been no war and no social revolution and had things gone on as they had done in his day,

---

[1] Six years later his enthusiasm for Ampleforth had declined. He wrote there to Mr Eyres, who in the meantime had had experience on the staff at Stonyhurst and the Oratory: 'The following statistics may have interest. Called here before tea-time on Monday [the first of term] Stonyhurst – freshers 4 (80%), seniors 5. Ampleforth: freshers 0, seniors 0. Called here at tea-time on Monday: Stonyhurst – freshers 1, seniors 1. Ampleforth – freshers 4 (80%), seniors 0. I doubt whether you will have the courage to report these statistics to Fr Paul. But, seriously, isn't it rather bad? I may say that, so far as freshers are concerned, Beaumont is best and Downside is way up.'

Ronald would (it may be conjectured) have resented any departure from the system he had so laboriously perfected and itemized. He believed he was founding a tradition where he was merely leaving a gracious memory.

In his valedictory conference Ronald described the chaplain's work as 'a series of frantic experiments made in the dark, based almost entirely on personal contact'.

The experiments, whose frantic character none of his flock suspected, must have belonged to his first term or two, and are neither recorded nor remembered. He seemed to all who knew him a man of undeviating routine. Every hour of his day and every day of the term were planned.

There was daily Mass at eight.

> I usually go out into the chapel when I have put on alb and girdle, taking a match-box with me, which I hand to a server chosen on the spur of the moment. The objection to having the same man every day, or a fixed server for any day of the week, is that the rest of the men forget how to serve Mass. I don't ask people who haven't been to Catholic schools because it embarrasses a man to explain that he doesn't know how. The average daily attendance in some terms has been over 12, in others under 7. . . . It is worth advertising beforehand, if one can remember them, first Fridays of the month; which have a special lure for the French Canadians.

On Sunday Ronald always said the first Mass at eight-fifteen. There was then a Mass for the townspeople of the district, served by the Jesuits, at nine. 'Undergraduates come to it rarely; with no encouragement from me. . . . The 10.30 or conference Mass is said by one of the Dominicans. The bother is that the Dominicans insist on saying an odd kind of Mass, which needs a server accustomed to the rite.'

There were collections on holidays of obligation. 'I think it is rather a good thing to get them interested in charitable objects, and also to accustom them to being cursed about money, since this will happen to them all the rest of their lives.'

Benediction was given elsewhere in the town with better music than Ronald could provide, and after failing on many occasions to assemble a quorum he gave up the attempt. Incense was used only once a year. 'On Shrove Tuesday he [the chaplain] will institute a search in the attics to find out where the thurible, incense boat, incense, charcoal and aspergillum have been packed away.

Sunday was the most exacting day of Ronald's week:

> The chaplain, having seen that the door is opened, put out the roll-call book, left the *Tablet* in the Newman room, fixed up on the glass swing-

door any notices about defunct members of the University, prepared a fresh ciborium etc. goes into the confessional about eight. He gets away as soon as he can. . . . Immediately after Mass, putting away his amice and purificator to make way for the next priest he goes down to the further end of the chapel, and rescues the collecting-plate, which is probably on the music-stool. This he takes to his room and decants into a box used for the purpose; then he takes the collecting plate back into the chapel (if the 9.0 Mass has started, going round outside and by the door at the west end of the chapel). He puts it in front of some respectable-looking male townee; then he rescues the roll-call book and takes it with him. If it is a conference preacher who is saying the Mass, the chaplain sees that he gets his breakfast at a suitable time.

About 10.20 the chaplain takes . . . a box of cigarettes into the Newman Room. . . . He talks to the earlier arrivals, who are beginning to turn up; at 10.30 or so he selects someone who knows how to serve Dominican, and takes him up to the sacristy. When the priest has vested . . . the chaplain goes downstairs and shoos the congregation into the chapel. If he is giving the conference himself, he waits at the back till the gospel is over. If there is a special preacher, the chaplain goes back, by the out-of-doors route, to his own room, picks up the special preacher and hides him in the sacristy, then opens the door into the chapel ever so slightly, to make things audible. . . . He comes back to the west end of the chapel just as the preacher appears, counts the congregation and listens to the conference from the stairs (where he is handy for dealing with stray cats, dog-fights, yodelling small boys and other interruptions to the sermon). It may be necessary for him to go up to the head of the stairs and make faces at the preacher if the conference is notably exceeding the statutory half-hour. Then he will go back to his room and offer the preacher a drink, still using the out-of-doors route; – in the winter months it is safest for the chaplain to wear an overcoat all through the early part of Sunday morning.

While telling the preacher how nice the conference was, the chaplain takes his stand at the window just inside the door of his room and watches for signs of the congregation going out. As soon as these appear, he dashes downstairs and picks off those members of the congregation he wants to have a word with. He invites, as a rule, any ex-members of the congregation who are up for the week-end to come upstairs and have some beer. He sees that breakfast is ready for the priest who has said the 10.30 Mass. He and the visitors probably stay till 12.15 or so; and now the chaplain can begin to think about saying some office . . . but it is more likely that fresh visitors will blow in. If there is a visiting preacher the chaplain will be occupied in entertaining him.

The luncheon guests will disappear about three. And now, unless the chaplain has to have a committee meeting of the O.U.C.A. in his room, or has to give a conference at Cherwell Edge, there is an interval between three and four with the chances, on the whole, against stray visitors. Not many people come to tea but they are in a leisurely mood and stay till nearly six. By then . . . the Newman speaker has probably appeared and has to be entertained till he is taken off to dinner. But the chaplain must excuse himself for ten minutes or so while he goes down to the Newman Room and makes a preliminary arrangement of the chairs. At five or ten minutes to seven the Newman speaker, duly washed, must be taken off to whatever club the Committee is dining at. He and the Committee must be lugged back to the Old Palace about 8.10 and given port in the chaplain's room. The chaplain will keep a look-out to see when the members have mostly arrived (he may even have to send an S.O.S. to Campion[1] to ask if a few people will turn up and conceal the sparsity of attendance); then he will take the Committee down to the Newman Room . . . and come to roost in a comfortable chair if he can still find one. During the five minute interval after the paper, the chaplain invites one or two of the more distinguished people present (Fr D'Arcy, Fr O'Hea, dons, senior week-end visitors etc.) to come up after the meeting. During question-time he tries to keep things going. . . . When the meeting has been declared closed . . . he locks the three doors of the Newman Room; draws the curtains over the swing doors to keep smoke out of the chapel (also opening a window or two if needed). . . . The visitors probably retire at eleven or soon after and the chaplain (unless he has the speaker to entertain) can now enjoy his own company.

If there was no meeting of the Newman, Ronald usually spent Sunday evenings at Trinity, where many of his old friends made a point of dining in to meet him.

On weekdays Ronald held himself continuously at the disposal of anyone who wanted him. Except for the hour of three to four, when he walked round Christ Church Meadow with his breviary, he was always at home. He had been early impressed by the great strength of the Oratorian system of 'keeping one's room'. It was the quality he had particularly noted in Fr Healy at St Edmund's. If serenity was the mark of Mugger Barnes's chaplaincy, accessibility and patience were the marks of Ronald's.

Whole days may pass without so much as a man wanting you to sign a passport form for him. But I have not discovered any other way of making sure of the rare undergraduate, perhaps one in a month, who screws up his courage to come and talk about something important and might, if I were out, not have the courage to come again.[2]

---

[1] See below p. 335. [2] *The Whole Art of Chaplaincraft.*

In the mornings he sat with his typewriter and patience cards (he played a difficult variety of Canfield, going through the pack once only, one card at a time. It came out once in a thousand times, and when it did he announced the event by word and letter) attending to his large correspondence, writing his sermons and articles for the Press. When possible he lunched alone or in silence, ritually turning the familiar pages of *The Path to Rome*, *The New Republic*, *The Egoist*, the Barchester novels, and, unaccountably, of *Guy and Pauline*. (He expressed a peculiar affection for the character of 'Pauline'.) At four he kept his watch over the tea-table and was very seldom alone. 'Getting to know undergraduates' was for him, though few suspected it, a laborious and intricate task. He kept an index, each year being entered on a differently coloured card from the last, and in later life would sometimes identify past members of his congregation, saying: 'So-and-so? So-and-so? Green, I think. That means he came up in 1930.' A freshman's first summons, if he did not call spontaneously on the advice of his Headmaster, was to fill in his card. One such invitation has been preserved:

> Oct. 16th 1936.
> Dear Pizzala,
>
> I gather I ought to be making your acquaintance; will you be very kind and look in some time to let me do this? Preferably some time (e.g. tea-time) tomorrow, Saturday.

Of such meetings he wrote:

> It will be found easiest, I think, to remember a crowd of 50 to 60 strangers if you get the name pinned down first as a fixed point in your memory, and tack a face on to it afterwards. If you *know* that you are going to meet a man called Jones who was brought up by the Christian Brothers at Silverbridge and is recommended to your care by the priest at Barchester, when the authentic Jones arrives his face will fit into an open niche in your memory.[1]

The first meeting was followed by an invitation to dinner.

> I have usually had three dinner parties a week all through the year . . . I start with the freshers in Michaelmas Term, reckoning to get through them in about five weeks. Then I go back to the senior people, and in a good year have been right through the congregation by the end of the Hilary Term. I can then devote the summer to more specialized hospitality, asking the people I want to encourage, or the people I want to introduce to one

[1] Ibid.

another. I never quite know what mixture of gratification, embarrassment and boredom an Old Palace invitation brings with it to the ordinary man. But I am sure it is a good thing to make a universal gesture of friendliness, even if some of the people affected seem to make absolutely no response. If a man (I) leaves two successive invitations altogether unanswered, or (II) tells me three times running he has a previous engagement without expressing much regret about it, I assume that for one reason or another the invitation is unwelcome, and try to investigate his dispositions from some different angle. . . . It is always hoped that the guests will leave about ten and lodgers can be useful in instilling this notion. From ten, when the house has to be locked up (if there are lodgers) by proctors' orders, I have not encouraged callers. This may be quite wrong; Fr Martindale once expressed himself surprised that undergraduates did not drop in to call at an hour when, he assures me, undergraduates are at their most communicative. But we have not all the same gifts.[1]

These short evenings were not as a rule very exhilarating. Ronald had neither the means nor the inclination to encourage luxury among the young. The cooking was excellent, the wine modest.[2] As in his old evenings at Trinity, bananas were the staple dessert; they were the ideal fruit, Ronald maintained, since they required no plates or knives or forks and could be eaten in any posture. Conversation was general and light. Argument was avoided. Ronald had to search anxiously for topics of common interest. He was quite ignorant of the vocabulary of Rugby football. He never went to the Cinema (he saw a talking-film for the first time in 1954 in a Rhodesian farm-house) and could not, as could Fr D'Arcy, discuss the relative merits of film stars. He read few new books. Those who enjoyed Ronald's foibles and shared his amusements were rather few among the undergraduates of the time. He had dedicated *Juxta Salices* to Patrick Shaw-Stewart as the only man who understood all his jokes. There was no one quite like that in his congregation; very few could appreciate his classical verses (indeed from 1926 he let that talent lie almost idle). For English topography as exemplified in Bradshaw he found few fellow enthusiasts. 'Wimbornes' were more popular.

These began, it seems, as a joke between himself and Maurice Baring which soon spread in a small circle who collected and exchanged them. A

---

[1] Ibid.

[2] Ronald was notably frugal in everything affecting his own tastes. He did not smoke cigarettes, and the cigarettes he provided were more expensive than those used by most undergraduates. He liked good wine and had the worst. He had a special taste for 'Gentleman's Relish'. A friend sent him a pot every birthday. He never bought one for himself.

'Wimborne' (taking its name from the photograph of a footballer which appeared in a newspaper over the title 'Lady Wimborne, who has adopted the new windswept style of hairdressing') was a picture cut from a newspaper with which was included from an adjoining column a particularly inappropriate caption. Ronald acquired an album in which he at first pasted his own articles from the Press; he quickly tired of this vanity and used the book instead for 'Wimbornes', which were passed round a party which needed enlivenment.

Ronald was always at greater pains to draw out the gauche and dull than to impress his guests with his own wit. If he ever in his mind contrasted wistfully his lost friends with his new, he gave no hint of it.

He preserved a curious souvenir which illustrates the impression he made on two very different generations of undergraduate. It is an envelope on which, presumably about 1912, Guy Lawrence had played the game of 'analogies'.[1] It reads:

Time: 2 a.m.
Place: Daniel's den of lions with one candle.
Period: 100 AD.
Dress: Cassock, cotta and biretta. Jewel: Uncut lapis lazuli.
Flower: Passion Flower.
Scent: Pot-pourri of John Cotton, incense and magazines.
Sound: Faint muttering.
Food: None.
Animal: A captive and emaciated raven.

In 1928 Mr Walker,[2] on the back of the same envelope, 'marked' Ronald as follows:

Time: Midnight.
Place: Oxford.
Period: Victorian (not quite Mid-).
Dress: Court jester's, only black.
Jewel: Jade.
Flower: Poppy.
Scent: Mint-sauce.
Sound: Anyone's dying breath.

---

[1] For readers unfamiliar with this game it may be explained that the player's aim is to itemize in set categories the objects which remind him of the subject, e.g., Mr Walker is not attributing to Ronald a partiality for devilled sardines nor is either he or Lawrence suggesting that he kept late hours. Both thought of him as having, presumably, something of the stillness, darkness, and solitude of night.

[2] See below, pp. 318–20.

Food: Devilled sardines.
Animal: A very tame ferret.

Ronald's question of 'what mixture of gratification, embarrassment and boredom' an invitation to the Old Palace brought to 'the ordinary man' would have been answered differently by each, but it is certain that these dinners served a purpose of reminding Catholic undergraduates that they were members of a society which transcended the distinctions of school and college and that Ronald was its visible head. So prodigal of his own privacy, Ronald was scrupulously respectful of others'.

> I never call on undergraduates except (I) when I know them well, (II) on special occasions like the old clothes collection or the preparation for a mission, (III) when they are ill. I don't ever ask undergraduates to go for a walk, except very rarely when they have expressed a desire to talk something over; I have always felt the invitation was rather a difficult one to refuse, and looked like forcing oneself into their confidence. . . . I doubt if any unsolicited advice ought to be given except in extreme cases. . . . Beer is always on tap, and is offered at any time, especially round the middle of the morning. I do not keep sherry, because I cannot believe it has a good effect on the livers of the rising generation. I keep two kinds of cigarette, one Egyptian and one Virginian. I am told it is quite unnecessary to keep anything so expensive. . . . I keep a canoe on the river in the summer term and take undergraduates out in it; it is a useful way of making people's better acquaintance.[1]

One defence only he maintained against intrusion:

> I have steadily refused the suggestion of the postal authorities that I should instal a telephone at the Old Palace. This is mainly personal; I hate using the instrument; I hate being interrupted by bells; I hate enquiries from the editors of Sunday newspapers about the existence of a future life. But there is this much of calculation about my attitude – that if you keep a telephone in Oxford the undergraduate can get directly at you, whereas you cannot get directly at him. If he wants a dispensation from abstaining next Friday, he can ring up, instead of coming round (and perhaps hearing Mass while he is about it). If you want to alter the time of an engagement with him, you can only send word to the lodge, with no certainty when it will be picked up. Thus the system is unilateral.[2]

In 1929 Ronald invited Mr David Walker, a man at the House chiefly interested in athletics, to come to the Old Palace as a lodger.

---

[1] *The Whole Art.*   [2] Ibid.

This was not entirely his innovation. Mugger Barnes had once or twice housed an undergraduate. Ronald made it a regular feature of the chaplaincy. When the new chapel was opened in 1931 and a further room made available as a common sitting-room, the number was increased to three. All were men in their last year, who were supposed to be reading for Schools. The atmosphere of the Old Palace was congenial to work, but few of its lodgers made any great show in the class-lists. Some were the sons of his friends, a few were men who, parents or college authorities thought, needed supervision, but most were ordinary members of his congregation to whom cheap, comfortable, and central lodgings were a convenience. Ronald made no profit from them. Mrs Lyons calculated the bills strictly according to what they cost him. It was part of his scrupulous generosity to feel uneasy in the possession of anything, house-space included, which could be of benefit to others. The lodgers provided a nucleus for Ronald's hospitality; he always chose men from different schools and colleges; they formed no clique; their chief function was to help maintain his close touch with other undergraduates.

The Old Palace had amenities which were lacking in all but the most expensive digs; but there were also restraints. The lodgers were fully within their rights when they stayed out until midnight, but Ronald did not disguise the reproach with which he came down to let them in after ten. He had other foibles. He thought it barbarous to open letters at the breakfast-table (but not to read Victorian novels at luncheon). He did not welcome female guests. Not everyone relished the task of helping freshers to feel at ease or of showing deference to visiting speakers and preachers. Mr Walker thus describes the beginning of the system:

> I had a horrible room in Meadow Buildings where I was studying mathematics and smoking a pipe when I would have very much preferred to play cricket, some summer-term-afternoon. Ronnie used the Meadows for his constitutional-cum-breviary. There was a knock at the door. Ronnie's invitation to take a room at the Old Palace for my third year did not appeal to me in the least. I did not want to become what the French call a 'sacristy louse' and had rather hoped to be a bit of a dog in digs. At the end of the talk I refused to commit myself; and it would be quite dishonest to pretend that I was anything but depressed at the prospect. When he went away I looked out of the window and saw the hunched figure returning to the O.P. I then decided that I would lodge at the old Palace, a decision made on the spot which I certainly never regretted even if now and then I sometimes wondered whether life might not have been more gay, say, in Beaumont Street.

He sums up the life at the Old Palace by saying:

> In some indefinable way his influence was, in dozens of cases, retrospective. It was only when we looked *back* that we realised how much this hopelessly shy, quiet creature had affected our thinking. Philosophy is far too high-falutin' a word for the sort of people we were. What happened was that Ronnie took quite a long time to sink into us; and by the time that he did we were stockbrokers, journalists or Inverness sheep-farmers. I do believe that this is immensely important, however silly it sounds. We were full of inhibitions about him when we were there, and perhaps he was too, about us, but we, in the long run, drew all the dividends. We gave him damn-all: he gave us a lot.

Ronald kept clear of non-Catholic undergraduates. It was not his business, he felt, to make converts. The goodwill which the chaplaincy enjoyed in the University would be compromised if he were thought to be poaching the preserves of the Anglican chaplains. His, he explained, was the crook of the shepherd, not the hook of the fisherman. Nor was he at any pains to cut a figure in the University. He spoke once a year at the Union in Eights Week, always with brilliant success; he was often invited to read papers to various literary societies. These, when he gave them, were always light and untendentious. Sometimes he brought out the yellow typescripts of before the War. Once when asked to address the French Club he composed in a morning the paper 'French with Tears', which he kept by him and read to a vast variety of audiences, with unvarying success. This and other papers of the kind have appeared posthumously in *Literary Distractions* (1958). But never (except on one occasion when the Union had departed from good usage and chosen for debate a question directly affecting Christian morals) did he, as Fr Martindale had often done, put himself forward in the University as a champion of the Faith beyond the limits of his own cure.

There was a succession of clever undergraduates during his thirteen years who then professed an atheism which many of them have since abandoned. No college chaplain could have justly resented an attempt to evangelize these, but Ronald showed awareness of their existence only in his efforts to keep his flock from association with them.

He kept clear of politics and that, in the mood of the time – a debilitating rancour that sprang from private fear rather than from any generous indignation – was a positive achievement requiring notable sagacity, patience, and courtesy. Between 1934 and 1939 the long tradition of witty debate almost died in the University. Instead, undergraduates and dons alike challenged one another to proclaim their party allegiance. One year there was a rowdy sort of pacificism,[1] next, a romantic attachment to the Abyssinian monarchy; next, fiery allegiance to the Communists and anarchists in Spain. Each access of emotion provoked its antithetical counterpart. The small Catholic body in that small community was in continual danger of breaking into personal enmities. Partisans of all opinions found some encouragement among the Jesuits and Dominicans; none at the Old Palace.[2] Ronald accepted as his first duty that of shepherd, to keep his whole flock together; not to enhance his popularity and influence among a part of them at the expense of others. So little were his political sympathies known that he was asked by Sandy Lindsay as Socialist candidate for Parliament to sign his nomination paper. No one was more sharply aware than he of the social and national dangers of the time. He measured them by other standards than the politicians, and saw no hope in the remedies presented.

Once only, on St James's Day, 1937, did he preach a political sermon. Passions were inflamed about the Spanish Civil War, and Ronald remained aloof, but consciences were also troubled, and he felt it his duty to give some guidance.

He preached on the text: 'James and John . . . said Lord wilt Thou that we command fire to come down from heaven and consume them? And turning He rebuked them.'

It was not a pronouncement calculated to stimulate either party. He reminded his congregation of the events that had preceded and followed the rising.

> During the last year Catholic Spaniards, invoking the protection of St James on their banners, have not been content to ask whether they should call down fire from heaven; they have rained down fire from heaven on their fellow countrymen. . . . Was General Franco justified in . . . taking upon himself the gravest responsibility that can be imagined, in plunging his country into the certain horrors of civil war to avoid the possible horrors of a Communist or an anarchist dictatorship? For myself I don't think there is any doubt that he was.

---

[1] At that time Ronald made one of his very few serious, secular speeches, at a meeting of the League of Nations Union in Glasgow City Hall. A hostile mob outside the Hall gave poignancy to the grave prescience with which he warned the pacifists inside that their hopes of peace depended on illusion.

[2] The only Catholic undergraduate of Ronald's time who explicitly left the Church did so on political grounds. But this apostate excludes Ronald from his general condemnation of the reactionary bias of the clergy.

But he emphasized the distinction which few leaders were drawing then (or later) between what is lawful and what is meritorious, between the ideal of the soldier and that of the martyr. 'The Church sanctions the use of arms in extreme cases; she canonizes non-resistance.' It was not a call for neutrality; battle was engaged, and for better or worse Christendom was committed. He prayed for a peace

> which will make it possible for the Church there to do its work unhindered. Not for vengeance on the enemies of the Church; that we leave to God. Not for clerical reaction, which will attempt to restore the fortunes of religion by enforcing the observance of it with the power of the secular arm; such triumphs of Christendom have been short-lived. Not for victory at all costs, but for the return of peace.

This had been Ronald's prayer in 1915, and was to be again in 1945. *Not for victory at all costs* reads commonsensical in retrospect; in time of war it is not a popular aspiration. It was repugnant to Ronald to make any political judgement. He did it on this one occasion as part of his mission as a teacher, which was the core of his work at Oxford. To that end all his activities – the card-index, the punt, the bananas – were serviceable means. He was there in the Old Palace to keep his flock faithful to their duties – if only because they knew it upset him if they neglected them – and to teach them their religion.

He wrote of John Wesley: 'It points, surely, to a danger of over-organization; suggests, surely, that the evangelist charged himself with a burden too great even for his powers, when he tried to keep himself accurately informed about the state of 70,000 souls "to Godward".'[1] If this was written at Oxford, as it well may have been (for it is impossible to date any passage in a work which occupied him on and off for thirty years), it must have been with an ironic eye cocked towards his own unexacting flock of 150.

As has been suggested above, Ronald used social means for getting the men to chapel. 'Spinal' was the word (meaning something which gave him 'the creeps') with which he reprobated any attempt to introduce edification into polite conversation, but seated before the altar at the Sunday conferences he spoke as their chaplain and tutor and dean. He wrote of visiting conferenciers: 'One does not want the fashionable preacher, whose talk savours too much of the pulpit; it is best that the

---

[1] Ronald Knox, *Enthusiasm* (1950), p. 430.

conferencier should carry the air of a lecturer who knows all about a single subject.'[1] And of his own:

> Cardinal Bourne, when I came here, told me he thought it was important that the conferences should form a continuous course of apologetic. Reference to my records will show the exact attempts I have made, year by year, to carry out this principle. I started in 1926 (October) with the existence of God; repeating this in 1929, 1932, 1935 and 1938. In the summer term of 1929, 1932, 1935 and 1938 we finished up the course with Birth Control. But I have varied the scheme, and never worked out the ideal arrangement. The first year is fairly simple; the autumn term goes to the existence of God; the spring term to the revelation made by Our Lord; the summer term to the position of the Church as the organ of revelation. In the second and third year I have tried courses on the four last things, on science and miracle, on the Mystical Body, on Faith, on the history of the Church or of the Holy See, on Science as it is sometimes represented in opposition to religion and so on. But always the ninth term has been devoted to a course on sex and marriage. At the beginning of each spring term I give a discourse known as 'the freshers' raspberry', in which I have adjured the freshers, and by implication their seniors, to pay their bills, not to get drunk and annoy the dean, to do more work, and to come to chapel at the Old Palace, communicating more frequently.

This three-year plan meant that only one generation in three heard the conferences in their logical order. Many freshmen were admonished about the responsibilities of matrimony as though these were their immediate danger. In their final form, selected and revised, the series was published in 1942 under the title of *In Soft Garments*. They were more forthright in language than any of his previous sermons; grave and didactic, designed for the man who was probably going to get a Third, who had been brought up in a Catholic home and a Catholic school and was for the first time finding himself in a society where the claims of the Church were repudiated or ignored. Their aim was less to counteract the teaching of the Schools, where Cardinal Manning had conceived lay the great danger, than the irreligious ethos of the general literature and conversation of the time. He provided simple, direct answers to obvious difficulties. He was not training apologists to speak in Hyde Park, but ordinary men living in the world, who should be able to give an account of their Faith when it was challenged in ordinary social intercourse; more especially – a consideration seldom far from his mind – when they found themselves getting

[1] *The Whole Art.*

engaged and married to non-Catholics; but, as always, his work extends beyond its immediate purpose and constitutes a book of permanent value in its own right.

After he went down he was invited almost every term to give one of the Sunday conferences. In these later appearances he was simply a visiting preacher without particular educational obligations towards his hearers. He was there to enhance the prestige and attractions of the chaplaincy and the sermons, the best of which he published in 1952 under the title of *The Hidden Stream* (giving the proceeds to the chaplaincy) are appropriately wittier and more diverse.

As chaplain Ronald gave his young men a conspectus in which the Anglican Reformation had no inordinate importance but took its place in the long succession of heresies and schisms. The problems which had tormented him in 1915 no longer existed for him. It was no satisfaction to him to see his own dark prophecies fulfilled and the question, which he had detected at the base of *Foundations* – 'How much will Jones swallow?' – become an increasingly popular test of dogma. He would have liked to find in the Church of England a strong and faithful ally in defence of the common theological and moral decencies, and where he took issue with her spokesmen it was not on the validity of their orders or the Petrine claims but on what seemed their abandonment of the creeds and the gospels and their compromise with the contemporary ethics. He did not greatly fear that his flock would be beguiled by any religious aberration of the sixteenth century, nor that they would totally renounce their Christian faith for any of the atheistic systems of the nineteenth. What he feared more for them was contamination and erosion of their faith by contemporary publicists.

These were a conspicuous and amorphous phenomenon in England between the two wars; events proved them to have served merely for a phase in the manipulation of popular taste in its transition from the educative notions of the Victorian age to its Elizabethan bifurcation into frivolity and brutality; but Ronald is not to be blamed for giving them importance in their brief heyday, and his exposures and refutations of them may be treated as a part of his teaching vocation as chaplain.

The decade opened with the dissemination of H. G. Wells' *Outline of History*. It is doubtful whether the author had planned it primarily as an attack on the Christian religion. He was the creature of his age and upbringing, and assumed that his ignorance and prejudice would be in sympathy with his readers'. He was disconcerted when, on the reissue of his book in more alluring form in 1925 and 1926, Hilaire Belloc tackled him in earnest and trounced him in a full series of articles syndicated through most of the English-speaking world. He was even more disconcerted when he found that editors were not interested in the controversy. He was obliged to print his reply as a pamphlet, *Mr Belloc Objects* (which provoked *Mr Belloc Still Objects*, another pamphlet). This refusal of the popular Press to give him a hearing at the height of his fame, on what in his youth had been a question of vital general interest, was striking evidence of the new trend. Fleet Street had decided that the truth or falsehood of theological assertions was no longer relevant; there remained, however, a vague residual curiosity in the common man about his ultimate destiny; people who no longer learned catechisms or listened to sermons were interested in the opinions of other common men, no better instructed but more articulate than themselves, on topics which had formerly been the concern of philosophers and clergymen. There was a fashion of some years' duration for symposia, to which all manner of notabilities, but chiefly popular writers, were invited to contribute; many of these were later issued as books. *The Daily Express* published series entitled 'Is Prayer Answered?', 'I Believe in – ', 'How I Look at Life', and 'My Religion'; the *Daily News* contributed 'Where Are the Dead?'; the *Sunday Chronicle*, 'The Outlook of the Churches'; the *Daily Telegraph*, 'If I Were a Preacher' and 'The Reality of Hell'; the *Sunday Dispatch*, 'When I Am Dead'; and so on. They were collected and handed to Ronald by a vigorous young man who had lately appeared in London, Mr Frank Sheed.

Mr Sheed is an Irish-Australian, largely educated in the United States. He was known to Ronald as the husband of Maisie Ward, later the biographer of Chesterton, the daughter of Wilfrid Ward[1] and sister of his friend Fr Leo Ward. In 1926 the publishing firm of Sheed & Ward was founded, with Belloc briefly advertised as literary adviser. It was at Mr Sheed's suggestion that Ronald collected *Essays in Satire* and his first volume of Catholic sermons, *The Mystery of the Kingdom*.[2] He now invited Ronald to conduct a vivisection of the symposiasts. The result was *Caliban in Grab Street*, which appeared in 1930.

The original title, held to be too recondite, was *Gigadibs upon Setebos*.

---

[1] Theologian, apologist and biographer, 1856–1916, second son of William 'Ideal' Ward of the Oxford Movement.

[2] Both published in 1928. *Essays in Satire* contains the best of his Anglican humorous writing, with some subsequent literary essays. *The Mystery of the Kingdom* comprises two series of sermons, one preached at the Carmelites' Church, Kensington, the other, on the parables, at St Charles', at Ogle Street.

'Grub Street' does not at first sight appear to be an apt description, for the symposiasts were not humble, working journalists but the chief popular writers of the day – Arnold Bennett, Hugh Walpole, John Drinkwater, Conan Doyle, E. Phillips Oppenheim, J. D. Beresford, Israel Zangwill, and others of equal contemporary prominence, including industrialists and prima donnas. 'Grub Street' was represented only by James Douglas. Ronald bore this accumulation of press-cuttings to Beaufort and earnestly attempted to make some order of them. It was not altogether a congenial task. His fine-trained mind was rather baffled by the naïvety, frivolity, and banality of those highly paid amateurs. It was easy enough to make fun of them:

> Mr Arnold Bennett [he wrote] begins with the confession: 'I do not believe, and never have at any time believed, in the divinity of Christ, the Immaculate Conception, heaven, hell, the immortality of the soul, the divine inspiration of the Bible.' The statement lacks, perhaps, scientific precision. Does Mr Bermett believe in original sin? I imagine not; and if he does not believe in original sin, then he believes in the Immaculate Conception; not merely in the Immaculate Conception of Our Lady, but in the immaculate conception of everybody else. Again, as Dr Norwood pointed out at the time, it was not easy to reconcile Mr Bennett's disbelief in the immortality of the soul with his subsequent admission: 'On a balance of probabilities, I am inclined to accept the theory of a future life.'

The symposia were replete with such absurdities, and there is much incidental fun in their exposure. But Ronald was trying to do more; he sought to identify and examine the ethos which his victims personified; to answer in a new form the question he posed in *Some Loose Stones*: 'How much *has* Jones swallowed?'

Conan Doyle had succinctly stated: 'The less dogma, the more Christ.' Dogma, Ronald patiently explains, is not derived from the Latin word meaning to teach, but from the Greek meaning to be acceptable; dogmas are the tenets on which a school or party are agreed; he wished to discover the dogmas of the symposiasts, and his quest led him through a miasma of undefined premises and irrational conclusions, of huge omissions and assumptions, of an almost meaningless vocabulary and fatuous self-complacency.

Most of the symposiasts made free use of the name of Christ. What did they mean by it? 'I have been at pains to rewrite the Gospel of St Matthew for the convenience of such persons, omitting no text which they could possibly want to quote.' His version occupies three pages.

He sifts out the agnostics, the atheists and the cranks, the vaguely ethical and the vaguely immoral. There is no consistent ethos. This, he concludes, is modern thought outside the Catholic Church; not the most acute thought, but what the newspapers find most purchasable. Gigadibs had in the late 1920s become transformed into Caliban.

Two years later, again at Mr Sheed's instigation, he turned his attention upon a more formidable group – the scientific publicists. Professor (Sir) Julian Huxley and Bertrand (Earl) Russell had contributed to the symposia, but their interests in the topic were stronger and their learning more considerable than their fellows'. In 1927 Julian Huxley had published *Religion without Revelation*; in 1930 Bertrand Russell published the *Conquest of Happiness*. In *Broadcast Minds* Ronald developed a full criticism of these works, associating them with Mr Gerald Heard's *The Emergence of Man*, Mr Langdon Davies's *Science and Common Sense*, and, as comic relief, H. L. Mencken's *Treatise on the Gods*.

He had already detected in the symposiasts what he called 'the Galileo Complex'; a vague belief that churchmen habitually discouraged inquiry in the natural sciences and that 'science' was in some way destructive of theology. This prevalent misconception is the theme of *Broadcast Minds*. Ronald had no specialized knowledge of anthropology, archaeology, astronomy, biology, chemistry and physiology, history, physics and chemistry, or psychology – the heads under which in his final chapter he countered the pretensions of the specialists. Each section of this chapter begins with the words: 'It is not true that . . .' It is a brilliant example of the old claim that a mind properly schooled in *Literae Humaniores* can turn itself effectively on any subject connected with man. In the bulk of the book he lets his exquisitely polite sense of the absurd play upon the pundits themselves. It is no mere sectarian loyalty (for inept championship causes much embarrassment) that prompts the judgement that he won a complete literary victory.

At the same time as he was writing *Broadcast Minds* he was engaged in a different kind of apologetics. Sir Arnold Lunn had not closed his mind to the questions he had raised in *Roman Converts*. He is by nature restlessly reasonable, and he has a particular talent for written controversy. In 1930 he published the *Flight from Reason*, an assault on popular 'thinkers' which has some affinities with *Caliban in Grub Street*. He was in a mood to challenge anyone to combat on almost any subject, and after reviewing *Caliban in Grub Street* he proposed to Ronald an exchange of letters for subsequent publication, in which he should choose the ground and advance all the objections he could conceive to the claims of the Catholic

Church. His own position had changed from his earlier agnosticism to an acceptance of enough of the Christian faith to give some hope of fruitful argument. Ronald accepted, and for more than a year the letters went to and fro. In 1932 they appeared as a book under the title, *Difficulties*, which aptly represents their character, for the matters discussed are in fact just that; problems capable of solution, which at one time or another suggest themselves to most reasonable Catholics; apparent anomalies capable of explanation. Sir Arnold stated his case with great vigour. Ronald's replies are briefer and superficially slighter; often he does no more than delicately rearrange in a different order the materials which Sir Arnold throws to him, and so reconciles them with their apparent contradictions; he is always 'away from his books' when answering and has to rely on an antiquated encyclopaedia, while Sir Arnold has all his authorities pat, but somehow the encyclopaedia suffices. There is a deceptive air of casualness about Ronald's handling of his case: some critics considered that Sir Arnold conceded more than he need have done, and that even so Ronald did not provide quite the conclusive answer which simpler minds expected. Ronald frankly admits that there are human oddities and logical puzzles which do not admit of a single, irrefutable explanation. He is plainly never the least disturbed in his own convictions. He simply admits that difficulties do exist and always will; that they are part of God's providence and that they never kept a man of good will from finding the faith. And that in fact was the outcome. Sir Arnold was received into the Church by Ronald in July 1933, less than two years after the last letter was put in the post, and became the most tireless Catholic apologist of his generation. Perhaps Ronald felt that in arming Sir Arnold and putting him in the field, he had fulfilled his own combatant duties. *Difficulties* was his last purely controversial work.

2

Throughout all his years at the Old Palace Ronald suffered from qualms about his own fitness for the work. The artist's and priest's insatiable thirst for perfection; the old-fashioned gentleman's sense of propriety; the scholar's respect for academic standards; his own particular husbandry of time and effort; his intellectual sophistication in the face of adolescent problems, which kept boredom at a distance only by a continuous exercise of the will, together with his horror of sin, especially of sins against purity, and the restless sense of responsibility which he felt for the delinquencies

and inadequacies of all his flock; the absolute primacy which he accorded
to the supernatural; all these qualities at one time and another, and
increasingly as the years passed, seemed to overburden him in the 'series
of frantic experiments made in the dark, based almost entirely on personal
contact'. In the *Whole Art of Chaplaincraft* he was deliberately putting
things at their driest; he was writing at the end of his time, when he was
already committed to a more congenial order of life; he was by nature
inclined to advert to his rare failures rather than to his numerous, manifest
successes; but with due allowance for all this the consistent undertone of
the document is unmistakably that of a man driven by duty rather than
joy. Those dinner parties; did he never want the evening to go so well
that time was forgotten and his guests had to race to their college gates
while Tom was striking? At the beginning of Michaelmas Term, 1937, he
wrote: 'My dinner party, mercifully, felt too bored to stay after 20 past 9.'
But none suspected *his* boredom except a few friends who were confident
of their own welcome.

It may occur to the busy parish priest that Ronald's limited responsibilities and his long vacations provided quite unprecedented leisure and that
his complaints of overwork have a neurotic flavour.

> I am under a great cloud of depression [he wrote at the beginning of
> Lent 1938] about my work here and the young generally. . . . It's 10.30
> p.m. and such a tiring day. You see Ash Wed. is the only day in the year
> when we have any ceremonies; and that always lays me out even when
> they are as simple as possible. Then I had to get ready 4 sermons (short) for
> a Holy Hour at a quarter past six. All morning I wrote, then had lunch
> with – at New College, the sort of lunch when he's collected his Protestant
> friends to say 'See what a bright chaplain I've got' and I was too hurried
> and harassed to say anything; got bad marks for leaving at a quarter to three:
> then more sermon; soon after 4 a mixed bag of undergraduates and I had
> to go on writing sermons and leave them to talk to one another. I only just
> got the stuff finished, and as there were only 8 undergraduates there, I hope
> they were appreciative. Hardly time to get my prayers finished and then a
> dinner party at which I didn't like the people. – is a very exhausting
> conversationalist.

And at Whitsun:

> Sunday looked as if it went off well: 69 people at 8.15 and 20 at 9.0; 75
> communions; 60 people at the late Mass to hear – , who talked unintelligi-
> bly about a lot of people I'd never heard of. But of course it's lamentable
> really. I only know of a little over a hundred men as definitely communi-
> cants, leaving 80 over of whom 30 are pretty well net loss. A man from

British Guiana came in on Sunday morning who was up some years back: he told me he goes to Mass every Sunday but hasn't been to his duties for 4 years, which is typical of what happens. I'm sure I ought to be leaving.

In a normal parish Communions are counted in hundreds where Ronald counted in tens; the absence of a few familiar faces at Mass raises no fear of disaffection. Ronald knew that all his parishioners ought to be at Mass every Sunday of term, and he knew who was there and who was not. His solicitude was unresting. Moreover, in a normal parish the priest can count on the help of responsible lay people; he does not have to be the sole source of energy in every organization.

In 1937 Ronald was forty-nine. Middle age brought him its normal concomitants of physical *malaise*. In summer he still punted his canoe on the river, and still swam. In winter his only exercise was an hour's walk with his breviary. He gave up the short walking-tours which had refreshed his youth. He was unwell in various ways. Insomnia, the occupational disease of writers, began to afflict him. He suffered from it for the rest of his life. In March 1936 he had to go into the Acland Home for a second operation for rupture. In December of that year and in the following February and March he had three separate attacks of influenza, each more severe than the last. In 1938 he had most of his teeth out. Dr Havard, his physican at Oxford, to whom he also had recourse for authentic medical details in his detective stories and to whom he dedicated *Still Dead*, recalls that he showed an infinitely polite, resigned scepticism about the powers of medicine.

> I sometimes thought [he writes] he would have preferred a doctor who was more 'active' in his outlook. But if that were so he was very patient with me and concealed any misgivings he may have felt, except on one or two occasions when he was really deep in 'post-'flu' depression and hopelessness in the spring of 1937. At that time he gave me the impression that he had grave misgivings about his condition and about my treatment of it. In spite of these he remained loyal to me and I think, looking back, that he probably showed no little courage in doing so.

There is something very typical of Ronald in this relationship.

In the summer term following he was heavily cast down by the sudden death of his housekeeper, Mrs Lyons. It was the loss not only of a friend to whom he had become deeply attached but of a support on which he had become heavily dependent. He took it hard. A good successor was found, but he never again enjoyed the domestic tranquillity at Oxford which she had inconspicuously provided. Uncertainty about plans which men of sturdier temperament endure almost with relish, always caused Ronald intense distress. He accepted the change of regime as an omen that his time at the chaplaincy was near its end.

Though undergraduates called more seldom than he would have liked, others from outside Oxford called too often. In the modern world men of eminence need protection. Ronald had no butler or secretary or chaplain or A.D.C. to preserve his privacy. He was there above his open door all day long inviting intrusion. As his fame spread he was increasingly the victim of idle trippers with inadequate introductions who took him in as one of the sights of Oxford. He was incapable of snubbing anyone, and he early decided that work which required continuous, prolonged attention must be left to the vacs. And he had to write for his living. His earnings were no longer, as they had been at St Edmund's, pocket-money to save or disburse in charities. During vacations he lived in the houses of his friends, chiefly at Beaufort,[1] but during term he had the Old Palace and its hospitality to maintain. The stipends of the chaplaincies at Oxford and at Cambridge were quite inadequate, and it was recognized that the posts could be held only by priests with other sources of income. The most impersonal, and for that reason the least exacting, form of popular writing was for Ronald the detective story. He wrote five[2] during his time at Oxford. They had their faithful, limited public. He also published collections of his secular essays, *The Open Air Pulpit* (1926) and *On Getting There* (1929). Cardinal Bourne is said to have disapproved of the detective stories. More human critics may regret that he was ever obliged to busy himself with ephemera. He was never at all straitened, but he was ill at ease about money. He could no longer save; the regular requirements of the chaplaincy fretted his nerves and any unforeseen expense caused him unreasonable anxiety. The books of Mr Watt who transacted most, though not all, of his literary business show a falling and fluctuating income. In 1927 he earned £904; in 1928, £846; in 1929, £700; in 1930, £917; in 1931, £244; in 1932, £310; in 1933, £408; in 1934, £511; in 1935, £367; in 1936, £85; in 1937, £457; in 1938, £47. These figures do not include his earnings from *The Tablet* or fees for lecturing and preaching which provided a modest surplus over his expenses of travel.

His most ambitious work of the period was *Barchester Pilgrimage*, published in 1935. Until black-out and bombardment brought Trollope

---

[1] In 1933 Lord Lovat died suddenly. In the same year the present Lord Lovat came of age. In 1938 he married and Laura, lady Lovat, moved from Beaufort.

[2] See footnote p. 287.

back into fashion, his cult was small and esoteric. In Ronald's letter of dedication to Maurice Baring he wrote: 'I owe you a deep debt of ingratitude for pointing out to me, when this book was nearly three parts written, that practically nobody would read it because practically nobody had ever heard of Barchester.' He himself had been saturated in the books since his schooldays and had already published an ingenious construction of the topography of Barsetshire. In *Barchester Pilgrimage* he narrates in imitation of Trollope's style the fortunes of the children and grandchildren of Trollope's characters up to the date of writing. He insinuates, not quite in the manner of the master, a brief passage of instruction on the Catholic regulations for mixed marriages. Otherwise it is a dry, gentle satire on the social, political, and religious changes of the twentieth century. It is a highly elegant accomplishment, but as the sole product in his forty-eighth year of a man of spectacular early promise, it gave some plausibility to the ever-ready criticism that the Church of Rome had not fostered his genius. Nothing Ronald wrote was ever ill done, but for twenty years, from 1918 to 1938, in the period when most writers are at their finest and most fecund, his literary work was subdued in tone and modest in scope, as though he were giving it minor importance.

When in 1938 he wished to make a present of one of his works, morocco bound, to commemorate the reception into the Church of a particularly dear catachumen, all he could find in his recent writing worthy of the occasion was *The Rich Young Man: a Fantasy*, a few pages of imaginative narrative, published in 1928, in which he identified the penitent thief on Calvary with the rich young man of the Gospel who turned away from his vocation.

In that year he wrote to a friend: 'I got my entry in *Who's Who* for revision today, and for the first time in many years found there was nothing to add to it.' But Ronald, more than most men of genius, was gifted with thrift; he husbanded his time and his talents, so that when in his fifties he emerged into his great period of literary work, his powers were unwearied and his sensibility acute.

Into his sermons he always put his best, and these are the permanent achievements of his forties. His was not an age of notable preachers. Disregarding the models of the past, Ronald created a new and entirely individual form for the traditional art. His sermons were prepared, revised, and rehearsed with every refinement of taste and skill. These were conceived not as literary essays but as oratory: they are idiomatic in phrase, the manuscripts are scored in pencil to indicate every pause and inflection of the voice – of his own quiet voice – and it was a unique gift of his to give by a sort of vocal legerdemain the impression, while reading, that he was talking simply and directly to his hearers.

'I have generally found,' he wrote in the Preface to *The Mystery of the Kingdom*, 'that the spoken word demands more preparation than the written; nor have I more regard for the susceptibilities of newspaper critics than I have for the pious ears of a Catholic congregation.'

Because there were none of the hesitations, repetitions, and discursions that intrude into almost all spontaneous oratory, he was able to say a great deal in a very short time. Because of his easy conversational tone, he was able to introduce the most subtle and original thoughts, usually by the juxtaposition of things not previously associated, without any parade of singularity. Versatility and consistency of tone kept an unstrained partnership. Whether addressing schoolboys at St Edmund's or nuns or undergraduates or priests or the congregations assembled at Westminster Cathedral for the requiem of some public figure, Ronald's tone remained the same; only the illustrations and allusions would differ with the audience.

A mark of his art was his reliance on Scripture. The text of each sermon is not simply an apt introductory quotation but the theme of the whole, on the words of which he delighted to disclose variations of meaning and emphasis. He had, too, a peculiar ingenuity in tracing analogies between Old Testament figures, barely known to many of his Catholic hearers, and familiar saints.

His Oxford conferences have been mentioned above. During term he could not fulfil other engagements, but in the vacations the invitations were always many more than he could accept, particularly to preach the panegyrics at patronal festivals. His exquisite wedding addresses came later when the young people whom he had known, grew up and married. As has been said above, Ronald exercised professional frugality with his sermons, filing, revising, and repeating them, and eventually selecting and arranging them for publication in books. His occasional sermons he was ready to give to the printer as soon as they were delivered. Some appeared as leaflets, others in various magazines. In 1936 a new vehicle offered.

The Tablet had sunk to an ignominious place in the last twelve years of the reign of Cardinal Bourne. It was his property. (Cardinal) Herbert Vaughan had purchased it from its lay owners in order that Cardinal Manning might not be embarrassed by criticism during the Vatican Council. When he succeeded to the archbishopric he made it the property of the see. He appointed a worthy editor to be his mouthpiece. In 1923 it fell to Cardinal Bourne to appoint a successor. He chose a man of meagre attainments and deplorable manners, under whom the paper became petty in its interests and low in tone. From having been a property of some value, it became a liability requiring regular subsidy. After Cardinal Bourne's death the paper was sold to a lay committee, and in April 1936 Mr Douglas Woodruff became editor with the aim of restoring it to its proper place as the Catholic counterpart to the established weekly organs of opinion.

Ronald was among those who had suffered from the rudeness of the former editor. He was one of the first whom Mr Woodruff consulted about the change. He promised his support and gave it consistently throughout his life; writing book reviews, translations, and special articles, and generally sending anything he had on hand which would be suitable to its columns. In particular, he sent all his occasional sermons, which thus reached a public far beyond the congregations to which they were addressed – beyond those who would readily sit down to a book of sermons – and while enriching *The Tablet* greatly he extended his own fame.

The succession of Archbishop Hinsley in April 1935, though he was an old and ailing man, was a grateful refreshment to English Catholics inside and outside the archdiocese. There was now at the head of the hierarchy a man amenable to suggestions, of deep human sympathies, who was also a shrewd judge of men, able and willing to recognize diversities of character and talent in his subordinates. As will appear, his coming to Westminster was the first bud of what may be called Ronald's 'Second Spring'. With his Ordinary at Oxford, the Archbishop of Birmingham, 'Tommy' Williams, who succeeded an aged and failing predecessor in 1929, Ronald quickly established terms of some cordiality, which were unclouded until 1942, by which year he had left the archdiocese. Archbishop Williams had spent most of his life in the government of scholastic institutions. He was a Cambridge man who appreciated that Oxford was a rather peculiar enclave in his industrial territory, and he left Ronald to do his work without interference. Lodgers at the Old Palace recall his visits as occasions of unstrained affability.

In the face of authority Ronald never entirely ceased to feel like a schoolboy – he once described it as a 'great coup' when the Archbishop, visiting him unexpectedly, found him in prayer in the chapel – but with Archbishop Williams he felt like a sixth-form boy at Eton or Shrewsbury rather than like one in Rudiments at Ushaw. Whether at Cardinal Hinsley's or at Archbishop Williams's instigation, Ronald, in 1936, was appointed Domestic Prelate to the Pope. The position was purely honor-ific. The title gave Ronald no particular gratification. 'Father Knox', a name prominent in letters since 1912 gave place to the less familiar 'Mgr Knox'. That was all. As will appear below, Cardinal Hinsley would have liked to start him on the road of official advancement, but this was not what Ronald desired or needed.

It would be a mistake to regard Ronald's last years at Oxford as being all weariness and frustration. There were many heartening events. He welcomed the children of many of his friends to the Old Palace, Frasers, Stirlings, Asquiths (Lady Helen Asquith, the daughter of Raymond Asquith and niece of Edward Homer, was the first person he instructed and received into the Church). From 1935 onwards he enjoyed the keen pleasure of having Fr Martin D'Arcy, S.J.[1] as an immediate neighbour, when Campion Hall moved from its cramped quarters at the top of St Giles into its new house, one of Lutyens's cleverest constructions, in Brewer Street with a garden door opening into Rose Place a few yards from the Old Palace. Ronald had always been happy in his relations with the regular clergy in Oxford. A Jesuit and a Dominican, as has been seen, usually said the two later Sunday Masses in his chapel. In the Master of Campion Ronald found a friend for whom he had boundless affection and esteem. Proximity fostered intimacy. In mind and taste he and Fr D'Arcy were widely different. Ronald took many problems, theological and personal, to Fr D'Arcy and, hearing them restated in Fr D'Arcy's terms, found himself stimulated to solve them. Once when Ronald was allowing himself one of his rare expressions of discontent, he was asked: 'Well, what *would* make you happier?' After some consideration he answered: 'If I could go for a walk every afternoon with Fr D'Arcy.' Even in practical, household matters Campion Hall was a help, relieving him of some of the burden of hospitality at his crowded week-ends by taking in many of the Newman speakers.

It is impossible for one who observed Ronald at the Old Palace in the late 1930s to believe that his ready welcome and gay hospitality sprang only from selfless charity; that the young men who treasured his friendship and faithfully sought him out all his life caused him nothing but anxiety; that it was only courtesy which infused his genial association with his clerical confreres. There was an abundance of frank, human friendliness. But his rare expressions of vexation were more than the mood of low health and occasional disappointment. He was approaching a decade of

---

[1] Appointed Master of Campion Hall 1933.

withdrawal. Superficial social relationships had ceased to stimulate him. He needed for his spiritual happiness greater seclusion; for the development of his literary genius he needed relief from the obligation of earning more money than his own modest requirements.

Shrewsbury, he had realized in time, threatened to confine him in 'golden chains'; Oxford was crustative. 'Ronnie', as he was universally addressed even by the most remote acquaintances, was tending to join 'Sligger' and 'Mugger' as a focal 'character'. The Universities delight to endow their denizens with quaintness; to allow spurious anecdotes and quips not theirs to accumulate and solidify about them; to mask them in an endearing but artificial *persona*. Small men are thus aggrandized, great men diminished. The shell which was being affectionately imposed on him irked Ronald; but diffident, humble, patient, he needed a liberator.

Chapter Three

THE SECOND SPRING

R onald's humility was remarked by all who met him, and was the more revered the better he was known. That supernatural grace illumined his every relationship and utterance and lay at the heart of all his devotion, but there coexisted with it a diffidence that was entirely human and not entirely healthy.

Depreciation of his own talents restrained him for twenty years from full literary exertion. His books in that period were written on commission from their publishers, whose advice was canvassed and accepted. When he was engaged without commitment on his most brilliant piece of secular work, *Let Dons Delight*, he repeatedly expressed doubts, which were none the less genuine for being absurd, that it would find a publisher. 'Watt' [his agent] 'says he thinks he can find somebody to publish anything I write, which is jolly of him,' he wrote of it on May 9th 1938. *Jolly of him.*

He was frequently haunted by the fear of failing powers. In March 1926 he wrote to Sligger: 'My literary style is rapidly vanishing, I never preach a new sermon and I find I can't even depend on my health.' In March 1930, when he had just finished *Caliban in Grub Street*, he wrote to Mr Eyres: 'Whenever I come across my old writings I am always struck with the sense (i) that they are very bad and (ii) that I could not do it so well now.' In March (always the cruellest month) 1949, when he was finishing *Enthusiasm*, he wrote to Mr Woodruff: 'How well I wrote in 1937. I find I can't write at all now.'

Depressive doubts of this sort are common to a certain kind of artist and are less injurious to his work than manic confidence, but there were also in Ronald the seeds of a weakness that was not a matter of mood; not the product of indigestion or influenza or the chill winds of March. The vision of himself *sub specie aeternitatis* threatened, and but for his reserves of spiritual strength might have overwhelmed him, with the sense of futility in all his occupations. He quite liked discriminating praise. He could not have written at all without the assurance that he was giving some pleasure

337

to someone. But the honours which gratified him were not favourable reviews or ecclesiastical promotions but those, such as his election as Honorary Fellow of Trinity and to the Old Brotherhood,[1] which were tokens of friendship. He needed human love.

Throughout *Enthusiasm* he particularly noted the number of religious leaders who had been upheld by an affinity with someone of the opposite sex, part disciple, part guide. Many canonized saints also have enjoyed on earth friendships which forecast the companionship of heaven.[2] In Guy Lawrence Ronald had found that fructifying intimacy of affection which was essential to his growth. For nineteen years that place in Ronald's heart had stood empty. In the summer of 1937 it was filled by a remarkable young married woman.

Daphne Strutt was the daughter of Lord Rayleigh. Both her father and grandfather were scientists of eminence.[3] Her father was an agnostic, her stepmother staunchly Protestant; for various reasons her brothers were united in anti-Catholicism and all her family were dismayed when, in 1931, she announced her intention of marrying Lord Acton, a light-hearted, sweet-tempered, old-fashioned, horsy young man, the grandson of the historian and head of the old Catholic family of Aldenham in Shropshire. She had no attachment to the Church of England and no religious beliefs, but at the time of her marriage she was entirely hostile to her husband's faith.

The historian's fortune had derived from estates in Germany (where he was Duke of Dalberg) which were forfeited in 1914. Lord Acton was not well off; he eked out his rents with a job in a firm of stockbrokers which obliged him and his wife to spend much of their time away from Aldenham moving among rich clients.

One of his sisters was married to Mr Douglas Woodruff. It was largely these two who aroused Lady Acton's curiosity and, later, sympathy, towards the Church. Within five years of her marriage she informed her family that she wished to become a Catholic. They feared that she might be suborned by a priest before her mind had cleared of what they assumed was a temporary aberration and in deference to their consternation she promised to wait a year before accepting formal instruction. This did not prevent her going regularly to Mass and pursuing her own studies. Mr

[1] See below, p. 396.

[2] E.g., St Francis de Sales and St Jeanne de Chantal.

[3] John William, third Baron Rayleigh, O.M., 1842–1919, the discoverer of argon 1894. Robert John, fourth Baron Rayleigh, F.R.S., 1875–1947, Professor of Physics at Imperial College of Science, President of British Association 1938.

Woodruff introduced her to a full course of theological, devotional, and liturgical works which might have daunted a seminarist, and by 1937 she was better informed about the Church than most life-long Catholics.

In June of that year she first met Ronald at Stanford Dingley in Berkshire, where the Woodruffs then lived. It was intimated that she was in need of a priest, and Ronald's nervous apprehension was thoroughly agitated at the prospect of the interview. It was a time of despondency for him, and he had little wish to add to his other cares the charge of what had been represented to him as a formidable blue-stocking. He found a girl of strong and original intellect, certainly; a tall, elegant beauty, but one who looked younger than her twenty-five years; was as shy as himself and fermenting with a radical, spontaneous humour in which there were echoes of the laughter of his lost friends of 1914. Her year of probation had still some weeks to run. She refused to discuss religion, and Ronald very readily fell in with her reticence. They got on well together, and partly as the result of the confidence and liking he inspired, she arranged to accompany her sister-in-law on a Hellenic cruise when Ronald and Mr Woodruff were to be lecturers.

Ronald had accepted this engagement in obedience to his doctor, who prescribed a voyage. He took it like medicine. He did not, at his present age, enjoy travel or sight-seeing or the promiscuous society of shipboard. The route was familiar. He had followed it with Lady Lovat in the Easter vacation of 1930, when he gave the lecture, 'The Greeks at Sea', which appears in *Literary Distractions*. He embarked with dismal expectations.

The miscellaneous tourists whom Sir Arnold Lunn used to coax into the delusion of being enthusiasts for classical culture were disposed to think that the price of their tickets included the acquaintance of the savants whose lectures they attended and whose holidays they subsidized. There was resentment on board when Ronald spent his time exclusively with Lady Acton. Through the crowded decks and saloons and on the excursions ashore which he perversely insisted on following – only at Constantinople in protest against the Turkish ban on clerical dress did he refuse to land – these two very shy people, diametrically apart in every outward particular, explored one another's personality and found everywhere an intricate dovetailing of complementary talents and tastes. They began the accumulation of common experiences, private jokes, and private language which lies at the foundations of English friendship. Within a few days of sailing she told him that she wished to be received into the Church and asked him to prepare her. Formal instruction was postponed until the late autumn, when she would be free to give her full mind to it, but their conversation ranged over a variety of questions of faith and morals. Ronald found he could talk to her on any subject without a tremor of the 'spinality' he abhorred.

What he gave Lady Acton in this friendship is her own possession. This book is his biography, not hers. It may be that at some future date she (or one of her descendants) may see fit to give an account of her debt to Ronald and to edit and publish their copious correspondence. If that day comes a charming and unconventional book will be added to the shelves of 'spiritual reading'. For the present it is enough to say that she sought the Faith not as an accommodation with her husband's family but quite simply as the means to perfection.

What she gave Ronald is written large in every detail of the next decade. She gave him in the human weakness suggested at the beginning of this chapter an infusion of strength and hope. He had felt alienated from the younger generation; here was one of them wholly captivated by him. His contemporaries considered him very happily situated at Oxford. They enjoyed his books as they did E. V. Lucas's and Maurice Baring's and thought he had made a comfortable and respectable place for himself in contemporary letters. They thought he kept up his standard very creditably, and they expected nothing better from him. Those who knew him least thought that perhaps he would one day be made a bishop; those who knew him better expected him to jog along at the Old Palace to the end of his working life. Lady Acton was the first person (so far as can be ascertained) to whom he confided his yearning for privacy and his ambition to write something of permanent value. She was certainly the first person to give him full-hearted and practical encouragement. Cardinal Bourne had disapproved of Ronald's detective stories and he had gone on writing them. She threw *Double Cross Purposes* overboard (after her own lipstick, of which Ronald had expressed dislike), and he never wrote another.

As for a place of retirement, what about Aldenham? Mass had not been said there for fifteen years. A cottage could be found or built for Ronald. He could come as chaplain, with no undergraduates to entertain, no visiting sight-seers, nothing to do except write important books and go for walks in the park with his new friend.

Ecclesiastical moves are not so easily arranged as Lady Acton impetuously supposed. It was not for two years, and over several obstacles, that Ronald finally settled at Aldenham, and then it was in circumstances very different from those originally imagined; but for those two years he had that delectable mountain continually in prospect.

At the end of the cruise Lady Acton went to Monte Carlo, Ronald to Scotland. Letters shuttled between them. Of recent years Ronald's letters had grown shorter and drier. Even to his oldest friends he wrote little but the times of trains. Now to Lady Acton he wrote as he used, long conversational exchanges comprising gossip, literary criticism, spiritual counsel, appeals for help in choosing new clothes, complaints of bores and of infirmities, exuberantly sharing all the details of his day. Not that he accepted this exhilarating new interest without scruple; there was too much of the ascetic in Ronald – too much perhaps of residual inherited puritanism – for him to regard anything quite delightful as being devoid of danger. His favourite spiritual writers were full of warnings against inordinate particular friendships. He sought the advice of the most severe monk of his acquaintance, and was with difficulty persuaded that it was really the will of God that he undertake a duty so congenial as Lady Acton's instruction.

Lord and Lady Acton returned to Aldenham before the beginning of term, and Ronald made his first visit there.

The romantic vicissitudes of the Acton family have left Aldenham a place of interest rather than beauty. The original seventeenth-century house is encased in a plain nineteenth-century structure in the German taste. The chapel, standing a little apart, is of the same style and has the air of a mausoleum rather than of a place of worship. Plate-glass windows look blankly across the flat park-land to a lake which has afforded pleasure to ornithologists. In the core of the building there is some woodwork of sombre magnificence, and the old library holds intact a typical collection of calf-bound volumes and a few family relics. The first Lord Acton's great historical library had been housed in a functional annexe whose iron shelves and galleries, emptied for the benefit of Cambridge, gave at the time of Ronald's first visit a premonition of the gymnasium it was later to become.

Nor were there in 1937 many evidences of ancient habitation. Most of the furniture had been dispersed before the present Lord Acton's succession. The bare drawing-room was used as a badminton court, and a few smaller living-rooms had been expensively decorated in the fashion of 1930. A lavatory upstairs had the singular feature of being flushed with hot water.

While Lord and Lady Acton were at home the house was always full of guests. There was only one occupant of the nursery in 1937, Pelline,[1] a delicate little girl of four years.

[1] The Hon. Mrs Marffy.

During this visit it was arranged that Lady Acton should come up to Oxford from London, where she had a flat, once or twice a week during term for her formal instruction.

It was at this time also that Ronald first mentioned (as far as is known to anyone) the ambition which may have been in his mind since, on his conversion, he was first introduced to the Douay Bible, of attempting his own translation of the Vulgate.

There had been indications during the preceding year that the project might be officially encouraged. At the Low Week meeting of the hierarchy in 1936 Ronald had been appointed to a committee to revise the *Westminster Hymnal*. Some converts from Protestantism repine at their lost opportunities for congregational singing. Indeed, many adult English Catholics do not hear a hymn from one year's end to another. Ronald attributed this silence to the low literary quality of many Catholic hymns. He took the work of revision very seriously, and his taste, more than that of any other individual, pervaded the committee, whose deliberations were protracted for two years. He attended every meeting, succeeded in introducing several hymns from Catholic sources which had previously been known only to those who used the *English Hymnal*, and the work of comparatively modern poets such as Francis Thompson, G. K. Chesterton, Lionel Johnson, Canon Gray, and 'Michael Field'. More than this he made 47 translations from the Latin, out of a total of 106, only 9 of which were by living writers, and contributed 4 original hymns. The new book bears his personal marks clearly; it was issued in 1940 and cordially welcomed by informed critics. Catholic parishes are slow to change their habits. They still sing what the oldest members learned at school. A full generation must pass before the innovations, so patiently debated, are allowed to fulfil their work of enrichment.

In the following year, 1937, Cardinal Hinsley and the hierarchy set up a commission for another much-needed reform. There is a copy of *The Manual of Prayers* somewhere in every presbytery, but it is seldom found in the possession of the laity or of the regular clergy. It was first compiled in 1886 and mildly revised in 1922. It comprises in their official form the extra-liturgical, vernacular prayers which are authorized for use in public services. The language of the current edition was in places stilted to the point of indecorum. Such invocations as: 'O glorious St Joseph, elected by God to be the reputed father of Jesus, the most pure spouse of Mary ever a Virgin, and head of the Holy Family' were offensive to sensitive ears. The committee appointed by the hierarchy to make recommendations for a new edition was under the presidency of Dr Moriarty, the

Bishop of Shrewsbury. He and Bishop Dey were chiefly responsible for the contents and arrangement, Ronald for the English translations of the Latin and Italian originals. Throughout the winter of 1937 and 1938 he gladly added this very appropriate task to his others, devoting to it all his habitual care and tact and also a particular enthusiasm for a civilizing mission in a Church whose forms still spoke too loud in the accents of the stultifying penal era and of the recent immigrations. Some years later he wrote to Archbishop Amigo, the Bishop of Southwark, to explain the principles on which he had worked.

> It [the draft revision of the Manual] was not intended, in the minds of those who suggested it, to consist of a few stray corrections here and there; it was to go much deeper. . . . We are not, it seems to me, converting England. . . . Among the barriers which divide us from our fellow-country-men and make it difficult for them to understand us there is one which has a certain, though a limited importance, and has always forced itself on my attention. In our vernacular devotions we do not use the same idiom as Christians outside the Church. And this is the more serious, in that the prayers used by the Church of England are, by general admission, models of dignity and faultless prose rhythm. No convert, I think, has ever failed to experience a sense of loss over this difference.
>
> The convert, however, may reasonably be expected to put up with such a minor deprivation, in return for all the treasures of grace which God's mercy has opened to him. What is more unfortunate is the effect produced by this same contrast on those who attend our churches before they have received the gift of faith; Protestants who have married or intend to marry Catholics, Protestants who are beginning to feel the weakness of their own position, etc. It is a pity if these go away with a sense that our prayer-idiom is something much inferior to their own, and that our priests rattle off the service as if conscious that it had no beauty of language to recommend it. The broadcasting of Catholic services in certain dioceses has given a far wider currency to this impression. And it is not uncommon to come across Catholics who have listened to Protestant services on the wireless, especially at the time of King George's coronation, and ask 'Why can't we have prayers like that?'
>
> These misgivings made me eagerly interested in the Bishop of Shrews-bury's suggestion that the Manual should be revised. When he wrote to me about it, I urged that such a revision should be entrusted to Father Martindale, who has a wonderful gift for translation from the Latin, or at least to a committee of which Father Martindale would be a member. The Bishop insisted that I should do it, since Father Martindale was so busy and he was anxious to have a draft made as soon as possible. I therefore drew up the suggested revision which was afterwards passed, with some altera-

tions, by your Committee. I left unchanged precisely those formulas in which the Catholic laity were accustomed to join – the Angelus, the Salve Regina, the Litany of Loretto, and so on. I left unchanged those older devotions, some of them very fine ones, which were originally composed in English; the Jesus Psalter, the devotions for the time of Jubilee and Indulgence, etc; or rather, I only altered a word here and there where the caprices of modern English seemed to make it advisable. I made no change, even, in Cardinal Wiseman's prayers for the conversion of England, not realizing at the time that he wrote them in Latin. But wherever it was a question of translation from Latin or from Italian I tried to go back to the spirit of the original, re-translating it with due attention to the claims of pure English and of rhythmical effect.

This work and the revision of the Hymnal, which commanded all the time and effort which he had been used to give to secular writing, were unpaid. The virtual cessation of Ronald's literary earnings in 1938 is attributable to them. The account of his labours quoted above gives little indication of their extent. Some of his translations – the *Pange Lingua*, *Te Deum*, *O Salutaris Hostia*, and *Tantum Ergo* – appear in both books. For the *Manual* he entirely re-wrote ninety-eight prayers. In numerous others his polite, correcting hand may be seen in single turns of phrase: 'my' for 'mine' throughout; in the *Regina Caeli* 'whom thou wast found worthy to bear' for 'whom thou didst merit to bear'; in the Litany of St Joseph 'Pattern of true workmanship' and 'Glory of the Christian home' for 'Model of Artisans' and 'Glory of home-life'. For the Stations of the Cross he resorted to earlier English manuals. The Shorter Morning and Night Prayers he took from the 1933 Ampleforth *Devotions and Prayers*. There was no syllable in the 276 pages but had received his scrupulous care.

A single example may be given to illustrate his method of translation. One of the morning prayers in the 1922 edition reads:

> Almighty Lord and God, who hast brought us to the beginning of this day, let Thy powerful grace so conduct us through it, that we may not fall into any sins, but that all our thoughts, words and actions, may be regulated according to the rules of Thy heavenly justice, and tend to the observance of Thy holy law.

Ronald's version reads:

> O Lord God Almighty, by whose mercy we are come to the beginning of this day, keep us while it lasts under Thy protection: that this day we may fall into no sin, but ever frame our speech, ever direct our thoughts and actions, to the fulfilling of Thy commandments.

He realized that familiarity and pious use had dulled many ears to the clumsiness of the earlier version; it was inconceivable to him that any could positively prefer it.

Ronald showed up his work in the confidence that he had deserved general gratitude. The Cardinal was delighted. In November 1938 he wrote: 'I have been ranting and raving to hurry up the publication of your revision of the Manual of Prayers on which you spent so much labour.'

Early in 1939 proofs were circulated to the hierarchy. Some resistance was expected from Archbishop Amigo, who constitutionally resented change of any kind.

It came promptly. On April 20th he wrote to the director of Burns, Oates, and Washbourne who had sent him proofs, wishing him 'every grace and blessing' and frankly declaring: 'I shall not have the Manual of Prayers in my Diocese.'

Ronald wrote to Lady Acton: 'I can only hope when the Bps meet again the Cardinal will tell him to go and make up his own Manual. They will hardly go back on the whole show for the sake of a notorious obstructionist of 75.'

But it was not only in Southwark that objections were made. In another letter of the same month Ronald wrote:

> I am having ups and downs over that dashed Manual, The Bp of Hexham and Newcastle wrote a letter which was terribly kind and said what a nice book it was, but when I came to read the long list of comments he'd enclosed, I found he'd confused the issues entirely. He minded any change except those he hadn't noticed which were fortunately numerous. He liked all the things he was accustomed to and simply loved the most hideous things, like the prayer to St Joseph.

Dr Poskitt, the Bishop of Leeds, was also firm in opposition, and Archbishop Mathew remarked that 'he looked forward to the year 1970 or so when as an aged prelate he would be defending the good old 1940 edition of the Manual against attempts at revision'.

The lightness with which Ronald accepted rebuffs at this time is plain evidence of Lady Acton's invigorating influence. Two years earlier (as was the case four years later) he would have been plunged in misery. Now after politely answering a number of nagging letters and soliciting personal interviews with the objectors, he quietly withdrew from the dispute.

In April he wrote to the Bishop of Hexham:

Thank you very much for your kindness in forwarding the criticisms. I am particularly grateful to your Lordship for indicating with so much care the exact points of disagreement, instead of anathematizing the whole revision; also for enclosing the sheets on which the danger-points occur (I return these for your Lordship's own use).

The enclosed sheets will be found to contain a few retractations and suggestions of compromise. But, under most of the headings, I have simply replied 'Will refer to Committee', because I feel they are points I am not capable of dealing with. These concern questions, not of faith or morals, but of good English and of accurate prose rhythm. Naturally I should not have made the changes if they had not commended themselves to my own taste, and I can't get outside my own skin sufficiently to see them with somebody else's eyes. I know your Lordship will excuse this contumacy on my part; if you have spent your whole life trying to translate Latin and trying to write good English, it is not easy to go to school again. What I should like to do would be to submit a few specimens of the variations to a competent critic who was brought up neither as a Catholic nor as an Anglican (such as Gordon, the President of Magdalen, who was Professor of English at Leeds), and ask him to choose between them without telling him which was which. But I'm afraid the hierarchy would think such a proceeding indecorous.

The only alternative I can see is to resign from the Committee, and let them appoint a fresh member, a Bishop for choice, who would approach the subject unbiassed. I would prepare all the work for them, by drawing up against the text your criticisms, and those of the Bishop of Nottingham, and any others I may receive, together with my own comments; my absence from the meeting would make it easier for them to discuss the alternatives in a dispassionate spirit. I need hardly say that I should not be resigning as a gesture of any kind; it is simply that I don't believe a man ought to sit in judgement on his own work, however good he thinks it is!

This is not the utterance of a man whose spirit was crushed by discouragement. He was confident in the quality of his work and in the support of the majority of the hierarchy and clergy.

This annoyance lay in the future. In 1937 Ronald returned to Oxford full of hope.

Lady Acton's instructions, forty in all, lasted until her reception at Aldenham on April 6th 1938. He began with the Cartesian 'Cogito ergo sum' and led her through the formal proofs of the existence of God. There were very few gaps in the theological grounding she had laid for herself. The recognition of analogies, he taught her, was one of the most important functions of the intelligence. He stressed the importance of liberty of conscience and the dangers of becoming rule-bound. Towards the end he went into great detail in explaining Catholic habits and practices and warning her of the human imperfections she would find in the society she was entering. But most of the instructions dealt with prayer.

At about this time Ronald gave two special conferences on prayer to a small group of undergraduates who asked for them. In the second of these he clearly refers to Lady Acton in saying: 'I should think it fairly certain that some souls reach the prayer of simplicity while they are still under instruction and before they are actually received into the Church.'

These conferences, later printed in the *Clergy Review*, give the most explicit account he left of his own habits of devotion. The first deals with 'the Prayer of Petition and the Prayer of Acts'. The logic of imperative verbal prayer had been an early difficulty to him, and in his Anglican days he had virtually abandoned it in private use. He accepted it as something plainly prescribed in the Gospels, but personally unsympathetic. As a Catholic he found himself constantly asked to say prayers for the 'intentions' of others – often rather frivolous ones, such as that an idle man should get through Divvers. He, of course, complied, but he never, it seems, prayed for anything for himself. In his first conference he is concerned to expound the economics of Grace in imperative prayers and acts of the will. In the second he deals with what he calls the 'Prayer of Stupidity', a phrase perhaps invented by Dom Hubert van Zeller. Here he speaks with unusual self-revelation of the distractions he found in formal, Ignatian meditation and the encouragement in the 'halfway house between meditation and contemplation'.

> The crucial point we have here to decide for ourselves [he said] is whether all contemplation is extraordinary and, as they say, 'infused', whether it must necessarily be written down among the mystic states, and cannot, therefore, be undertaken without grave fear of presumption, and of illusion; or whether there is a prayer short of this, making no pretensions to extraordinary graces, which does, nevertheless, bypass the whole course of formal meditation, not only its intellectual considerations, but its consciously elicited acts of the will and the affections as well? . . . I believe there is an infra-mystical form of prayer which you can call the prayer of simplicity, as distinct from the prayer of quiet which is the lowest of the mystical states. . . . I must come to God (it seems to me) without any plan or programme in my mind at all, leaving myself in his hands. The will seems to turn towards God of itself; I do not know why a human will, belonging to a redeemed soul in a state of grace, should need any

extraordinary mystical illumination to make it turn towards God of itself. The mystery is rather that it turns as easily towards creatures. Commonly, at least in a limited experience like mine, the attraction . . . does not last for half an hour continuously; but it is there, at least ordinarily, reasserting itself at intervals. . . . In the great bulk of my prayers, vocal and mental, all my life, I have not felt I was talking to God in his presence, but rather apostrophising him in his absence. The more I attend to what I am saying, the less I seem to attend to him. 'The prayer of stupidity,' he found, 'overflowed' into his other prayers, when saying his Office for instance.' 'Should we allow it, if it wants to, to flood out the whole of our prayer? . . . The whole subject is one to make a mere man afraid of having said too much, rather than of having said too little.'

Thus he concluded. This much he felt bound in conscience to reveal to the undergraduates who came to him for practical advice at an early stage of their spiritual growth. How much else he knew, and how much else he learned in the following twenty years, is without record.

During his last two years at Oxford Ronald spent the greater part of every vacation at Aldenham. His friendship with Lady Acton infused every detail of both their lives. Their converse was not exclusively pious. When they were apart they kept one another informed of what they were doing every day, whom they were meeting, what they were reading. They introduced one another to their friends. Lady Acton became an *habituée* of the Asquiths' circle at Mells. Ronald wrestled in argument with Lady Acton's brothers. He shared the elation of Lord Acton's successes on the Turf, his vexations with his partners in business, his solicitude in 'bringing out' his younger sisters in London. Lady Acton took Ronald to a new tailor and tried to impose on him a course of reading in modern fiction. There she failed. 'Aren't you getting a bit strict?' was his protest when Vita Sackville-West's *The Edwardians* was put into his hands; and of another novelist: 'If books are going to be like this, it's *all no good*', in a note of cosmic despair. When they were at Aldenham they went through his post together. Lady Acton opened and destroyed his Press-cuttings, showing him, on his instructions, only those which were 'stinkers'. She gave him a notebook. 'Daphne made me start this book,' is written on the cover, 'because my memory was going.' He filled thirty-three pages with *pensées* which – although few of them were ever used in his published work – reveal his habits of thought.

> Everybody who writes about grace makes the doctrine either harder to understand or harder to believe.

Prayer is perhaps not trying to make our voices heard above the chorus of the angels but hoping that in all that noise their inadequacy will go unnoticed.

Prayer is a mist God sucks out of our marsh.

Are creature comforts more demoralizing when consciously enjoyed or when taken for granted?

These and many others were probably remarks which occurred in conversation with Lady Acton, to which she replied: 'Write it down before you forget.'

Let Dons Delight was written at Aldenham during the vacations of 1938. The dedication of that book – 'To Daphne: all this waste of time' – has been misread. The phrase sprang from a private joke. At the time of its publication he wrote to her:

> Of course Let Dons Delight is due entirely to your influence. You (i) forbade me to write a detective story, (ii) gave me the idea of the book, (iii) gingered me up to read all those books about it, (iv) let me bore you about it all the time it was being written, (v) marooned me at various times so that I had to write it, (vi) told me it was worth going on with, (vii) made me in a hurry to get it finished, so that I could dedicate it to you. In fact you are the formal, efficient, material and final cause of it. The Vulgate would never have been written but for St Paula saying 'Come on, now'.

The two friends awaited news of the book's reception with equal interest.

On January 13th 1939 Belloc wrote to Lady Lovat:

> I have been sent proofs of R. Knox's book called 'Let Dons Delight'. It is a masterpiece. I was quite bowled over by it. It is astonishing. I've not written the author because I don't think my appreciation would make much difference to him, but I am telling everyone I know what a revelation it is. It saddens me to think that, as England is today, the book will probably be little noticed and little read. It is one of the very best things that have been done anywhere in my lifetime, and I remain gasping at it.

At the end of February, when it was published, Belloc gave his opinion in *The Tablet* in more measured terms but in the same spirit of unqualified admiration. It was, perhaps, the last new book he read with full comprehension; certainly the last he read with delight.

Belloc's fear that it would pass unnoticed was not realized. Almost every respectable paper greeted it with enthusiasm (though it was the end of July before *The Observer* joined in the chorus). Everyone with an eye for style was dazzled by the brilliance of pastiche and by the superb balance and completeness of its construction. It was Ronald's farewell to secular literature, and in it, under the new exhilaration of that year, he completely fulfilled the promise of his youth. The eight half-centuries between the Armada and the Munich agreement fall precisely into place, like the combination of a lock, as though especially designed to open the heavy door of the theme. Every fifty years as the dons of St Simon Magnus sit over their wine, a great change is impending. Their idiom changes. Continuity is maintained by names only; the old men who survive from one generation to the next have changed beyond recognition. Most of the critics were so captivated by the technical skill, invention, and wit, particularly in the notes parodying contemporary sources, that they missed the theme. One of them, indeed, ingenuously remarked that the dons of the early periods seemed strangely preoccupied with the fortunes of the Church of England. By doing so, he illustrated Ronald's point. There is a sense, of the same order as Belloc's much-quoted and much-misunderstood assertion that 'Europe is the Faith and the Faith is Europe', in which it can be said that for 350 years Oxford and Cambridge (and Oxford especially) *were* the Church of England; that the secularization of the Universities, an inevitable though long-postponed consequence of the Reformation, was national apostasy. A great part of Ronald's purpose was to show that when the Universities attempted to be centres of a general education which excluded theology they found themselves not knowing what they were to teach, to whom, or why. The society of the Senior Common-room breaks up into a miscellaneous collection of specialists with neither common ground for discussion nor interest in one another's opinions. By 1938 even the massive confidence in false prediction which has characterized the older fellows has given way to bewilderment.

Let Dons Delight is Ronald's farewell to Oxford, the expression of a long love-hate. Not every reader has observed the tender note of valediction which haunts its pages.

> All these last weeks, I know not why [says Mr Lee in 1588 (he was going out to join the recusants at Douay, to return to martyrdom)] that of the shepherd in Virgil hath been coming back to my mind continually; *At nos hinc alii sitientes ibimus Afros*: we are exiled from you now across the seas, and we shall be exiled yet longer from your thoughts and memories in England, and most in Oxford. Anyone that will be absolute over a point of doctrine shall find himself a stranger here. And we above all, that will stick to the old religion, shall have no part with you.

It is the voice of Ronald twenty-one years before, when he resigned his fellowship at Trinity; it is his voice at the time of writing, when he resigned the chaplaincy. The Virgilian quotation recurs. The type of the exile changes – to the Scholar Gipsy, to Mr Savile the Tractarian, to Ronald himself.

It is, as has been said, his farewell to Oxford but it was not his last word. That can be read in the Preface to the *Hidden Stream*, written in 1952.

> The lane which runs past the Old Palace bears every mark of being a closed-in water-course, and so indeed it is; here the Trill Mill Stream, a true branch of Isis that has flowed modestly through the less frequented parts of Oxford, goes underground for a few hundred yards. . . . Five centuries ago it must have hurried past the walls of the Franciscan, then of the Dominican friary, accepting its tribute of grey cowls and black competitively washed. Those rivalries have vanished; invisible now, it burrows its way under the discreet postern of Campion Hall, the pious uproar of the Old Palace. But it is the same channel, and a true water-course; not all the Isis flows under Folly Bridge or meanders about the shoals of the Seacourt Stream.[1] And (if I must drag my parable to the light) not all the philosophies of Oxford are philosophies of negation and despair; she is fed by secret streams, not less influential to her life or less native to her genius.

2

Ronald's withdrawal from Oxford comprised three distinct operations: his resignation from the chaplaincy, his commission to translate the Vulgate, and his installation as private chaplain at Aldenham. Until all three had been approved, he was anxious to keep the project a secret between himself and Lady Acton. But by January 4th 1938 he wrote to say that 'the cat was out of the bag'. Catholic gossips had got wind of the proposed move. On May 9th 1938 Archbishop Williams visited the Old Palace, and Ronald wrote that evening that he had pursued the subject of 'not staying on here for ever. He [the Archbishop] thought at first I was fishing for compliments but got rather sensible afterwards. I think I've prepared now for a breakaway when necessary, though he is one of the people who has got the silly idea of their wanting to make me a Bishop.'

---

[1] The Seacourt Stream leaves the Thames at Hagley Pool, a little west of King's Weir, breaks up into a network of shallow little streams which eventually find their way back into the Thames between Osney Lock and Hinksey.

On June 10th Cardinal Hinsley offered Ronald the Presidency of St Edmund's.

> I know something of your innate modesty [he wrote] but I also know that the Catholic world does not share your opinion of yourself and your desire to be away from the footlights. I am persuaded that no one whom I know could or would fulfil the post as you and no one would give so much prestige to the grand old College which you have already served so admirably.

The proposal was entirely repugnant to every personal wish of Ronald's. He had found a new friend, a new home, and, it seemed probable, new work. Now all these were in jeopardy. Characteristically he put his own preferences aside and addressed himself to the problem: was it his duty to accept?

He consulted Mr Eyres, who had not yet heard of the Aldenham project and replied in a formal statement of the arguments for and against the appointment.

> *Pro.* 1) Authority has invited you to accept what it, and the general public, would consider an honour. 2) If Ward and Burton are any criterion, you would have ample time for serious writing. 3) You would be in a position, almost unique in Christendom, of being able to bring a fresh mind to the running of a seminary, through never having been yourself a seminarian. *Con.* 1) Your creature comforts and general amenities would be noticeably diminished. 2) Your holidays would be curtailed. 3) 'Unhappy far-off things' have left memories behind which it may be difficult to eradicate. 4) You would be difficult to replace at Oxford. 5) You would from time to time have to rebuke individually boys, divines, and even priests.

Under both columns is entered: 'It would in all probability lead ultimately to a bishopric.'

These considerations were designed to make Ronald accept, but he also consulted Fr D'Arcy and his confessor, who both advised refusal. To Mr Eyres he replied: 'I am *quite certain* I should not be able to write another line, except perhaps in the summer holiday. Forgive me if I've asked your advice and not taken it; both Fr D'Arcy and Fr Justin were quite clear about it.'

To the Cardinal he wrote:

> I have been consulting, in confidence, one or two friends about the suggestion of my going to St Edmund's, and I haven't had time to hear from all of them, but I thought it best not to wait any longer. Even as it is,

I am afraid my answer is delayed, but I have been away the last two nights, to address the Maynooth Union, and have only just got back.

I'm sorry to say that, according to the best light I can get, I don't think it would be right for me to accept the position, as far as your kindness allows me to have any say in the matter. I agree with my confessor here, who said unhesitatingly that it was not my *métier*; and I hope you will acquit me of modesty when I say that. For indeed, it is a kind of vanity which tells me that one thing is my *métier* rather than another. The root trouble is, I really believe I am abnormally disqualified for organizing and administrative work. When it is a case for decision, or for ordering something to be done, I let weeks and months pass without doing anything. Any success I have had here has been entirely on the personal side, and wherever organization is concerned, I have been a failure. (Any official of the Universities' Catholic Federation will cordially bear out this view.) If I went to St Edmund's I should see changes that I should think ought to be made (at least, all Presidents do). But I shouldn't make them; from a mixture, I suppose, of shyness and procrastination I should leave things as they are; and if people on the staff made suggestions in this sense, I should say it was an excellent idea and we must see about it some time. I don't know whether a psycho-analyst could cure me of this habit; but I know I can't cure myself, because I have tried often and failed. My present house-keeper has been here for two terms, and I haven't really begun to get my own way yet.

There's another defect which may or may not be connected with this, but it seems to me equally ineradicable and at least equally dangerous – I cannot take the stern line, or impress people with my dignity. To be called by my Christian name by second-year undergraduates may be a gift, but it is not the gift needed if you are to be the Awful Presence in the background which the Presidency of a seminary demands. I realize, of course, that the President can make the mistake of being too distant, and I understand that Mgr Bickford has been successful in bringing a good deal of human approachableness into his work. But I feel quite sure that my temperament would make me a parody of him in that respect. I think I might easily be popular, but it is because I find it very hard to say No to people; and with the best will in the world I imagine that the head of a seminary ought to spend a good deal of his time in saying No; you cannot ride everybody with a light rein, and I feel that here I have been a failure with most of the people who do not respond to kindness. I feel that if I went to Old Hall the whole discipline of the place would be subtly relaxed. Worse still, I think I should lack the sternness needed when it is a question of getting rid of somebody, boy or divine. I know that the Orders Council can be a help here; but a great deal must depend on the President; and I feel terrified of what might be the results of over-indulgence strewn towards the diffcult cases. At the Orders Council I was nearly always in favour of lenity, and I am sure I was often wrong. Another disadvantage about an over-complaisant President is that he is in danger of being too much influenced by his subordinates; and I know how easily this can lead to jealousies and spiteful criticisms.

I have tried to explain the dangers which I fear for the College as the result of these flaws in my own temperament. I am less ready to base my refusal on the dangers which they would have for myself in such a position; but I think it would make me perfectly miserable. I know when I am being inefficient, and I should realize that I was not making the right changes or taking the right decisions or keeping a proper check of expenditure etc., and the knowledge would make me constantly worried. I am a born worrier, and any kind of unpleasantness, any difficult decision which had to be faced, would interfere with my sleep and my health as it used to with Fr Sich when he was at the Oratory. My tenure of office would, I suspect, be no longer than Canon Burton's (a man for whom I always felt an extraordinary sympathy), and would end for the same reasons.

As I said at the beginning of this letter, I suppose the feeling that my gifts do not lie in this direction is at bottom a less modest belief that they lie in other directions. I had hoped, in a year or two's time, to be allowed to resign the chaplaincy here and take on some purely nominal work, such as would enable me to accept more of the preaching and lecturing invitations I get, and at the same time do some real writing, after so many years of pot-boiling. I started a book in 1918, of which I have still no more written than some four or five chapters. And if I don't write, soon, some of the things I feel I could write, I shall have become too rusty and perhaps too flabby to write them at all. Of course, it is for my superiors to judge whether such a life of half-retirement is suitable to my priesthood, and I would not undertake it rashly. But the acceptance of the Presidency would mean saying good-bye to all that side of my work. I am sure the President ought not to be continually away from the College; and I am sure that, given my temperament, I could not find the time, the leisure, or the peace of mind for effective literary work, such as might be of benefit to the Church, if I could really do it. We all have our heroes, and mine is Newman rather than Manning.

In saying all this, I do not disguise from myself the fact that I have more selfish reasons for dreading the change. The life at St Edmund's never seemed to agree with my health or my digestion. But I hope I should have enough devotion to duty to waive all that, if I felt that I could do the work well. (So far as personal relations are concerned, I have none but the warmest memories of St Edmund's, and I think I should find it easy to work with the people there, though I do not know how I should play the superior with a man like Canon Smith, who, besides being my very good

friend, has always been a theological oracle to me). Both my confessor and
Fr D'Arcy, who I think knows me better than any other priest in Oxford,
are in general agreement with what I have written. I am very sorry indeed
to involve your Eminence in fresh difficulties over filling the post; but I
can say, with definite alternatives in my mind, *detur digniori*.

The Cardinal replied on June 30th:

> We [he and the Vicar General] are both agreed that I ought not to press
> my suit with you further in view of your reluctance to accept. I understand
> perfectly. . . . Your interests and wishes are decisive; I bow submissively . . .
> I do agree completely with you that you should have time and opportunity
> to *write*. If I can do anything to secure this – either by releasing you from
> distractions, or by finding you a place where you can do the great work of
> the pen-apostolate, you will please let me know, and I will do my best.

The generosity and humility of this letter are none the less remarkable
for being typical of its writer.

Warmed and exhilarated by the confidence shown him, Ronald
broached the subject nearest to his heart. For a hundred years or more the
Douay version of the Bible, as amended by Challoner the official text of
the Catholic Church in England, had been generally recognized as
unsatisfactory. The second Synod of Oscott in 1855 had recommended
that Newman should edit a new English version. The editorship as then
conceived was more than the composition of the philosophic *Prolegomena*
which he had in mind, and the choice of the translators; Newman's
literary taste was to inform the whole work. As W. G. Ward wrote: 'It
will be most pleasing to your friends in making your *name* immortal; for
every Catholic reading his vernacular Bible will have your name on his
lips. Your memory will be embedded as it were in the English Bible.'[1]

A number of causes – the commercial interests of a bookseller, the
apathy of Cardinal Wiseman, Newman's diffidence – contributed to
frustrate this great project, but the primary impediment was the protest of
the American Bishops on the ground that Archbishop Kendrick of
Baltimore was already engaged on the same task and that it was undesirable
that there should be two competing English versions (of which Newman's
would without doubt have been the superior).[2] To Newman's chagrin the
matter was dropped with few expressions of regret. The Baltimore Bible
was not adopted in England; the Douay stayed in use; but the sense of the

---

[1] Wilfrid Ward, *Life of Cardinal Newman* (1913), I, p. 420. Cf. R. A. Knox, *On Englishing the
Bible* (1949), p. v.
[2] Ward, op. cit., 418–24.

resolution of 1855 was never entirely forgotten. All that was required was human energy to put it into effect. In 1938 the matter was recognized as being urgent, for the American bishops were again busy preparing their own new version.

On September 19th the Archbishop of Birmingham wrote:

> Shrewsbury has sent me the letter you received from the U.S.A. about revising S. John's Gospel or the whole bible 'in the idiom of our time'. I can well imagine what that will be. Can you wait till after the bishops' meeting on October 25th and 26th for an answer? I am proposing to put it to them that they appoint you our representative with power to coopt any other workers you desire. But I should also like to put to them, if you do not strongly object, that they appoint you to do a new version of the New Testament first of all, and then the O.T. if the work goes on as I trust it will. This is a big job, and will mean your giving up the chaplaincy, I fear. But I've been thinking it over seriously, and it seems to me that no one is better fitted for the work than you are, and the work itself is needed badly. Let me know what you think, and I'll try to do what you would like me to do. I shall never be quite reconciled to your leaving Oxford – but there you are, it just can't be helped.

News of the hierarchy's decision was sent by the Cardinal on November 8th.

> With all the other Bishops I welcomed the proposal to commission you to translate the New Testament. We have confidence in you as the one man who can give us an English text readable and understood of the people.
>
> I quite appreciate that the task will necessitate freedom from your present duties. You have had more than enough of a very trying position.
>
> The resignation will, I note, take place half-way through next year.
>
> You will understand me, I am sure, when I say that I am anxious to keep hold of you for Westminster. At the same time the work of translation will require that you should have peace and leisure. The offer of the Actons is most suitable. But it is just possible we may be able to find you something even more suitable and within easier access to libraries &c. in London. Of course I shall consult your own desires in this matter. Only do not desert Westminster for good and all. You may be badly wanted here when your task is done.

The terms of this invitation are important in the light of subsequent misunderstandings.

3

The news that Ronald was leaving Oxford at the end of the summer was made public in January 1939. It had been kept a fairly close secret, and the announcement on the wireless brought a heavy post of letters of expostulation. His removal from the University seemed to accentuate the uncertainties of the period, and the imminent loss was felt far beyond his congregation and his college. Only his closest friends understood the strong pull of Aldenham, and most others were puzzled at the choice of a remote rural chaplaincy by one who had seemed so sociable. His fellow clergy, especially those who had looked to him as a future leader in the public life of the Church, were disconcerted by his withdrawal from the course of clerical life. Some few among both the higher and lower clergy who did not know Ronald personally or appreciate his peculiar gifts may have been troubled by a tinge of professional resentment of the kind felt by regimental officers towards a man who is seconded for special duties. The Oxford chaplaincy itself had been, in a sense, an extra-regimental posting. It was known that most of his very long vacations had been spent at Beaufort. Now, once again instead of gratefully embracing the normal clerical preferments open to him, Ronald, it seemed, chose to sequester himself among patrician converts, whose habits of thought and devotion were strange to the generality of industrial parishes and whose way of life was assumed, quite wrongly as things turned out, to be more luxurious than that of the presbytery. The hostility shown later to the *Manual of Prayers* may in part be attributed to half-conscious jealousy.

Members of his congregation, present and past, rather suddenly recognized how much they owed to him. No one had foreseen the time when he would not be there, always accessible, at the top of his narrow stairs.

He had hid his plans even from his friends at Trinity. Mr Philip Landon, sole survivor of the Orthodox Club, wrote to express his regret and on January 20th Ronald answered, making no mention of the friendship eighteen months old, that was drawing him away.

The Old Palace.
Jan. 20.

Dear Philip,

You said not to answer your letter; but I feel you've been so much the welcoming person in the University ever since I came back here, that I ought to put my apology on record to you.

I think, if this hadn't turned up, I should have given myself two more years here, and then offered my resignation. It's partly, I admit, a selfish decision; I do find that Oxford wears one out inside in the most extraordinary way; not, heaven knows, that I work hard; but incessant contact with human beings does seem to drain one's vitality and unfit one for serious writing or the formation of independent judgements. You'll say that applies equally to you, and to lots of other people here; if Sligger stuck it out till his health cracked, why shouldn't the rest of us? But then, I shouldn't mind so much if it were only the undergraduates. But I am such a target both for visits and for correspondence from people who aren't really my business: strangers (especially clerical) passing through Oxford who simply want to waste time, people who have schemes for setting the world right and find me a convenient waste-paper basket for them; parents of boys who might possibly come up to Oxford but probably won't; and you can't be always at home to your own congregation without being also at home to these time-wasters, who prey like vampires on one's faculty of attention.

Only I don't think it's entirely selfishness; there's an admixture of vanity. It's difficult to get over the feeling that one is meant to write; and all the writing I have done since Some Loose Stones has been, from my point of view, not perhaps mere pot-boiling, but spare-time writing.[1] I started on the idea of a book in 1918 which has so far only reached four chapters or so. To put off these literary schemes till you are overtaken by old age means that you can't carry them out effectively; look at Gore, and how much more influence those last books of his would have had if people hadn't been able to dismiss them by saying, 'Oh, he's ga-ga.' This Bible business will take a lot of time, but I don't mean it to take all my time. I want to write other things, and if possible put up some kind of barrage against this revolting age.

You may say, Yes, but I could go and live in North Oxford to do it. I know, but I think Oxford is an awfully depressing atmosphere if one's work isn't connected with the University; and I should still be at the mercy of the time-wasters, perhaps more than ever. I've at least got to try the idea of tucking myself away in the country, and only emerging at intervals when I'm wanted to do sermons etc. (this will mean coming back to Oxford a good deal); if it doesn't work, I must start all over again.

'Trinity had never been unkind to me'; that sentiment I shall always be able to echo. And your letter was about the best instance of it I've had. Thank you awfully, and try to forgive me.

---

[1] Let Dons Delight had not yet appeared. It is certain that Ronald did not regard that book as 'pot-boiling'. It is typical of him not to refer to it before publication while he was still in doubt of how it would be received.

Lady Acton was pregnant and obliged to lie up in her flat in London for most of Hilary Term. Letters went between them almost daily. Already, by February 9th, Ronald was beginning to fuss about moving his furniture; what should he leave, what take with him to Aldenham?

> I want to know about the china in the corner cupboard which was only bought at all to have something in the corner cupboard. It would be fantastic to buy a corner cupboard for Aldenham so as to have something to keep the china in.

The proposition at this time was that a cottage near the house should be adapted for his and a housekeeper's use.

> As far as I know [he wrote to Mr Eyres on January 30th] the only pay offered for my new job is the absence of any necessity to live in a large house and entertain undergraduates. But with a house rent free I think I ought to be able to manage, helped out to some extent by preacher's expenses, etc.

Archbishop Williams considered that the hierarchy should take the risk of subsidizing the translation in return for the copyright. A stipend of £200 a year was voted at the Low Week meeting, each Bishop to contribute in proportion to the Catholic population of his diocese (the Bishop of Northampton dissenting). 'Goodness knows where the money is to come from' was Archbishop Williams's comment on this transaction. In the event the hierarchy found the stipend for three and a half years and enjoyed the profits of the New Testament. They were unwilling to continue while Ronald completed the Old Testament, but on his appointment in 1944 Cardinal Griffin charged the Archdiocese of Westminster with this sum until 1947, receiving in return the copyright of those volumes. For a few hundred pounds the Bishops acquired a thriving property, which at the time of Ronald's death had yielded some £50,000. At a later date Ronald remarked drily, but without bitterness, that no word of thanks was ever said to him for this substantial benefaction.

Lady Acton was still laid up in London during Easter. Ronald gave the retreat at Ampleforth and spent most of the vacation at the Old Palace, beginning to teach himself Hebrew, a language to whose orthography his cross-word mind aptly responded. The Summer Term was much distracted and overshadowed by the cares of departure. His successor in the chaplaincy, Fr Alfonso de Zulueta, eased his anxieties by taking over at a generous price whatever furniture he wished to leave behind him, but his letters to Lady Acton are full of the dimensions of curtains and carpets, the quantities of kitchen ware and bed linen that he would need at Aldenham. On all these problems she gave decisive, written directions.

In Eights Week Ronald spoke at the Union, a gay conclusion to the series, in which he performed a memorable pantomime of reading a newspaper in a railway-carriage. The last weeks of term were full of social engagements and several speeches, culminating in a dinner at the Randolph Hotel at which the Newman Society presented him with an early folio of the Douay Bible, a silver mug, a water-colour of the Old Palace, and £50. Mr Douglas Woodruff proposed the health; he and a subsequent speaker emphasized the great lustre which Ronald had brought to the chaplaincy; in replying Ronald said: 'I should like to feel that during the time I have been in Oxford I have not been engaged in putting myself across as a public figure, but rather in putting the Old Palace more and more on the map as an integral part of Oxford.' Fr de Zulueta spent two days at the Old Palace, and Ronald arranged tea parties for him to meet those of the congregation who were staying up the following year.

The Press were disposed to make an event of Ronald's retirement, and many hours of his last days were spent away from the Old Palace, dodging interviewers and photographers.

> A horrible sort of conspiracy seems to have sprung up [he wrote to Lady Acton] to treat me as if I were something of importance. The Daily Sketch wanted to send a man to take photographs of me working in my study. I wrote back and said I hadn't a study and didn't do any work. Still more annoying a thing called Paramount Films wrote and wanted me to do something for a revolting thing called a news reel. I hope I've choked them off.

A more agreeable attention was paid to him in the Creweian (Latin) Oration, given that year by the Rev. Adam Fox.[1] In recounting, according to custom, the events of the University year he bade farewell to Ronald in the peculiarly felicitous phrase 'deliciae Academicorum' – the Dons' delight.

On June 23rd he attended the Balliol gaudy given for Cyril Bailey's old pupils. At last, by June 26th, all his farewells were made, his superfluous books were sold, anything he was taking with him was packed, and he was able to move to Aldenham.

The cottage was not yet ready for him, and the housekeeper who had been engaged was not free until the autumn. He came to live in the

---

[1] Now Archdeacon of Westminster.

house, arranging his working books in the old library and taking possession of the writing-table there. Lady Acton's baby was due at the beginning of September. Meanwhile she gave him her full attention. Lord Acton had left his London firm and was engaged on the Birmingham Stock Exchange, to which he was able to go daily and return at night. At week-ends as usual the house was full of congenial guests. He settled down to a routine of hard, uninterrupted work. He started again on the book he had begun in 1918, which had of late been so much in his mind. In his new, serene mood he scrapped much which he had conceived when his mind was still sodden with controversy. Lady Acton worked with him, finding his references and discussing his plan. He set aside certain hours for Hebrew. For two idyllic months he led the life to which for two years he had fondly aspired.

Aldenham in August 1939 bore a faint but recognizable flavour of the reading party he had planned twenty-five years before, at More Hall with Guy Lawrence and C: the party that never met.

Chapter Four

KEEPING ANOTHER ARMAGEDDON

Aldenham 1939–1947

For the past eighteen months the possibility of a second world war had been present in Ronald's mind no less than in everybody else's, but he suffered less than others, perhaps, from particular anxiety in matters outside his own responsibility. The English politicians he knew were mostly Conservatives who encouraged the hope of peace; the few foreigners he met were mostly *ancien régime* Catholics with a faith in the unity of Europe and a disdain for Nazism. From time to time in his letters of this period he records what he heard said by people who seemed to know, about the intentions and strength of the various powers, but he suspected the cocksure everywhere and himself eschewed speculation. The veering emotions of contemporary Oxford, now pacificist, now interventionist, encouraged him in his aloofness. When issued with a gas-mask he used it as the comic climax of his Eights Week speech at the Union. A man's first duty was still to his own plans.

These plans, however, were entirely dependent on the peace being kept. Lord Acton held a commission in his county yeomanry. On mobilization his work in Birmingham would cease, and with it the greater part of his income. Lady Acton could not afford to maintain Aldenham alone even were it not, like all large houses in the country, liable to requisition as a hostel for refugees from the cities, which were expected to be laid waste within a few days of the declaration of war. Early in 1938 Lord and Lady Acton had been in negotiation with two London convents, and it was eventually arranged that the Assumption nuns and their school, from Kensington Square, should occupy Aldenham in the event of war.

Ronald was to act as their chaplain without pay, receiving food, fuel, and laundry; he stipulated only that a substitute should be found for him when he was asked to preach elsewhere and that he should not be expected to sing Mass or perform any ceremony except giving the ashes on Ash Wednesday. The project of his keeping his own cottage and housekeeper in the village was abandoned. Instead he took a room in the original priest's house adjoining the chapel, then occupied by Bazley, the bailiff, who was married to a former lady's-maid. The Bazleys, to whom Ronald was grateful for countless attentions, also kept a spare room for Lord Acton's use when he came on leave. Lady Acton retained the nursery of the main house, a dressing-room for herself and a small sitting-room near the front door for herself and Ronald. For six years this room, shared with her, often with Pelline and sometimes with a visitor, was where Ronald stored his reference library, laid out his patience cards, ate, typed, read. It was there, in circumstances very different from what he and Lady Acton had planned, that the greater part of the Knox Bible was written.

On Friday, September 1st the first detachment of the convent arrived in a charabanc. There were ten nuns, six or seven foreign girls who were spending their holidays in England, and a huge variety of luggage and equipment. Lord Acton was at home at the time to greet them with his habitual geniality. Fr Brodrick, S.J., was staying the week-end, as Ronald had expected to be with friends in Gloucestershire who, themselves invaded by 'evacuees', had put him off. He stood rather wistfully in the background of the welcoming circle. In private with Lady Acton he did not dissemble his dejection.

For three weeks furniture and stores arrived from Kensington Square and the house was in a turmoil of rearrangement. Lady Acton was in the last month of her pregnancy. Lord Acton was with his regiment. The weather alone was kind. Ronald bathed in the lake and pursued his study of Hebrew; then went to fulfil a long-standing engagement to give a retreat at Grayshott.

In his absence term started with the arrival of some forty girls. This number was barely enough to support the convent. The school received none of the subsidies provided by the State for its own institutions. Later in the term ten more girls arrived, but there was no certainty that parents would keep their children permanently in the country. At half-term the headmistress gave notice of their return to London, and Ronald and Lady Acton were anxiously discussing the economics of the coming year. All over England the anti-climax and disillusionment of the diaspora were expressed in scenes of farce and fury. There were no bombs, no poison gas in the cities; none of the accustomed amenities in the country. Everywhere the 'evacuees' began drifting home. At Aldenham good sense and goodwill prevailed. There was need of both in adjusting the rather casual agreement into which Lady Acton had entered. 'We were allowed the use of everything,' the headmistress wrote in 'News from Aldenham' in the *Assumption Chronicle*,[1] 'the home atmosphere remained and in such lovely surroundings the children were soon perfectly happy', but there were anxieties about the gardeners' wages, leaks in the roof, and similar problems of tenancy which were overcome by the nuns' patience and Lady Acton's generosity. Eventually a thriving school of 55 girls, 15 nuns, 3 lay teachers, and a lay matron lived at Aldenham until the end of the War.

Lady Acton's baby, Catherine, was born on September 30th, and Ronald celebrated the occasion by translating the first chapter of Genesis. He went to Bridgnorth to ask the parish priest's permission to baptize her, but found that he had not made his meaning plain. Fr Cronin supposed he was being asked to come out for the ceremony and kindly consented; Ronald acquiesced.

Aldenham was unsuitable for convalescence, and Lady Acton removed with her baby and the nurse to spend some weeks with more comfortable neighbours, leaving Ronald alone to make closer acquaintance with the school and community. He was seldom quite at his ease with nuns, and his long association with the Congregation of the Assumption did not completely mitigate his shyness. He said Mass for them, heard their confessions, and gave them retreats – nine of the conferences later adapted for *A Retreat for Priests*[2] were first given to them. He read as lectures to them parts of his work in progress which later appeared in *Enthusiasm*; each Christmas he took charge of the crib; they were more appreciative than the Fraser children of his elaborate decorations; but none are known to have gone to him for spiritual direction. They respected his need for privacy in his work, and his daily intercourse with them was limited to the exchange of courtesies.

The school, however, whose coming he had awaited with consternation, proved a source of unexpected pleasure. One or two of the girls were already known to him through their parents; most were strangers. It was impressed on them that the Monsignor was engaged in grave studies and that they must keep out of his way. It was in the chapel that he made his first impression by his gentle sympathy as a confessor and his humour as a preacher. None of them had expected to enjoy sermons, still less to laugh during them. He gave them a short instruction after Benediction every Sunday of term when he was at Aldenham, and with his peculiar versatility and felicity he evolved a new, entirely original style, specially designed for his new, unfamiliar audience. As he came to know the girls

---

[1] War Issue No. 1, April 1942.　　　[2] Sheed & Ward, 1946.

individually and to enter their lives he adopted their habits of speech and introduced allusions to their routine. These talks were so popular that one girl, who was being taken out for the day by her parents, insisted on returning for Benediction rather than go to the cinema. Most of them have been printed in the books *The Mass in Slow Motion* (1948), *The Creed in Slow Motion* (1949), and *The Gospel in Slow Motion* (1950), which have proved the most popular of all his writings. The first, in particular, has found a large adult public and is regarded by many as the ideal present for a convert of any age or intellectual equipment. Each of these is dedicated to an Aldenham girl; the first two to Claudia and Nicola,[1] the twin daughters of Mr N. L. C. Macaskie, K.C., who attained and retained a particular place in his affections.

These two pretty children arrived in the autumn of 1943 when Ronald's popularity and fame were well established in the school but when he was suffering from a dismal sense of discouragement in his more public life. They first attracted his attention when Nicola, for a 'dare', burst into his sanctum and asked whether he liked pink blancmange. Shortly afterwards there was a more solemn encounter. Claudia was quite suddenly struck alarmingly ill, and Ronald was called to anoint her. It was the first and only time he gave the last sacraments; he had often spoken of them in his sermons but always with the implied assumption that they were something brought in extreme old age. The summons to the apparently dying child was an incident of poignant emotion. The twins invited him to stay in the holidays, and soon their house in Kensington Square became his regular lodging in London. He said they should put up a plaque: 'Ronald Knox practically lived here.' Later they were among the very few of his friends to whom he wrote letters in his old, free, affectionate manner. In May 1947 he wrote to Nicola: 'You and Claudia are the only people I want to write to except on business.' In the drab and sour period of victory their friendship was a substantial solace. With his habitual reticence, he seldom spoke of them. At the dinner given to him in London on his sixtieth birthday the appearance of Claudia, dressed for a ball and prematurely called away by a young man in a white tie, created a stir of curiosity among his elderly friends.

For a time Ronald took a weekly discussion class for the Sixth Form. He read several of his old, humorous papers to the school, including the never-failing *French with Tears*. Sometimes he chid the girls in a bantering way which they understood and enjoyed; about their answering Mass he

---

[1] Mrs Joly de Lotbinière and Mrs John Roberts.

wrote: 'When you come to a difficult word in the Latin, don't think simultaneously, "That looks a bit of a stinker, I'll leave it to Mary Jane." *Laetabitur* is pronounced like "late arbiter", not like "later bitter".' He introduced some of the old verbal games he had played at Trinity in 1912 and at Beaufort with Maurice Baring; 'Peach-Each', a kind of spoken cypher 'calculated', as he described it in the *Assumption Chronicle*,

> to make your conversation even more exasperating than it is at present. The principle is that whenever you find yourself on the point of pronouncing two consecutive syllables which rhyme (as, 'I hate waiting') you should substitute the two syllables 'peach each' (and say, 'I peach eaching'). Occasionally [he adds] it obscures your meaning; when you say, 'I have just been to Peacheach' it is difficult for the other person to know whether you have been to Walsall (say) or Goodwood

and he appended a letter to a parent written in this argot which requires long efforts to translate.

Also for the *Assumption Chronicle* he composed what at first reading appears to be thirty-one lines of a curiously worded anecdote of a missionary priest. It concludes: 'Read through these edifying lines again and you will find the Christian names of twenty-four of your School friends buried in them.'

It was pleasant to grow old among the very young, to whom there is no appreciable difference of age between forty and sixty. It was a pleasant experience to find in late middle life a new, eager audience for the entertainments which had seemed rather antiquated at Oxford. But it was not as an entertainer that he most impressed the children at Aldenham. Their clear young minds recognized holiness and loved it. He explained the action of the liturgy as they had never heard it explained before, but it was in participation in his Masses that their understanding flowered. A girl had occasion to go through the chapel one morning as he was making his thanksgiving; he knelt completely absorbed in prayer, and she later told a nun that passing between him and the altar was like 'cutting through the supernatural'.

The routine of Ronald's life varied little during the convent tenancy. Unlike the first war the second was not for him a time of tragedy. Few of his friends were killed. No bombs fell near him. It was rather for him, as for all the elderly, a time of cumulative strain and frustration, of scarcities and restrictions, meagre rations, black-out; of lack of information, growing resentment of the ugly tones of official propaganda and growing foreboding of a world where the springs of civilization seemed to be fast running dry. The very simplicity of Ronald's needs – a box of matches, a razor-blade, a handful of coal, a seat in a railway-carriage – made their deprivation the more irksome. He lived always in spirit so near the edge of misery, in a scheme so narrowly calculated, that he was peculiarly vulnerable to diminution and change. He scrupulously eschewed the many opportunities of advantage; he accepted the hard conditions of civilian war-time life and aggravated them by self-denial – by saving, for example, all his marmalade for Pelline – but he was unable to make a continual show of cheerfulness, and in their close quarters the delights of his companionship became somewhat rarer to Lady Acton.

She changed; the delicate, pensive girl rather suddenly grew into a robust active woman. She bore two sons, Richard in July 1941 and John in January 1943. At times dressed in Girl Guide uniform, at times in corduroy trousers, she let her intellectual interests lie fallow and devoted herself furiously to pig-farming. Where she had been Ronald's pupil, he became hers; less aptly. He followed her ineffectually about the fields, helping to mend the fences. 'Poor old chap,' said Vaughan, the factor, 'it gives him an interest.' He picked damsons, fell and sprained an ankle. He lent her money to buy a tractor, a vehicle which at that time exercised an irresistible fascination over the women of the English countryside. She spent long days with it. She took out her luncheon and munched under the hedges, leaving Ronald to coax Pelline into eating the convent puddings; she returned in the evenings weary and in no mood for literary exercises. In the hours she spared from the nursery, Ronald read agricul-tural manuals to her in place of Bremond and Pascal, and himself memorized the vocabulary of the pigsty and the root-crop.

While his regiment remained in England, Lord Acton came on regular leave. There were few visitors except the priests who did duty in Ronald's absences. He spent a yearly average of about thirty-five days away from Aldenham, few of them in very exhilarating surroundings. He gave retreats to the clergy, to seminarists, and to schoolboys; he preached in industrial cities. Travelling was exhausting and exasperating at that time, particularly for one who had made a hobby of the railway system. His engagement books for those years give few hints of pleasure – a few dinners at Trinity, when he preached at the chaplaincy; a few weddings; once a year a day or two at Mells or Keir or Beaufort or in Edinburgh with his sister; a day in 1944 at Kingsland with Belloc who was then much broken in strength and in mind, sometimes a luncheon engagement in London, when he gave his annual sermon at Maiden Lane. Apart from these, there is only a grim catalogue of professional duties. His correspondence is almost exclusively with biblical scholars. His election in 1941 to an honorary fellowship at Trinity was the happiest human event of those years. He spoke of it, indeed, as 'the nicest thing that ever happened' to him.

A typically gracious episode may be recorded here. In the third week of April 1942 he gave a retreat to the community at Belmont Abbey, Hereford. A young novice, Michael Oakley (now Brother James, O.S.B.), came to him for advice, and in the course of their conversation mentioned that he wished to learn to write Latin verse. Ronald undertook to give him instruction by post and for five years among all his other occupations he conducted the course, correcting the exercises and sending fair copies, encouraging him – 'This is great fun. You've got all the right instincts' (September 1943) – until, in September 1947, he could write, 'your prosody has got altogether away from leading strings'.

They never met again, but continued to correspond. At Ronald's instigation Michael Oakley translated the *Aeneid* for the Everyman Library, and Ronald entrusted him with the completion of the *Imitation of Christ*, which was left unfinished at his death.

2

The translation of the Bible was not Ronald's only work at Aldenham. He wrote many sermons and some 'talks' for broadcasting; he added intermittently to *Enthusiasm*; from February 18th 1940 he contributed every month five hundred words to the *Sunday Times*; 'lightning meditations' as he later described them when collecting them into a book.[1] In 1945, as will appear later, he wrote the masterly essay, *God and the Atom*. But for 'nine years hard', as he described it on the wireless, he was dominated by his Bible. He earned very little money and spent less while he served his sentence.

St Jerome was not more solitary in his task. Some years later an American asked Lord Oxford whether it was not true that the translation was completed at his home: 'it must be an enormous place'. 'Not particularly.' 'But to accommodate the Monsignor *and all his staff*?' By transatlantic standards of 'team-projects' the individual achievement was stupendous. In fact, some years earlier a German priest, Fr Rosch, had produced, on his own responsibility, a vernacular Bible that had enjoyed

---

[1] *Stimuli* (1951).

great success, but he had worked with greater amenities than Ronald. With his books of reference heaped on window-ledges and his typewriter poised on the corner of a table littered with files, between the clearing of one meal and the laying of another, Ronald worked alone through the War and into the chilly peace with no help at all and very little encouragement.

As has been seen above, Ronald's commission was to translate the New Testament, yet his first act on leaving Oxford was to set about learning Hebrew, and the first words actually set down were: 'God, at the beginning of time, created heaven and earth.' From the first, with or without official recognition, he was determined to make his own translation of the whole Bible. He had heard a vocation which would take no denial. Diffident about so much else, on this one question he was completely confident in his powers and judgement.

As has been seen, he had received, as far as the New Testament was concerned, direct personal authority to make a translation, and he did not read that to mean edit, revise, or collaborate. His committee was to correct slips and advise on doubtful renderings, but the whole style and temper of the work were to be his alone. His old friend from St Edmund's, Bishop Flynn of Lancaster, was chairman; the other members were Mgr John Barton, also an Edmundian colleague, Dr Bird, Fr Hugh Pope, O.P., Fr Martindale, S.J., and Fr Christopher Butler, now Abbot of Downside. All these had other multifarious duties. It was not likely that they would often meet. It was rather vaguely recognized that Ronald would do most of the work. But there was at first some uncertainty about their authority. The Bishop of Lancaster wrote: 'I did not myself know what was the exact nature of his commission and I ventured to wonder whether any precise directions had been given.'

Fr Martindale writes:

> I certainly thought at first that the members of the committee were, so to say, on an equality under (I presumed) a sort of chairmanship held by the Bp of Lancaster. . . . When I understood that R.K. was really to do it himself, I wrote to say how glad I was that he – who had expressed different *kinds* of talk so well in 'Let Dons Delight' – would make readers feel the real delicate differences between the naive Mark, the cultured Luke, the rather stiff Matthew: I also said I hoped he would let Catholics down easily and not make his work *too* different from what they were accustomed to, and not change 'consecrated phrases'. He said (1) there were now *no* 'consecrated phrases'; that (2) he wanted to write an entirely new version without special attention to Cath/s or anyone else; and (3) that he was

paying no attention to differences of style in the evangelists but, in the N.T. would use a 'timeless English' (as if there ever could be one!) and, in the O.T., a kind of pseudo-archaist style. Since I could not agree at all (especially as he kept saying a translator ought to get 'into the skin' of his subject), there arose that 'paroxysm' – sharp difference of opinion (Acts 15: 39).

He here summarizes a personal controversy which was the subject of several letters in the winter of 1939–40. In December Ronald submitted a draft of St Matthew's Gospel to each member of the Committee. Fr Martindale, Dr Bird, and Mgr Barton replied with detailed criticisms, tabulated by Ronald: 'In the first six chapters; objections by C.C.M. [Martindale] alone, 64; by Barton alone, 19, by Bird alone, 18. Objections by all three, 2.' It was clear that Ronald could not expect consistent advice from his committee. Fr Hugh Pope, whose opinion had not been received when Ronald enumerated these objections, proved a pertinacious critic and the member of the committee who caused Ronald the greatest labour. He was delighted when he came across the verb, ὑπωπιάζω to which Liddell and Scott give the literal meaning 'to give a man a black eye' and the metaphorical sense of 'to annoy greatly' and 'to wear out'. Mgr Barton, though critical in matters of detail, was the sole staunch supporter of Ronald's intention of totally disregarding the current Douay–Challoner version; Fr Martindale alone was ruthlessly hostile to his whole conception.

Ronald wrote to him on February 8th 1940:

> It is a nightmare, disagreeing with you. Partly on the 'sed non multos patres' principle, because of Hickleton 1915; partly because I have an inveterate habit of thinking you right wherever you say anything, and the present paroxusmos makes me wonder whether I have gone mad.

The Bishop of Lancaster was disconcerted but kept an open mind. 'His version was not at all the thing that I had anticipated,' he wrote, 'and it was only after I had read a number of chapters that I began to see what he was at.'

He called a meeting of the committee for January 30th in Birmingham, but only Ronald came. He was then able to explain at length what his intentions were, and persuaded the Bishop that there was reason in them. Another meeting was called for February 27th, at which all attended except Fr Martindale, who had made his views abundantly clear, though he did not write officially to the committee, and Fr Butler, who wrote to say he would have preferred the new version to be a revision of Douay–

Challoner. The committee decided to refer the question back to the hierarchy. Ronald agreed that if he had misunderstood the terms of his commission he would, under obedience, abandon his work and produce a mere revision. In order to help the hierarchy in its decision he undertook to make a sample revision of St Matthew. It was a dire undertaking, destructive of all his hopes. With heroic humility he set himself to prepare the case for his opponents; exerting all his skill in their cause, he produced a lucid and graceful rendering. One chapter of it, the thirteenth, he had printed together with his own translation (which is not identical with the final publication) on alternate pages, prefaced with the request: 'Mgr Knox will be glad to have a ruling on the question raised, viz, whether he was wrong in supposing that the hierarchy, in asking him to submit "a new version", meant a new version altogether, not merely a reconditioning of the older model.'

This document was circulated to the hierarchy before their Low Week meeting 1940. There are no very sensational contrasts between the two versions. Indeed, a lazy reader might well have to remind himself by a glance at the heading which version was which.

A single sample may be taken of the flavour of the three versions. Verse 52 of the current Douay-Challoner Bible reads: 'Therefore every scribe instructed in the kingdom of heaven is like to a man that is a householder; who bringeth forth out of his treasure new things and old.'

Ronald's adaptation read: 'Therefore every scribe whose instruction befits him for the kingdom of heaven is like a man that is a householder, and brings forth from his treasure-house things new and old.'

His translation reads: 'Every scholar, then, whose learning is of the kingdom of heaven must be like a rich man, who knows how to bring out from his treasure-house things new and old.'

It is unlikely that the hierarchy were greatly exercised by aesthetic scruples. Those who knew Ronald were disposed in favour of what, they were aware, he so ardently wished. There was a further consideration of general interest. If Ronald produced his own new version, it would be copyright. No such certain claim attached to a revision of the existing text. Fr Rosch in Germany had sold 300,000 copies of his translation.

On March 27th Archbishop Williams wrote:

> I have to spend 3 weeks in bed so I cannot go to the Low Week meeting of the bishops. I'm sorry for this because I should like to have heard some of them arguing about your new version. But as I cannot go, I've just sent off to each bishop a strong recommendation to leave you

alone to produce what version you judge best, and urging them not to appoint any other committee. . . . so please don't worry any more about revising Douay–Challoner. Let's have R.A.K. in your best 20th Century style.

The support of Cardinal Hinsley and Archbishop Williams proved decisive at the meeting. The hierarchy were not committed to approving the publication of Ronald's version, still less to its use in church, but they made clear the task they had set him. At about this time Fr Martindale went to Denmark, was caught in the German invasion, and held incommunicado for the rest of the War. Without him the committee worked smoothly. It never met. Ronald submitted his text as he wrote it, and received much valuable help in *minutiae*.

In April 1941 he received a rather chilling intimation that his superiors did not attach as much importance as he did to his work. The chaplaincy at Oxford unexpectedly fell vacant, and the Archbishop of Birmingham wrote:

> My own feeling is that the best and happiest of all solutions would be that you should come out of your hermitage at Aldenham and return to Oxford for the duration. I have a suspicion that you won't want to do this; but setting aside the question of the Scripture work which you are doing, you can be very useful to England at present (probably most useful especially in Oxford itself) by counteracting some of the confounded left-wingers and pro-Russians of whom Oxford seems to be full and who seem to be powerful at the Foreign Office. If you are at Oxford in these days, you will be doing good war work. Well, what about it?

As the Archbishop suspected, Ronald did not welcome the suggestion. The University was a ghost of itself, thinly peopled by invalids, very young men taking short courses before joining the Forces, technicians, and women. (The town had temporarily become one of the most crowded and ill-supplied in the country.) At no time would Ronald have thought of himself as an effective political instrument. He countered by suggesting that, since men were few, the chaplaincies of the male and female undergraduates should be combined under Mgr Vernon Johnson. This solution was accepted. Women became members of the Newman Society and of the congregation at the Old Palace. It has often been said that Ronald was a last-ditcher for the divided chaplaincy and that women came in with the telephone, in defiance of his sentiments. In fact, he was the author of the temporary amalgamation, which persists to this day.

He resumed work. It seemed that his way was now clear ahead. By September 1941 he was finishing *II Corinthians*, when Archbishop Amigo, who had concurred in the Low Week decision of 1940, became more alive to what was afoot. He cast an eye over St Matthew's Gospel and condemned it.

Ronald wrote:

> I am very sensible of the kind intention with which your letter was written. None of us is any the better for living in a fool's paradise. . . . It is notorious that a short sample can easily be misleading; and I have no right at all to complain that a fresh reading of the whole gospel should have altered your Grace's opinion. It seems to me that I have to accept the award as a final blow to the hopes I had entertained; a correction here and a correction there would not be enough to win my version acceptance in your Grace's diocese, and that means that I cannot hope for its unanimous adoption by the hierarchy, even as an alternative official version. An official version only current in certain dioceses would evidently be undesirable, and probably impracticable. I am therefore asking the Bishop of Lancaster to suggest to his Eminence the discontinuance of the whole project. Fortunately, I am in a position to refund to the hierarchy the sum – four hundred pounds – which they have so generously contributed for the purpose. Later on, perhaps, if I can secure a diocesan *imprimatur*, I might publish a translation of the New Testament at my own risk. (I do not think the American version will stand in the way; it is priced at a guinea, and comment on this side has not been favourable.) But that would only be for private reading; and I might, in those altered circumstances, be bold enough to ask afresh for your Grace's approval.
>
> Meanwhile, I can only accept as God's will a decision so generously communicated, and hope for the opportunity to serve him in some other way.

Perhaps on receiving this letter the Archbishop suffered some misgivings; he may have felt he had gone farther than he intended; he may, on the other hand, have felt the need of support; he may merely have realized that he was not observing strict etiquette in exchanging letters in this way with the priest of another diocese. Whatever his motives, he now sent copies of the correspondence to the Archbishop of Westminster. If he had hoped for encouragement or connivance, he was sharply disappointed. The Cardinal rose loyally and wrathfully to the defence. 'H.E.' (His Eminence), an official at Archbishop's House wrote to Ronald, 'has sent a real snorter to H.G.' (His Grace).

As a result Archbishop Amigo made an immediate retreat, writing to

Ronald on September 8th that it would be 'a disaster' if he abandoned his work of translation.

He bided his time and had not long to wait for his retaliation.

3

Absorbed in his greater work, Ronald had given little thought to the *Manual of Prayers* since leaving Oxford. There had been objections which had been met, some minor criticisms had been accepted, and, as far as he knew, all was going slowly but smoothly. At the Low Week meeting 1942 the entire hierarchy appended their signatures to the preface, and the book appeared later that year, finely printed for Messrs Burns, Oates, and Washbourne at the Cambridge University Press.

In March 1943 Cardinal Hinsley died. Within six weeks of his funeral the hierarchy met under the chairmanship of the Archbishop of Liverpool, in Low Week, May 3rd–8th.

On May 22nd the Bishop of Leeds issued a letter *ad Clerum* stating: 'We have to inform you that the new Manual of Prayers has had to be withdrawn from publication and circulation on account of the number of errors found in the text.' On May 26th the Bishop of Nottingham followed suit. It was not until May 27th that any word was sent to Ronald. Dr King, the Bishop of Portsmouth, then wrote with warmth and courtesy:

> Dear Monsignore,
>
> I have just received an order from the Archbishop of Liverpool to send you extracts from the minutes of the Low Week meetings. This is my thankless job as secretary. May I say that I do it 'without prejudice'? I hope you will keep your sense of humour in spite of all.

The minutes of their meeting read:

> 13. The Archbishop of Birmingham unfolded the defects of the Manual of Prayers. Agreed to request the Archbishop to enquire of the publishers the size of the edition with a view of buying it in: and that a special small Committee, headed by Bishop Myers, should undertake the revision and preparation of an amended edition.

Delegation of any task to Bishop Myers notoriously meant its relegation to oblivion.

It was not until July 11th that Ronald's old friend Tommy Williams wrote:

> When I saw Mia Woodruff yesterday she told me you were much cut up about the Manual of Prayers – so I thought I'd write to you. I did intend to write to you before any official notice was issued, but Bishop King had sent you an extract from the minutes of the meeting before I had a chance of writing [as appears above, three weeks had passed] and Leeds issued a notice *ad clerum* to say the book was withdrawn before I had even settled with Burns and Oates. So, the blow having fallen, I thought I would leave things as they were for the time.

He then proceeds to itemize certain defects of editing, for which Ronald had no responsibility.

Ronald's answer, by return of post, reads:

> Thank you very much for your letter; it was very good of you indeed to send me such a full statement of the situation. If I may comment on it without offence, surely the objections you allege to the late Manual are of two wholly disparate kinds. (i) There are certain errors of inadvertency, errors about indulgences (you don't say how many) and the strange Latinity of p. 174. These aren't my fault, because I refused to touch the final revision of the indulgences, and there was no Latin rubric on p. 174 when I handed in my stuff to the Committee; I think I know the name of the Westminster priest who was responsible for these last touches. But I know that there are one or two slips in what I did; probably there are many more. (By the way, what makes you say the prayer for the King was 'omitted'? It was never in the old Manual, in spite of the *Daily Mail*.) But these things could all have been put right by a private interview with Braybrooke at Burns and Oates; there was no controversy over them; no need, therefore, for a new edition or for any public scandal.
>
> (ii) There are various changes deliberately introduced into the text of the Manual by way of making the English of it less hideous. These changes you all imposed on the clergy the other day, and now, when the clergy don't like them (any more than they like the new Hymnal), you explain that you were too busy to read them. (As for the bishop who is under the impression that his comments weren't attended to, I have the documents to show that the statement is untrue, but I can't do anything about it till he makes it in public.) Haven't you used the immediate necessity for making the corrections given under (i) as an opportunity for immediately satisfying the demands made under (ii)? Did you give the revised Manual a fair trial?
>
> I hope you will forgive me expressing so much in the way of comment; and I hope you will forgive me for expressing no more. My feeling about the whole thing is still so strong, that I should be afraid of seeming to write

without charity, or without due respect and it would be unpardonable in me to fail of charity or respect, in writing to one from whom I have received so much kindness in the past. I can only hope to forget about the whole thing as soon as possible.

He did not forget, but he kept silent. Lady Acton has no memory of his inviting her sympathy in his evident dejection or even of his mentioning the cause of it.

Too many pages, the reader may think, have been given to this dismal episode. It has been treated at length with deliberation for a number of reasons.

It affords a fine example of his scrupulous courtesy in dealing with opponents who were not especially graced by that quality.

It is an example of the official frustration of his talents. There were unique services which he might have done for the Church and was not allowed to do. His great influence on his contemporaries was largely, in the title of his second volume of Oxford conferences, a 'hidden stream'.

It illustrates the ethos of the Church in which he was working. In 1915–17 when he was canvassing the advice of his Anglican friends and relations about his change of obedience, they all warned him that whatever the historic grandeurs of the Church of Rome, he would find himself in twentieth-century England associating with men who were notoriously deficient in taste and manners. The humiliation of 1943 might be read as the price exacted by an ironic Providence for the well-bred fun of the Society of SS. Peter and Paul.

It should be noted that Ronald's opponents belonged to no specific party or tradition, as did the 'old Catholics' who troubled Newman. Archbishop Amigo was a Gibraltarian, educated at St Edmund's and at Cardinal Manning's short-lived seminary in Hammersmith. Dr McNulty of Nottingham was a Manchester-Irishman, a priest of late vocation who had spent some years in business before taking his theological course at Fribourg. Dr Poskitt was a Yorkshireman, a convert Anglican clergyman of only two years seniority in the Church to Ronald. They were a fair cross-section of the clergy of the time. None of them was a personal friend or enemy. The Archbishop of Birmingham was in a rather different position. He had ample knowledge of Ronald's character, his tenderness, diffidence, and scrupulous artistry. He was Ronald's Ordinary when the proofs were circulated; he had given his approval to them without any expression of doubt or any warning to Ronald; he had committed himself to imposing the book on his archdiocese. At the first grumbles he not only failed to support Ronald but took immediate advantage of the Cardinal's death to lead the attack. He delayed two months before sending a word to his friend and then, not on his own initiative, wrote a letter which reads, at the best, off-hand.

Ronald had struck on something quite outside his experience or comprehension. It confirmed him in his sense of singularity and in his inclination to hide himself the more securely in private life.

The Church has a faculty of retrieving her losses, often in unexpected ways. The new edition of the *Manual* appeared in 1953. Bishop (later Archbishop) Myers had no hand in its preparation. Ronald, without comment, substituted the new volume for his own in the chapel at Mells. All trace of his style had been obliterated, but the gross language of 1882 had gone with it. The revision had been more drastic than anything proposed by him. The prayers, many fewer in number, had been rewritten lucidly and with dignity. There is little in the new book to distress the convert of 1917; much to outrage the hierarchy of 1942. Though the letter of Ronald's work is lost, the spirit, its hidden stream, has achieved its cleansing purpose.

As soon as the last page of the New Testament had gone to the publishers, Ronald started on the Old. The history of this work may conveniently be summarized here. It was mostly done at Aldenham between 1942 and 1947 and finished at Mells in 1948. The preface is dated from St Jerome's day of that year. He expected it to take longer. In February 1944 he wrote to Mgr Barton: 'If I am given health and life I think I ought to be through by 1950. The Psalms took nine months, but Genesis only 3, and Isaiah, at my present rate of going will be hardly as much as 3.' There was no single committee responsible for its revision. Instead, sections of 200 pages each were sent for preliminary censorship to seminaries and religious houses, whose experts without remuneration for their labour issued certificates stating that in their opinion the passages they had studied were an adequate rendering of the Latin. It received the Westminster *imprimatur* in October 1948 and was published by Messrs Burns and Oates in two volumes 'for private use' in 1949.

The Old Testament was an altogether more formidable and, in general, more thankless, task than the New. As an eminent biblical scholar, not wholly sympathetic to Ronald's treatment, wrote to Cardinal Griffin:

> It is of course, a very heavy undertaking for one man, since even OT specialists do not usually claim to be specialists for more than a part of their

immense subject. So the excellent Protestant version (*The Bible, an American Translation*, University of Chicago Press, 1935) while allowing a single scholar to translate the NT, divided the OT among four. Neither Newman nor the new American Catholic Board ever considered entrusting the whole venture to one man.

Ronald worked with a freedom of spirit which has been thought audacious.

> Cut the Old Testament in half at the end of Esther [he wrote],[1] and you may say the first half is intelligible. . . . The second half contains Maccabees which is narrative again; contains the Psalms, Proverbs and Ecclesiasticus, in which you do not expect, from the nature of the case, a continuous argument. All the rest of Part 2, except Daniel and Jonas, is unintelligible unless you translate it, not verse by verse, but chapter by chapter. . . . The prophets, practically a quarter of the old Testament and yet, apart from Daniel and Jonas, hardly a chapter you can read with your feet on the fender.

And of the 'experts' he wrote:[2]

> The modern reader is at the mercy of a set of commentators, who take fantastic liberties with the text. They assume from the first that it has reached us in the form of a broken-up jigsaw, and proceed to reassemble it; they make up their minds from the first what the prophet's message is, and ring off, with dark allusions to the Maccabean period, when he starts talking about anything else. What they never seem to allow for is *defective* text; and yet in real life a copyist is far more likely to drop things out than to foist things in. . . . The word 'paraphrase' is a bogey of the half-educated. . . . It is a paraphrase when you translate 'Comment vous portez-vous?' by 'How are you?'.

For the rest of his life Ronald suffered extreme vexation from critics who attributed to him failure in a task he had from the first explicitly abjured. 'Why did you change such and such a rendering?' from the Douay or the Authorized version, was a question with which he had no patience. Butcher and Lang were not asked why they had 'changed' Chapman, nor were subsequent translators of the Odyssey challenged to justify divergences from Butcher and Lang. He had been commissioned to make his own new translation, and had done so without deference to his predecessors, whose reputation as stylists and scholars he held to be inordinate. The Authorized Version, he pointed out, was written in the

---

[1] *On Englishing the Bible*, p. 88.   [2] Ibid., p. 91.

language of a century earlier and had perpetuated Hebraisms which were alien to pure English. There were memorable passages whose rhythm, by constant repetition, had mesmerized English readers so that they failed to observe the many passages of gibberish – Amos iv. 2, 3 was a favourite example. The affection for the Douay–Challoner Bible, which was so strongly expressed by his opponents, he regarded as purely factitious.

> The clergy, no doubt, search the Scriptures more eagerly [he wrote],[1] and yet, when I used to go round preaching a good deal, and would ask the Parish Priest for a Bible to verify my text from, there was generally an ominous pause of twenty minutes or so before he returned, banging the leaves of the sacred volume and visibly blowing on the top.

As he had told Fr Martindale at the start, there were for him no 'consecrated phrases'.

But he was translating a translation; the Clementine rescript of St Jerome's Latin. That, whatever its deficiencies, was the official text. When he spoke of 'getting into the skin' of the author, he referred to St Jerome's. Not all the texts from which St Jerome worked are now extant; not all of them, presumably, had been transcribed free of error from the inspired originals. By going behind St Jerome to the available Hebrew and Greek texts and to the Masoretic commentaries, he was seeking to learn what precisely had been in St Jerome's mind when he framed his sentences. Having found that, he sought to put it into entirely lucid English. He was prepared when necessary to sacrifice elegance for lucidity, particularly in the order of words. An attractive rhythm and sonorous vocabulary may give a false meaning. He had always in mind the refectory readers whom he had so often heard falsify the sense of a passage by unintelligent emphasis. He contrived a version that could not be misread.

His Old Testament raised squabbles among professional exegetes, but in spite of its great feats of ingenuity and imagination, it has caused less stir in the general public, largely because it is so seldom read or heard by the Roman Catholic laity. A broadcast performance of the *Song of Songs* spoken, as he had written it, as a dramatic dialogue was the nearest any part of it has come to wide popularity. The publication, as has been seen, took place smoothly. The battle had been fought and hardly won over the New Testament, whose success silenced effective opposition. The current verdict of the general run of Mass-goers seems to be that the Epistles are at last intelligible. They were quite unintelligible before. The Gospels do

---

[1] Ibid., p. 17.

not appear to them greatly changed nor, where changes are apparent, do they seem improved. Most people, perhaps, do not resent or even detect a modicum of ambiguity in their spiritual reading.

Ronald answered his critics in a number of articles and addresses which he collected in *On Englishing the Bible*. It is not in the scope of this biography nor in the ability of its writer to examine the countless technical problems which Ronald sought to solve. He had a very good reason for everything he did. There are no errors of inadvertence. Every word and sentence was deliberated over the patience cards. He had an answer to every objection. But he grew very weary of the objectors.

> For some reason, when the authorized edition was at last produced, I fell to imagining that the voice of criticism would be silent. . . . I get much more angry with the people who like me and don't like my Bible, than with the people who like my Bible and don't like me. It is a humiliating reflection, that a careful perusal of the Holy Scriptures should engender (or perhaps reveal) in one's character this unreasonable streak of touchiness. I can only comfort myself with the thought that, among canonized Saints, none has been more frequently accused of touchiness than St Jerome.[1]
>
> If you translate, say, the *Summa* of St Thomas, you expect to be cross-examined by people who understand philosophy and by people who understand Latin; no one else. If you translate the Bible, you are liable to be cross-examined by anybody; because everybody thinks he knows already what the Bible means.[2]

To precise scholars like Mr Laurence Eyres, who figures as 'Glaucon', he delighted to justify himself, but the correspondence which ended only at his death, and came to him from all quarters, from cranks and prigs and bores, raising as though for the first time points which had been tediously debated, asking questions which were already answered in the footnotes, or in *On Englishing the Bible*; that made him shrink from the letters on his breakfast-table and provoked occasional asperities from his heroic courtesy.

Ronald finished the Apocalypse on September 30th 1942, a date deliberately chosen; St Jerome's day, the third anniversary of his setting down the first chapter of Genesis. Since that symbolic act of initiation he had worked solely on the New Testament. The long technical discussions carried on by letter with his committee, the patient consideration of all their criticism had been as great a part of his labour as the process of translation. There remained ahead of him more than two years of often

[1] Ibid., p. vi.   [2] Ibid., p. 66.

exasperating negotiations before the bishops could be persuaded to authorize his version for public use.

The immediate need was to give them a fair chance – and the clergy and the laity also – to form their opinions of the work. Extracts from the Epistles had appeared in *The Tablet* and excited anticipation. Mgr John Barton wrote in November 1942: 'It would be an advantage if the version could be given some sort of preliminary canter.' This coincided with Ronald's own intentions. From early in July he had been in correspondence with Mr Christopher Hollis of Burns, Oates and Washbourne, uging him to print an edition and issue it to private subscribers. Mr Hollis considered that a few hundred 'manifolded' copies would meet the demand; his firm would not risk the expense of setting up type without some assurance that the book would later be officially authorized and entrusted to them to publish. Ronald was sharper to appreciate the difference of impression which is made on the reader by a book properly printed and bound, as distinct from a sheaf of typescript carrying the air of a film scenario or an inordinately bulky departmental report. He proposed that the 'trial' edition should be made to pay for itself; a sale of 1,500 copies at ten shillings should cover expenses. Mr Hollis had no hope of selling half as many. Eventually it was decided to insert advertisements in the religious Press announcing an edition 'for private use'. No copies were to be issued to booksellers or anywhere exposed for sale. Those who wanted them must apply in writing. The Cardinal gave his sanction. After much discussion, the advertisements appeared in January 1943. The conditions were scrupulously observed. No attempt, other than the bare announcement, was made to promote the venture. Everyone – Ronald himself, his supporters and his opponents alike – were dumbfounded by the result. More than 9,500 individual applications were received.

The irksome conditions of war-time book production delayed publication (or, rather, the issue to subscribers) until April 1944. Ronald was momentarily exasperated, for he had been promised that it should appear before Christmas 1943. He was anxious that the hierarchy should have full opportunity to study the book and, more important (for none of the bishops at that time had any pretension to biblical scholarship; none had even taught Scripture in a seminary), to hear the opinions of the educated public before their Low Week meeting, when it was expected they would make their decision about authorization. When at the end of February he learned that sheets were only then going to be bound, he wrote:

That means the whole thing is absolutely ruined. . . . I could have given the thing to the Orphans' Press at Leominster and got it all through in three months. . . . You cannot expect the bishops to make up their minds in a fortnight whether they are going to like the thing or not. . . . I can't trust myself to write to – , for fear of laying myself open to a libel action. . . . The point was that a whole crowd of priests and laymen were to have the opportunity of seeing the stuff and discussing it and seeing what the public reaction was BEFORE the bishops met on April 17; and of course that is now out of the question. Nor can the bishops' decision be delayed, because we have fixed up with Sheed for the States [in order to preserve copyright there] and he must know where he stands before he publishes.

But the decision of the bishops was delayed. The renewal of bombardment on London postponed their meeting until autumn.

In 1944 the see of Westminster was filled by Archbishop (later Cardinal) Griffin, who continued his predecessor's policy of personal support of Ronald, though without his forthrightness in sending 'snorters' to his colleagues. On September 19th 1944, three weeks before the meeting, he wrote:

I find that there are some Bishops who would be opposed to having the Epistles and Gospels read in churches. I really think that your best way would be to bring out the work with an Imprimatur from me, which I should be delighted to give when it has been submitted to censorship, and then leave it to the different dioceses, through their Bishops, to allow the text to be used in the pulpit. It would be like a snowball, and I think when once it was passed round from one diocese to another, you would find that practically every diocese, with one or two exceptions, would adopt it as an official version.

Ronald replied in a letter which he preserved in its draft and its final form:

I wish, now, that I had never worried the unfortunate hierarchy about it [*Original draft*: 'I wish, now, that I had had nothing to do with the hierarchy']; it would have made everything very much simpler, and of course it would have been more satisfying to my vanity to let the translation succeed, if it is going to succeed, purely on its own merits and without any recommendation from authorities. As it is, I have said in the preface that this version is offered to the hierarchy for their acceptance, and if it is now published under my name with a Westminster imprimatur, there is no disguising the fact that the offer has been met with a refusal.

All this is ridiculously unimportant in itself [*Original draft*: 'For myself, I've had so much trouble with the thing first and last that I think I am past caring']; but ever since I was received, *twenty-seven years ago* tomorrow, I have been incurably propaganda-minded, and the question, 'What will the Protestants think of this?' has never been absent from my thoughts. It is obvious that the Newman centenary will be written up by the *Church Times* and all its unfallen sisters; and they will say what they have always said – That the Church of Rome does not want converts, finds them an embarrassment and does not know what to do with them. That Newman, like all converts after him, found himself entirely wasted as a Roman Catholic, whenever he tried to do anything, authority always let him go a little way with it and then crushed him. So it was over the Irish University scheme, so it was with the Oxford Oratory scheme, so it was, above all, with the projected new version of the Scriptures.

If, in the very year of the centenary, a new version of the Scriptures is offered by a convert to the Hierarchy, and the offer is turned down, you can hardly blame the *Church Times* if it draws the moral: 'There you are! What did we tell you?' It *will* draw that moral; it knows quite enough about Catholic procedure to know all about *imprimaturs*. A book which is prefaced by the assurance that George Smith sees nothing wrong with its faith or morals is not thereby identifiable as an authoritative book; rather the contrary. It is a private venture which authority finds no reason for suppressing. And I can see the *Church Times* writing, 'Father Knox should have known the Church of Rome better by now. He would have been wiser to stick to detective stories.'

I am not much happier about the effect on Catholics. It would be silly to pretend that there are not a great many Catholics who complain that the Hierarchy never gives them a lead. If, as you suggest, the book is published simply as my own production, and if, as you're kind enough to forecast, it manages to infiltrate until diocese after diocese adopts it for official use, won't it inevitably be said that the Bishops didn't like the book, but were forced to sanction it owing to the persistent demands of the laity? ('Is not a Patron, my Lord, one who looks with unconcern on a man struggling for life in the water, and when he has reached ground, encumbers him with help?') [*Original draft*: 'I could say much more about this, but I don't think I will.'] From this point of view, I would much rather that the Hierarchy would publicly express disapproval of my translation, than that they should be accused of waiting to see which way the cat jumps. [*Original draft*: 'I'm afraid I'm not being very helpful. But it doesn't seem to me that I could do any good by being more accommodating; the public effect would be no less disastrous. Isn't it possible, somehow, to find a formula? Yours v. sincerely.']

Please forgive all this, and believe that I'm only trying to put an objective view of what will be *said*. If, after all, you can't find a formula to avoid this, I shall never doubt, for a moment, your good will.

At the meeting in the second week of October the bishops decided to postpone their decision for three months, but they were more sympathetic than had been expected. Cardinal Griffin wrote on October 19th:

> There will be no difficulty whatever in your version being approved as an official version, provided that your committee sends in a favourable report.
>
> I do not think that having to put off the decision for three months will really affect the issue. If I could have the report by January 10th, I could then let the Bishops see a copy, and we can, I hope, proceed.

The report, of course, was satisfactory. As the result of suggestions made by readers of the 'trial' edition, some 500 minute changes were made. On January 10th 1945 the Cardinal issued a letter to the bishops, enclosing for their approval a foreword which contained the sentence: 'Not the least happy circumstance connected with the publication of this translation is that it has received the official recognition of the Hierarchy of England and Wales in the year when we are celebrating the centenary of the reception into the Church of . . . John Henry Newman.'

At long last, in October 1945, six years after it had been begun and three years after it had been finished, there appeared *The New Testament of Our Lord and Saviour Jesus Christ newly translated from the Vulgate Latin and authorized by the Archbishops and Bishops of England and Wales*, which has won the hearts and minds of a yearly increasing number of English-speaking Catholics far beyond the dominions of the English and Welsh hierarchy.

5

As peace approached the physical privations of civilians became more acute. Military success kept close company with political disaster. The schoolgirls, who brightened Ronald's brief periods of relaxation, had little conception of the strain and distress which beset him during their last year at Aldenham. His happiest sermons were preached to them in this unhappy time.

In 1943 Lord Acton went with his regiment to Italy. His sister, Princess Rospigliosi, came with her three children to live in the village. There was now a change from the nuns' cooking and a lively companion for Lady Acton, but her presence accentuated rather than mitigated Ronald's loneliness.

Peace in Europe and the Socialist regime in England brought him little comfort. The destruction of Hiroshima and Nagasaki appalled him. The event, which others were greeting with jubilation (one popular newspaper even adopted a new chronology and for a time dated its issues by 'Days of the Atomic Age'), constituted for Ronald a triple outrage on Faith, Hope, and Charity; on Faith in that the actual mechanics of the device, the discovery, as he phrased it, of 'an indeterminate element in the heart of things' seemed at first flush to cast a doubt on the hypothesis of causality and so on the five classical proofs of the existence of God; on Hope by 'the prospect of an age in which the possibilities of evil are increased by an increase in the possibilities of destruction'; on Charity by 'the news that men fighting for a good cause have taken, at one particular moment of decision, the easier, not the nobler path'. 'At the moment of victory a sign appeared in heaven; not the comforting Labarum of the Milvian Bridge, but the bright, evil cloud which hung over Hiroshima. In this sign we were to conquer.'[1]

He very rarely felt moved to make a public pronouncement on a general topic. He waited, but no guidance was given in the name of the Church. At last on August 14th he wrote to *The Times*:

> If no word is to be spoken from any authoritative quarter, may I be allowed to express the idea which is (I suppose) simmering in most people's minds? The idea, namely, that it would be a fine gesture if the Allied Powers, having shown what the new bomb can do, cease to use it? A self denying ordinance now would make a much deeper impression on the conscience of humanity than any amount of between-war resolutions.

He was on his way to post this letter when he heard the news of the Japanese surrender. He carried it back and kept it. Instead he wrote *God and the Atom*.

This essay, scarcely more than a pamphlet, of 143 pages, a masterpiece of construction and expression which gives no evidence of the speed with which it was written, fell quite flat. Consciences were dulled by war and minds agitated by the superficial problems of peace. It was a moral and philosophical tract offered to a public obsessed by practical politics. It appeared out of due time, nearly a year before the *New Yorker* startled America by devoting an entire issue to Mr John Hersey's gruesome report of the physical effects on Hiroshima; more than five years before the public to whom it was addressed, awoke to the fact they themselves were

---

[1] *God and the Atom* (1945).

threatened by the invention they had applauded; ten years before the publicists began to exploit the panic. Ronald had not sought to raise the alarm. He felt himself charged with an urgent message of consolation to a people who did not then know that they had been hurt. The failure of *God and the Atom* was added to Ronald's many other disappointments.

The Assumption nuns remained at Aldenham until Easter 1946. In September 1945 Lord Acton returned from the Army and took up quarters with Ronald in Bazley's cottage. Throughout that winter the little study remained the only sitting-room and Princess Rospigliosi's cottage the only resort. Ronald seldom went away; a week-end at Mells, after a week's retreat at Downside, was his only holiday from his work of translation. He gave longer hours to it, wrestling with a chapter a day, and sometimes more, of the intractable prophets. He cut down his smoking when the price of tobacco was raised, and at one time limited himself to twenty-five pipes a week.

Lord Acton, like many soldiers returning from the wars, had imagined greater opportunities in peace than the harsh times allowed. He had decided to give up the stock market and devote himself to agriculture. He began with enthusiasm. After Easter he and Ronald and the Rospigliosis moved into the house, but it was impossible to re-establish the broken contentment of the household; absurd servants came and went. There was abundant space, now, but little comfort, and the children of the family caused more disturbance than the school. 'They are such leavers of things about,' he wrote to Claudia Macaskie, 'that the house and even the garden are turning into a dump.' He was underfed, cold, hard-up, growing old and shabby, and apprehensive of the future; so that at moments he felt himself estranged from the young lives teeming round him; his natural ripe melancholy turned sour and he appeared sulky and querulous.

At this time he wrote an uncharacteristic letter to a young man who solicited the help of his 'influential friends' in getting a play produced:

Dear—,

I don't know you very well, and I don't know your friend at all. What the hell does he write plays for? Anyhow, I haven't any influential friends, and if I had I wouldn't risk the loss of their patronage by fussing them about plays.

Yours
R. A. Knox.

He never posted it, but he kept it. Why? To show posterity the kind of absurd distraction to which he was subject? To remind himself of his own lapse from charity? Who shall say?

In June another son, Robert, was born to Lady Acton. Summer on the farm was arduous and unprofitable. Lord Acton met official obstruction in every project of improvement. Finally, in February 1947 he decided to emigrate and impetuously bought a property, unseen, in Southern Rhodesia, and left in May to take possession. Lady Acton's father, Lord Rayleigh, bought the Aldenham property as an inheritance for a younger son. She was again pregnant (Jill, June 1947) and was to follow with the Rospigliosis, the pigs, and the family portraits as soon as she was fit to travel and a passage – no easy matter at that time – could be obtained.

Ronald in his sixtieth year had to find a new home. He had put himself outside the normal course of ecclesiastical appointments. His translation of the Old Testament was still unfinished. The dire prospect of a convent chaplaincy impended.

On March 30th he wrote to Mgr Vernon Johnson, who was retiring from the Oxford chaplaincy:

(i) Are you still in the position of the evil spirit seeking rest and finding none? Or have they found a convent for you?

(ii) The point is that I met a non-Catholic friend of Wall's the other day, who lives at Hare street; and he says that the Cardinal is *never* there.[1] Is this true, or is it notably exaggerated?

(iii) The other point is, that John and Daphne, with their family and the governess and (as Jeremias would say) all the carpenters and smiths in Israel are removing permanently to Southern Rhodesia, as from this autumn. Hence it is the Embankment for me, unless I can find a perch somewhere.

(iv) Do you think it conceivable that, if the facts are as represented, you and I could make a bid to rent Hare Street from the Cardinal and live there?

This is only exploring an avenue; other things might offer. E. G. Laura [Lady Lovat] might want to instal me in the house she and Hugh have taken in the Stone area (Hugh's constituency). Or Katharine [Mrs Asquith] might want me to come and live in a cottage at Mells and serve her chapel there. But I thought it would be a good thing to find out what your reactions are to this Hare Street idea, in case there should be anything in it. There are several crabs; the railway facilities, as you know, are vile; I don't know whether the housekeeper there would want permanent tenants, or whether she could be replaced; and so on. I dare say the house is much too

---

[1] R. H. Benson's house in Hertfordshire which he left to the archdiocese of Westminster.

big for two people to live in. But I'd like to know what you feel about it all, because I'm not clear that it is good for man to be alone, and if you aren't going to be alone there's something to be said for having known your house-mate for forty years rather than picking him up from an advertisement.

But this project was not pursued. Mrs Asquith, as soon as she heard of his predicament, invited him to Mells. At the beginning of May she visited Aldenham, and it was then decided that he should come to her in the autumn as a paying guest for six months' trial. He spent ten days there in June, when he first met and struck up an immediate friendship with Anne Palairet, who was engaged to Mrs Asquith's son, the Earl of Oxford and Asquith. On August 28th he preached their marriage sermon at Brompton Oratory[1] and returned to Aldenham to pack. On September 28th he wrote to Claudia Macaskie: 'It's rather beastly to feel that on Tuesday I shut up the chapel for (as far as I know) good and all.'

Three years before, it so happened, a novelist had asked his help in describing just such a scene, and he had then explained the procedure in a letter which began: 'If, which heaven forbid, I should ever have to close the chapel here, I suppose I should . . .' On September 30th he said his last Mass at the altar, removed the consecrated stone from its slot, and left the chapel, so full of memories, as empty as he had found it. Only the sepulchral monuments kept watch. The tabernacle from which he had given Lady Acton her first Communion nine and a half years ago, and the ambry from which he had taken the oil to anoint Claudia, stood open and bare.

He went straight into retreat at Downside, and from there moved to Mells on Saturday, October 4th, and began his life as chaplain on the twenty-seventh anniversary of his ordination as priest.

---

[1] *Bridgeroom and Bride* XXIV.

Chapter Five

HORTUS CONCLUSUS

Mells 1947–1957

Mells has often been mentioned in the foregoing pages. It is a small, ancient, irregular, rather extended, stone-built village once the property of the Abbots of Glastonbury, lying some 15 miles south of Bath, off the main roads and just clear of the coal-mining district of Radstock. Frome serves it as market town and railway-station. The estate, once much larger, has been held by the Horner family since the dissolution of the monasteries.

Ronald was moving into a close circle of old association and present friends. Downside Abbey, where Dom Hubert van Zeller, his confessor and confidant, is a monk, is seven miles distant. Less than three miles away stands Ammerdown, the seat of Lord Hylton, who is married to Mrs Asquith's younger daughter, who had played trains with him in the billiard-room at Beaufort. In the village lives Mr Christopher Hollis, then Member of Parliament for the adjoining constituency.

His ties with the Manor House extended back to Summer Fields. Mrs Asquith, as has been mentioned above, is the sister of his early friend, Edward Horner. Her unmarried daughter, Lady Helen, whom Ronald had received into the Church, and her son, Lord Oxford, who had been a lodger at the Old Palace (with his wife and later his children), inhabited the house intermittently during their leave from Government service, the one in Oxford, the other in Tripoli and Zanzibar.

The Manor House is in complete contrast to Aldenham; smaller, older, deeply sheltered behind high stone walls in the heart of the village; between the Rectory – an eighteenth-century mansion built by the Horners for their younger sons – and the fifteenth-century church where Patrick Shaw-Stewart had once read the lesson and Edward Horner's equestrian statue now stands among the tombs of his ancestors; whose splendid tower grows, as it seems, straight from the formal gardens and, rather too often for Ronald's comfort, fills them with the sound of its bells.

The hand of Art never laid a finger on Aldenham. Mells Manor (and indeed much of the village) is an achievement of individual taste. For thirty years, until her death in 1940, Mrs Asquith's mother, Lady Horner, never rested in her work of enrichment and embellishment.

Outside, when Ronald first came to live there, the War had left its mark of enforced neglect and misuse. The great north court was under plough, and the yew hedges, which had been rows of young plants on Ronald's first visit forty years before, were unkempt. Ronald lived to see them massive and neat as ashlar, the lawns resown and re-established.

Inside, wherever the eye moves it lights on something lovely. The residue of the notable William Graham[1] collection of Italian Masters hangs beside Rossettis and Burne-Joneses and panels of Lady Horner's needle-work. Two libraries divide the leather-bound volumes inherited from Mells Park and Lady Horner's own collection of all the chief publications of her lifetime, a great part of them the gift of their authors. Open Tudor fireplaces are discreetly reinforced by central-heating. Lady Horner was renowned for her hospitality, which was, at the same time, informal, illustrious, and affectionate, and its aura lingered into the straitened and hungry 'forties.

Mrs Asquith had added an oratory, a converted bothy, and hung over its altar one of her finest pictures, a crucifixion by Matteo di Giovanni. When Maurice Baring died she inherited the Stations of the Cross which Mrs Arthur Pollen had painted for his chapel at Rottingdean. Plain oak benches completed the furniture.

Ronald was given for his study the room rising three steps up from the dining-room, which Lady Horner had used as her own. It has mullioned windows on three sides, on the fourth an open stone fire-place. The wall-space is lined with bookshelves except where hang a quaint painted map of the Mendips and the veil of Mary Stuart. Here Ronald unpacked his books and settled down to finish the Old Testament. 'I don't know how I shall manage to work in a place where life goes on so dreamily,' he had written to Nicola Macaskie during his visit in June; and two months later:

> This place is being great fun but awfully demoralizing and rather bad for work compared with Aldenham. I think Somersetshire is partly responsible. I never want to do anything here but sit still and wait for the next time the church chimes will go off. Also there are no children in the house so that after meals one sits about and talks. . . . One curious effect of my present move is that for the first time in nearly forty years I am not living with

[1] Mrs Asquith's grandfather.

people noticeably younger than myself. In fact, believe it or not, I am *under* the average age at the Manor House.

And to Claudia Macaskie, in February 1948:

> I am leading a very quiet not to say hoggishly self-indulgent life. I am facing the prospect of being sixty on Tuesday with comparative equanimity, bred of the surroundings. Nanny (80) is at all meals and Aunt Muriel (96) is hard at work reading books of Tractarian devotion upstairs.

He might have added that no one knew the age of Mrs Gould, the cook, who first entered service at the Manor in 1908 and had won the esteem of an august procession of gourmets. Soon after Ronald's arrival she officially retired but lived on in the house and kept a benevolent eye on every process of the kitchen.

In April he wrote in the same vein of satisfaction:

> Here I go on with my ultra peaceful existence, and a fire at the Hollises constitutes a major excitement. It only burned out the nursery but I've been rushing round buying toys for Nigel Hollis (aged 4) so as to prevent his becoming a pyromaniac as the result of losing all his worldly possessions.

At that time food-parcels from the Dominions and the United States were a feature of English life. Those who had access neither to restaurants nor factory-canteens nor to the (largely illicit) produce of their own farms were scarcely better fed in the first years of peace than during the attempted German blockade. The Government of the time resented anomalous mitigations of their system of rationing and were only with difficulty persuaded by the donors that, by a vagary of the human heart, generosity cannot be regulated; an attempt to confiscate presents to individuals and distribute them to those officially recognized as needy had to be abandoned, and writers in particular benefited from the munificence of remote readers; Ronald among them. Parcels which had vanished almost unnoticed into the many ravening mouths of Aldenham became a considerable addition to the smaller table at Mells, and it was a keen satisfaction to him to be able sometimes to give, not always only to receive kindness.

> It looks as if the arrangement was going on [he wrote to Claudia Macaskie]. I'm frightfully comfortable here and on the other side my parcels come in useful for housekeeping – one arrived the other day from a total stranger in Australia who thought I was doing good work for the Church.

It was March 1948 before Lady Acton was able to get a passage to Africa for her party (now seventeen strong). She came twice to Mells before she left and found that Ronald had put on several pounds in weight and recovered much of his equanimity. In spite of his laments over his idleness he was working, and continued to work, assiduously.

His major task was still the Bible. When in 1948, as has been mentioned above, his translation of the Old Testament was given the Westminster *imprimatur* 'for private use' there were six years' work ahead of him. The committees of experts who were examining his text section by section, continued to send in recommendations until 1953; each had to be considered and discussed; some 1,500 were adopted. There were also independent and less responsible critics to be answered. *On Englishing the Bible* appeared in 1949, and deals mostly with the New Testament. Later critics, both public and private, encumbered his day's work. He undertook the drudgery of proof-reading; for the first time since he was an undergraduate he showed a concern for a book's appearance, and in 1954 gave detailed help to Mr Burns of Burns and Oates in the arrangement of the pages of the definitive edition.

This was published on November 14th 1955. A luncheon, at which Cardinal Griffin presided, was given by the publishers to more than 200 notables, clerical and lay, Roman Catholic and Anglican. In a speech of peculiar felicity Ronald distributed the largess of his courtesy broadcast. He said nothing of the opposition and neglect he had suffered; he specifically thanked all who had helped and encouraged him, from the learned exegetes to the proof-readers of the Cambridge University Press – 'You wouldn't have thought it possible for any human being to notice that you had spelt "ill-will" with a hyphen on page 249 when you spell it without a hyphen on page 868.' Finally, he said that his many anonymous assistants 'must not be taken to task, if they failed to correct the incorrigible'.

> For better or worse, there the thing is; the Knox version has a treatment of its own; if I may borrow a phrase from my laundress, it is past mending. Will it live? I can't guess. Already I am beginning to regard it with that somewhat distant affection which we authors bestow on the books that do not bring in royalties. Will it live to become dated? According to a reviewer in *The Times Literary Supplement*, a translation of the Bible gets dated in fifty years. Will somebody suggest, fifty years hence, 'It is time that the Knox Bible was revised, and brought up to date?' Then, oh, then, gentlemen, I have a charge to leave with you. If any such suggestion is made, then let the youngest person who is present today rise in his bath-chair and cry out,

'No! The whole point and protest of the Knox Bible was that it is a mistake, this continual revising and refurbishing of existing Scripture translations, this continual cutting down of father's pants to fit Willie. To revise the Knox Bible would be a treachery to the memory of its translator. If it is dated, then let it be scrapped; let somebody else sit down and undertake the whole task afresh, in a style of his own, and with a treatment of his own; let him give us, not a pale rehash of the Knox Bible, but a new Bible, and a better!'[1]

There was also his Commentary on the New Testament. This was finished in August 1955. It comprises a summary of all the processes of the translation and his meditations on the verbal meaning. It was published in three volumes, without the text, and in its present form makes rather forbidding matter for the general reader, to whom it is addressed as much as to the expert. It was Ronald's wish that text and commentary should be printed together, and doubtless in the fullness of time this will be done, when the light of his studies will show more vividly.

In 1949 he completed the work which had occupied him intermittently since 1918.

> There is a kind of book [he wrote in the dedicatory letter] about which you may say, almost without exaggeration, that it is the whole of a man's literary life, the unique child of his thought. Other writings he may have published. . . . It was all beside the mark. The Book was what mattered – he had lived with it all these years. . . . Did he find himself in a library, he made straight for the shelves which promised light on one cherished subject; did he hit upon a telling quotation, a just metaphor, an adroit phrase, it was treasured up, in miser's fashion, for the Book. . . .
>
> Such a thing, for better or worse, is this book which follows. . . . To be sure, when the plan of the Book was first conceived, all those years ago, it was to have been a broadside, a trumpet-blast, an end of controversy. It was to fill up the picture outlined in Bossuet's *Variations*, in Moehler's *Symbolik*; here, I would say, is what happens inevitably, if once the principle of Catholic unity is lost! All this confusion, this priggishness, this pedantry, this eccentricity and worse, follows directly from the rash step that takes you outside the fold of Peter! . . . But, somehow, in the writing, my whole treatment of the subject became different; the more you got to know the men, the more human did they become. . . . The result, I am afraid is a hotchpotch. . . . But I could not go on for ever revising my estimates. . . .
>
> It is not to be supposed that this haphazard process of composition will

---

[1] *The Tablet*, November 19th 1995, p. 502.

have justified my selection of material, or produced a literary unity; but how it endears the pages to their author!

It was published at the Clarendon Press in 1950 under the title *Enthusiasm: a chapter in the history of religion with a special reference to the XVII and XVIII centuries.*

Ronald was pleased to have the University imprint on his favourite book. It was received with suitable respect by all the respectable reviewers. He had forestalled criticism by his description of its origins. It enshrines much of his finest writing. On Jansenism, on Mme Guyon, on the convulsionaries of Saint-Médard, on John Wesley, he writes with a mastery which he never excelled. There are many long-sustained passages that are fit to stand beside the most illustrious prose in the language. But he himself called it a 'hotch-potch' and doubted whether it had literary unity. The revealing phrase in the foregoing quotation is, perhaps: 'I could not go on for ever revising my estimates.' The book had lost its impetus. The achievement must be made manifest. In the introduction to the seventeenth and eighteenth centuries he is in a world of dry theology; in the conclusion he is in a world that has been well travelled by psychologists and satirists – the world of wild aberration without theological significance. The heart of the book is in those centuries, in the heroic companionship of Bossuet and Fénelon and Pascal. His ever-growing charity tempered his judgement. He had to call a halt and deliver his accumulated studies as they stood, not imposing an argument but presenting a scene.

Enthusiasm was the most notable of many publications in this decade, most of which were compilations of earlier work. Sermons which had originally been preached for small fees or for nothing, found a large public when printed and bound. In 1948 *The Mass in Slow Motion* appeared; in 1948, *The Creed in Slow Motion, On Englishing the Bible,* and a limited *edition de luxe* by the Dropmore Press of his *Occasional Sermons.* In 1950, *St Paul's Gospel,* a collection of Lenten conferences; in 1951, *Stimuli,* a selection of his monthly contributions to the *Sunday Times;* in 1952, *The Hidden Stream,* a second volume of Oxford conferences; in 1953, *Off the Record,* comprising letters of general interest addressed from time to time to individual inquirers; in 1955, *A Retreat for Lay People;* in 1956, *The Window in the Wall,* a collection of his Corpus Christi sermons at Maiden Lane; in 1957, *Bridegroom and Bride,* wedding addresses.

As paper restrictions became less severe, his earlier books were reissued and found new readers. The New World became interested in him. In 1949 he was called to the telephone by an American priest who wished to

import him to New York for a single sermon. Popular American magazines began to send him long cables soliciting his opinions; they sent
photographers to Mells to prepare a composite portrait; they offered him
very generous terms for contributions which they never printed. His fame
grew and his finances became easier.

It is not quite correct to say, as has been said above, that he was ever
'hard up'. He was never in debt or overdrawn at his bank. He never
dissipated his capital. With him money was a matter of mood. If his
current balance fell below £1,000 he felt poor; when it rose above that
figure he felt indecently rich. At Aldenham his income and his expenses
had both been negligible. By 1950 he was feeling the weight of taxation.
He never ceased to give and, with returning prosperity, he gave more
abundantly. Often he told needy acquaintances that he knew of a public
fund which would relieve them, and then entered into a private arrangement with the treasurer so that he could supply them from his own pocket
without their knowledge. When his stepmother died and his patrimony
was slightly augmented, he at once increased a stipend he had been
secretly paying through the Converts' Aid Society. He was not called to
heroic poverty, but his extravagances were always designed to give
pleasure to others – pleasures he shared, but never indulged alone.

Certain public honours came to Ronald in these years. In 1951 he was
appointed Protonotary Apostolic *ad instar*, a grade in the papal service
defined in the *Catholic Encyclopaedia* as enjoying 'the same external insignia
as the real protonotaries'. This elevation meant little to the majority of his
fellow countrymen. He used to say that it entitled him to wear a mitre
once a year, but he never availed himself of this privilege. The polysyllables
of his new title quickened his old appetite for parody, and in reply to
some verses of congratulation from Cyril Alington he wrote the imitation
of Gilbert's 'Modern Major General', which is printed in Mr Eyres's
compilation *In Three Tongues*.

It has been suggested that his name had been put forward for a higher
honour and that, in a society of very old men, he was regarded as being
still young in his career. It was still fresh in Vatican memories that Cardinal
Gasquet had been given his red hat in the mistaken belief that he was a
historian of impeccable accuracy. Perhaps they were in consequence a
little sceptical of English scholarship and did not want to give too
resounding a welcome too early.

All this is conjecture. It is certain that Ronald could not have borne the
cares of a diocese and would not have liked to live half his year in Rome.

He had been a great pot-hunter in youth. All ambition of that kind was behind him. But he was not insensible to gratitude. It is possible that he might have liked some formal recognition of the work he had done. Neither his appointment as Protonotary nor his election five years later to the Pontifical Academy[1] expressed quite the full-hearted appreciation which his friends would have wished for him.

In July 1954 he went to Dublin to receive an honorary D.Litt. from Mr de Valera, the Chancellor of the National University of Ireland.

Honours of a more private character which particularly gratified him were his election in 1949 to the 'Old Brotherhood of the English Secular Clergy' and the invitation, which he received in the autumn of 1956, to deliver the Romanes Lecture for the coming year.

The Old Brotherhood has its roots deep in penal times. It was founded in 1623 as the Old English Chapter, to take over the government of the Church in England from the Arch-priests who had succeeded Cardinal Allen in 1594. Episcopal jurisdiction was in their hands in the absence of a bishop. From 1631 to 1655 the only English bishop lived in France, and after his death the Chapter corresponded directly with Rome for thirty years, pleading for the appointment of an Ordinary rather than a Vicar-Apostolic. With the re-establishment of the hierarchy the body gave up all claims to jurisdiction, and in 1862 took its present name. There are twenty-four members, all secular priests, who resign when raised to the hierarchy. They administer certain trusts and meet together at dinner-parties which are called 'Consults'. They preserve the strict tradition of the pre-emancipation clergy, and Ronald rightly regarded his co-option to them as the full recognition of his status. He was no longer, as far as his English brethren were concerned, a convert on trial, but one of themselves.

The Romanes Lecture is not of great antiquity. It was founded by a scientist, G. J. Romanes, a Cambridge man of Canadian origin, who moved to Oxford in 1890 and left £1,000 to the University for the endowment of an annual lecture. There are many such benefactions, but in the inexplicable process by which certain prizes and appointments irrespective of their monetary value achieve a prestige denied to others, the Romanes Lecture has maintained a peculiar lustre even beyond the limits of the University. The appointment is made by the Vice-Chancellor; the terms of reference are wide, Science, Art, and Literature being equally

---

[1] A body recently revived, ten of whose forty members are nominated from countries outside Italy.

eligible in subject. Gladstone gave the first in 1892. He has been followed by Bryce, Curzon, Balfour, Theodore Roosevelt, J. J. Thomson, Asquith, G. M. Trevelyan, Sir Winston Churchill, Gilbert Murray, John Galsworthy, and a succession of scholars eminent in their special subjects, though less known to the general public.

2

Ronald's routine at Mells varied little. He was never called in the morning, and his Mass at eight o'clock came at the end of morning prayers, whose duration only he knew. After a long thanksgiving he returned to the house for breakfast, at which he left newspapers and letters untouched. He then retired to his study, where, unless there were guests to entertain, he spent his day. After luncheon he read *The Times* and answered his correspondence. He said his office and, rather rarely, read a new book. *The Tablet* and the *Clergy Review* were the only periodicals he studied regularly. Every afternoon he made the short walk to the village shop to post his letters and, when it was needed, buy tobacco. He worked again after tea. He never attempted at Mells the outdoor tasks he had performed at Beaufort, Keir, and Aldenham. Sometimes he walked up the village to visit the Hollises, but he preferred to be driven.

The evening was always devoted to recreation. There was often reading aloud. He devised a way of doing the crossword which some of his friends found too laborious. He allowed himself to read only the horizontal clues. When these were complete he filled in the perpendiculars by guesswork, and only then verified them from their clues. Every Christmas he composed a crossword which he copied out, not always quite accurately, and sent to his friends; they were expected to send him the solutions and held in disgrace if they neglected this duty. In Lent he denied himself the crossword entirely. In the last years of his life the American game 'Scrabble' greatly took his fancy. He made a copy in cardboard and paper of the first set which he saw. It was a mitigation for his friends when he acquired a real set, but the intensity with which he played and the solemn silence he demanded were especially trying to visitors who came to Mells in the hope of enjoying their host's and hostess's conversation.

He developed, without the discouragement they had sometimes met at Aldenham, a number of amiable crotchets. Once in his absence Mrs Asquith, finding herself without stamps, took some from the sheet on his table. Later he said: 'Of course, Katherine, I am delighted you should do so, but will you, please, in future, tear them horizontally *not* perpendicularly?'

He made few new friends; the chief of them were the poet, Mr Siegfried Sassoon, who lived not far away in Wiltshire and who, partly by Ronald's influence, was received into the Church, and Mr Cavendish, the rector of Mells, who came to the Manor every Sunday evening. Ronald held him in great esteem and affection, totally unembarrassed by their differences of religion. The novelist, Anthony Powell, whose books, Ronald used to complain, were 'too difficult' for him, came to live in the neighbourhood, and Ronald spent some happy hours bottling wine with him.

Ronald had been starved of company during the War. He had left Oxford believing that he needed solitude. That phase was over and his old sociability returned; he enjoyed the comings and goings at Mells. He even insisted on giving two or three cocktail-parties to the neighbours, a thing that had never been known before at the Manor House.

In London, in 1953, after preaching one of his noblest panegyrics at Belloc's Requiem Mass, he was carried off by a friend, unprotesting, to luncheon at Mrs Ian Fleming's, a lively modern hostess unknown to him. There he met Mrs Rodd (Nancy Mitford), Mr Cecil Beaton, Mr Osbert Lancaster, and a number of sharp-witted, middle-aged strangers quite unconnected with the ceremonies at which he had been assisting. He wrote later:

> I loved my luncheon party and very nearly wrote to say so only I couldn't remember the address. If it hadn't broken up I'd have found myself asking Cecil Beaton to do a passport photograph of me. It's very sad, considering my years and profession, but I still find it fun meeting the young and gay, even though I know I'm talking boringly to them.

He was not happy alone and, when Mrs Asquith went away, he made a round of visits to a few familiar houses. He particularly delighted in the young children (and grandchildren) of his friends. He kept up and enlarged his circuit of sermons and retreats and latterly allowed himself the indulgence of travelling in the first class. Wherever he went he left kind memories. At Dursley in Gloucestershire his Mass was served by an old schoolmaster who was on the point of superannuation. Ronald secured for him a permanent post in the sacristy at Westminster Cathedral.

In August 1953 he went abroad for the first time since the Hellenic cruise of 1937. Mrs Asquith and Lady Helen drove him to Germany to visit a former lodger[1] at the Old Palace, and his wife, who were quartered near Bonn. They spent a night at Bruges, but Ronald showed no desire to review the scenes which had once so fascinated him, and was impatient to get to their destination. Once settled with their hosts, he enjoyed a week of expeditions and entertainment but refused to go on with the Asquiths to Porto Fino, and returned directly and alone.

Early in 1954 he set out on what was, to him, a high adventure: a journey to visit the Oxfords in Zanzibar and the Actons in Rhodesia. He left on February 4th and returned on March 28th. Mrs Asquith accompanied him on the first part of the journey. Wherever he stopped old friends and acquaintances turned out to greet him and smooth his way. He moved entirely among Europeans of the sort he was used to. It was a series of neighbourly calls, rather than a voyage of discovery, and the diary he kept shows little curiosity about the exotic.

He noticed what has long been notorious, that aeroplanes are very much less comfortable than trains, that their portholes provide few spectacles of interest, that the booking of a seat does not guarantee a passage, that the formalities at airports are irksome, that the impersonal solicitude of their staff is not particularly endearing. 'People kept coming round and offering you cups of coffee or the last number of *Picture Post*. I had a copy of the Father Brown Omnibus with me, but a Dutch neighbour started reading this under the impression that it was laid on like everything else, so I let him have it.' When he was met at Nairobi by Sir Evelyn Baring's A.D.C. he noted: 'Hitherto you felt everybody had been nice because he was paid to be nice; with Mr Shelley you felt he was being nice because it was his nature to.'

He and Mrs Asquith spent two nights at Government House and then flew on to Zanzibar. It came as a surprise to him to find that sunny days on the equator are not, by analogy with the Highlands, inordinately long. 'Zanzibar midsummer,' he naïvely notes, 'is not like that at all.'

He said Mass in the Cathedral and gave Communion to many native women from the mainland whose lips were marked by tribal, pagan scars and silver studs, 'a touching reminder that they were your fellow converts'.

He spent a very hot but very happy week at Zanzibar bathing and sailing and being entertained, endearing himself to the Asquith children. Zanzibar has been known to evoke images of the Arabian Nights in the minds of romantic tourists; not in Ronald's.

---

[1] The Hon. Miles Fitzalan Howard, eldest son of Lord Howard of Glossop.

I don't know how it is with other people of a certain age; but for myself I find the longer one lives the more one's pleasures are conditioned by memory. Even your new friends, if you look into the matter closely, often appeal to you because they remind you of old friends. And I knew when I set out on my travels, that I was too old to get a kick out of 'going places'. Vistas of coconut-palms, with their slim trunks and mop-like heads, silhouetted against the colours of dawn and sunset in a perfect sky – how can they not be beautiful? But they only remind me of missionary magazines.

He gratefully received *The Times* and daily solved the crossword puzzle.

On his way to Rhodesia he stopped at Dar-es-Salaam with an old friend from the chaplaincy, Mr Robert Risley; found next day that the place booked for him on the aeroplane to Salisbury was not available and returned to keep his birthday in Zanzibar. 'My ignominious return was soothed by a more than patient reception.' He was there for another six days, and his restless industry asserted itself. On February 19th, in the great heat and in the intervals of a full day of picnic and entertainment, he translated the first chapter of *The Imitation of Christ*.

On February 23rd he at last reached Salisbury and drove out in the darkness the forty miles to the Actons' farm, M'Bebi, near Mazoe. The house 'has no front door exactly, but Daphne was waiting for me on the stoep, with nothing about her (except her attendant children) to suggest that time had moved since 1947'. She found him, then and throughout his stay, a much happier man than she had left. His plans had been dislocated by the air-service; the booking for his return was uncertain; but he, who seven years before was abnormally dejected at missing a railway connexion and losing half an hour on a short journey across the Midlands, now calmly accepted delays of a week and divagations of hundreds of miles. This was one of many signs of a new serenity he evinced, as though Mells had permeated him with its own tranquillity.

The two elder Acton boys were at school. Seven other children were at home. Pelline had lately married a Hungarian tobacco-planter and lived a long drive away. Lord Acton was there to greet him, but during Ronald's visit they saw little of one another except at week-ends. He came home to dine and sleep, but during the hours of daylight his commercial, agricultural, and sporting interests kept him fully employed.

On his first evening Ronald went early to bed with the sound of rain drumming on the iron roof (for the seasons had not kept to the calendar that year), and it was not until after Mass next morning, which he said in the drawing-room for the Acton family against 'a background of some twenty boys from the school, nearly all pagans, but apparently dead keen on hearing Mass', that he began to notice his surroundings.

> The smell of pigs brings back Aldenham. I can't as yet distinguish the crops from the meadows, because nature here has no sense of restraint, and all the grasses and weeds grow breast-high. On all sides the prospect is bounded by hills no great distance off, with the height of minor Welsh or Scottish hills, like the best of the Quantocks.

The house is a long, one-storied building standing on a slope. A wing has since been added which is, supposedly, banned to children. When Ronald stayed, the wide stoep which serves as day-nursery and recreation-ground enclosed the living-rooms and bedrooms ineluctably.

He spent a month at M'Bebi in great contentment and spoke of retiring there finally when his work in England was done. There was a full round of hospitality – official, ecclesiastical, social (Rhodesia, he remarked, seemed to be peopled entirely with Shropshire county families and Central European refugees), and domestic. He was prevailed on to preach at the Cathedral and to address St George's College and a Catholic luncheon club in Salisbury, but most of his days were spent at M'Bebi, back once more in the old, happy friendship of 1938.

> There is not a great deal of sitting about [he wrote in his diary], because Daphne really works a 24 hour day; not only attending all the time to a rather obstreperous family, teaching them lessons, calming their tantrums, saying prayers with them and dosing them, but answering the telephone – which is in the middle of the house and disastrously audible from most corners of it [he might have added: it is served by a party-line] – dishing out medicine and plasters to native boys and even going out by lantern light to attend the *accouchement* of a cow.

On March 1st after dinner –

> John [Lord Acton] produced a talkie – he does at intervals – for the benefit of the household and the compound. My principle of always letting people be kind to you involved me in breaking a third negative record; I have not only left Europe and flown, but been present at a talkie. The illusion was greater than I expected but I was too stupid to understand the story properly. Subsequent conversation made it all clearer to me; the younger Actons can have understood little of it and the natives nothing whatever.

He saw, altogether, three films at M'Bebi and wept at one – *The Song of Bernadette* – but the habit did not take him and later, in Gloucestershire, being cajoled to *Julius Caesar*, he remarked that it was less effective than Shakespeare readings at Eton. *The Rhodesian Herald* had a headline about Famous Scholar seeing First Talkie.

Between visits and engagements he kept his regular stint on *The Imitation*, working in his bedroom until summoned by Jill: 'Ronnee! Drinks!'

He returned to Zanzibar for a week and then flew back to England, noting:

> The things that make you glad to be going home (i) The sight of the Nile and the reflection that this belongs to the history of the world, whereas everything else you have seen in Africa dates from Livingstone. (ii) The conversation of waiters in Rome; speech of which you can catch the inflections, and understand a few fragments. (iii) Getting into a *train* at Paddington; catching it at the last moment, while the guard keeps his flag unwaved, because the porter has not yet appeared with the luggage.
>
> The twins saw me off by the 3.30 train, on which I was overcome by such profound sleep that I did not notice when the carriage was slipped. At Mells all the daffodils were out on the front drive.

3

In the knowledge that they were to be his last, these ten happy years at Mells may be seen now in an autumnal light, as the season of garnering the fruits of what has here been called his 'second spring'. It was not thus that Ronald regarded them. He had seen his father in full vigour at eighty, and he seems never to have doubted, until a few weeks of his death, that he owed multitudinous and heavy duties. There was his translation of *The Imitation*; a series of meditations on the words of our Lord; an autobiography; but more than anything his mind was occupied with a work of apologetics.

His *Belief of Catholics*, which has run into many editions, was originally written (in 1927) for a series[1] in which the exponents of various prevalent creeds and doubts concisely defined their opinions. It was perfectly adapted to its function, and has served as the text-book for countless catechumens, but it may be doubted if it has often been read by those whose curiosity was not previously aroused. Ronald had long pondered something more

---

[1] *What I Believe*, edited by Ernest Benn.

ambitious and often mentioned it as one of the tasks which awaited his completion of the Bible.

The answers to the problems of the age provided by the professors at the seminaries, seemed to him to display a glibness which commanded only half-hearted assent.

On January 1st 1956 he began work, knowing what he wanted to do but uncertain of the way of doing it. On February 1st when the season of self-distrust was on him, he wrote to Lady Acton:

> It's only got one chapter finished at present and quite a short one. I am so worried at my incompetence about apologetics that I'm putting it all in the form 'Why can't somebody write a really good book about apologetics? I mean, this *sort* of thing – ' all through.

Or, as he wrote in his opening chapter:

> What I am concerned with is our apologetics, and that great work of apologetic, some day to be written, which shall suggest to the reader that in approaching Christian theology he is approaching something that is alive, not a series of diagrams. The hardest part of the author's task, as I see it, will be to introduce some human element into natural theology; to prove that God is, and what God is, not merely with the effect of intellectual satisfaction, but with a glow of assent that springs from the whole being; 'did not our hearts burn within us when he talked to us by the way?' But his task will not end here. He will vindicate the prophecies, not by raking up a score of familiar quotations, but by exhibiting the Old Testament *in extenso* as a cipher message imposed on history. He will prove the divineness of our Lord's mission, not by presenting us with a series of logical dilemmas, but by trying to reconstruct the picture of our Lord Himself, what it was that met the gaze of the Apostles, and the touch of their hands. He will read the New Testament, not as a set of 'passages' which must somehow be reconciled with one another, but as the breathless confidences of living men, reacting to human situations, and inflamed with zeal for their Master. He will portray the teaching Church, not as a harassed official 'handing out' information at a series of Press-conferences, but as a patient pioneer washing out the gold from the turbid stream of her own memories. Everything will come alive at his touch; he will not merely know what he is talking about, but feel what he is talking about.
>
> *Exoriare aliquis!*

In June he was hesitating between two forms, those of plain disquisition and of dialogue. As has been said above, he had always been fascinated by Mallock's *New Republic*. He appreciated that in 1956 it was impossible to maintain the fiction of a party in a country-house as the setting for debate;

modern pundits did not squander their talents in private conversation; they gathered round the microphone. Accordingly, he attempted to recast his second chapter in the form of a professional 'brains-trust' with a 'question-master' in the place of the host. In July he wrote that he was 'stuck'; he showed the two versions to various friends, including Mr Frank Sheed, Dom Sebastian Moore of Downside, and Mr Siegfried Sassoon, whose opinions seem to have favoured the direct method of exposition. While he was still undecided, he was deflected to a new task.[1]

No religious book of the last hundred years has had so great an influence as *The Story of a Soul*, first printed in 1898. It was believed that this was the full autobiography of St Thérèse of the Child Jesus, as she had written it and left it to her Superior. In fact, it was an abridgement and compilation from three distinct documents. Mother Agnes, the saint's sister, was their editor and custodian. She died in July 1951, and in September 1952 permission was given in Rome for the publication of the complete text. A facsimile edition of the manuscripts was made by Fr François de Sainte Marie, O.C.D. It was a work of the highest importance, and in 1954 Ronald promised to make the English translation. He had not, as had his friend Mgr Vernon Johnson, any particular devotion to the saint. He undertook the work because it was the wish of the Carmel of Lisieux and because he felt confident that he could avoid the infelicities which the saint's language sometimes invites. 'I have a superstition,' he wrote to Lady Acton on December 14th 1956, 'that she [St Thérèse] was asked in Heaven whom she'd like as her translator, and replied "Ronald Knox – he'll mind my style so terribly, and the great thing is always to do something you don't like."'

The photostats of the manuscripts reached him in September 1956. He had them copied by his friend, Miss Antoinette Lambert, and worked from her transcription. He regarded it as an interruption of his major writing, but it proved to be his last completed work.

In the winter of 1956 visitors to Mells were alarmed at a deterioration in his health that was more apparent to them than to those who lived with him, or to himself. He complained only of indigestion and the general enervation which the winter brought. Various medicines and changes of diet were tried without result. Early in January 1957 an X-ray examination revealed an obstruction of the colon. His doctor in Frome suspected cancer, but of an operable kind from which the sufferer often

---

[1] The preliminary chapter and the alternative versions were published in *The Month* in March, April, and May 1959.

rallies for a long period of comfort and activity. The disease was not named to Ronald, and on January 20th he went into a London hospital for the operation. The immediate cause of his trouble was successfully removed, but the surgeon then found a malignant and inoperable growth in the liver. Ronald was not informed of this discovery. He returned to Mells on February 7th hoping soon to resume his writing and, more important, his office as a priest.

On February 18th he wrote to Dom Hubert van Zeller thanking him for the dedication of a book: 'I am still so weak that I can only read with languid attention; and I want to keep this book until I am physically convalescent, and can hope to become morally convalescent from all the selfishness, querulousness and general unsupernaturalness which hospital life breeds.'

At the beginning of March Mrs Asquith had herself to go into hospital for treatment for arthritis. Ronald was a little stronger, but he was not making ground as he expected. Thinking that the soft air of Mells might be responsible for his lassitude and despondence, he decided to try the seaside and went to Torquay accompanied by two friends, a husband and wife. It was his last, most cruel March. He had lost all appetite for food, wine, and tobacco; it rained almost continuously; the large, expensive hotel was uncongenial and so placed that it was impossible to walk out without encountering steps and steep hills. He drooped miserably over the table in the garish dining-room, forcing himself to eat with evident revulsion. On some afternoons he took short motor-drives, and once showed fleeting pleasure in a neighbouring cave full of stalactites which had for him the extraneous interest of having been first explored by a priest. He was notably slower in speech and thought. He could not write, and read only with an effort of concentration. After a week he and one of these friends moved to an hotel at Sidmouth, where he was slightly happier. The parish priest was a fellow-member of the Old Brotherhood. He visited some of the churches of the district and laboriously made a few notes for his Romanes Lecture, but he was baffled by the realization that he was not mending. He believed that through lack of will he was falling into the habits of an invalid and that he should be able by effort to achieve his normal activities. The excruciating deprivation was his inability to say Mass, which, whatever his other occupations, had always been the vitalizing force of his day. After a week he moved to the house of the same friends near Taunton, but here he was too far from a church even to hear Mass, and he went at week-ends to Lady Eldon at Rackenford. During two weeks near Taunton he wrote most of his Romanes Lecture,

On English Translation.[1] It was an extraordinary feat of will. He was oppressed with lassitude and nausea. He had only his host's modest library to draw on. But the paper is as sharp and sparkling as any written in his youth.

Early in April he rejoined Mrs Asquith at Mells. Here he concentrated on the attempt to regain the altar. On Holy Saturday, April 20th, he performed a full rehearsal, and on Easter Day said Mass without failure. For a month he said Mass every other day, then on Sundays only. Each morning found him weaker. At length on June 9th, with Dom Aelred Watkin of Downside standing by, he said his last Mass.

From the middle of April it was clear to all about him that he was suffering, not from the effects of the operation, but from a graver illness. The unmistakable marks of jaundice suggested disease of the liver. On May 16th his sister, Lady Peck, came to visit him. Medical etiquette required that she, as the nearest accessible relative, should be officially informed of what all suspected. At the end of the month Ronald himself, the last of those concerned, was told he was fatally ill. Sceptical as always of the pronouncements of science, he asked for a second opinion, and an appointment was made for him to see Sir Horace (now Lord) Evans in London.

The date fixed for the Romanes Lecture was June 11th. By the end of May Ronald was so weak that those round him doubted whether he would be able to deliver it. His colour was ghastly, and his speech slow and broken by pauses. Dom Hubert van Zeller, visiting him from Downside, saw that he could not make the journey alone, and obtained the Abbot's leave to go with him. He was a little surprised by the readiness with which Ronald accepted the offer of companionship. They drove to Oxford in the morning, Ronald scarcely speaking during the two hours' journey. Both stayed with the Vice-Chancellor, Mr J. C. Masterman, at Worcester: Ronald rested in the afternoon and was taken early to the Sheldonian, so that he was in his place before the audience arrived, and thus escaped the fatigue of the usual ceremonious entry. He had been given a drug to stimulate him, and without his knowledge a doctor was posted near the rostrum; also a reader who would take over his manuscript if he were unable to continue. The theatre was crowded. Many of his audience knew he was dying and that this was to be his last performance in the University he had regaled for just fifty years.

[1] R. A. Knox, *Literary Distractions* (1958), pp. 36–58.

I was in a fever of anxiety [Dom Hubert writes] as to how it would all go off. But I need not have worried. From the opening sentences the lecture seemed to give R. strength, and more strength came to him from the people who were listening. At times one almost forgot he was ill at all: voice, gestures, mannerisms – everything as usual. He spoke, sitting down and reading it, of course, for what must have been more than an hour.

When, half-way through, to illustrate a point, he recited in full Cory's familiar rendering of the Greek epigram, 'They told me, Heraclitus, they told me you were dead', most of those present recognized the words as his own farewell to Oxford, and some with whom of old he had 'tired the sun with talking', did not restrain their tears.

The applause at the end was terrific [Dom Hubert continues]. He was less tired than was to be expected, sitting up till eleven while friends from various colleges – dons, mostly from Trinity – talked with him while he sipped fruit juice. J. C. Masterman could not have been a better host and I think Ronnie was as happy as I have ever seen him. But it must have been a strain because when I called him in the morning he looked desperately ill.

Mr Harold Macmillan, a friend of long standing, had invited him to stay at 10 Downing Street and see Sir Horace Evans there. Dom Hubert took him by train to London and left him with his host. Sir Horace came that afternoon, confirmed that he had cancer of the liver and could not live long.

Ronald's primary question was: how long? How much work could he hope to finish? At first glimpse death appeared neither as an awful summons to judgment nor as a recall from exile, but as the final disruption and frustration of plans.

Next morning they were trooping the colour on Horse Guards Parade, and only the Prime Minister's car could make a way through the traffic. Mr Macmillan came with him to Paddington and satisfied himself that Dom Hubert had the carriage reserved. 'We got back to Mells,' Dom Hubert continues, 'in time for luncheon. He was exhausted but also in a curious way elated. He was glad to know that he had pulled it off. At lunch he told us more of what the specialist had said and how kind the Macmillans had been over everything.'

Almost immediately afterwards Sir Horace Evans was raised to the peerage. Ronald wrote to congratulate him, at the same time as thanking him for his attention. One of them, he remarked, had left Downing Street with a patent of nobility in his pocket; the other with a death warrant.

★

Eighteen years before he had written to Lady Acton: 'I always pray for a prepared death because that seems the Christian thing to do, but really if I died unexpectedly in my sleep just after making a general confession in retreat, I believe it's what I'd like.'

Now he wrote to tell her how he was ordained to die. Characteristically he gave the news as something of secondary interest. The first half of the letter, written immediately on his return to Mells, deals with the entrance of her eldest son to Oxford. At the party at Worcester after his lecture he had consulted the President of Trinity; he encourages her hopes of her boy's admission and tells her what should be done to make formal application. Then he says:

> Sir Horace Evans confirms the diagnosis of cancer of the liver and says nothing can be done about it. I asked him whether he thought I was likely to live a matter of weeks or a matter of months and he said months – it would be worth trying to finish off one of the books I've started on (Ste Thérèse, thank God, is finished). K [Mrs Asquith] is very keen that I should go on living here, and I suppose I shall, though I feel increasingly an incubus. It doesn't look as if we are likely to meet again in this world, but partings are unsatisfactory things and perhaps best done without. Please ask our Lord to let me have the gift of *perseverance*.

He then gives directions for the disposal of some investments he held in Rhodesia and expresses the wish to contribute to the church which the Actons were building at M'Bebi, and ends: 'Don't worry about me because I'm not getting much fun out of things at present with perpetual discomfort (though no pain). I just seem to drift. God bless you, Daphne, always.'

In all the letters he wrote to priests, and many to lay people, he asked them to pray for his perseverance. To Mgr Vernon Johnson he added: 'I gather this kind of cancer doesn't mean suffering in any acute form – I expect I'm not worthy of it.'

There is no scale for measuring pain. During his last weeks Ronald had to battle against temptations to *accidia* which may have been as grievous as any physical suffering the disease can inflict.

Sir Horace's prognosis erred on the side of generosity. Ronald was not able to work again. He attempted to resume his translation of *The Imitation* but made no progress. Instead he rallied his failing strength to put his affairs in order so that his death should give as little trouble as possible to others. On June 27th he saw his literary executor and speaking very slowly and clearly gave his directions; on July 1st his publisher, Mr Frank Sheed, was invited to Mells and given the typescripts of various essays and sermons for posthumous publication. On July 23rd he saw his old friend and literary agent, Mr W. P. Watt.

His will had been made in 1950 and, with the addition of two codicils, remained unchanged. The greater part of the money he had inherited and saved was left to his family; future royalties on his books to Lord Oxford, his library to Prinknash Abbey, which was especially dear to him as embodying both the old Anglican community of Caldey and the Benedictines of Farnborough, where he had been received into the Church. He desired to be buried in the village churchyard at Mells. He knew that a Requiem would be said for him in London and suggested Fr Martin D'Arcy as the preacher. It was a surprise to him to learn that the Westminster authorities wished to take his body to the Cathedral for the ceremonies, and he apologized for the trouble he was causing.

His last public appearance was on June 22nd at a fête held in the gardens of the Manor to raise funds for the carillon of the Anglican parish church. The house was on view that day, and Ronald, after walking a little on the lawn and greeting friends, drove off to take refuge at Ammerdown.

On June 27th the Pope, being told of his condition, sent him a relic of the Blessed Innocent XI and a 'warm commendation' of his 'praiseworthy achievement' in the translation of the Vulgate which His Holiness described as 'a monument of many years of patient study and toil'.

Other letters flowed in from the most diverse sources – old members of his undergraduate congregations, old girls from the Assumption Convent, fellow priests, total strangers – all assuring him of their prayers. There was, in macrocosm, a repetition of his departure from the Old Palace. People who had taken his presence for granted, suddenly awoke to their impending loss.

From the beginning of July he remained in his bedroom attended first by one and later by two nurses. He made some listless attempts to read Jane Austen. Mrs Asquith read aloud to him Stevenson's *Master of Ballantrae*, but his attention wandered. There was a concourse of visitors lay and clerical throughout that month. Dom Hubert van Zeller, who was leaving for America, came to say good-bye on the 19th. 'Whatever his attitude later on,' he writes, 'he did not then want to die.' A few days earlier Dom Hubert had offered to anoint him, but with his unfailing punctilio Ronald said that it should be done by the parish priest. From the beginning of August Mrs Asquith was obliged to tell visitors that he was too weak to see them. On August 11th he was brought Holy Communion for the last time.

On August 20th Lady Eldon came to stay. She and Mrs Asquith watched alternately beside him day and night, counting the seconds between one breath and the next, knowing that each might be the last. For three days he lay in a coma, but once Lady Eldon saw a stir of consciousness and asked whether he would like her to read to him from his own New Testament. He answered very faintly, but distinctly: 'No'; and then after a long pause in which he seemed to have lapsed again into unconsciousness, there came from the death-bed, just audibly, in the idiom of his youth: 'Awfully jolly of you to suggest it, though.'

They were his last words.

He died on the evening of August 24th. His body was taken to Westminster Cathedral on Wednesday, August 28th, and on the following day a Solemn Requiem Mass was offered by Bishop Craven. The Archbishop of Westminster presided and gave the absolution. Fr Martin D'Arcy preached the panegyric from the text: 'But the wise man will be learning the love of former times, the prophets will be their study. Theirs it is to support this unchanging world of God's creation; craftsmanship is their title to live – lending themselves freely and making their study in the law of the most High' (Ecclesiasticus xxxviii. 39).

'I wonder,' Fr D'Arcy said, 'when he translated the words of my text, whether he realized how well they fitted him.'

A great congregation listened while the Jesuit philosopher, so far from Ronald in mind, so near him in friendship, expounded his achievements.

> He did not attempt to invent something new; he did not try to keep up with the latest fashions in philosophy, art or literature. . . . Many of his friends were startled and confused to find that he apparently thought them superior to himself. . . . He tried to speak as a ranker and even as an outsider in the spiritual army of the Church, though it was so obvious that he was a favourite of God as well as of man. . . . As a Catholic he was universal, but he had no wish to mix his strain with the strain of other cultures. . . . He who thought himself of such little worth, could use the gifts which God had given him . . . to insure that the word Roman in Roman Catholic should no longer feel foreign. . . . What that long companionship with the word of God, so close to the Holy Spirit, meant to him, he was too shy to say. It could be guessed from his ever-growing gentleness and charity. This was the great work of his life. He had lived with God's mystery and revelation for a long while, from the first fruit of creation to the last words, those of the Beloved Disciple in the Apocalypse: 'Be it so, then; come Lord Jesus.' He himself had not long to wait. His Lord and Master has said to

him: Come; no longer to serve as his amanuensis and special interpreter, but, please God, to see him face to face.

After the Mass the body was taken back to Mells and buried in the churchyard there on the afternoon of the 30th, by the parish priest of Frome, accompanied by a few relations, friends, and neighbours.

Among his papers was the following, which was designed to be the preface of the book of apologetics which he never finished; indeed hardly began. It may stand as the epitaph of his life's work.

INVOCATION

Let me say what is in my mind; what ought to be in all minds at all times.

My God, when I dedicate something I have written to any human creature, I am taking away something which does not belong to me, and giving it to one who is not competent to receive it.

What I have written does not belong to me. If I have written the truth, then it is 'God's truth'; it would be true if every human mind denied it, or if there were no human minds in existence to recognize it. It is the obverse of that reality, that factualness, which belongs to some of our ideas and not to others; belongs to them, not in their own right — how could it? — but as lent to them by you, who are the focus and the background of all existence. If I have written well, that is not because Hobbs, Nobbs, Noakes and Stokes unite in praising it, but because it contains that interior excellence which is some strange refraction of your own perfect beauty; and of that excellence you alone are the judge. If it proves useful to others, that is because you have seen fit to make use of it as a weak tool, to achieve something in them of that supernatural end which is their destiny, and your secret.

Nor is any human creature, in the last resort, competent to receive the poorest of our tributes. When we dedicate a book to any name that is named on earth, we owe it (so we tell ourselves) to the love we bear him, or the admiration he excites in us, or the aid he has given us in the writing of it. But all we can love or admire in him is only some glimpse of your glory that peeps through the ragged garments of humanity; all the contribution he has made is only a part, and a small part, of the sufficiency which is your gift. If, in the computation of our indebtedness, we stop short now and again at the thought of some creature, it is only through a kind of fatigue, such as persuades the traveller to accept a night's lodging, and delay his journey till the morrow. You yourself are the fountain of all our activities, and they cannot round off the cycle of their being until they have returned, like water finding its own level, to you.

Into your hands, then, I remit this book, undedicated. Nor do I seek, after the fashion of authors, to forestall criticism by any modest disclaimers; I know well that in your sight every thought of the human mind is full of ignorances and misapprehensions. But some of us — and perhaps, at the roots of our being, all of us — cannot forgo that search for truth in which full satisfaction is denied us here. We apprehend that there is no encounter with reality, from without or from within, that does not echo with your foot-fall. We scrutinize the values, and can give no account of them except as a mask of the divine. Something of all these elusive considerations finds a place in my book. And you, who need nobody's service, can use anybody's. So I would ask that, among all the millions of souls you cherish, some few, upon the occasion of reading it, may learn to understand you a little, and to love you much.

Appendix

Chronological list of the chief published works of Ronald Knox, not including the various editions of his translation of the Bible.

Signa Severa. By R. A. K. (Eton, 1906).

Juxta Salices (Alden & Co: Oxford, 1910).

Remigium alarum. Carmen Latinum Praemio Cancellari donatum etc. (B. H. Blackwell: Oxford, 1910).

A Still more Sporting Adventure! Humbly dedicated to the authoresses of 'An Adventure' and transcribed by the Misses Lavinia and Priscilla Daisyfield (A skit on Charlotte A. E. Moberly and E. F. Jourdain's 'An Adventure', by R. A. Knox and C. R. L. Fletcher) (1911).

Some Loose Stones. Being a consideration of certain tendencies in modern theology illustrated by reference to the book called 'Foundations' (Longmans & Co: London, 1913) (Reprinted).

Naboth's Vineyard in Pawn. Three sermons later reprinted in *The Church in Bondage* below. (Society of SS. Peter and Paul: London, 1913).

Absolute and Abitofhell (Society of SS. Peter and Paul: London, 1913(?) (Often reprinted)).

The Church in Bondage (Sermons) (Society of SS. Peter and Paul: London, 1914).

Reunion all Round . . . By the author of 'Absolute and Abitofhell' (R. A. Knox) (Society of SS. Peter and Paul: London, 1914).

Bread or Stone. Four conferences on impetative prayer (Society of SS. Peter and Paul: London, 1915).

A Spiritual Aeneid (Longmans & Co: London, 1918). (Reprinted).

The Essentials of Spiritual Unity (Catholic Truth Society: London, 1918) (Reprinted).

Meditations on the Psalms (London, 1919).

Q Horati Flacci Carminum Liber Quintus . . . edidit A. D. Godley. (The Latin texts by R. A. Knox, J. U. Powell, A. B. Ramsay, and A. D. Godley.) (1920.) (Reprinted.)

Patrick Shaw-Stewart (W. Collins, Sons & Co: London, 1920).

Memories of the Future: being memories of the years 1915–1972, written in the year of grace 1988 by Opal, Lady Porstock, edited by R. A. Knox (Methuen & Co: London, 1923).

Æneid. Books vii to ix . . . edited by R. A. Knox (London, 1924).

A Book of Acrostics (Methuen & Co: London, 1924).

Sanctions: a frivolity (Methuen & Co: London, 1924).

The Viaduct Murder (Methuen & Co: London, 1925).

Other Eyes than Ours (Methuen & Co: London, 1926).

An Open-Air Pulpit (Essays) (Constable & Co: London, 1926).

The Three Taps, A detective story without a moral (Methuen & Co: London, 1927).

The Belief of Catholics (Ernest Benn: London) (What I Believe Series) (Reprinted).

Essays in Satire (Sheed & Ward: London, 1928) (Reprinted).

Anglican Cobwebs (Sheed & Ward: London, 1928) (Twelvepenny Series No. 5).

The Footsteps at the Lock (Methuen & Co: London, 1928).

The Rich Young Man. A fantasy (Sheed & Ward: London, 1928).

The Mystery of the Kingdom and other sermons (Sheed & Ward: London, 1928).

The Church on Earth (Burns, Oates & Co: London, 1929) (Treasury of the Faith No. 20).

On Getting There (Essays) (Methuen & Co: London, 1929).

Caliban in Grub Street (Sheed & Ward: London, 1930).

Broadcast Minds (Sheed & Ward: London, 1932).

Difficulties. Being a correspondence about the Catholic religion between Ronald Knox and Arnold Lunn (Eyre & Spottiswoode: London, 1932) (Reprinted).

The Body in the Silo (Hodder & Stoughton: London, 1933)(Reprinted).

Still Dead (Hodder & Stoughton: London, 1934).

Heaven and Charing Cross. Sermons on the Holy Eucharist (Burns, Oates & Co: London, 1935).

Barchester Pilgrimage (Sheed & Ward: London, 1935).

Double Cross Purposes (Hodder & Stoughton: London, 1937).

Let Dons Delight. Being variations on a theme in an Oxford commonroom (Sheed & Ward: London, 1939) (Reprinted).

Captive Flames. A collection of panegyrics (Burns, Oates & Co: London, 1940).

In Soft Garments. A collection of Oxford conferences (Burns, Oates & Co: London, 1942) (Reprinted).

I Believe. The religion of the Apostles' Creed. Reprinted from *The Tablet* (Tablet Office: Reading, 1944).

God and the Atom (Sheed & Ward: London, 1945).

A Retreat for Priests (Sheed & Ward: London, 1946).

The Mass in Slow Motion (Sheed & Ward: London, 1948).

The Creed in Slow Motion (Sheed & Ward: London, 1949).

On Englishing the Bible (Burns, Oates: London, 1949).

A Selection from the Occasional Sermons of the Right Reverend Monsignor R. A. Knox . . . (Dropmore Press: London, 1949).

The Gospel in Slow Motion (Sheed & Ward: London and New York, 1950).

St Paul's Gospel (Lenten conferences preached in 1950) (Catholic Truth Society: London, 1950) (Reprinted).

Enthusiasm. A chapter in the history of religion, with special reference to the xvii and xviii centuries (Clarendon Press: Oxford, 1950).

Stimuli (Sheed & Ward: London, 1951).

The Hidden Stream. A further collection of Oxford conferences (1952).

Off the Record (Selected letters) (Sheed & Ward: London and New York, 1953).

A Retreat for Lay People (Sheed & Ward: London, 1955).

Commentary on the New Testament (Burns, Oates: London, 3 vols., 1955).

The Window in the Wall and other sermons on the Holy Eucharist (Burns, Oates: London, 1956).

Bridegroom and Bride (Sheed & Ward: London, 1957).

Posthumous

Literary Distractions (Sheed & Ward: London, 1958).

Autobiography of a Saint (translation) (Harvill Press: London, 1958).

In Three Tongues (edited by Laurence Eyres. Chapman & Hall: London, 1959).

The Priestly Life (Sheed & Ward, 1959).

Others in preparation.

BIBLIOGRAPHY

List of books referred to in the text, other than those by Ronald Knox.

Anon (Lady Desborough). *Pages from a Family Journal*
Anson, Peter F. *The Benedictines of Caldey.* 1940
Assumption Chronicle, 1942
Bailey, Cyril. *Francis Fortescue Urquhart.* 1936
Birks, Rev. Herbert. *Life and Correspondence of Thomas Valpy French.* 1895
Chesterton, G. K. *Collected Poems.* 1927
Clay, Charles (ed.). *D. R. Brandt; Some of His Letters.* 1920
Dearmer, Rev. Percy. *Parsons' Handbook.* 1899
Edmundian, The, April 1923, July 1937 and Autumn 1957
Eyres, Laurence. 'Some Edmundian Memories', *The Edmundian*, Autumn 1957
George, Kenneth Wykeham, O.P., and Gervase Mathew, O.P. *Bede Jarrett.* 1952
Jones, L. E. *A Victorian Boyhood.* 1955
Knox, Rt. Rev. Edmund Arbuthnott. *Reminiscences of an Octogenarian.* 1935
Lindley, Francis. *Lord Lovat. circa* 1934
Lovat, Laura. *Maurice Baring.* 1947
Lunn, Arnold. *And Yet so New.* 1958
Mackenzie, Compton. *Sinister Street*, Vol. II. 1913
Micklem, Nathaniel. *The Box and the Puppets.* 1957
Month, The, 1959
Oldham, J. Basil. *A History of Shrewsbury School.* 1952
Oldmeadow, Ernest. *Francis, Cardinal Bourne*, Vol. II. 1944
Parsons, Alan. *Alan Parsons's Book: a Story in Anthology.* 1937.
Pax, 1910, 1940, 1956, and 1957
Peck, Winifred. *A Little Learning.* 1952
——— *Home for the Holidays.* 1955
Ribblesdale, Lord. *Charles Lister.* 1917
Smyth, Ethel. *Maurice Baring.* 1938
Speaight, Robert (ed.). *Letters from Hilaire Belloc.* 1958
Tablet, The, 1936 and 1955
Universe, The, 1926
Ward, Maisie. *Gilbert Keith Chesterton.* 1944
Ward, Wilfrid. *Life of Cardinal Newman.* 1913